Decline & Fall of the American Programmer

Edward Yourdon

YOURDON PRESS
Prentice Hall Building
Englewood Cliffs, New Jersey 07632

Yourdon, Edward.
    Decline and fall of the American programmer / Edward Yourdon.
        p.   cm. — (Yourdon Press computing series)
    Includes bibliographical references and index.
    ISBN 0-13-191958-X
    1. Computer software—Development.   2. Computer programmers—
United States.   I. Title.   II. Series.
ZA76.76.D47Y678   1993
005.1—dc20   93-3153
                                                                       CIP

DEDICATION: *to Darlene Eno (1921–1991)*
                whose quiet efforts helped reunite
                a father and his son,
                a brother and his sisters

Editorial/production supervision: *Ann Sullivan*
Cover designer: *Bruce Kenselaar*
Cover illustration source: *The Image Bank*
Illustrator: *Jean-Francois Podevin*
Buyer: *Mary Elizabeth McCartney*
Acquisitions editor: *Paul W. Becker*
Editorial assistant: *Maureen Diana*

©1993 by PTR Prentice Hall, Inc.
A Simon & Schuster Company
Englewood Cliffs, New Jersey 07632

The publisher offers discounts on this book when ordered in bulk quantities.
For more information, contact:

    Corporate Sales - PTR Prentice Hall
    113 Sylvan Avenue
    Englewood Cliffs, NJ 07632
    Phone: 201-592-2863   FAX: 201-592-2249

Printed in the United States of America
10 9 8 7

ISBN 0-13-191958-X

Prentice-Hall International (UK) Limited, *London*
Prentice-Hall of Australia Pty. Limited, *Sydney*
Prentice-Hall Canada Inc., *Toronto*
Prentice-Hall Hispanoamericana, S.A., *Mexico*
Prentice-Hall of India Private Limited, *New Delhi*
Prentice-Hall of Japan, Inc., *Tokyo*
Simon & Schuster Asia Pte. Ltd., *Singapore*
Editora Prentice-Hall do Brasil, Ltda., *Rio de Janero*

About The Book

Today, veteran programmers are watching their jobs being out-sourced to the far corners of the earth; unless things change drastically, this situation will only worsen. During the 1990s, software development may well move out of the U.S. into software factories in a dozen countries whose workers are well educated, less expensive, and more passionately devoted to quality and productivity. In DECLINE & FALL OF THE AMERICAN PROGRAMMER, Ed Yourdon demonstrates how U.S. software organizations can become world-class shops if they exploit the key software technologies of the 1990s.

Companies that master these new technologies can be sure of superior productivity and quality; those that don't won't be here when the 21st Century begins! What are these technologies whose implementation holds the key to survival for the U.S. software industry:

- Object-Oriented Methods
- CASE Tools
- Software Quality Assurance
- Structured Methods
- Software Metrics
- Re-engineering

Separate chapters are devoted to each of these topics. Each chapter can be read on its own, although the sequence of chapters reflects Yourdon's opinions about the ideal order in which critical issues should be tackled by an organization.

Yourdon also discusses critical "peopleware" issues (hiring practices, training methods, motivational strategies, performance management procedures, and project team coordination), which are crucial to running an effective software development operation.

Yourdon's "Decline and Fall of the American Programmer" received the **Jolt Award for Product Excellence** from *Computer Language Magazine.*

". . . the book clearly and convincingly argues irrefutable truths about our industry. If the American software community ignores this message, as surely as we import our VCRs, in 10 years we'll be importing our software."
— **Larry O'Brien, Computer Language, April 1993**

"Yourdon's books are usually entertaining as well as interesting. *Decline and Fall* is no exception. Anecdotes, quotes, "war stories," and "sound bytes" provide entertainment and occasionally offer astute insights as well. . . . it is provocative and readable, and the section on India provides useful information available nowhere else in the West."
— **Capers Jones, IEEE SPECTRUM Magazine, March 1993**

"The heart of this book is it's thorough look at the latest techniques for rationally organizing software development. . . . cutting edge . . . extensive, well-commented bibliography. . ."
— **Walter Zintz, UNIXWORLD, February 1993**

"If you read no other computer book this fall, read *Decline and Fall of the American Programmer.*"
— **Data Based Advisor, January 1993**

"Yourdon's book includes interesting, useful, and (unfortunately) depressing data about the state of software development."
— **Paul Gray, Information System Management, Winter 1993**

"I recently had the pleasure of reading Mr. Yourdon's book . . . Even though it's directed at Americans, he brings up some very interesting points that every Canadian developer should be aware of."
— **Scott Ambler, Computing Canada, November 23, 1992**

"... essential reading. Whilst the stated objective of Mr. Yourdon's book was to alert the U.S. software industry. . . the benefit is the provision of a guide to contemporary software practice in an eminently readable form complete with caveats, written in a manner that can be appreciated by both managers and coding operatives."

> — **Database and Network Journal, United Kingdom, September 1992**

"*Decline and Fall* is an entertaining and readable book; *Decline and Fall's* attitude and lucidity recommend it. It's also scarier, in parts, than most horror books."

> — **Dan O'Brien, EXE Magazine, London**

"This is a book *Software Futures* believes every serious software industry professional should read, as quickly as possible. It's informative, well written, funny and timely."

> — **Software Futures, June 1992**

Contents

Preface

All over the world, software development organizations are grappling with staggering problems of productivity and quality. But while most organizations see the current situation as a problem, a few—the *world-class* software organizations—see it as an opportunity, and have publicly commited to bringing about ten-fold improvements by the mid-1990s. What is most astonishing is that some of these companies have *already* begun to achieve these great leaps forward. I have visited many of these organizations around the world—not only in the United States, Japan, and Europe, but also in Manila, Bombay, Buenos Aires, Hong Kong, and a dozen other places. I have studied their methods, interviewed their managers, assessed the practicality of their approach for other organizations. In this book, I will show you how your organization can be a "world class" leader in software development by applying practical ideas of software metrics, reengineering, reusability, CASE, and other concepts.

But before I plunge into the details, I need to explain and defend the main premise of the book: that the American programmer is likely to suffer the same fate as the dodo bird and the dinosaur, because of low software productivity and low software quality, as compared to the leading-edge software organizations in other countries around the world. I have included some lively debate and commentary from consultants and experts around the U.S. to provide several different perspectives on this controversial conclusion. If you have been brought up in a culture that glorifies the American software industry as the world leader, I ask simply that you remember that it was only a few years ago that we had the same opinion of our automobile industry. Already, computer hardware has become a world-wide commodity; during the 1990s, software development may well move out of the U.S. into software factories in a dozen countries whose people are well educated, less expensive, and more passionately devoted to quality and productivity.

But this is not necessarily a foregone conclusion: U.S. software organizations can remain (or become) world-class software shops if they exploit the key software technologies of the 1990s. These new techniques are the wave of the future, and will eclipse the productivity improvements promised by fourth generation languages and other techniques of the 70s and 80s. Companies that master these new technologies can be sure of superior productivity and quality; those that don't won't be here when the 21st century begins.

The bulk of the book is devoted to these key software technologies. Separate chapters discuss CASE tools, software metrics, software quality assurance, reengineering, software process models, software methodologies (incudling information engineering, object-oriented techniques, and structured techniques) and the concept of "peopleware." An appendix describes the state of software development in India, not because India is the *only* example of an emerging software power, but simply because it is one of the more colorful ones that I have visited. And a final appendix provides a list and brief review of some 80 software books that should form the core of an essential library for the world-class software shop; one reason for including this is to emphasize that the tenfold productivity improvements enjoyed by a few software organizations is not based on black magic, but on widely available technology that has been well documented in readily available textbooks.

Each chapter can be read on its own, and the associated software technology discussed in that chapter can be implemented by an organization without necessarily implementing any other technology. However, most organizations will want to implement new productivity techniques in some kind of logical order, and the sequence of chapters reflects my strong opinion about the ideal order. Thus, it is worth emphasizing that *peopleware* issues are likely to be more important than CASE tools or object-oriented techniques.

I have written this book for a broad range of people involved in the software development process: programmers, systems analysts, software engineers, and various levels of project managers. Though the material obviously assumes a basic understanding of current software terminology and concepts, you don't have to be a rocket scientist to understand most of the material in the book. And since many of the technically-oriented attendees at my seminars and conferences around the world often remark to me, "Boy, I wish our management could hear this!", I am hoping that the book will find its way into the hands of senior management and that mysterious form of life we call "end-users" who must suffer the consequences of the software systems we build.

In a university environment, the material in the book would be quite suitable for a one-semester survey of software engineering techniques, particularly in the third or fourth year undergraduate level, after the student has mastered the basics of programming and systems design. If nothing else, it may provide a rude awakening for students who blissfully anticipate a lifetime job in the software field, free of the annoying problems of layoffs and outsourcing. Veteran programmers are watching their jobs being outsourced to the far corners of the earth right now; unless things change drastically, it will only get worse.

The Decline and Fall of the American Programmer covers a wide range of technical subjects, and I have drawn on the expertise, advice, and guidance of a number of talented professionals in the field. Wherever possible, I have provided credit and attribution for verbal comments, as well as published works, from consultants, educators, and researchers around the world. I have also benefited enormously from the careful review and critique of the manuscript by Capers Jones, John Johns, Charles Martin, Robert Glass, and Neil Iscoe.

In addition to the various cited sources, I want to pay tribute to the many thousands of conference attendees, seminar participants, and students who have borne the brunt of various draft versions of the material in this book. Our software industry is blessed by an extraordinary number of highly talented, professional, concerned people; they don't always have an opportunity to speak out on the topics discussed in this book, but many hundreds have shared their ideas with me. I can't acknowledge all of them by name, but anyone who has ever attended one of my presentations should realize that he has my personal thanks for contributing to whatever good ideas may be in this book. My intention has been to synthesize all of this into something greater than the sum of the parts; but if any errors have occurred in the process, they are entirely my responsibility.

Finally, my thanks to the many unseen hands that transformed a rough manuscript into the book that you are holding. Sally Ann Bailey did a magnificent job of editing my atrocious attacks upon the English language; my wife, Toni, did yet another yeoman's job (I hope Sally Ann will forgive me if I eschew the use of "yeoperson" here!) of transcribing all of the corrections onto our Macintosh system. Paul Becker and the editorial production staff at Prentice Hall broke all speed records in producing the book while maintaining a superb level of quality. My thanks to everyone who gave freely of their time and help. I hope the result will play a role in helping as many organizations as possible into becoming the world-class software shops of the 1990s.

Edward Yourdon
New York City
December, 1991

The Decline and Fall of the American Programmer

The American programmer is about to share the fate of the dodo bird. By the end of this decade, I foresee massive unemployment among the ranks of American programmers, systems analysts, and software engineers. Not because fifth generation computers will eliminate the need for programming, or because users will begin writing their own programs. No, the reason will be far simpler: *international competition will put American programmers out of work, just as Japanese competition put American automobile workers out of work in the 1970s.* And just as the American automobile industry was shocked and unprepared for its loss of dominance, so the American software industry will find its fall from preeminence difficult and unexpected.

Figure 1.1: The American programmer, circa 1999

From my visits to data processing organizations in the United States and around the world, I am firmly convinced that most American programmers (and their managers) do not yet fully understand, deep in their psyches, that every product and every service provided by today's society depends on productive, high-quality information systems [1, 2]. An increasing number of manufactured products contain one or more embedded computer systems, systems that are software intensive, with 100,000 or more lines of code. And though the term "service economy" conjures up images of low-paid workers dishing out hamburgers at Burger King, today's service economy is information intensive and would collapse almost instantly without smoothly functioning information systems. So it's not just the EDSs, the Microsofts, and the IBMs that are at risk; all the Blatzco Widget companies with embedded computers in their widget products are at risk too. The companies that face up to this risk will be the ones with *world-class software.*

The average company spends a minuscule 1 to 3 percent of its revenues on data processing. But this paltry figure fails to emphasize the point that a company's information technology is its Achilles' heel. As a project manager at the Jet Propulsion Laboratories remarked to me a few years ago, "Software represents only 10 to 15 percent of the money we spend around here, but it's 'in series' with 90 percent of what we do: if the software fails, the mission fails." And thus the people who build those information systems—the programmers, systems analysts, database designers, telecommunication specialists, and others—play an increasingly crucial role in the fiscal health, and the very survival, of their employers. In the 1990s, a company whose programmers and systems analysts are an order of magnitude better than its competitors will have a dramatic advantage—and the company whose software folks are an order of magnitude worse than its competitors will go out of business.

The key comparisons between the *world-class* software organization and the run-of-the-mill software organizations will be these:

- Cost of the staff—salaries and benefits
- Productivity of the staff
- Quality of the systems developed

1.1 THE COST ISSUE

Just as American automobile workers labored for decades in blissful ignorance that similar workers in other countries were earning 5 to 10 times less, so it seems that American software engineers are equally unaware that their foreign counterparts are earning substantially less. Of course, this changes from month to month: as the U.S. dollar becomes stronger or weaker, the salary differential between American programmers and, say, Canadian or British or French programmers may not be that significant. But programmers in Manila, Singapore, India, Brazil, and other parts of the world typically earn 5 to 6 times less than an American programmer. For an even more dramatic comparison, consider the People's Republic of China: as of June 1990, Hong Kong newspapers reported job openings for a PRC programmer at a salary of $180 per month [3]—and this is for a programmer with a college engineering degree and two years' experience in Unix and C!

When wage differentials like these began to be publicized in other manufacturing industries in the 1970s, many American workers reacted by proclaiming that they had some kind of inalienable, God-given right to high wages. Foreign workers with their low wages were ridiculed—often because it was assumed that they were working in "sweatshop" conditions building low-quality products. To the extent that the wage differentials were seen as a competitive threat, high American wages were often protected through a combination of strong union negotiating practices and government-sponsored tariffs and import quotas.

What about the comparable situation in the data processing industry? The computer hardware situation is fairly well known: every major country is trying to nurture its native hardware industry and/or protect it from foreign "threats." Government involvement takes a variety of forms:

- Import duties on foreign computer equipment
- Subsidies to foster local R&D efforts
- Restrictions on exports to "unfriendly" nations
- Preferential treatment for local computer companies for government contracts
- Restrictions on foreign companies wanting to start a local manufacturing facility

This will continue, but it will be less and less significant in the 1990s—simply because software will finally be recognized as the dominant factor in the computer industry. For years, it has been known that software and related expenditures represent 50 percent or more of the overall corporate EDP budget; indeed, in some organizations the figure is closer to 80 percent. This inevitably means that a larger and larger percentage of the revenues generated by the computer industry will be related to software products and services.

Does this mean that governments will begin "protecting" their software industries to the same extent that they now protect their hardware industries? Very probably, but not until they realize that software matters. And thus far, hardly anybody seems to be paying attention to the fact that a programmer in India earns five times less than a programmer in Indianapolis. A few companies in the business of creating software products have indeed noticed this and have established their own offshore "software factories" or have set up joint ventures with software companies such as Tata in India.

But if you ask the DP manager in a typical company in Middle America whether he or she is doing anything about the situation, you're likely to get a blank look or a loud guffaw. "Why should I care if there are programmers in Bangladesh who make $1 a day?" they'll ask. "They're not here, and *here* is where I need my programs written. Besides, they don't speak English. And they're probably illiterate. And anyway, they don't understand the business issues that concern my users."

Unfortunately, the fact that programmers are "there" rather than "here" is increasingly irrelevant. Back in the 1970s, a Japanese software firm offered to provide programming services to a San Francisco bank by parking a boat full of programmers just outside the international limit near San Francisco harbor; one could imagine programmers, analysts, and users frantically rowing back and forth, carrying their specifications and COBOL programs. Today, of course, things are a lot more sophisticated: there is no reason why a software development group anywhere in the world couldn't communicate via satellite with customers or users anywhere else in the world.

And is English really that much of an issue? It may be for the Brazilian programmers who really wish the rest of the world spoke Portuguese, or for the Chinese programmers who are still struggling with their 40,000 ideograms. But it's not so much of a problem for most of the world: English became a de facto language for the computer industry in the 1950s and 1960s as a result of the early development efforts in England and the United States. But a far more important reason for the dominance of English is the educational system. Many of the countries that are now able to offer low-cost software development services are former British colonies, that have inherited an excellent English-based educational infrastructure. And those countries that don't have good universities of their own can simply send their students abroad: more than 50 percent of the U.S. computer science Ph.D. students these days are foreign nationals.

So it's increasingly true that foreign programmers and systems analysts do speak English, are literate, and can transport their software products anywhere in the world. The only thing they can't do, perhaps, is deal with the nuances and idiosyncrasies of individual, local user communities in world markets. But even this is not a problem: it may mean that individual companies retain a few of their own native systems analysts to develop specifications for their systems those specifications can then be transmitted by satellite to remote software development facilities for implementation. Or the foreign software developers can set up their own local marketing/analysis teams on U.S. soil, with the intention of soaking up the local culture. Or joint ventures may emerge between the American software developers who want to stay in business and those foreign software companies that want to concentrate on the design and coding part of systems development. Meanwhile, many of the multinational companies have already solved this problem in a variety of other industries and disciplines; they will use whatever methods they have already developed for this new issue of information systems development.

1.2 THE PRODUCTIVITY ISSUE

Wage differences are one issue but by no means the only one when comparing one programmer with another or one DP organization with another. Productivity is certainly another key issue: Which person (or project team or organization) turns out the most source statements (or function points or delivered systems)? We know from Barry Boehm [4] and Capers Jones [5] that there are dozens of factors influencing software development productivity within any individual organization; Capers Jones [5] has also published recent figures comparing software productivity and quality between different industries in the United States. As of the end of 1991, there was no published data comparing software development productivity at the international level, though Capers Jones has begun gathering impressive research data in this area [6].

To the extent that productivity is influenced by better programming languages (for example, Ada, Smalltalk, or 4GLs) and CASE tools, the American programmer might be at a slight advantage—simply because the American software industry tends to be somewhat susceptible to new fads and gadgets (for an interesting discussion of this, see Nomura's analysis of Japanese usage of CASE tools [7]). But to the extent that productivity is influenced by common, rigorous use of a standardized systems development methodology, I think Americans are at a disadvantage. The American programmer is still too much of a loner and a cowboy. Hotshot programmers like Bill Atkinson (developer of Apple's MacPaint and the new HyperCard software) are accorded superhuman status, even though virtually all the truly difficult software projects involve hordes of hundreds of programmers and systems analysts.

And, finally, there is the issue of a programmer's propensity for hard work: How many hours of hard work does the American programmer put in each week? Capers Jones [8] claims that the average American programmer works 50-hour weeks. Maybe so. Maybe I've only seen the below-average half of the American EDP industry. But I have to say I have not been impressed with the energy level of the average programmer in the vast majority of DP shops I've visited in the United States. Most of them have a difficult time remaining in an upright position all day. I'm convinced that many organizations play Muzak just to hide the sound of snoring.

What's the bottom line? Though Capers Jones has some excellent statistics on software productivity *by industry* [5], I think it will be a few more years before we begin to see large-scale evidence of programming productivity on a national basis. But when it appears, I think we will see a reaffirmation of the Boehm–Jones statistics indicating the possibility of a 10:1 variation in productivity. And I doubt the United States will be at the top of the spectrum of national programming productivity rates.

1.3 THE QUALITY ISSUE

Obviously, it doesn't do much good to write lots and lots of software if it doesn't work, or if (to steal David Parnas's term) it can't be trusted, or if it can't be easily modified and maintained. The quality of software is just as important (if not more important) than the productivity with which it is generated. This, I think, is going to be the key issue of the 1990s—and it is an area where I think the American programmer is at a terrible disadvantage. I'm tempted to say that it's a cultural disadvantage, because I see so much evidence of sloppy, low-quality work all around me in my day-to-day life—in all fields, not just in software development.

There is no shortage of data about the bugginess of American software. If you've been in a monastery for the past 10 years and haven't read any scary stories, start with Peter Neumann's software bug documentary [9], which begins in the mid-1980s and continues up to the present day. Or read Jon Jacky's critique of the safety of the Star Wars software [10]. Or contact the Computer Professionals for Social Responsibility (P.O. Box 717, Palo Alto, CA 94301) for some of their horror stories.

There have been at least a few reports in the literature of systems developed with 10 times fewer errors than the "typical" system; such reports date back to the classic IBM "superprogrammer" project involving Harlan Mills and Terry Baker. More important, it appears that in at least a few cases, Japanese software has been delivered with 100 times fewer errors than typical American software [11].

Of course, software reliability and software quality involve much more than just counting the (visible) bugs in a system during some period of time. And once again, nobody (to my knowledge) has yet attempted any large-scale surveys of software quality on a national basis. But I would be willing to bet my Macintosh (and all its buggy software) that if such a survey were made, American software would rank near the bottom.

1.4 OTHER POINTS OF VIEW

As you can imagine, there are different opinions on this subject; while preparing this material, I solicited comments and opinions from a number of consultants, experts, and authors around the United States. A sampling of their opinion follows.

Seattle-based author and consultant Meilir Page-Jones [12] had this to say:

> First of all, it's news to me that the American Programmer ever rose or triumphed. [Ten years ago], there was a wealth of ignorance out there. Today, there still is. Indeed, it seems that many a programmer in a large corporation whiles away his entire career without being troubled by the burdens of professional competence.
>
> What are the reasons for all of this? The first is a lack of education: few older programmers were trained in structured programming, and few programmers of any era have read a book of any kind since *Huckleberry Finn*. Most programmers are not even aware of

the personalities in our field; they know only two names: Michael Jackson and James Martin. However, they think that Michael Jackson is a rock star and that James Martin is a computer scientist. Doth ignorance know no bounds?

The second reason for poor programmer quality is the value system that surrounds programmers every day of their working lives. The message is explicit: Get the crap out as fast as possible and it doesn't matter that it is crap. Someone else can worry about that in next year's budget. In many cases, managers can't tell the difference between complete rubbish and primo-grade systems, probably because most DP managers have never seen systems of any quality in their entire lives.

Well, programmers may be ignorant, but they're not stupid. When they're given the chance, students do well in classes turning out rigorous specs and many of them actually get enthusiastic about doing good work. After all, in class they're rewarded by my value system (as well as, perhaps, their own internal quests for quality). But, back at the ranch, my alien, in-town-for-a-week value system is no more, and the so called "real world" with its surreal, topsy-turvy values takes over again.

I think you're right in your speculation that certain Asian countries are ready to pull the rug out from under American programmers' slothful feet. Earlier this year, I was approached by the Indian Government, which was interested in my views on how to set up an establishment capable of training $N \times 100,000$ young, educated people in modern software engineering techniques. What a prospect! However, not wanting to spend the rest of my days in Monsoonland, I politely made a hurried excuse and left.

But someone will take up the challenge (and doubtless make some rupees). And then what? Cheap, hard-working, disciplined, logical programmers by the millions, reinforced with values of quality by their national government (no less). Have we seen this before? And what did those folks do to Detroit?

Independent software developer David Gedeon, based in Athens, Ohio, disagrees with Page-Jones's assessment [13]:

Your outrageous predictions on the demise of the American programmer have moved me to this response: Rubbish! At least partly.

One of your points was that the loner or cowboy programmers were doomed. I feel just the opposite—they are the future. What does a small group of programmers (say 1–4) working away with little or no overhead have to fear from a horde of programmers slaving away along the Pacific rim?

Take me, for example. I'm a sole proprietor who writes engineering software for NASA and private industry. I can respond to market whims instantly. My capital investment consists of a PC, printer, and a few accessories. With the software aids available today, I can bookkeep, wordprocess, typeset, program, debug, and market all by myself and still have time left over to play with the kids. In other words, I can be a one-man multinational corporation.

So what if Mitsubishi has 1000 programmers working on a better spreadsheet? I compete in markets too small for them and besides, how can 1000 programmers do much of anything besides get in each others' way? I do modular programs too, but constantly revise all the pieces and their common data structure. Can a large team of programmers do this effectively? I doubt it.

Gedeon is right: sole proprietors, working in their own electronic cottages, can be much more competitive than the typical bloated American corporation. However, a PC and a laser printer are about all they can afford in terms of a capital investment; there are lots of other expensive CASE-oriented software productivity tools, which we discuss in Chapter 6, that they can't afford. The lone programmer will be able to compete effectively in parts of the PC marketplace, and in various other small niches—but not on the projects that are intrinsically huge and complex, requiring teams of people or even teams of companies; nor will they compete on projects that are intrinsically mundane and boring, for example, making maintenance changes to 20-year-old COBOL programs. That is where I see the foreign competition.

Capers Jones wrote to me with the following comments [14]:

Your theme of the decline of the American programmer is a melancholy one, and it needs to be taken seriously. Software would not be the only high-technology occupation where the United States lost out due to misunderstanding the ground rules of international competition.

Tom DeMarco, on the other hand, disagrees. DeMarco is dubious about futurist pronouncements in general, and mine are no exception. He and I shared a panel in Singapore at the 10th International Software Engineering Conference, and he confronted me with a blunt question: "If the American programmer is in such peril, why is the U.S. share of the world software market increasing?" Ummm . . . err . . . ahhh . . . . I had no answer, but I wasn't sure I trusted the statistics DeMarco flung into the air with such wild abandon. However, a small squib in the July 1988 *Communications of the ACM* supports his point:

> The U.S. has sustained its dominance of the world's software and services market over the last five years, with its market share of 70.8 percent in 1982 rising to 73.2 percent in 1987, according to a study by CBEMA and the Center for Economic Analysis, in Stamford, CT. Customizing software, systems support, training, and data base access are included in the services category. Revenues of the world software and services market increased from $51 billion in 1982 to $108 billion in 1987, with $36 billion generated by U.S. companies (including subsidiaries and plants outside the U.S.) in 1982 and $79 billion in 1987. The compound annual growth rate for American companies during this period was 17 percent a year, whereas non-U.S. companies experienced 14.1 percent per year.

But notice a few things about the CBEMA report:

- U.S. figures include work done by offshore subsidiaries and plants, for example, IBM's software shops in England, Texas Instruments' software shops in India, Andersen Consulting's development center in Manila, and a dozen other examples. This may be great for the balance sheet of the American firms, but it's not so great for American programmers.

- The market share increased but not by much. As a mathematician friend of mine would say, the first derivative is still positive, but the second derivative may have turned negative. The acceleration of the growth in market share may have stopped. We won't know until we see the next five-year report.

- The 1982–1987 time period covered by the study corresponds to the period during which England's Alvey Directorate, Europe's Esprit program, and Japan's SIGMA project (among many others) began. The results of these nationally funded programs, which could be devastating to the American software market, won't be seen until the early to mid-1990s.

- The CBEMA report, and DeMarco's challenge to me, ignore the more insidious problem: the loss of market share for American corporations in general caused by low productivity and sloppy quality of the information systems that drive their businesses. It's not just Microsoft, IBM, and Computer Sciences that I'm worried about; it's all the General Foods and Bank of Americas that are competing against similar companies in countries around the world.

Author Leon Levy [15, 16] wrote from Bell Labs with an example of the "technology will save us" argument:

> Our present methods of developing software were developed two decades ago when machines were expensive and programmers weren't—at least not cumulatively because there weren't that many of them. With the changing relative cost of machines vs. programmers there will be increasing pressure to mechanize. Those of us with elephantine memories recall when machine time cost $300 per hour, and a week's worth of programming time was about the same. Today, a week's worth of programming time is about the cost of a PC-AT, so the ratio has shifted by orders of magnitude. Another shift in the economics is the cost of memory. When I last did the calculation, one week of programmer time came out to about 20 Mbytes of RAM!
>
> The bottom line is that I don't believe Fred Brooks' argument about the "silver bullet," at least not in substance. Yes, there will always be hard problems, but they will be research problems requiring specialized skills. Development of the transaction type applications that are the bread-and-butter of the application programmers of today will be sufficiently automated that only very few applications programmers will be needed to supply the demand.
>
> In short, I have high hopes for CASE being able to solve the "routine" problems—the kind that most programmers deal with.

Irv Wendel, a consultant in Oakland, California, disagreed with my criticism of American programmers for a different reason:

> You blame U.S. programmers for rotten systems, crap code, and not having a decent DP education. *Bullshit*. Blame the people who control the situation—management. Management sets the tone and determines strategic goals. Management is responsible for a company's (or division's or project's) success or failure. Management sets deadlines, dress codes, corporate educational policies, and even determines if incompetents stay in the company.

One interesting indicator of job trends in a profession is the number of students who major in that discipline in college. In 1986 and 1987, for example, the number of people applying to U.S. graduate business schools increased by 30 to 40 percent. But after the October 1987 stock market crash, enrollments leveled off and even declined in some schools. Similarly, *Investor's Daily* [17] reported that enrollments in undergraduate computer science courses declined by 30 percent in 1987—and this follows 10 percent declines each year since enrollments peaked in 1983. As David Gries, former chairman of the Computer

Science Department at Cornell said, "Unless you're a one-in-a-million Steve Jobs, students just don't see the rewards either in fame or fortune in a technical discipline any more."

To put it more bluntly, around 1983, college students began to see that a degree in computer science would not guarantee them a job. In 1984, 10 percent of the 2.7 million U.S. high school graduates expressed a desire to major in computer science when they got to college. But in that same year, universities were turning out 50,000 computer science graduates who competed for 25,000 jobs. Despite the doom-and-gloom headlines, the sad truth is that industry doesn't want or need all those trainee programmers. There is an ironic "catch-22" situation here: the shortage everyone bemoans is a shortage of trained, competent programmers and systems analysts—but the only way industry can get the trained people it needs is to hire the relatively useless college graduates and educate them on the job. Meanwhile, universities are turning out a pitifully small number of people with advanced computer science degrees. In 1984, the United States produced 268 doctorates in computer science; by 1987, the figure had climbed to 466, far short of the 1000 doctorates per year needed by academia and industry.[1]

Meanwhile, other countries are working hard to provide educated programmers of their own. The National Computer Board of Singapore, for example, announced at the 10th ICSE conference [18] that it has increased the number of trained software engineers by a factor of 10 in the past eight years. And the National Institute for Information Technology in Delhi, India is now educating approximately 8000 students each year in data processing.

Richard Harrison, who recently retired as director of the Federal Software Management Center, wrote with the following commentary [19]:

> Despite what I see as a coming shakeout in the programming ranks, I remain optimistic regarding our national ability to maintain a strong, commanding, and global grip on control of information technology. I believe that our corporations, our universities, and our governing bodies have, in spite of themselves, managed to

---

[1] Capers Jones has pointed out that the U.S. *Fortune* 500 companies provide more inhouse software training than all American universities combined, and that much of it is better than that provided by universities. This could be regarded as a practical effort by industry to fill a vacuum created by academia, or it could mean that society is slowly downgrading the software profession to that of a mechanical trade, not worthy of a university degree.

produce a handful of bright and capable people skilled in both the techniques and the business of information processing. During the next ten years or so, we're going to naturally attrite not a few management and programming Neanderthals. Those bright few, together with the graduating classes and some pretty powerful technology, will step into their shoes. I have faith that they will do a considerably better job of running the shop than we have.

In the interim I guess we'll just bite our nails, cross our fingers (hard to do simultaneously), and hope for the best. No doubt there will be fewer of us in this business in the future; but I still think it's going to be our business.

Author Eric Vesely [20] wrote to me with some personal experiences about "offshore programming":

> I think it will take more than seven years [for the American industry to collapse] simply because of the sheer stubbornness of Americans. Japan made significant inroads into America because it was essentially selling consumer goods of better quality and lower price. Mainframe software is an industrial good purchased normally by data processing people who will protect their own by stating that the quality is insufficient, or support is inadequate because it is an overseas product, or . . . regardless of the price difference.
>
> Sooner or later, the price difference will force DP to purchase overseas contract programming, but not soon. I know this from personal experience, since I am a director of an offshore programming company [Data Systems International (DSI)] located in Kathmandu, Nepal. They paid Nepalese graduates with masters or doctorate degrees to learn COBOL. After six months or so of intensive training, they became full-fledged business programmers. DSI currently has a staff of about fifty DP professionals, and I believe that the highest salary is about US$250 monthly. This would appear to most Americans as sweatshop wages, but it is approximately the wage of a government minister.

Vesely overlooks one point: software development is no longer a business of secretly writing programs to run on mainframe computers. Software has come out of the closet. In addition to showing up on PCs, it is showing up in what Vesely calls "consumer goods" in the form of embedded systems. The Japanese are very good at building and marketing electronic gadgets, household appliances and many other products; now those gadgets are becoming "smart" software-controlled gadgets.

Back in the United States, author John Boddie [21] has looked at the situation from a different perspective:

There are lots of expensive programmers in the United States who are not very productive. There are lots of underlying reasons, one of the main ones being that most programmers learn their trade by patching up inadequate systems instead of learning how to build good ones. There are also more than a few programmers who aren't much good at it and probably shouldn't be in this business.

Nevertheless, I think that the American programmer will be around for a good while. His (her) resilience will be a direct consequence of the ineptitude of the people who specify the work the programmer is to do.

Let's face it. Most programs spring from truly wretched specifications, if, indeed, there are any specifications at all. Throughout the development process, users, programmers, and analysts are engaged in a ritual dance of successive approximation to the required product. In order to join the dance, one needs to have not only a knowledge of programming, but also an appreciation of the cultural aspects of the problem and the user's agenda for its solution. The twin problems of distance and cultural difference make it very difficult for the programmer in New Delhi to respond to requests from the manufacturer in Kansas City.

However, if we can improve our ability to create specifications (and I believe CASE has a role to play in this process), the need for the aforementioned dance disappears. Now, armed with detailed design documentation and specifications for the system to be delivered, the programmer needs only to translate the requirements into code. However, better specifications will also improve our ability to generate systems by using the computers themselves to produce the code.

In either case, the result is the same: the American programmer will find himself imperiled by the actions of the American systems analyst. It is the analyst, through improved specifications, that allows the foreign programmer to do an acceptable job.

Carol Covin, a consultant in Falls Church, Virginia, is very dubious that offshore systems development will work successfully. As she points out [22],

Despite increased communications via satellite negating the need for users and systems analysts to sit down together and work out specifications jointly, I have yet to see a project where specs could be delivered and the programmers code in isolation and deliver a useful product.

Your point about former English colonies is one I had not considered. However, I do not think you can overestimate cultural differences between user and programmer. It all has to do with assumptions, and these are difficult enough when you are crossing from the accounting department to the programming department, never mind crossing country/cultural borders.

In China, for instance, being late is not simply a matter of being impolite, or encountering unforeseen circumstances. It is taken as a direct, intentional insult. . . . Such misunderstandings might never be resolved, or even uncovered, when there is no direct communication.

Phil Howard, president of Applied Computer Research and publisher of the newsletter *System Development*, offered this opinion [23]:

I have some difficulty convincing myself that your prediction will come true. In the first place, upper management will have a tough time with this one. By and large, I think they have a negative view of the MIS function as it is now, due to missed promises in the past, and I doubt that they will buy the idea that it can be done any more successfully elsewhere. Besides the MIS function generally represents no more than one to two percent of gross revenue so the savings won't look that impressive either.

At the MIS level, top management already has overwhelming problems with poor (or missing) documentation, endless maintenance, and the inability to write good requirements, let alone specs. Besides the natural human desire to keep one's empire intact, I have a tough time visualizing most MIS directors going for this based solely on the economics. The area for savings probably doesn't represent more than 15 percent or so of the total MIS budget.

I agree with many of the things you say in your article, but am less inclined to conclude that we are heading toward "massive unemployment among the ranks of American programmers." Who was it that said "The more things change, the more they stay the same"?

Good point. Senior management is rightfully suspicious of all programmers—they think of us as characters in *Revenge of the Nerds*. But if indeed they are ignoring this issue because the MIS function represents "only" 1 to 2 percent of gross revenues, they are sitting on a time bomb. If the software doesn't work, then the company's product—be it airplanes or dishwashers—won't work. The economics of overseas software is only part of the issue. More important than the claim that India-based software is 30 percent cheaper than American software is the likelihood that it is has 10 times fewer bugs and can be maintained 10 times more easily.

Eric Vesely sent me the front page of an interesting newsletter, *Software Success* (4684 Blanco Drive, San Jose, CA 95129), which carried this story in the September 1987 issue:

> On-Line Software International last week began selling CasePac, a front end development environment for IBM DB2 MVS sites. CasePac is priced at $200,000. It was developed by Tata Consultancy Service, Bombay, India. This is the largest application, that I know of, which was developed offshore in conjunction with a U.S. marketing firm. I continue to be impressed with the quality of some of the new offshore software.
>
> I am also surprised by the complacency of many U.S. software development firms. I find that very few developers believe that software can be developed offshore. At the same time, U.S. software developers are slow to adopt the tools and technology to improve programmer productivity. If the software industry doesn't wake up to the possibility of software development moving offshore, we may be just another U.S. industry which is asleep at the wheel.

Tata is the largest software consulting and development firm in India and has been working with a number of U.S. and U.K. firms for several years. In addition to its own work, it now has the benefit of support from the Indian government, which is setting up a dedicated satellite communication system to enable local Indian "software factories" to interface with clients around the world.

I talked about this with Professor Kesav Nori, who heads up Tata's research center in Pune, India.[2] Nori emphatically disagreed with the notion that Third World countries will use the "Mongolian horde" approach to compete against the American Software industry—that is, using armies of low-paid programmers to overwhelm American software organizations by brute force. He pointed out that, at least in India, the supply of trained, educated software engineers can't grow fast enough to keep up with the overall growth in the worldwide software market. While the 5-to-1 wage differential obvi-

---

[2] See Appendix A for a lengthy discussion of software technology in India.

ously provides a competitive advantage, Nori argues that it may only be a (relatively) short-term advantage that could disappear over the next 10 to 15 years. Thus, Tata is focusing on capital-intensive software technologies with which it hopes to "leverage" the work of its people.

1.5 WHERE DO WE GO FROM HERE?

Let's accept my premise for the moment: American software is developed at a higher cost, less productively, and with less quality than that of several other countries. So what? Does this mean that Congress is going to awaken from its usual stupor one morning and declare a national software initiative? Hardly! Does it mean that the CEOs of the U.S. *Fortune* 500 companies will insist that their five-year capital expenditure budget include an item for investing in software productivity and quality? Maybe, but I doubt it.

Does it mean that individual project teams will try to be more productive? Yes, but in the context of an organization that doesn't care about *enterprise* productivity, such project-level efforts will probably prove futile; the efforts of a productive few are often overwhelmed in companies where 25 percent of large system development projects are canceled before completion.

Does it mean that individual programmers and systems analysts will take it upon themselves to develop higher-quality systems at a higher level of productivity, and thus begin to change the overall culture in which such systems are developed? Maybe; after all, the Ayatollah Khomeni showed us that grass-roots revolutions still do work from time to time. But I wouldn't bet on it.

Obviously, there are some initiatives at the national level. In the United States, we have Microelectronics and Computer Technology Corporation (MCC), the Software Engineering Institute (SEI), and the Software Productivity Consortium (SPC). These are interesting organizations, and some innovative technology will certainly emerge from them,[3] as well as from the smaller, innovative research firms like Capers Jones's Software Productivity Research, Inc. But I doubt they will have much impact on "mainstream" American computing, be-

---

[3] Unfortunately, though, MCC virtually shut down its heralded Software Technology Program in 1991, and its premier software researchers have moved on to greener pastures. Human interface expert Bill Curtis has moved to the Software Engineering Institute, where he heads up the process maturity effort described in Chapter 4, and the former director of the Software Technology Program, Laszlo Belady, is now heading up the software research program at the Mitsubishi Electric Research Laboratory (MERL) facility in Cambridge, Massachusetts.

cause the fundamental problem is more one of technology transfer and cultural change than of technology development. Meanwhile, we will have much to watch over the next few years as Japan's SIGMA Project reaches its conclusions [24] and as similar projects in Europe (Esprit, Eureka, Alvey, etc.), Brazil, Korea, and Singapore unfold. And we will also have to watch such slumbering giants as Russia and the People's Republic of China as they struggle with the challenges of the Information Age.

1.6 THE WORLD-CLASS SOFTWARE ORGANIZATION

More important are the initiatives at the corporate level: the efforts of a few companies to develop *world-class software organizations* with the same level of passion and intensity that we have seen in other manufacturing and service industries throughout the United States in the past few years.

A key issue here is the recognition that *enterprise* productivity is much more important than project productivity or programmer productivity. This will require measuring aspects of productivity that many organizations ignore today: turnover, training, idle programmer time between projects, systems that are scrapped before (or after) they are developed, and so forth. And it will require a capital investment perspective (for programming tools, development environments, etc.) notoriously lacking in organizations that budget all their DP activities on a year-to-year, quarter-to-quarter basis.

This book is for the world-class software organizations who want to *stay* world-class and for all the other software shops that aspire to *become* world class. The fundamental questions raised in the chapters that follow are: What do the world-class software organizations do differently from your organization? What tools do they use? What methods, procedures, and techniques do they use? What do you have to do to be like them?

1.7 VOTING WITH YOUR FEET

Finally, there is the personal level of initiative. As a programmer, systems analyst, software engineer, or junior project manager, you can vote with your feet. You can change jobs freely, and (a little less easily) you can even change countries. Most American programmers are blissfully unaware of the issues raised in this chapter, and they will continue working, slothlike, until their employers go out of business. But those who are concerned will begin looking more closely at the environment in which they find themselves today. And they will begin asking questions like these:

- Does your company *care* about software quality—does it care enough, for example, to delay putting a new system into production because its software reliability models indicate an unacceptable number of latent errors? Does it even have software reliability models? (Software quality is discussed in Chapter 8.)

- Does your company *care* about its people? Has it invested time and money to train its DP managers to do a better job in hiring people? Does it invest an adequate amount of time training its technicians, or does it simply assume that its software engineers are replaceable commodities, not worth any investment? Does it use modern "performance management" methods to ensure that its corporate goals are aligned with personal consequences of those goals, or does it rely on lies and threats? Do the people in the organization even understand what the organizational goals really are, and how they are supposed to fit into those goals? (Peopleware issues are discussed in Chapter 3.)

- Does your company use modern programming tools, languages, and methodologies—or does it still defend assembly language and the waterfall life cycle as the greatest inventions of the twentieth century? (Software processes and methodologies are discussed in Chapters 4 and 5.)

- Does your company measure everything it does in the software arena? Does it measure the *process* of software development as well as the final *product*? Does it have a separate software metrics group? Are its metrics of project size, defects, and effort available for all to see? Are the metrics used in a positive way, so that everyone in the organization can see how they can improve? (Software metrics are discussed in Chapter 7.)

- Does your company support the concept of software reusability? More important, does it provide some incentive—for example, cash royalties—to its software engineers to create reusable components? Has it considered a separate "Software Parts Department" whose *only* job is to create reusable components? Does it estimate the degree of expected reusability at the *beginning* of projects and base its schedules and resource requirements on that estimate, or does it simply discover by accident, after the fact, whether anyone paid attention to reusability during the project? (Software reusability is discussed in Chapter 9.)

- Does your company have CASE tools? Does it believe that CASE tools are like toothbrushes, that is, they're not meant to be shared? Does it provide an adequately equipped PC or workstations for everyone? (CASE is discussed in Chapter 6.)

- Is it running scared, as if its very existence were at stake?

Unless the answer to most of these questions is an enthusiastic "yes!" the smart programmer will update his resume and move on.

The smart DP manager will look at the questions just posed, and the recommendations in subsequent chapters, as a mandate for change. Few, if any, of the changes can be accomplished overnight; indeed, many of the most ambitious U.S. software organizations realize that it will take them until the end of this decade to reach "best of breed" status where they can compete, and win, against virtually any software organization in the world—*if they start today*. It took a long time for most of our organizations to dig themselves into a hole, and it will take a long time to dig themselves out.

Smart senior executives, or end users, may wish to use the questions posed throughout this book to see if they should replace their DP organization. "Outsourcing" is not just an idea for getting rid of the hardware and the DP operations staff: you can use it to get rid of your programmers, too. If your slovenly bunch of software engineers doesn't want to play at the world-class level of performance, trade them in for a new bunch from Ireland or Singapore.

END NOTES

1. Yourdon, Edward. *Nations at Risk*. New York: Yourdon Press, 1986. See Chapter 23 for a discussion of the size of the information technology industry in the United States.
2. Porat, Marc. *Information Economy: Definition and Measurement*. Washington, D.C.: U.S. Government Printing Office, Special Publication 77-12(a), May 1977.
3. Yourdon, Edward. "Hong Kong: Countdown to 1997," *American Programmer*, June 1990.
4. Boehm, Barry. *Software Engineering Economics*. Englewood Cliffs, NJ: Prentice Hall, 1981.

5. Jones, Capers. *Applied Software Measurement: Assuring Productivity and Quality*. New York: McGraw-Hill, 1991.

6. Jones, Capers. "Evaluating International Software Productivity Levels," Version 3.0. Burlington, MA: Software Productivity Research, Inc., July 31, 1991.

7. Nomura, Toshitsugu. "Use of Software Engineering Tools in Japan," *Proceedings of the 9th International Conference on Software Engineering*, Monterey, California, April 1987.

8. Jones, Capers. *Programming Productivity*. New York: John Wiley & Sons, 1985.

9. Neumann, Peter. "Some Computer-Related Disasters and Other Egregious Horrors," *ACM SIGSOFT Software Engineering Notes*, January 1985. Each month's issue of this technical journal usually contains a new batch of software horror stories.

10. Jacky, Jon. "The Star Wars Defense Won't Compute," *Atlantic Monthly*, June 1985. Other stories on the possible defects in Star Wars have appeared in newspapers and technical journals around the world, most notably when David Parnas publicly questioned the viability of the software in 1985 in *The New York Times*. For a discussion of the current testing strategy for the SDI software, see John Morrison's article, "A Wicked Problem—Software Testing in Large-Scale Systems," *American Programmer*, April 1991.

11. Jones, Capers. *Programming Productivity: Issues for the Eighties*, IEEE Catalog No. EHO 186-7. Jones has also written a paper reporting on the tenth anniversary of the creation of ITT's Programming Technology Center in Stratford, Connecticut. I found it fascinating reading and suggest you write Jones for a copy at Software Productivity Research, Inc., 77 South Bedford St., Burlington, MA 01803-5154; phone 617-273-5176.

12. Page-Jones, Meilir. *The Practical Guide to Structured Systems Design*, 2nd ed. Englewood Cliffs, NJ: Yourdon Press/Prentice Hall, 1988.

13. Gedeon, D. Personal correspondence with the author.

14. Jones, T. Capers. Personal correspondence with the author.

15. Levy, Leon. *Taming the Tiger: Software Engineering and Software Economics*. New York: Springer-Verlag, 1987.

16. Levy, Leon. *Fundamental Concepts of Computer Science: Mathematical Foundations of Programming*. New York: Dorset House, 1988.

17. "U.S. Faces a Difficult Technological Future as Number of Engineers, Scientists Declines," *Investor's Daily*, July 11, 1987.

18. Also reported in *ITI Innovator*, available from the director of the

Information Technology Institute, National Computer Board, 71 Science Park Drive, Singapore 0511, Republic of Singapore.

19. Harrison, R. Personal correspondence with the author.
20. Vesely, Eric. *The Practitioner's Blueprint for Logical and Physical Database Design*. Englewood Cliffs, NJ: Prentice Hall, 1986.
21. Boddie, John. *Crunch Mode*. Englewood Cliffs, NJ: Yourdon Press/ Prentice Hall, 1987.
22. Covin, C. Personal correspondence with the author.
23. Howard, P. Personal correspondence with the author.
24. As reported in the February 1991 issue of *American Programmer*, the SIGMA project has not yet produced any significant results and is characterized in the Japanese computer trade press as a "$200 million failure." But it may be too early to tell: the project finished its five-year research phase in 1990 and is now a self-sustaining, revenue-generating entity. It may yet have an impact on the Japanese software industry.

2

The Lure of the Silver Bullet

Of all the monsters that fill the nightmares of our folklore, none terrify more than werewolves, because they transform unexpectedly from the familiar into horrors. For these, one seeks bullets of silver that can magically lay them to rest.

The familiar software project, at least as seen by the nontechnical manager, has something of this character; it is usually innocent and straightforward, but is capable of becoming a monster of missed schedules, blown budgets, and flawed products. So we hear desperate cries for a silver bullet—something to make software costs drop as rapidly as computer hardware costs do.

But, as we look to the horizon of a decade hence, we see no silver bullet. There is no single development, in either technology or in management technique, that by itself promises even one order-of-magnitude improvement in productivity, in reliability, in simplicity.

Fred Brooks, "No Silver Bullet,"
IEEE Computer, April 1987

Though he has made numerous contributions to the field of software engineering, many people know Fred Brooks only as the author of two phrases: "the mythical man-month" (the title of his best-known book) and "no silver bullet" (the title of a paper that has become an instant classic).

With the exception of a few hysterical CASE vendors and religious zealots, most software professionals would agree that there is no single silver bullet that will exorcise our software demons. That doesn't mean we should give up and accept today's world of "missed schedules, blown budgets, and flawed products" as inevitable. As Brooks points out toward the end of his paper [1],

> Even though no technological breakthrough promises to give the sort of magical results with which we are so familiar in the hardware area, there is both an abundance of good work going on now, and the promise of steady, if unspectacular progress.

In the previous chapter, I argued that American software organizations must begin paying attention to the problems of software productivity and software quality if they are to become (or remain) world-class competitors. But though the global scale of competition may be new, the problems themselves are not. For years, we have known that the day-to-day operation of our companies has depended on software-intensive computer systems. And for decades, we have known that the productivity of our software engineers is abysmally low; the figures produced by metrics guru Capers Jones in the 1990s are now expressed in function points,[1] but we first began to hear reports of 10 to 15 lines of debugged code per person per day in the 1960s. Nearly a decade ago, Tom DeMarco [4] pointed out that 25 percent of large system development projects *never* finish, and a more recent study by Capers Jones [2] documented the gloomy statistic that the average MIS development project is one year late and 100 percent over budget.

Senior MIS executives in world-class software organizations must be familiar with the kinds of "good work" going on in the software field today and must develop long-term game plans to implement the "steady, unspectacular progress" suggested by Fred Brooks in tools,

---

[1] One of the great difficulties, of course, is that everyone measures different software development activities in different ways; we will discuss this in more detail in Chapter 7. Jones [2, 3] documents minimum, median, and maximum productivity rates for 25 different software development activities (e.g., requirements analysis, coding, unit testing, and management) and a wide range of industries.

techniques, and other forms of improved productivity and quality. Without this awareness, there is a tendency to view software productivity problems as the end result of a programmer shortage. Indeed, this is exactly how the general public often hears about the situation; in Japan, MITI has extrapolated the supply and demand for software engineers from 1985 through the year 2000 and predicts a shortage of nearly a million people [5].

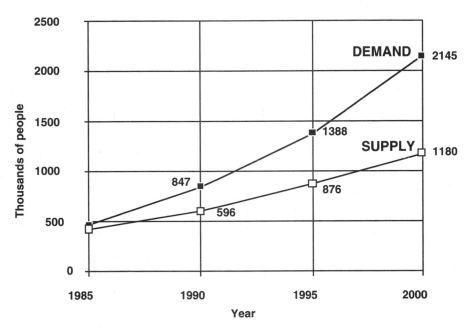

Figure 2.2: Supply and demand of Japanese software engineers, 1985–2000

When programmers, systems analysts, or MIS managers ask me, "Which silver bullet are you recommending today?" I answer, "There is no *one* silver bullet, but there may be a dozen or so that are worth exploring." My personal list of 11 silver bullets is summarized as follows:

1. Better programming languages
2. Better people
3. Automated tools
4. JAD
5. RAD
6. Prototyping

7. Structured techniques
8. Information engineering
9. Object-oriented methodologies
10. Software reusability
11. Software reengineering

2.1 BETTER PROGRAMMING LANGUAGES

Newer and more powerful programming languages are a perennial favorite of the tech weenies and propeller heads in the organization. If third generation languages didn't solve our productivity problems, then fourth generation languages will; if fourth generation languages won't do the job, the fifth generation languages will.

In any reasonable situation, nobody is going to argue against an assertion that high-level languages are better than low-level languages. However, such an argument typically ignores the problem of maintaining *existing* programs written in older languages during the past 20 years. Since we're spending between 50 and 80 percent of our MIS budget maintaining these old systems, perhaps *that* is what we should be focusing on: upgrading the old programs from a 3GL technology to a 4GL technology may be a great idea, but the focus has to start with the existing programs, in whatever generation of programming language they were written in.

Similarly, the argument about newer and better programming languages typically ignores the problem of retraining existing *programmers* who have spent the past 5 to 10 years muddling around in their old languages. An upgrade from COBOL '74 to COBOL '85 is hard enough for these folks; an upgrade from COBOL '85 to object-oriented COBOL (which will appear sometime in the early to mid-1990s) is likely to knock their socks off. An upgrade from FORTRAN to Ada, or from Pascal to Smalltalk is equally mind-blowing. An upgrade from C to C++ may appear simpler, because C is a proper subset of C++, but of course, this just masks the problem—old programmers may continue to write old programs in their new language. In any event, a new language is typically *not* something you can just drop into the organization the way you might replace an 80286 PC with an 80386 or a Mac Plus with a Macintosh Quadra unless you give the existing programmers a lobotomy and "refresh" their memories with the elements of a new programming language; it's going to be an expensive, time-consuming process.

But the real problem with programming languages as the silver bullet solution to software problems is that it puts the emphasis at the wrong level: *better coding techniques may do nothing more than help you arrive at a disaster sooner than before.* Better programming languages, used without anything else, may be just what your programmers need to develop a brilliant solution to the wrong problem. Certainly one major lesson we have learned from the past 20 years of software engineering experience is that there is more to be gained from attention to design, analysis, and business strategy issues than from attention to programming-level issues.

Ultimately, most of us won't care very much about the issue of programming languages, because it will be hidden by the CASE tools we use. As an analogy, harken back to the days of the 1960s when the concept of "high-level" third generation languages was relatively new and many programmers distrusted compilers. *Everyone* insisted that the compilers generate assembly language as their output rather than a direct translation to machine language. Why? So the programmers could examine the compiler output to see if it was as tight and efficient as they could have done on their own; also (though we often forget it), the assembly language code was important during debugging sessions, since the debugging tools available to the programmer typically didn't operate at the same level as the third generation language.

Today, we have a comparable situation. Everyone insists that modern CASE tools generate COBOL, even though nobody in his or her right mind should want to *look* at the COBOL. But we're all curious about the quality of the code produced by the CASE code generators. And besides, if the code doesn't work, we have to use our COBOL debugging tools rather than debugging at the level of data flow diagrams, action diagrams, or some other high-level abstraction.

By 1995, all this will seem like an anachronism. Programming languages will still be a matter of some academic interest, but the world-class software organization will greet the announcement of yet another new and sexy language (the seventh generation? maybe the eighth) with a loud yawn. The real productivity gains are to be found elsewhere. Based on this expectation, I won't discuss new/better/higher-level programming languages any further in this book.

2.2 BETTER PEOPLE

Mediocre people with good tools and languages will still develop mediocre systems, but good people, even when burdened with poor tools and mediocre languages, can turn out damn good software. This has been true in the past, and it will continue to be true for the foreseeable future. As DeMarco and Lister [6] argue,

> The major problems of our work are not so much *technological* as *sociological* in nature.
>
> Most managers are willing to concede the idea that they've got more people worries than technical worries. *But they seldom manage that way.*

Because of this, many organizations are focusing their software improvement efforts on the human resource component—often referred to as "peopleware." As we will see in Chapter 3, attention to peopleware issues can literally cause 10-fold productivity improvements, while investments in CASE, methodologies, or other technologies rarely cause more than a 30–40 percent improvement.

Peopleware efforts are directed at several related issues:

- Hiring the best people
- Engaging in the ongoing training and education of existing staff
- Motivating people for higher levels of performance
- Developing performance management ideas to align personal goals with corporate goals
- Offering an adequate working environment, with particular emphasis on adequate office facilities rather than the pigsties in which most software engineers find themselves squatting for 10 hours a day.
- Placing more emphasis on creating and maintaining effective *teams* of people who can work together to create high-quality software products.

These ideas are discussed in more detail in Chapter 3.

2.3 AUTOMATED TOOLS

Automated tools—in particular, CASE tools—are currently a favorite approach to improving software quality and productivity; from a shaky beginning as avant-garde toys in the mid-1980s to robust, industrial-strength tools in the early 1990s, CASE is becoming a mainstream technology: by the middle of the 1990s, most market forecasters expect that 50 percent of the professional software engineers in the United States will have their own personal CASE tools.

This is clearly a technology that is separating the world-class players from the wishy-washy mediocre shops. One reason for the separation between the "big guys" and the "little guys" is the cost issue: as of 1991, the cost for a reasonably well-equipped CASE environment in the United States is $30,000–50,000 per person.[2] While this kind of investment can usually be justified by a 20–30 percent improvement in productivity, it nevertheless represents a "big-ticket" investment: one study [7] estimated that installation and five-year maintenance costs of CASE tools for a 200-person MIS shop would be approximately $6.5 million. No matter what the cost–benefit study says, or how reasonable the return on investment (ROI) looks, $6.5 million investments in productivity tools can easily be delayed, sidetracked, or mothballed in tough economic times.

The situation is compounded by some short-term problems: CASE users often experience a productivity *decrease* for the first 3 to 6 months, and it often takes 12 to 18 months before productivity gains are visible. So the organization expecting a "quick fix" from the CASE silver bullet can be in for a rude shock.[3]

But even with short-term problems, there is a growing consensus that CASE will be a necessary component of the software development community in the 1990s—just as the software development community began arguing about the efficacy of dumb time-sharing terminals in the late 1960s, and finally concluded sometime in the 1970s that sooner or later everyone would move away from the IBM 029 keypunch machines and insist on having a terminal on their desk. In 1991, only 10–15 percent of the software engineers in the United States had the luxury of a personal CASE workstation; thus, this is an area where the world-class companies have an opportunity to move ahead of their competition. More on this is found in Chapter 6.

---

[2] One would expect the cost of this technology to drop over the next several years, as the CASE vendors recoup their development expenses and as they look forward with greater confidence to large-volume sales. On the other hand, the functionality offered by today's CASE tools is only a small fraction of what we expect to find in the fully integrated CASE tools of the mid-1990s; thus, it is quite possible that the price tag will remain relatively constant over the next several years as the functionality of the tools increase. More on this is found in Chapter 6.

[3] In our discussion of software metrics in Chapter 7, we will point out another interesting "backlash" problem associated with CASE tools: if the organization does not measure unpaid overtime, then it may not see any visible evidence of productivity improvement from the introduction of CASE tools (other than a small decrease in the electric utility bills caused by programmers turning off the office lights when they go home at 5 PM). It's quite possible for CASE to make the software engineers happy, but managers frustrated.

2.4 JAD, RAD, AND PROTOTYPING

JAD is not new, but it has been given a new life. "Joint application design," as it was originally called, was created by IBM Canada in the 1970s as a mechanism for bringing users and systems analysts together for intensive, highly productive mediated sessions to elicit the requirements of a new system. JAD was widely practiced in North America for several years, but gradually lost its glamor and pizzazz until the advent of CASE tools revived the concept. Today, there are a number of books, articles, and consultants supporting the JAD concept [8–11]; it is indeed alive and well and credited with providing significant improvements in software productivity.

A modern variant of JAD is known as RAD, for "rapid application development." As we will discuss in more detail in Chapter 5, RAD is usually described as a combination of JAD sessions to determine user requirements quickly, as well as CASE tools, prototyping techniques, Rambo-style SWAT teams, and a formal software development methodology to implement those requirements quickly; in some cases, though, it is interpreted simply as a form of prototyping. As a *combination* of tools and techniques, RAD has much to offer, but any of the techniques used alone—whether JAD sessions, prototyping, or CASE tools—almost certainly will *not* turn out to be the silver bullet that some vendors are promising.

It is particularly important to emphasize this point about prototyping, since many current languages, tools, and methodologies emphasize the benefits of prototyping. Everyone knows the benefits of building a prototype for an end user who is unsure of his or her requirements, but prototyping cannot eliminate the need for formal analysis and design work on large, complex projects.

It has already become clear that JAD sessions will be strongly affected by the nature of tools used by software engineers; already there is great debate about the adequacy of current CASE tools in JAD sessions.[4] In our discussion of CASE tools in Chapter 6, we will emphasize the need for "groupware" tools that facilitate cooperative work activities of software engineers.

[4] For an example of the debate, see the articles by Crawford [11], Wood [12], and Hill [10]. My personal feeling is that the vast majority of current CASE tools are a disaster in JAD sessions, for they completely distract the discussion away from the subject matter of the user's application and focus instead on the artistic elegance of the diagrams drawn by the CASE tool. I strongly recommend an electronic whiteboard with a capability to produce hard copy of anything drawn on it; the hand-drawn diagrams can then be given to clerical drones (sometimes disguised as computer science students) to be carefully entered into the "official" CASE tool.

2.5 STRUCTURED TECHNIQUES

In the 1970s, a number of my colleagues and I—people like Larry Constantine, Tom DeMarco, Tim Lister, Chris Gane, Trish Sarson, Steve McMenamin, John Palmer, Paul Ward, Steve Mellor, and many others—developed a collection of software development ideas that have come to be known as "structured techniques" or "structured methodologies." We weren't exactly sure what we were doing in those days, but the ideas caught on, and by the mid-1980s many of us were convinced that structured techniques would save the world from communism and protect the American way of life.

Well, it turned out that the American way of life didn't need to be defended by us; it remains to be seen whether structured techniques have had any impact on Western civilization. But in the early 1990s, it appears that structured techniques are the most widely practiced form of systems analysis and design in North America and one of the two or three most widely popular techniques in the world.[5]

For the organization that has *no* methodology, structured techniques may indeed appear to be a communism-defeating life-saver; this, then, has become the silver bullet solution for some organizations looking for dramatic improvements in productivity and quality. And for the organization that wants CASE support of its methodology, structured techniques are attractive: nearly every major CASE vendors offers support for the Gane–Sarson, or Yourdon–DeMarco, or Ward–Mellor, or Yourdon–Constantine variant of structured analysis and structured design.

Unfortunately, some of these CASE tools provide automated support for only the older dialects of structured techniques—the ones my colleagues and I developed in the mid-1970s.[6] The original form of these methodologies were all right for their time but are woefully inadequate by today's standards. In particular, the original form of

---

[5] A survey in 1990, *The Second Annual Report on CASE*, provided statistics indicating that various forms of structured techniques are by far the most popular in the United States, by a factor of approximately 5 to 1.

[6] It is important to note that the "bibles" of structured analysis are Tom DeMarco's *Structured Analysis and System Specification*, published by Yourdon Press in 1978 and still available from Prentice Hall in its original first edition form, as well as Chris Gane and Trish Sarson's *Structured Analysis: Tools and Techniques*, first published by Improved Systems Technologies in 1977 and also still available from Prentice Hall in its first edition form. Larry Constantine and I published *Structured Design* in 1975 and made only cosmetic changes in the Prentice Hall version, which appeared in 1978. For an interesting history of the early days of the structured movement, see Ward [14].

structured analysis gave great emphasis to the modeling of *functions* in a system, using the ubiquitous data flow diagram as the graphical modeling tool. The *data* component was incorporated in structured analysis, but was not given proper emphasis; not until the mid-1980s did more "modern" forms of structured analysis appear, incorporating the entity–relationship diagram for data modeling and the state–transition diagram for models of real-time systems. McMenamin and Palmer added a crucial concept of *events* and *event partitioning*, as well as a critical emphasis on modeling the "essence" of a system. A number of current textbooks [13, 15, 16] discuss these modern variants of structured analysis and design; some of the more recent ones, including Martin's *User-Centered Requirements Analysis* [16], shift the perspective of systems analysis noticeably toward the end user.

Much of this important work, unfortunately, seems to have escaped the attention of many CASE vendors; their tools are still based on vintage-1978 versions of the structured techniques. It is still not clear how quickly this situation will change.

This does not mean that something is wrong with the concept of structured techniques, but merely that a software development organization hoping that structured techniques will be its silver bullet could be badly disappointed. The bottom-line advice should be obvious: if you are going to adopt structured techniques, be sure that you pick a modern variant, and make sure that your CASE vendor supports a modern variant.

But the situation just described suggests that something more fundamental is going on: software development methodologies are created (by someone, or by some motley crew of people) and introduced into the field. If they survive, inevitably they evolve over a period of time. Meanwhile, CASE tools evolve too—but the key point is that they may lag behind the methodologies (by several years, in the case of structured techniques!) *until the CASE tools themselves become the driving force for methodology creation and evolution.* We will discuss the phenomenon of methodology "paradigm shifts"—a phenomenon of far more concern to the world-class software shop than the esoteric details of any specific methodology—in Chapter 5.

2.6 INFORMATION ENGINEERING

Information engineering, as popularized by James Martin and others, found itself in an interesting position at the beginning of the 1990s: as a methodology, it was used by as many as 10 percent DP organizations than those using structured techniques, but it had nevertheless acquired the momentum and fervor that had been associated with structured techniques in the late 1970s and early 1980s. It is, quite possibly, the fastest-growing methodology in the United States in the early 1990s.

The technical components of information engineering will be discussed in a little more detail in Chapter 5, but references like [17] are probably the best source of complete, detailed information. At this juncture, suffice it to say that information engineering emphasizes *data* as a corporate asset and as the basis for systems analysis and design. Though it can be for the analysis and design phases of individual projects, information engineering is most often perceived as a methodology for *enterprisewide* modeling activities.[7]

Because information engineering is a somewhat newer (and less widely used) methodology, the CASE "methodology lag" discussed earlier does not exist: there are fewer full-spectrum information engineering CASE vendors, and those that exist support an up-to-date version of the information engineering methodology.

But here again, there is an interesting issue lurking behind the surface: one reason for the adherence of CASE tools like Texas Instruments' IEF and KnowledgeWare's IEW CASE products to the "official" information engineering methodology is the business relationship that existed in the developmental stage of the product, between the CASE vendor and the methodology developer (James Martin). This is in stark contrast to the large number of CASE vendors who claim, for example, to support the DeMarco form of structured analysis, but who have never spoken to Tom DeMarco and who have evidently never read past Chapter 2 of his book on the subject.

The issue of symbiotic relationships between methodologies and CASE tools—for example, the existence of CASE "methodology companions," "methodology copycats," and "methodology-neutral" tools—is discussed in more detail in Chapter 6.

2.7 OBJECT-ORIENTED METHODOLOGIES

If information engineering was the hot new methodology of the late 1980s and early 1990s, it's a safe bet that object-oriented methodologies will be the hot new methodology of the mid-1990s. A whole new

---

[7] By contrast, structured analysis is generally perceived as a methodology for modeling individual systems within an organization, but it can be (and has been) used to model entire enterprises.

generation of hackers and hucksters, gurus and methodologists, language developers, tool builders, and assorted others are proclaiming that *this* is the methodology that will change Western civilization like no other methodology before it.

Unfortunately, the vast majority of public discussion on the subject of "OO-stuff"—in the form of books, newspaper articles, seminars, and conference presentations—is devoted to the subject of object-oriented *programming*. Is Smalltalk better than C++? Is Eiffel better than Smalltalk? Can Ada ever be object oriented, and would anyone really care? The discussions that do not revolve around programming languages typically concern low-level design issues within specific operating system environments: What's the best way to implement a scroll bar in Microsoft Windows?

Alas, OO-stuff will never be the silver bullet if the discussion remains at such a low level. World-class organizations looking to object-oriented technology to improve their productivity and software quality dramatically are strongly advised to focus their attention on object-oriented *analysis*, object-oriented *design*, and object-oriented *databases*. In all these forms of object orientation, we find the universal concept of encapsulating data and function together into highly reusable *objects*. But the argument made earlier in this chapter that better programming languages might allow us to arrive at a disaster sooner than before is an argument that applies equally well to object-oriented programming languages. If you don't understand the user's requirements, it doesn't matter how you code it.

Other technical concepts of object orientation—inheritance, messages between objects, and so forth—will be discussed in more detail in Chapter 5. Of more importance is the discussion in Chapter 5 about methodology paradigm shifts. For many organizations, the *real* question today is: *Is this the time to switch to an object-oriented methodology?*

Another issue becomes evident when discussing OO-stuff: the *generational* issue. It is no accident that object-oriented methodologies are largely supported by a generation of software engineers in their twenties—a generation that tends to disparage the methodologies of the 1970s precisely *because* they were developed in the 1970s. It is hard enough to compare the strengths and weaknesses of various methodologies in even the most neutral setting; when the emotions of mothers and daughters, fathers and sons, youngsters and old-timers enter the argument, it's difficult to arrive at any rational conclusions. More about this also in Chapter 5.

2.8 SOFTWARE REUSABILITY

An interesting characteristic of silver bullet productivity solutions is their tendency to be recycled every 10 or 20 years. Software reusability is a good example: promoted with great fanfare in the 1960s, reusability faded away in the 1970s and 1980s, but is now back with us again. Some software development organizations are convinced that achieving a higher level of reuse is more important than which methodology they use, or even which people they employ.

As we will see in Chapter 9, some of the world-class organizations are achieving reuse levels of 60–70 percent; that is, most of the code in any new system consists of components taken from a library of reusable components. The typical organization is achieving only a 20–30 percent level of reuse.

How is reuse accomplished? Some organizations argue that *technology* is the answer: new programming languages, new (object-oriented) analysis and design paradigms, and aggressive use of CASE tools with repositories of reusable data and code elements.

But in Chapter 9, I will argue that the key issues for success in reusability initiatives are managerial and cultural in nature. *Motivation* plays a big role: if software engineers see no personal incentive for reusing components from a library, then it doesn't matter very much whether management thinks it's a good idea. *Passive* versus *active* reuse is also a factor: if management assesses the level of reuse only at the end of a project, rather than building it into the project plan from the beginning, it's likely that the extent of reusability will be random and accidental. And the creation of a separate group with the responsibility for creating reusable components may be a big factor, too.

Some organizations—especially the Japanese software shops—have addressed these issues. While the creation of a software reuse environment is expensive, and while it may require a massive culture shift in the organization, the end results can be impressive: both the productivity gain and the quality improvement associated with a 80 percent reuse organization are obviously far higher than that associated with a 20 percent reuse organization.

2.9 SOFTWARE REENGINEERING

It is no secret that many organizations spend more than half of their MIS resources keeping old software alive. Whether it's called maintenance, enhancement, upgrades, ongoing development, refurbishing, or bug-fixing, it all has to do with *existing* systems rather than the more glamorous work of developing new systems from scratch.

For the organization spending 50, 60, or 80 percent of its data processing dollars in this fashion, greater productivity gains may be achieved in the maintenance area than in the new systems area. This may be achieved in the form of reduced defects (or increased mean time between failures) in existing systems or a shorter time to respond to requests from the users for new features. Or it may be achieved in the form of a reduced staff requirement for maintenance—after all, if some of the maintenance programmers can be freed up to work on new systems, it should make everyone happy!

One of the technologies that has long been advocated for decreasing maintenance costs is *restructuring*—transforming old, unstructured code in functionally equivalent structured code. While it does offer some benefits, we will show in Chapter 10 that only approximately 10 percent of the candidate companies are currently making significant use of this technology. Most companies are currently using a variety of *reengineering* tools, which provide the means for maintenance programmers to understand more easily "alien" programs written years earlier by people no longer with the organization. There is also a slow but steady growth of interest in *reverse engineering*, which attempts to reconstruct design models and specification-level models directly from the source code.

As we will see in Chapter 10, reengineering technologies are considered by many to be a subset of CASE technology; indeed, reengineering does depend heavily on automated tools. But as with most of the other software productivity technologies, success in reengineering depends heavily on management issues and cultural factors. This is particularly true in a software maintenance environment, where a single individual may be the "sole living expert" who keeps a mission-critical system alive.

But if there are management problems here, there are also management opportunities. After all, the organization may only have the opportunity to develop one or two major new systems each year—but it has an existing portfolio of 20 years of accumulated software, upon which the entire enterprise depends. A significant improvement in this existing mass of software can have profound consequences for the organization—and the world-class software shop looks at this opportunity from a variety of different perspectives. For example, what better place to look for potential reusable components for the software reusability library than the inventory of existing applications?

2.10 CONCLUSION

Of course, there are many other productivity tools and methods besides the ones here. And individual organizations will assign different priorities to the productivity approaches I have listed. But each is important and deserves to be reviewed thoroughly on an ongoing basis.

No rational DP organization can implement all these productivity approaches simultaneously. It would cost too much, and it would throw the technical staff into such a state of hysteria that the organization would never recover. But management must have a plan for implementing these and other productivity techniques over a period of 3, 5, or possible even 10 years.[8]

There is no one single bullet. But taken together, perhaps a collection of small silver pellets will help to slay the werewolves of software development quality and productivity.

END NOTES

1. Brooks, Fred. "No Silver Bullets," *IEEE Computer,* April 1987.
2. Jones, Capers. *Applied Software Measurement.* New York: McGraw-Hill, 1991.
3. Jones, Capers. "Applied Software Measurement: The Software Industry Starts to Mature," *American Programmer,* June 1991.
4. DeMarco, Tom. *Controlling Software Projects.* Englewood Cliffs, NJ: Yourdon Press/Prentice Hall, 1982.
5. Yourdon, Edward. "Japan Revisited," *American Programmer,* February 1990.
6. DeMarco, Tom, and Timothy R. Lister. *Peopleware.* New York: Dorset House, 1987.
7. Yourdon, Edward. "The Future of CASE," Technical Report TR-3. New York: American Programmer, Inc., 1990.
8. August, Judy. *Joint Application Design: The Group Session Approach to System Design.* Englewood Cliffs, NJ: Prentice Hall, 1991.

[8] For a discussion of the problems associated with implementing such organizational changes, and some good strategies for overcoming these obstacles, see Barbara Bouldin's *Agents of Change* [18].

9. Wood, Jane, and Denise Silver. *Joint Application Design*. New York: John Wiley & Sons, 1989.

10. Hill, Inez Marino. "Not All JADs Are Created Equal," *American Programmer*, January 1991.

11. Crawford, Tony. "People Considerations for a More Successful JAD," *American Programmer*, January 1991.

12. Wood, Jane, "The 10-Minute JAD Quiz," *American Programmer*, January 1991.

13. Yourdon, Edward. *Modern Structured Analysis*. Englewood Cliffs, NJ: Yourdon Press/Prentice Hall, 1989.

14. Ward, Paul. "The Evolution of Structured Analysis: Part I—The Early Years," *American Programmer*, November 1991.

15. Ward, Paul, and Stephen J. Mellor. *Structured Development of Real-Time Systems*. Englewood Cliffs, NJ: Yourdon Press/Prentice Hall, 1985.

16. Martin, Charles. *User-Centered Requirements Analysis*. Englewood Cliffs, NJ: Prentice Hall, 1988.

17. Martin, James. *Information Engineering*, Vols. 1–3. Englewood Cliffs, NJ: Prentice Hall, 1990.

18. Bouldin, Barbara. *Agents of Change*. Englewood Cliffs, NJ: Yourdon Press/Prentice Hall, 1989.

3

Peopleware

*Imagine that you had a one-hour conference with the senior data process-
ing manager in your shop and that you had enough clout and credibility
that he or she would actually pay attention to what you said. My
questions are (1) What three things would you tell him or her that he or
she does not know is going on down in the trenches? (2) What three things
would you tell him or her must be done to improve the working conditions
of the people down in the trenches? (3) What three things would you tell
him or her to stop doing to the people down in the trenches?*

I posted this message on one of CompuServe's electronic bulletin
boards recently, curious to see if I would get any reaction. To my
surprise, during the next two weeks I received more than 100 replies
from programmers, systems analysts, database administrators, and
consultants all over the United States. Here is a typical comment from
a senior programmer in a midwestern organization:

> Tell them to learn how to be leaders rather than dictators, and to
> see people rather than parts. Our company motto proclaims that
> "people are our most important resource." Unfortunately, "re-
> sources" happen to be things that get used up, and what's left is
> discarded. When people see that management views them in that
> light, how can anyone expect them to give their best?

If you're a manager, read this chapter as if it were a memo from one of
those programmers whose name you can't remember, whose scruffy

face you see only at Christmas parties and other ceremonial gatherings. Your programmers wish they could express these ideas to you themselves, but they're afraid you'll fire them. Messengers bearing bad news never have had much job security. For example, when I asked one consultant, via CompuServe, why he didn't point out some of the organization's problems to his clients, he e-mailed back:

> They didn't fire me when I did just that. The director of operations did, though, call me into his office for a private conference and spent a full two hours telling me (in quite carefully phrased words intended to keep me from walking out in a huff) to bring my complaints to him privately and to no one else. Then a week later he quit to assume the presidency of a firm in another city.

3.1 THE PREMISE

My CompuServe electronic message began with the following introduction:

> The January issue of *American Programmer* will discuss the "peopleware" issues of improving MIS productivity and software quality, and I would like to get comments from members of this illustrious forum. The theme is that better people, better motivation, and better working conditions can often yield greater productivity/quality improvements than technological gadgets (CASE, OOD, Ada, prototyping, etc.), methods, methodologies, and so on.

And indeed I believe this to be true. Some grizzled veterans probably knew this back in the 1950s; I began to get a sense of it as I learned about programming at MIT, and in my first couple of jobs at DEC and General Electric. I learned, for example, that tiny miracles could sometimes be accomplished by individuals or small groups if management would just leave us alone. I even participated in a small miracle myself: during a one-week winter break my senior year at college, I locked myself in my room and produced a new assembler for DEC's fledgling PDP-8 minicomputer. I was severely chastised by management when they saw my time sheet showing an 80-hour workweek—but at $3 per hour, DEC got a pretty good bargain for what came to be known as the PAL-III assembler.

The scientific evidence supporting the importance of the human element began in a classic 1968 paper by Sackman, Erickson, and Grant [1]. In a study intended to determine whether programmers were more productive with time-sharing terminals, the authors discovered something even more important: independent of tools, techniques, and programming environments, some programmers are much better than others. In their own pithy words, Sackman, Erickson, and Grant observed that

> When a programmer is good,
> He is very, very good,
> But when he is bad,
> He is horrid.

This conclusion was based on the results of a programming exercise given to a group of 12 experienced programmers. Careful records were kept to see how long the programmers took to finish various phases of the programming job, and what results they produced. The outcome was staggering: the best person in the group finished coding and debugging the exercise 28 times faster than the worst person, and the best program was approximately 10 times more efficient (in terms of memory and CPU cycles) than the worst.

Equally important was the discovery that the actual performance of the programmers had no significant correlation with years of programming experience or scores on standard programming aptitude tests. As the authors said,

> This situation suggests that general programming skill may dominate early training and initial on-the-job experience, but that such skill is progressively transformed and displaced by more specialized skills with increasing experience.

That was in 1968, before many of today's programmers were even born. But studies at General Electric in 1979 [2], and the University of Maryland in 1989 [3] continue to confirm that the phenomenon is as true today as it was 20 years ago. Barry Boehm's classic study of programming productivity factors in *Software Engineering Economics* [4] found that the productivity of the 90th-percentile *teams* is four times higher than that of the 15th-percentile teams. And Capers Jones has reported [5] that the development and maintenance costs of projects using experienced people were half that of projects using inexperienced people.[1]

You've heard all this before? Well, consider the "downside" scenario: if good people can increase the productivity of your MIS

[1] In all these studies, little correlation has been found between performance and years of experience in the field. Actual productivity is better correlated with the number of programming languages that the person knows.

organization, then below-average people—or good people who have become discouraged, demoralized, even disgusted with their environment—can decrease your productivity.

Morale in your MIS organization is probably worse than you think. No doubt you have heard that on average, programmer/analysts change jobs every year and a half. Why do you think that's true? It's not because they've grown tired of the menu in the company cafeteria, but because they've grown tired of the management milieu, tired of working on doomed projects, tired of being deceived.

3.2 MURMURS FROM THE TRENCHES

An outsider can sense a low-morale DP shop as soon as he walks in the door: the smell of death and decay is in the air. Consultants learn to sniff the air for the telltale odor. (Perhaps that's why so many of the CompuServe messages I received were from consultants.)

For example, the programmer who argued that managers should not consider their people replaceable parts sent the following comment:

> I really don't have any quibble at all with the NewSpeak redefinition of "quality" to mean "meeting the requirements," just so long as senior management itself accepts the definition. But since the essence of Crosby's approach is that "quality" is a Boolean quantity (it either is present, or is not, with no in-between states), any time that management uses phrases like "high quality" or "superior quality" that simply shouts that they themselves either (1) do not comprehend that they are spending horrendous amounts to teach all employees and are therefore total incompetents or (2) have not themselves accepted the definitions they want the rest of us to work by and are therefore hypocritically incompetent!

> Another cornerstone of the Crosby system is that all changes must be initiated from the top, BY EXAMPLE. Again, when senior management fails to set forth a quantifiable list of requirements for tasks and products, then sends the strong message by their actions that the only real requirement is to "meet the schedule," they demonstrate a lack of commitment which most definitely teaches the rest of us to "do as I do, not as I say," and the net result is totally counterproductive. This is, I think, the #1 Quality Killer. . . .

> Little things like "functional products" and "customer satisfaction" are not even considered; the proof is that they are always being talked about, but the only thing that can bring the top dogs down to the factory floor is a threatened schedule slippage.

That being the case, we obviously run a "quality" operation, since we always ship on schedule even if we have to backdate the shipping ticket to do so <grin> . . . .

Another example of discontent and cynicism on the part of programmers came from John James, a Dallas-based consultant:

I've worked for some really terrible managers. In fact, one of the poorer ones I've ever worked for—real yes man, had no idea how to interview or select employees, was not a leader or a decision maker, could not relate to his employees—was just selected the company's manager of the year. In the term of the year he was selected for, his center was shut down permanently, he was moved to the location that had the poorest performance levels in the country, and as of the week he was selected the levels had dropped since his arrival.

I think the people who put poor management in place, then do nothing about it, should be thrown up against a wall or two. It might only help vent a little frustration, but [a] blow to the head has been known to knock a little sense into people at times.

If managers do a lousy job but are left in place or—scarier still—are rewarded for such performance, the problem isn't all theirs . . . .

Consultant Tom Rawson sent me the following observations:

I am an independent consultant and have been for four years. My comments are based mostly on watching people manage in organizations I consult for.

Basically I think senior management in most companies really doesn't know what it is doing. Seriously. And nobody wants to own up to it (of course). The senior managers who are not in it purely for personal gain (i.e., those who care about doing a good job—and that is many of them, don't get me wrong) know plenty about business, but almost nothing about software.

In particular they don't understand the design process. Recently I've dealt with a couple of embedded systems projects. I was dealing with engineering managers, who should (in my opinion) have at least as good an understanding of how to manage a technical project as an MIS or general business manager, and probably (on average) are considerably better. But in both cases there were no specs, and then they wanted to know why it "took so long."

Even the most rudimentary things, e.g., Brooks' Law (adding manpower to a late software project simply makes it later), seem to be unknown to people who are supposed to be managing this process . . . .

Washington-based independent consultant Rich Cohen remarked:

> I wonder how much management is paying to replace workers lost through stupid management policies. In Washington, D.C., in the consulting sector, the average turnover is under two years. On the other hand, I know of a few well run companies that hold their people a lot longer.
>
> What I would tell a senior manager:
>
> 1. Managers are not reviewing work products (designs and programs) and acting on the results.
> 2. Time must be invested in internal training to ensure that all workers have a common understanding of the methods used to develop software within the organization.
> 3. Reviews that are held at the end of a project are worthless in preventing or correcting errors.
>
> Three things to do:
>
> 1. Hold weekly four-hour study and discussion periods with everyone required to read selections from a good book on analysis, design. or programming.
> 2. Obtain one or more CompuServe accounts and encourage employees to visit this forum [the CompuServe electronic mail bulletin board system] on their own time, at company expense.
> 3. The first review of a product should be held after one to two staff weeks of effort have been invested and no later.
>
> Tell him to stop:
>
> 1. Setting unrealistic schedules.
> 2. Treating people like interchangeable parts.
> 3. Acting like quality isn't important.

Steve Kalman sent in the following comment to Cohen's statistic on job turnovers:

> Regarding the turnover statistic . . . looking back at an old resume, I see that my average tenure was about 1.5 years. There was one job that I held for 3.2 years, and I remember the reason for that phenomenon—the director of DP. In a shop with lots of hardships (low pay increases, tougher than usual commute, poor environment), there were only three people who left during the last two

years that I was there. Of them, one went to another job and two moved away from New York for personal reasons. After that manager was fired (for no good reason except that his bosses changed and brought in their own people), the entire staff turned over in less than a year, with the exception of the few folks who knew that they could not compete in the job market.

In other words, the reason we all stayed on was that the manager provided a superb, challenging environment in which to get things done.

Jeffrey Jacobs, president of a Manhattan Beach, California, consulting firm, continued on in the same vein:

I think the biggest problems are to be found in management. In particular:

(a) Managers who have no experience as a programmer (or analyst). You can't manage a process that you don't understand. Ideally, the manager should be better than the people being managed. Particularly in the aerospace/defense industry, far too many managers come to their position via hardware or some other type of background, and do not understand the process. These managers may or may not have good people skills; it seldom matters.

I've seen a manager get up in front of his own people, the prime contractor, and the Air Force and proclaim that if he only had 3 more real-time programmers who would work hard, he could have the job done in three months. It took 35 people and nine months!

(b) Managers who may have the necessary technical background, but have no management training, and in particular, terrible people skills. It doesn't matter a bit if you are the world's greatest software architect if you can't motivate and/or get along with people. Such managers range from the Type X, who manage by intimidating, to the Type W (wimp), who can't string more than 15 words together without choking.

Solving (b) is usually easier; Dale Carnegie courses are great training for managers. Other similar courses abound . . .

Stan Dvoskin, president of Boston-based OASYS Consultants, sent the following note:

It is said that the most important part of the business plan is knowing what and when to change. That holds for most plans, including MIS. The key to the morale issue, as far as I've been able to determine over the years, is that management seems to think that they are the only ones who should be aware of why the changes have to occur. It's the old adage: they must think the people who work for them are mushrooms, since they keep them in the dark and feed them.

Anyway, if I could counsel one significant change in policy for management, I'd suggest telling everyone what the hell is going on on a regular basis, and more often when sudden changes need to be made.

It shows a measure of respect for the people who work for you. And it does one more important thing—it establishes communications. And if you're lucky, the communication will become a two-way street and you (management) will find out what's going on in the "real" world from your employees, rather than from a newsletter (no matter how fine <grin>).

(Comments like <grin>, <chuckle>, and <snicker> are part of conversational protocol used by CompuServe subscribers to deal with the nonvisual nature of electronic mail.) Meanwhile, Daniel Opperman, of Opperman Associates in New Jersey, responded to Dvoskin's mail with the following comment:

The biggest barrier to getting management to tell people what in the hell is going on is that old cliche that we've all seen much too often. "Information is power—information that only you have is absolute power." It's not always management either; I've seen far too many examples of people refusing to share information with peers because it would make them appear "smarter" to their boss. I was in a situation where a VP of IS almost got fired because after a corporate takeover he held weekly staff meetings to keep all 110 of his people informed on what was happening in terms of reorganization and how it would impact them! What made it all the more absurd was that the info was all positive (the new owners were going to keep hands off and let us continue on our highly successful (profitable) ways). The VP was attempting to stop a mass exodus based on fear of the unknown!

Steve McMenamin, coauthor of *Essential Systems Analysis* [6], sent the following electronic mail:

Here's what I'd want to get across to the MIS manager in your scenario:

1. Those promising young analysts and designers you promoted to become supervisors and managers have changed their focus from the product to the process of system development. . . . The

gifted minds that once tried to envision the very best system are now mesmerized by the task of plotting the very best path to *any* deliverable system. So . . .

2. The task of thinking up just what the project's destination ought to be is too often delegated to the most junior members of the technical staff. The natural result is a system that more closely resembles a quilt than a tapestry. In the best cases, it is a successful quilting of dozens of separately conceived designs. The other 98 percent of the time it's Route 22. As the project crashes to a conclusion, everybody wonders why nothing hangs together except the Gantt charts lovingly crafted by senior people who should have been thinking more about the destination than the itinerary. As a manager of my acquaintance once said, "Most of the business policy decisions around here are dictated by a junior clerk to a junior programmer/ analyst.

Not everyone feels management is to blame for all the problems in data processing. For example, a Utah-based consultant sent me the following electronic mail:

The first thing I would discuss with my manager is how to get the systems analysts out of the rut they are in. No interest in trying anything new, as long as they can get by with what they know now. Very stagnant. The programmers are always looking for new ways to do things.

Secondly, I would try to get some input from our group into corporate data processing management. As it stands now, it is a one-way street, bad enough locally but terrible corporate-wide. No input into standards or future technologies.

Thirdly, at my exit interview (resulting from the above) I would discuss cronyism and favoritism toward old drinking buddies.

And Martin Schiff, president of Custom Data Solutions, sent a comment suggesting the problem may not be managers but the "system" in which managers work:

Regarding the peopleware premise that productivity can be improved by using better people, better motivation, better working conditions, etc.:

This is absolutely true. Unfortunately, with companies who work on a cost plus basis, there is a vested interest in not being as efficient as possible since to complete a job in fewer hours results in lower profits. So there are shops where people who try to be more productive are discouraged from doing so. These shops would not be likely to provide any incentives for higher production.

Ignoring the fact that these answers would not win any points for the software specialist that proposed them (and might get you fired), here are the answers to your questions:

Question 1. There are people who are not pulling their weight, who are making the work load for the rest of the group higher. These people are well known, but are not being reprimanded or fired.

Question 2. People are being overlooked due to nepotism or favoritism.

Another (anonymous) respondent made the following comment:

I have no doubt that better working conditions would lead to greater productivity. The real question is what constitutes better conditions to programmers and systems analysts? My managers know pretty much what's going on "in the trenches," they just make business decisions to ignore much of it. As for improving the working conditions, I want (a) more pay (better raises), (b) state-of-the-art equipment, and (c) time to play with the advancing technology. One V.P. of systems I know (not at my company, alas) ordered his people to take one afternoon a week and play with their computers. He didn't care what they played with—games, new tools, whatever. The only requirement was that they write one paragraph telling him what they did with their playtime. In eight months, there were three new active production applications being used by the company that originated in the play sessions!

As for your third question: I want my managers to stop giving me multiple jobs with conflicting priorities, and I want tools (an electronic conferencing system would be nice) that would cut the time required to produce and communicate weekly status reports. The most demoralizing thing about where I work is that the company's business is changing so rapidly that there is no coherent system strategy. This means projects are started, killed, switched around, and sometimes started again months later, only to be killed again, etc. One cannot build sophisticated DBMS systems unless the company has a reasonable (say, three- to five-year) idea of where it wants to go with its systems. Right now, we operate on a three- to six-month change of mind cycle!

As the "thread" of electronic messages continued, the subject of "doomed" projects came up. Bill Hamaker, for example, commented on the need for decisiveness on the part of managers:

. . . I wasn't referring to problems requiring "wisdom." I was talking about problems that require "decisiveness" and "power" to solve.

Stuff like "the project is obviously going to be three years late if we don't do something about it," or "our computer response time is 10 seconds per character so I can't get any work done," or "I was chatting with the user the other day and from what he tells me it sounds like what we are developing is useless to him."

Generally people working on doomed projects know they are doomed quite early on. They just never tell their bosses because they assume that that's a waste of time (frequently a true assumption).

And, finally, a consultant who requested anonymity responded with the following note:

Re: Doomed Projects

As a consultant working on a doomed project, let me report what I see as the range of reactions among my fellows. All of the other people involved are employees, not consultants. Group 1 has the attitude of "let's milk this for all we can get in terms of new hardware and software." Since it's doomed, they feel they ultimately won't have to deliver anything, so why not play in the meantime. Group 2 seems to be on what a colleague calls the ROADS program (Retired on Active Duty Status). They come to work, put in their hours doing virtually nothing or attending to personal business, and go home promptly at quitting time (or earlier if possible). Group 3 people are giving themselves ulcers because they want to do a good job, but see it as a pointless exercise. The waste of resources and their time bothers them.

I responded to several of these messages by asking why programmers who were so discouraged by management—especially on "doomed" projects—didn't just quit and go somewhere else. Typical of the responses was this one from Jeffrey Jacobs:

Simply quitting and finding another job is usually a pretty traumatic experience, especially if you have other mouths to feed.

Further, a lot of people (a) develop loyalty to the company, even if the individual project is doomed, (b) hope to get off the doomed project and onto a better one, (c) hope things might get better, and (d) are taken by surprise because they have already worked on one or more successful projects.

And there is no assurance that things will be any better at a new job!

There was a final word from Janet Ruhl, author of *The Programmer's Survival Guide* [7]:

> Why do people work in these places? (1) They get paid in American Dollars, which still retain some sentimental value. (2) In a nation that just elected George Bush president, do you really believe anywhere else is different?

Obviously, the situation may be either better or worse in your organization. And if it's as bad as suggested by the preceding remarks, this review won't be able to offer instant, easy solutions. But I can offer some advice on how to get started. What follows, then, is what I would say if I had an hour with you, the senior DP manager, to talk about things you should do, and things you should stop doing.

3.3 THE SOLUTION: STEP 1

An old cliche says you can't solve a problem until you know (and accept) that you have a problem. If you're already at this stage, you may want to skip forward to the next section. But perhaps your feeling about the people situation is closer to that espoused by Tony Hoare [8]:

> Basically all problems are technical. If you know what you want to do and you have the necessary technical background, there is no point in making a great management problem out of it. Obviously, a certain amount of resource control and personnel work have to go on but that's all.

In this case, I suggest you begin with some reading. The books in the end notes to this chapter may not be a comprehensive bibliography on the subject of programmer motivation, but it's a good start. Though the material spans 20 years—from 1971 through 1990—and though the authors provide a variety of perspectives, one message comes through loud and clear: though sometimes strange and different, programmers are people, and in the end they react to political, environmental, and managerial situations more or less the same way other kinds of people do.

If you respect consultants, or if you've just been brought in to head up (or save) a software organization of several hundred people, you might consider bringing in consultants to provide an independent, objective survey of the caliber and morale of your people. Personally, I don't recommend it. Even if the consultants are objective (which is a subject in itself), their presence in the organization for such an assignment is likely to cause more trouble than it's worth—unless you've already decided the organization is infested with a cancerous sickness and you're preparing for a wholesale sacking of staff.

My recommendation in this area is the MBWA philosophy— managing by walking around. Wander around the terminal rooms, the programming cubicles, the cafeteria, the water cooler and coffee machine, and wherever else programmers and systems analysts may be found. Do your wandering at various times of the day and night; much of the important work and many of the more enlightening "bull sessions" are likely to take place outside the 9-to-5 hours. People are not going to, as Tom DeMarco likes to say, "open their kimono" and share their innermost feelings with you the first time they see you, but eventually you should be able to pick up an overall sense of the mood and atmosphere in the trenches where the real work is being done. It's not hard: as I pointed out earlier, consultants do this all the time, and they're no smarter than you.

If you come to the conclusion that you really do have good, well-motivated, happy people, you can pat yourself on the back and continue doing whatever you've done to create such an admirable situation.

What should you do if you discover—as I suspect you might— that your staff is generally poorly motivated and downright unhappy? If you're one of the hard-driving, tough-as-nails, competitive senior MIS managers I've had the dubious honor of meeting over the years, your reaction might be, "Tough! Life is tough! Business is tough! We've got a lot of tough competition, and we don't have time to play nursemaid to these people! If they're not happy, and if they're going to whine and complain about things they don't understand, then they should get out!"

I won't comment on this credo: it either works for you or it doesn't. My only advice is: if you've got a large shop with serious morale and motivation problems, don't think that you can make significant improvements to productivity and quality with technological solutions such as CASE, prototyping, or fourth generation languages. Grumpy programmers will ignore, misuse, or subvert the technology.

3.4 THE SOLUTION: WHAT TO STOP

1. *Stop lying to your people.* Don't tell them the Super Megalith project is going to be a smashing success if you both know it's not; they may

admire your desire to accomplish miracles by sheer willpower, but they no longer believe in Santa Claus and the tooth fairy. Don't tell them you're totally committed to quality if you're not; the first time they see you sacrificing quality—for example, putting a bug-ridden system into production in order to meet a schedule—they'll know you're lying.

2. *Stop being a wimp.* Face up to the deadbeats and malingerers in your organization; throw them out and you'll get a lot more respect from your staff. One of the CompuServe messages I received commented on this:

> In the years of putting up with stuff, I can recall two very good managers in my command chain. One was an Operations Director (now, I believe, CEO for one of the *Fortune* 500) who impressed one and all when he summarily fired one of his direct reports (i.e., a senior staff level manager) for lying to him. Seems the guy had been claiming all was well in his area, when it was really a mess. Then the fellow went on vacation, and his second in command represented him at the Operations staff meeting. When asked about status, he told the truth. The O.D. questioned him closely, discovered the true situation, and had the manager's office cleaned out; when the manager returned from vacation he found his office empty and his personal things stored in a locker!
>
> So far as I know that was the only time the O.D. ever had to do anything of that sort; he made the point crystal clear that the firing was not for getting into trouble, but for lying about it. Afterward people were quite willing to keep him up to date on all the problems, and he was able to keep most all of them from getting to be major ones! (I saw him break down an office door one afternoon, when a couple of goldbricks had locked themselves in to play chess all afternoon, and refused to believe it was really him outside. His sense of humor led him not to fire them, just enjoy their discomfiture when he broke through the door! And they did reform, never trying that trick again . . .)

Your staff would particularly appreciate it if you would stop being a wimp when dealing with the corporate bureaucracy. For example, my CompuServe dialogues brought up the issue of "telecommuting"—allowing the programmers and systems analysts to have a terminal or PC at home, so that they can work at home when (and if) it's more productive to do so. A typical reaction to this idea was this message from Dan Opperman:

Most corporate personnel departments are taking a very conservative approach when it comes to granting "favors" or what can be seen as "special consideration" when it comes to things like telecommuting or flex-time, etc., etc. They live "in fear" of anything that smacks of discrimination or management subjectivity. Sad but true . . .

3. *Stop setting unrealistic deadlines.* This has been a problem since the first systems development project was conceived in the time of the Pharaohs. When you tell your staff that a three-year project absolutely, positively must be finished in two years or the world will come to an end, your staff concludes that (a) you're lying, (b) you expect them to abandon their personal lives for the next two years and work nights and weekends, or (c) you're willing to sacrifice a substantial amount of quality to achieve the deadline. Or all of the above. The young hot-shots and the macho types will accept the challenge and throw all their energy into the project. But when they finally finish two years later and compare the personal sacrifices (divorce, stress, etc.) against the fact that the Integrated Universal On-Line System did not save the human race from alien invaders, or eliminate hunger and disease, or even cause a "blip" anyone noticed, then they are likely to react to the next project as indicated by this message from my electronic dialogue:

> A prior general manager, for instance, issued a decree that every person in the engineering department would work a minimum of 24 hours unpaid overtime per week, whether it was needed or not. I responded by cutting my workweek from 40 hours to 32 by coming in late each day and leaving early, thus putting in just half the hours he had decreed. Nevertheless I kept all my assignments up to date, and had enough time left over to provide PC support for the rest of the plant. Obviously there was no need for me to be there 64 hours a week. And I think he did two things wrong in this case: (1) issuing the decree in the first place and (2) letting me get by with flagrantly flaunting it!

4. *Stop setting fuzzy goals.* Vacuous phrases like "We're committed to quality" or "Productivity improvement is our number 1 priority" are not only a waste of time, they are an insult to your staff. Unless you can quantify the goals you want your staff to achieve, you're wasting your time. If fuzzy goals are the source of your staff's discontent, I strongly suggest you read one of Tom Gilb's recent books on the subject [9].

3.5 THE SOLUTION: WHAT TO DO

In my hypothetical one-hour discussion with the senior MIS manager, I would summarize my advice on "what to do" as follows:

- Hire the best people you can.
- Pay special attention to proper training of your people.
- Provide an exemplary environment in which your people can feel motivated to *have fun and do good work.*
- Pay attention to effective project *teams.*

Would management listen? Perhaps, perhaps not. My track record of authoring nearly 20 books on software engineering methodologies is certainly no evidence of expertise in managing people; my experience of managing a software consulting and training firm of 150 people for 12 years provides some credentials, but many hard-boiled managers feel they know just as much about managing people as anyone else in the field.

And in any case, the advice I offer here is just common sense. But as Will Rogers once said, "Common sense isn't common." Decide for yourself whether *your* organization does a good job in these areas.[2]

3.6 HIRING THE BEST PEOPLE

Hiring better people is one of the best ways to improve the productivity and quality of systems in your organization. One software manager emphasized the importance of good hiring in a recent article [10]:

> The most important ingredient on this successful project was having smart people . . . . Very little else matters in my opinion . . . . The most important thing you do for a project is selecting the staff . . . . Really, the success of the software development organization is very, very much associated with its ability to recruit good people.

Or in the words of the immortal baseball manager, Casey Stengel, "I just know I'm a better manager when I have Joe DiMaggio in center field."

[2]Obviously, there are cultural difference from country to country, and from company to company; things that work in Japan or Europe might not work in the United States, and vice versa. The things that work for one organization may not work for others; this is particularly true when you see the differences between large organizations and small organizations. Nevertheless, if you pick up only one or two ideas in this chapter that can be applied to *your* shop, it could have a major impact.

Wouldn't *you* be a better manager if you have the software equivalent of Joe DiMaggio in the center field of your software project rather than the faceless drones that populate many of the Mongolian horde projects you've seen?[3]

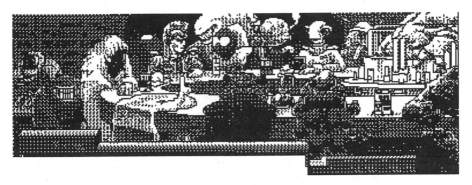

Figure 3.1: Starfighter versus the mongol hordes

The analogy with baseball teams is deliberate. Sports teams live or die by their recruiting skills, but we don't seem to recognize the importance of recruiting in the software industry. Specifically, the vast majority of DP managers have no training (and often no interest) in interviewing and/or recruiting people. Watch what happens in most interviews, and you'll find the DP manager dominating the conversation, telling long war stories about his early career, or pontificating on some aspect of the current project. The first thing I advise companies to do if they want to increase the quality of the people they hire is *train the DP managers in interviewing skills.* One source of information is Uris's interviewing checklist [11].

Let me add one new strategy to your recruiting and interviewing approach that evolved over a period of years in the consulting firm I ran in the 1970s and 1980s: the "audition" process. In addition to whatever interviewing and reference-checking processes you now use, ask a candidate programmer or analyst to give a 30- to 60-minute presentation on some technical subject to the group that would normally interview him. Typically, the candidate will talk about the last project he or she worked on, why it succeeded or failed, what role he or she played in it, what the design looked like, and so on. During or after

---

[3] This is not intended as a slur on the Mongol peoples, but rather a reference to the military tactics of Genghis Khan. Others have referred to it as the "Chinese army" approach: overwhelming the objective with sheer masses of people. It can be a terrific strategy if people are cheap and expendable, but is hard to justify in many of today's software projects.

the audition, the audience should ask relevant questions to ensure (1) that the candidate is not pulling the wool over everyone's eyes about technical issues he or she really doesn't understand, (2) that he or she has some minimum level of communication skills, and (3) that he or she has some degree of excitement and passion about his or her work, and a sufficient energy level to carry out the work. Two important things come out of this: (1) everyone in the audience sees the same presentation at the same time, and can thus discuss the candidate's strengths and weaknesses more objectively, and (2) everyone in the audience is able to get a sense of whether the candidate would "fit" into the human dynamics of the organization. There's no point hiring a genius who can't communicate and who can't get along with anyone on the staff.[4]

The recruiting skills of the individual manager, and the company as a whole, are likely to matter more and more in the 1990s, because we are likely to face a continuing shortage of skilled software engineering professionals. Because of falling birth rates, the United States will produce fewer college-aged students through most of the 1990s; more important, college-level interest in computing as a career has fallen from roughly 9 percent of the entering freshman class in 1983 to approximately 2 percent in 1990. Thus, there is likely to be more intense competition for the skilled software professionals for the rest of this decade.

Thus, the world-class software organizations are working hard to develop a good relationship with local universities who may be a spawning ground for new people; they offer research grants and consulting assignments to the university professors at least partly to gain some exposure to the student body. They offer bonuses to existing staff members who can recommend friends and acquaintances for hiring; people are unlikely to recommend incompetent idiots for a professional-level position, and in any case the process is cheaper than headhunter fees. Other organizations are striking up a relationship with consulting firms that allows them to hire the "body shop" contractors after a period of three to six months if both parties feel it's a good match.

---

[4] DeMarco and Lister [12], who were associated with my company for a number of years and helped polish the audition approach, point out two more advantages: employee morale is typically improved both by the people who pass the audition and the people who fail. The people who pass feel they have gone through a "trial by fire" and are now part of an elite group rather than part of a faceless herd of programmers. And when people fail the audition, it reconfirms to the people in the organization that management really does care about quality and won't hire any bozo who happens to wander in the door.

3.7 FIRING AND QUITTING

Firing people is something we would prefer not to talk about; indeed, I was loath to write this section of the chapter, because I worried that people would think I was in favor of firing people. On the other hand, company policies and government regulations have eliminated the ugly act of employee firing from the experience of many managers: in a large company, it's about as common as using a gun or a switchblade to resolve an argument. As a result, most managers have little or no experience with firing people, and they find it emotionally traumatic; as a result, they often delay the act interminably, much as an unhappy spouse will prolong a bad marriage. And when the firing is done, it's often done clumsily, with far worse side effects than are necessary.

Do the world-class software organizations have a different way of firing people? No, but they do the deed swiftly, humanely, and professionally. If ever there was a place for the human resources organization (which is typically useless during the hiring process), this is it: they can give advice on the formalities to be followed, and they can help coach the manager (as well as the employee) who feels traumatized by the process.

The key point here is to view the fired employee as a "failed product" and to ask how the *process* allowed such a phenomenon to occur in the first place. The process begins with recruiting, and then continues with activities of training, motivation, career counseling, and so on. Thus, what distinguishes the world-class software organization is not that they are better at firing, but rather that they are better at hiring; thus, they create a situation where they have fewer people to fire in the first place, because the act of firing represents a failure in the organization's process.

But even in the best of companies, indeed even when nobody is fired from the company, it may still be necessary to remove someone from a project team. As Schulmeyer [13] argues, "Taking a poor performer off your team can often be more productive than adding a good one." Schulmeyer argues that in a software project of 10, there are probably 3 people who produce enough defects to make them "net-negative" producers; the probability that there is not even 1 net-negative producer out of 10 is negligible. And if the team as a whole is turning out a low-quality product (with, say, 30 defects per 1000 lines of code), there is a good chance that *half* the project team is in the negative production category.

This is a sobering thought, particularly since the lack of software metrics in most organizations means that the phenomenon usually goes completely undiscovered. But when it *is* discovered, it may simply indicate a need for more training, better tools, or more appropriate methodologies for developing software. Or it may indicate a need for the project manager to switch the roles of his or her people: some software professionals should be kept away from coding, and some of the best programmers should not be allowed to test. This may not be a popular concept in an organization where testers are considered "lower" than programmers, but as John Gardner [14] observes, "An excellent plumber is infinitely more admirable than an incompetent philosopher."

By contrast, some organizations make a point of *not* removing people from a project team if they are performing poorly. Tomoo Matsubara, one of Japan's most respected software engineers, describes a policy at Hitachi Software Engineering [15]:

> This ["don't-withdraw"] policy may sound a little strange to Westerners, I suppose, but it is our long-standing policy that "an individual who has participated in a project from the initial stages should not be removed from the project even if it flounders because of his sloppy design or code or because of his mistakes." We have a notion that people's experience will accumulate only if they complete their work and observe the results of their ideas during development. If they leave the project in the midst of development, it becomes a negative experience because of resignation, frustration, or heartbreaking mentality. This policy also applies to key people on the project team, and I believe it nurtures many skilled people for project and technical management.

Of course, firing isn't the only reason people don't leave an organization; it's far more common for them to quit. Some people quit in order to avoid being fired, but U.S. surveys indicate that the people most likely to quit in a DP organization are those with the highest performance level. Thus, the greatest risk for many large, stodgy organizations is that the best people quit, the worst people are fired, and what you're left with is all the mediocre people in the middle. Another consequence: in the high-turnover companies, the workers at the bottom of the organization are typically *very* junior, often with no more than 6 to 12 months of experience.

Why do people voluntarily leave an organization? Sometimes to join the Peace Corp or the Marines, or to sail around the world;

sometimes for personal reasons ranging from marriage to divorce to child-rearing to a desire to write the Great American Novel; sometimes to take a job elsewhere that pays more money or has a better dental plan. But if you think these are the reasons why most people are leaving *your* organization, you're probably wrong: the most common reason for resignations in professional DP jobs is dissatisfaction with management. From the comments earlier in this chapter, you should not be surprised to learn this: most software engineers think their managers are idiots, liars, or spineless wimps.

Is this a significant point? It may not have seemed so when this book was written, for the 1990–91 recession reduced employee turnover to a 10-year low. But in normal economic times, turnover ranges from 10 percent to 100 percent per year in DP shops across the country; the turnover among a representative group of companies—for example, banks in New York City or insurance companies in Hartford—is likely to vary by at least a factor of 2. And when turnover becomes part of the corporate culture, it has some nasty side effects, as DeMarco and Lister point out [12]

> . . . turnover engenders turnover. People leave quickly, so there's no use spending money on training. Since the company has invested nothing in the individual, the individual thinks nothing of moving on. New people are not hired for their extraordinary qualities, since replacing extraordinary qualities is too difficult. The feeling that the company sees nothing extraordinary in the worker makes the worker feel unappreciated as an individual. Other people are leaving all the time, so there's something wrong with you if you're still here next year.

Hence, if you have any hope of becoming (or remaining) a world-class organization, *exit interviews* are extremely important; current employees may not give you a candid assessment for fear of losing their job or their next promotion, but disgruntled employees on their way out the door have much less hesitation about telling you what they think is wrong with the organization. Any manager who has participated in exit interviews will tell you that it's frustrating, annoying, and discouraging—but as the old proverb says, your enemies are your best critics.

A key point to remember, though: departing employees are *not* the enemy, and it's downright stupid to think of them this way or treat them this way. The former employee may become a valuable contact in his next organization, and—most important—he or she may decide to come back. The grass always seems greener on the other side of the fence, and it often doesn't occur to the disgruntled employee that the next organization may be just as screwed up as the one he left. I'm always amazed at the organizations who refuse, on principle, to rehire former employees; it seems to me they are passing up a golden opportunity to take advantage of known talent.

3.8 TRAINING

Another clear distinction between the world-class organization and the run-of-the-mill DP shop is the quantity and quality of training provided to its professional employees. The average shop provides only 1 to 2 days of training per year; the training is rarely customized for the software engineer's real needs and is rarely reinforced back on the job. The exemplary organization, on the other hand, provides 5 to 10 days per year as a minimum and sometimes provides as much as 20 days per year.

Why does training matter, aside from the obvious fact that it may be absolutely necessary for people to do their job in a fast-changing world of technology? Because employee surveys [16] indicate that software professionals have a deep-seated fear of obsolescence. Thus, investment in education is a message that the organization cares about its staff. Tom DeMarco suggests a simple policy for a company to demonstrate to its employees that it is committed to education: allow them to "carry over" their training days from one year to the next, just as they can carry over their vacation days. If you want to be even more convincing, try the approach used at Apple Computer: offer a paid sabbatical to your professional employees after seven years.

Some managers disagree with this view. "My shop is just a training ground for the other companies in town," they'll argue. "As soon as my new hires go through six months of training, they quit and take a job somewhere else for a much higher salary." Ergo, training is something they would prefer to abolish. But in such organizations, the entry-level training has typically become institutionalized and cannot easily be abolished, but the expectation of a high turnover has also become institutionalized. Thus, the organization may hire 100 fledgling university graduates and train them all, fully expecting that 50 will quit as soon as the training has finished.

Something is terribly wrong about this scenario, and it's not the training.[5] The reason newly trained people leave such organizations in droves is usually quite simple: the marketplace puts a higher value on their skills than the very organization that trained them. So the employee thinks to himself, "I've just gone through six months of intensive training, and I know an awful lot more than I did when I started. But my employer still thinks I'm only worth $X per year, while the people across the street think I'm worth 20 percent more. Hmmm . . .". As Tom DeMarco once commented in a software engineering conference, not recognizing individual excellence—such as the excellence gained from an intensive training process—sends out a strong message by default to the employee: "We don't know, or care, about the difference between mediocre work and excellent work."[6]

Meilir Page-Jones [17] has another perspective on the training issue: contrary to what most organizations seem to think, training is not a binary proposition. People do not exist in just a "trained" or "untrained" state, but in one of several stages of increasing expertise. Page-Jones proposes seven levels of expertise:

Stage 1   *Innocent* (has never heard of technology X)

Stage 2   *Aware* (has read an article about X)

Stage 3   *Apprentice* (has attended a three-day seminar)

Stage 4   *Practitioner* (ready to use X on a real project)

Stage 5   *Journeyman* (uses X naturally and automatically in his job)

Stage 6   *Master* (has internalized X; knows when to break the rules)

---

[5] On the other hand, sometimes the high "wash-out" is *not* wrong, but is a healthy way for both employee and employer to discover that the marriage was not meant to be. The training experience at Andersen Consulting's St. Claire facility, for example, is as much a cultural acclimatization process as it is a technical training process; if the new recruit and/or the employer don't feel good about the results at the end of the process, it's in everyone's best interest to sever the relationship.

[6] So instead of hiring 100 people and losing half at the end of the training process, perhaps the organization should plan on hiring 55 people, and losing only 10 percent through normal attrition. But to keep the remaining 90 percent, it should provide a market-level salary increase to the people who survive the training process; this may require adjusting the salaries of other veterans with even more tenure. Too expensive? Perhaps—but if you pay peanuts, you get monkeys. Charles Martin, author of *User-Centered Requirements Analysis*, suggests that this contradicts my argument in Chapter 1 that *all* U.S. programmers are overpaid, but the real issue is the level of salaries relative to productivity.

Stage 7   *Expert* (writes books, gives lectures, looks for ways to
extend X)

Page-Jones wisely recommends that an organization should never
attempt a crucial project solely with stage 3 or lower levels of expertise
in a crucial technology. Such project should be seeded with stage 4s,
and should have access (perhaps through the medium of external
consultants) to stage 5s and stage 6s. Most important, the organization
should nurture inhouse expertise at the stage 6 level in fundamental
software engineering methodologies and principles.

3.9 MOTIVATING PEOPLE: THE CLASSICAL ISSUES

It's a shame that we have to give any thought to the idea of motivating
software professionals. As DeMarco and Lister [12] argue,

> There is nothing more discouraging to any worker than the sense
> that his own motivation is inadequate and has to be "supple-
> mented" by that of the boss.... You seldom need to take Draconian
> measures to keep your people working; most of them love their
> work.

Indeed, most software professionals *do* love their jobs, but they
don't always love every aspect of their jobs. Sometimes they don't like
the rules and procedures; sometimes they don't particularly like the
projects they're working on, or the people with whom (or *for* whom)
they have been assigned. Most often, they don't like *change*: if we
change the rules, the procedures, the tools, the programming language, the hardware, or the software development methodology,
we're likely to get loud squawks of complaint.[7] Thus, even assuming
that they have hired the best people and trained them well, many DP
managers worry about how best to motivate their people.

Is money the answer? Big salaries, bonuses, stock options, royalties, and other forms of financial remuneration are always exciting,
and some managers feel that the easiest way to a software engineer's
heart is simply through his pocketbook. But the world-class companies that I have seen around the world generally don't bribe their
professional people; they pay competitive wages (relative to other
organizations in their area), but not always the very highest

---

[7] It's somewhat ironic that this should be so, since software professionals often accuse end
users of being stodgy, refusing to accept computers, refusing to accept new ways of thinking
about their systems.

wages.[8] In general, high wages alone are not enough to create a world-class software shop, as Fred Herzberg [18] argues:

> Money, benefits, comfort, and so on are "hygiene" factors—they create dissatisfaction if they're absent, but they don't make people feel good about their jobs and give them the needed internal generator. What does produce the generator are recognition of achievement, pride in doing a good job, more responsibility, advancement, and personal growth. The secret is job enrichment.

This doesn't mean that classical techniques such as performance reviews are going to disappear from the typical company. But performance reviews typically take place at 6-month or 12-month intervals, long after the software engineer has forgotten the details of the performance being reviewed. Gerald Weinberg [19] points out that

> Many programmers—probably *most* programmers—work in environments in which they receive essentially no real feedback embodying the consequences of what they do. Lacking this feedback, they lack the motivation to attempt changes, and they also lack the information needed to make the correct changes.

Performance reviews are also associated with a management-by-objectives (MBO) style of management, which is regarded by many companies today as incompatible with a total quality management (TQM) approach that emphasizes the *process* rather than the *product*.

DeMarco and Lister [12] discuss a number of other interesting motivation techniques:

- *Pilot projects*, in which the participating members know they are the first to try some innovative technology in their organization
- *War games*, where groups of programmers compete against each other in "mock" software competitions
- *Brainstorming sessions*, specifically devoted to exploring innovative solutions to thorny software problems
- *Provocative training experiences*, for example, seminars on problem-solving techniques, or unusual seminars, conferences, or "retreats" that are outside the narrow scope of the software engineer's daily work

[8] Of course, if a whole segment of the marketplace has gone stark raving mad, as was the case in the brokerage and financial services industry in the 1980s, it's possible to see ridiculous situations like 25-year-old "rocket scientist" programmers making $100,000 per year writing FORTRAN programs. But this phenomenon largely disappeared after the October 1987 stock market crash. Thank goodness: it's time we got rid of FORTRAN anyway.

3.10 PERFORMANCE MANAGEMENT

Another way to motivate people is to have a better understanding of the personal *consequences* of the behavior management is trying to impose upon them. As Weinberg [19] points out,

> If you want people to change what they're doing, make sure they are fed back the consequences of what they're doing.

In more colloquial terms, as Henry Ford suggested in a congressional hearing, this means that if people are going to throw sewage into the same river from which they obtain their drinking water, you should make sure they dump their sewage *upstream* rather than downstream; this will ensure that they have the proper motivation to think about pollution control.

Another approach, described eloquently by Susan Webber [20], is simply to understand better the chain of events from "antecedents" to behavior to *consequences* of the behavior:

antecedents → behavior → consequences

Antecedents are all the things managers do in order to *cause* the desired behavior to occur; these may include memos, meetings, threats, warnings, pleas, bribes, and so forth. And *consequences*, in this case, means the *personal* consequences experienced by the individual, not such corporate consequences as higher profitability, strategic competitive advantage, and the like.

Webber's performance management approach is best described with an example. Suppose that management has decided that software reusability, as discussed in Chapter 9, is the new "silver bullet" that will dramatically improve software productivity and quality. In addition to investing in reusability libraries, new object-oriented methodologies, and other approaches, management has also informed all the software engineers that they should devote some of their time, while designing and programming, to see whether the modules they are creating could be "generalized" and put into the software reusability library.

What are the antecedents? In addition to memos from the boss, there may be training sessions; "commitment" meetings where, in the fashion of a religious revival meeting, everyone vows his eternal devotion to management's new dictum; publication of standards from the ever-popular standards group on the characteristics of the ideal reusable module; and so forth. And if these antecedents aren't enough, management typically responds by adding more: more memos, more meetings, more standards. Despite the effort, management is likely to find at the end of a year that the software engineers have fundamentally ignored all the noise and commotion; the reusable library is still empty. *Why don't the antecedents work?*

The reason the antecedents typically don't work is that nobody (including the software engineer) has bothered thinking about the consequences of the desired behavior, *as seen by the individual*. When the desired behavior is "spend some time and effort creating reusable components," here are some of the *possible* consequences:

- After spending some time studying the software module he has just finished creating for the project he is working on, the software engineer discovers that he *can* generalize it and create a reusable component for submission to the library.

- After spending some time, the software engineer decides that it's *not* possible to create a reusable component.

- Two weeks after creating a potentially reusable general-purpose component from his own special-purpose component, the software engineer discovers that the quality-control group in charge of the reusable library has rejected his submission.

- The software engineer's manager recognizes his effort, thanks him publicly, and remembers to include the item in the next performance review.

- The software engineer does not accomplish other more enjoyable tasks, such as coding another of his own modules.

- The software engineer is late completing his own deliverables, because of the time invested in generalizing one of the modules for the library.

- The software engineer has to work overtime in order to carry out the work required to generalize his special-purpose modules.

There may be other consequences as well, but this should give you the general flavor of consequences that are of significance to the individual—but that are typically of no concern whatsoever to the organization. Furthermore, each of these consequences can be characterized as

- Positive (P) or negative (N)
- Immediate (I) or future (F)
- Certain (C) or uncertain (U)

People naturally gravitate toward consequences that are positive, immediate, and certain—or PICs. And human nature is such that we tend to shy away from consequences that are negative, immediate, and certain—so-called NICs; consequences that are uncertain, or that take place in the future, are less likely to lead to decisive behavior. Thus, the performance management approach tries to evaluate the consequences of the desired behavior to see if the PICs outweigh the NICs.

If we examine management's desire to create reusable modules from this perspective, we might end up with the following assessment:

Consequences	P/N	I/F	C/U
Creating a reusable component	P	I	U
Not being able to create a reusable component	N	I	U
Rejecting the component by quality-control group	N	F	U
Gaining recognition from the manager	P	F	U
Not accomplishing other, more enjoyable tasks	N	I	C
Being late with other deliverables	N	F	U
Working overtime to develop the reusable components	N	I	C

In this analysis, there are two NICs and no PICs. Guess what? The software engineer may try to "follow the rules" during the initial few weeks when software reusability is introduced with great fanfare—but within a few months, he will gradually (perhaps unconsciously) decide that it's all a waste of time, and the whole idea will fade into oblivion.

What does management do in this case? Some managers automatically try to inject some NICs to offset the "natural" NICs—for example, they may announce: "Anyone who fails to create at least one reusable component a month will be fired." The software engineer's natural reaction to this is: "I'm damned if I do and damned if I don't; I think I'll find some other company to work for."

A better response is to discuss each of the consequences in an open, candid fashion to see if some of the innate NICs can be eliminated, or whether they can be mitigated by converting some of the PIUs or PFUs into PICs. In the example, there may not be any obvious way to eliminate the NIC associated with the software engineer's inability to spend his or her time accomplishing other, more enjoyable tasks. But there *is* a way to eliminate the NIC associated with overtime: schedule some time—formally and explicitly—in the project to concentrate on the creation of reusable components.[9] Another approach would be to give the generalization activity to a separate group—for example, the Software Parts Department, as discussed in Chapter 9—rather than asking the original software engineer to do the work. And some of the uncertain, future consequences can also be addressed: as a matter of management policy, the project manager could be instructed *always* to thank the software engineer, *immediately*, for his efforts, regardless of whether he was successful at creating a reusable component.[10]

Performance management is not a panacea and will not solve motivation problems by itself. But it is a simple and powerful mechanism for explaining the human reaction to management's requests for behavioral changes. Most of the technology discussed in this book—software reusability, CASE, object-oriented methodologies, and so on—require behavioral changes, and ignorance of performance management issues is probably the single greatest explanation for the failure of these technologies.

3.11 PROJECT TEAMS

Only in rare cases today do software engineers work entirely alone, on one-person projects; in most cases, people work in *teams*. Therefore, the productivity, and to some extent the degree of staff turnover, is related to the effectiveness of the team environment. Thus, the world-class organizations are devoting significant effort today to the issue of building effective, harmonious, well-balanced teams.

This is in stark contrast to the practice of the average organization, in which management simply herds a bunch of people together and says to them, "You . . . and you . . . and you . . . you are now the Project X team. Be teamlike!" Teams can be created by management decree for accounting purposes; strangers can be herded together and told to work on a common project. But *effective* teams are not created by edict.

Unfortunately, even in the world-class organizations, effective teams are created more by accident than by conscious planning. The personal chemistry and social dynamics of a group of people within a high-pressure project are such that, even with the best of intentions,

---

[9] One organization does this by including the activity in the normal inspection/review process. In addition to reviewing the software component for defects, the group discusses the viability of generalizing the component.

[10] Of course, this represents a potentially new behavior for the project manager, and the consequences of *that* behavior should be examined.

the team members may not be able to work effectively. DeMarco and Lister [12] concentrate their advice not on how to *create* teams but, rather, how to avoid "teamicide" in those lucky situations when an effective team does "gell."[11]

Typically, the team that has gelled can be recognized by such external signs as a strong sense of identity (e.g., the team adopts a name for itself), a sense of eliteness, a feeling of joint ownership of the product (the product developers are proud to have their names grouped together on the final product), and an attitude of enjoyment.[12] And the cohesive team typically feels a sense of *empowerment*: it knows its strengths, and it knows when it can "push back" against the organization when it gets unreasonable requests (e.g., "don't worry about testing—we'll do that in the field."). As Apple Computer's Mike West [21] points out, though, empowerment of employees is something that most organizations find difficult to accept; only the world-class companies are even considering it.

And the typical team has no sense of empowerment, for it lacks the member(s) who can articulate that empowerment when communicating with software engineers, users, or managers outside the team; while it may seem an oversimplification, the typical team is dominated by serious, quiet, introverted people who are not interested in subjects for which they see no immediate use. Rob Thomsett [22] has confirmed this with a survey of some 600 Australian software professionals to see where they fit in the Briggs–Meyers personality-type model. Some 38 percent fell into the sensing-thinking-introverted-judging category, whose personality type is summarized as

> serious, quiet, earns success by concentration and thoroughness. Practical, orderly, matter-of-fact, logical, realistic, and dependable. Takes responsibility.

And another 25 percent fell into the sensing-thinking-extrovert-judging category, whose personality type is summarized as

> practical, realistic, matter-of-fact, with a natural head for business or mechanics. Not interested in subjects they see no use for. Likes to organize and run activities.

Software engineers, when asked, typically describe their profile

[11] First you have to recognize that the team *has* gelled.

[12] It is this last characteristic that seems to cause a knee-jerk reaction in old-line managers: *something must be wrong if they're having fun.*

of the ideal manager as an intuitive-feeling-extrovert-judging person, someone whose personality type is summarized as

> responsive and responsible. Generally feels real concern for what others think or want. Sociable, popular. Sensitive to praise and criticism.

The irony, of course, is that most organizations promote people from the technical ranks into the managerial ranks; this does not change ugly ducklings into swans, and it rarely causes people to undergo a fundamental personality transformation.

But there is more to building an effective team than just finding bosses and workers (and avoiding the dilemma of a team composed only of workers, or only of leaders). Thomsett, Constantine, and others have done some important work recently identifying the critical roles that make up an effective team. Thomsett's [22] team model consists of the following eight critical roles:

- *Chairman:* controlling the way in which a team moves forward toward the group objectives by making the best use of team resources, recognizing where the team's strengths and weaknesses lie, and ensuring that the best use is made of each team member's potential

- *Shaper:* shaping the way in which team effort is applied, directing attention, and seeking to impose some shape or pattern on group discussion and on the outcome of group activities

- *Plant:* advancing new ideas and strategies with special attention to major issues and looking for possible new approaches to the problems with which the group is confronted

- *Monitor-Evaluator:* analyzing problems in a practical manner and evaluating ideas and suggestions so that the team is better placed to make balanced decisions

- *Company Worker:* turning concepts and plans into practical working procedures and carrying out agreed-upon plans systematically and efficiently

- *Team Worker:* supporting members in their strengths (e.g., building on suggestions), underpinning members in their shortcomings, improving communications between members, and generally fostering team spirit

- *Resource Investigator:* exploring and reporting on ideas, developments, and resources outside the group; creating external contacts that may be useful to the team; and conducting any subsequent negotiations

- *Completer:* ensuring that the team is protected as far as possible from mistakes of both commission and omission and actively searching for aspects of work that need a more than usual degree of attention; maintaining a sense of urgency within the team

The first two personality types described, which account for some 63 percent of the software engineering community, are appropriate for the company worker, monitor-evaluator, completer, and technical shaper roles. But the other roles are better suited to different personality types, typically those involving an intuitive, extrovert personality.

Does this mean that all introverts should be shot, or that we should refuse to allow teams to be created without the necessary personality types? Obviously not. But as one seminar participant remarked to me recently, "Simply *knowing* of the roles and the personality types makes everyone much more sensitive and aware of the team's strengths and weaknesses." This awareness can also help make the team, as well as external managers, aware of the importance of the "team worker" (a role I prefer to think of as the "diplomat") even if that person does not appear to be a "work horse" who knuckles down and churns out thousands of lines of code.

The world-class software organization are, at the very least, *aware* of these team-role and performance management issues. The aggressive ones are providing training to their professional staff in these areas, and the very best have added professional experts—for example, industrial psychologists—to their staff of consultants and advisors.

3.12 SUMMARY

You may have additional criteria to add to my list. Perhaps you feel that the ideal DP shop should pay its programmers a salary of $100,000 and throw wild parties every Friday afternoon. Maybe you think a model DP organization has to be located in San Francisco or within a 20-mile radius of Sydney Harbor. You could argue that the exemplary organization can't have more than 1000 professionals (or 100, or 10, or 2). But these are, for the most part, personal issues. Everyone will have a different opinion, and each will gravitate to the environment in which he or she is most comfortable.

You could also argue that a DP organization can only be exemplary if the overall enterprise within which it operates is exemplary, in the sense described in such books as Tom Peters's *In Search of Excellence*. I think this is probably true in the long term—but not necessarily in the short term. I have seen some absolutely sterling DP groups flourishing within the most stagnant enterprises imaginable; in most cases, the situation can be attributed to the DP leader, who is trying to make the best of an otherwise untenable situation. In the long run, though, it's hard to maintain a record of excellence when surrounded by mediocrity. If you can't stand the company you work for, don't think you can hide in its DP department for more than a couple of years before it gets to you.

END NOTES

1. Sackman, Harold, W. J. Erickson, and E. E. Grant. "Exploratory Experimental Studies Comparing Online and Offline Programming Performance," *Communications of the ACM*, January 1968.

2. Sheppard, S. B., B. Curtis, P. Milliman, and T. Love. "Modern Coding Practices and Programmer Performance," *IEEE Computer*, Vol. 12, no. 12, 1979, pp. 41–49.

3. Valett, J. D., and F. E. McGarry. "A Summary of Software Measurement Experiences in the Software Engineering Laboratory," *Journal of Systems and Software*, Vol. 9, no. 2, 1989, pp. 137–148.

4. Boehm, Barry W. *Software Engineering Economics*. Englewood Cliffs, NJ: Prentice Hall, 1981.

5. Jones, Capers. *Programming Productivity*. New York: McGraw-Hill, 1985.

6. McMenamin, Steven, and John Palmer. *Essential Systems Analysis*. Englewood Cliffs, NJ: Yourdon Press/Prentice Hall, 1984.

7. Ruhl, Janet. *The Programmer's Survival Guide*. Englewood Cliffs, NJ: Yourdon Press/Prentice Hall, 1989.

8. Hoare, C. A. R. *Proceedings of the 2nd NATO Conference on Software Engineering*, April 1970. J. N. Buxton and B. Randell, eds. Brussels, Belgium: NATO Scientific Affairs Division, 1970.

9. Gilb, Tom. *Principles of Software Engineering Management*. Reading, MA: Addison-Wesley, 1989.

10. Curtis, B., H. Krasner, and N. Iscoe. "A Field Study of the Software Design Process for Large Systems," *Communications of the ACM*, November 1988, pp. 1268–1287.
11. Uris, Auren. *88 Mistakes Interviewers Make and How to Avoid Them.* New York: American Management Association, 1988.
12. DeMarco, Tom, and Timothy Lister. *Peopleware.* New York: Dorset House, 1987.
13. Schulmeyer, G. Gordon. *Zero Defect Software.* New York: McGraw-Hill, 1990.
14. Gardner, John. *Excellences.* New York: W. W. Norton, 1987.
15. Matsubara, Tomoo. "Project Management in Japan," *American Programmer*, June 1991.
16. Couger, J. Daniel, and Robert A. Zawacki. *Motivating and Managing Computer Personnel.* New York: John Wiley & Sons, 1980.
17. Page-Jones, Meilir. "The Seven Stages of Expertise in Software Engineering," *American Programmer*, July–August 1990.
18. Herzberg, Frederick. "One More Time: How Do You Motivate Employees?" *Harvard Business Review*, September–October 1987.
19. Weinberg, Gerald M. *Understanding the Professional Programmer.* New York: Dorset House, 1988.
20. Webber, Susan. "Performance Management: A New Approach to Software Engineering Management," *American Programmer*, July–August 1990.
21. West, Mike. "Empowerment: Five Meditations on the Soul of Software Development," *American Programmer*, July–August 1990.
22. Thomsett, Rob. "Effective Project Teams: A Dilemma, a Model, a Solution," *American Programmer*, July–August 1990.

4

Software Processes

Despite the emphasis on peopleware in the previous chapter, most organizations emphasize technology-oriented solutions—for example, CASE tools or new methodologies—to solve their productivity problems. But before embarking on an ambitious plan to provide every software engineer with an expensive CASE workstation, and before deciding to abandon structured design in favor of object-oriented design, there is a critical question the organization must ask: *Are we ready for new technology?*[1]

The majority of software development organizations today are, unfortunately, far too primitive to take advantage of CASE, new methodologies, or virtually *any* complex technology. In the best case, newly introduced tools and techniques become "shelfware"—after the initial fanfare, software engineers simply put the manuals and the floppy disks on their bookshelves, alongside the ponderous tomes produced by the Standards Department. In the worst case, newly introduced technology can prove chaotic and may be the straw the breaks the camel's back in a critical project; in this unhappy scenario, the new technology is banished from the organization and may not be allowed back in until a generation of managers is replaced.

Probably the "hottest" idea in the software development industry in the early 1990s is the notion of organizational maturity, particularly with regard to the *process* used by the organization to develop its systems. The notion of "process maturity" and "process assessment" is now widely discussed within aerospace and defense software organizations, as well as a number of other firms in the United States and other parts of the world. Traditional MIS organizations, however, are largely unaware of the work done in this field and consequently run the risk of falling far behind their competitors.

Without a doubt, the most influential work in this field has been carried out by Watts Humphrey and his colleagues at the Software Engineering Institute (SEI), affiliated with Carnegie Mellon Univer-

---

[1] Note that there is a difference between *organizational* readiness and *industry* readiness. Studies by Sam Redwine indicate that it takes 14 to 20 years for new technologies to become accepted and widely practiced in the software industry. If this seems discouraging, Capers Jones reminds us that it took the military 75 years to go from the technology of muskets to the technology of rifles.

sity; the definitive reference book is Humphrey's *Managing the Software Process* [1], though a number of other papers and research reports have begun to appear. This chapter introduces the concept of process assessment for those unfamiliar with the topic and comments on some of the current issues associated with process assessment.

It should be emphasized that while the SEI assessment model is the most visible, it is by no means the only one available; a number of consulting firms have traditionally provided assessment questionnaires and advice, and some—such as the one provided by Software Productivity Research—have been highly praised. Also, the intense publicity afforded the SEI model described in this chapter has already led to a major revision, due to take effect in late 1992. And there is considerable controversy about the applicability of the SEI model to small, innovative organizations; as Tom DeMarco remarked to me, only partly in jest, "according to the SEI model, Apple Computer should not exist." Indeed, a small software organization probably could not afford the overhead required by the SEI model.

Notwithstanding these criticisms and concerns, the very existence of the SEI process maturity concept is an important development in the field—just as Nolan's "stages of growth" model of corporate computerization was important in the 1970s. No doubt it will be improved and revised, and no doubt it will be joined by a number of other models, but for now, the DP organization striving to be a world-class organization must, at a minimum, familiarize itself with the SEI model.

4.1 THE SEI PROCESS MATURITY MODEL

The essence of the SEI model is that software development organizations can exist at one of five levels of maturity:

- The initial level
- The repeatable level
- The defined level
- The managed level
- The optimizing level

Rubin [2] characterizes these levels as an evolutionary scale, as shown in Figure 4.1. The key point is not whether there are 5 levels, or 10 levels, or 347 levels—but, rather, that there are marked, recognizable differences between organizations as they progress from anarchy to maturity. The assessment is based on a complex questionnaire, involving over 100 questions; the questionnaire and the assessment process has its strengths and weaknesses, as will be discussed shortly, but the overall rating summary is tremendously useful for organizations who want to know where they stand.

In particular, as we will see, the SEI process maturity model helps to prioritize the things an organization must do to improve. A primitive organization at level one does *not* need CASE to improve; it needs much more basic things.

4.2 LEVEL 1—THE INITIAL LEVEL

The level 1 organization is one in which anarchy prevails—for example, where programmers consider themselves to be creative artists, not subject to rules or common procedures. There may be standards, but they are generally ignored; there may be tools, but they are used on a haphazard basis; there may be officially endorsed methodologies like structured analysis and design, but they are practiced "informally" according to the whims of the developers.

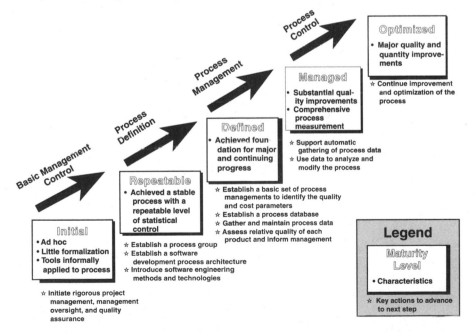

Figure 4.1: The SEI process maturity levels

This does not mean that the developers or the managers are stupid or that they are doomed to failure in all their projects; it simply means that their results are not predictable. A project is just as likely to be finished three months ahead of schedule as it is likely to be three months behind schedule. It may be over budget or under budget. It may turn out that it only needed 1 person when 10 were assigned, or 10 people when only 1 was assigned. *Nobody knows.* The success or failure of projects in the level 1 organization is not dependent on the nature of the process being followed (for there is none), or even the skill of the mangers; it depends entirely on the skill (and perhaps the mood or temperament) of the individual(s) on the project.

How do you know if yours is a level 1 organization? Humphrey [1] suggests a simple test:

> . . . the best test is to observe how such an organization behaves in a crisis. If it abandons established procedures and essentially reverts to coding and testing, it is likely to be at the Initial Process Level. After all, if the techniques and methods are appropriate, then they should be used in a crisis; if they are not appropriate in a crisis, they should not be used at all.

So if your organization is filled with software managers who behave like the one shown in Figure 4.2, you probably work in a level 1 organization.[2]

Figure 4.2: Behavior of the level 1 software manager

[2] Similarly, if your manager pounds his or her fist on the desk and announces, "We're going to get to level 3 within 18 months, whatever it takes!" you can be reasonably sure that you are deeply mired in a level 1 company. And, by the way, you probably won't get to level 3 in 18 months, no matter how many fists are pounded on tables.

Ironically, the level 1 organization often *knows* that things are screwed up; a visitor from outside will often hear everyone complain about the sorry state of affairs. But the level 1 organization often has little idea of how to improve, and often makes the fatal mistake of assuming its problems can be solved by hiring more people. *If the current horde of 1000 programmers isn't enough to get rid of the backlog,* says management, *let's hire another thousand!*

But if more people isn't the answer, what do the level 1 companies need to do in order to improve—that is, to advance to level 2? Surveys by Humphrey [3] and his colleagues of several hundred U.S. organizations indicate that the key issues for level 1 companies are these:

66% *Estimating software size.* If you don't know how big the job is, it doesn't matter too much what tools or methodologies you use. The level 1 organization often underestimates the size of the project by a factor of 2, a factor of 4, or even a factor of 10.

64% *Tracking software size changes.* The "teeny-weeny change" requested by the user, midway through the project, often turns out to be a killer; if it is accepted by the software development organization without a proper readjustment of schedules, budgets, and personnel assignments, it can doom the project. The level 1 organization doesn't know how big or how small a change it is taking on, and the decision is often made by the lowest-level technical people on the project.

58% *Tracking code and test errors.* The more sophisticated organizations track errors at the earlier stages of analysis and design; the less sophisticated organizations don't focus on the problem until they reach the coding and testing stages. But the level 1 organization has no organized process for tracking errors (and the fixes to those errors) even at this stage.

49% *Scheduling and estimating.* The level 1 organization uses informal estimates, typically concocted by the bottom-level technicians in a "seat of the pants" fashion. Schedules are equally informal, often without the use of even the most rudimentary PC-based project management package for creation of Gantt and PERT charts.

45% *Software commitment review.* The software organization will take on projects and agree to utterly impossible schedules and budgets if there is enough political pressure; indeed, politics and personalities dominate the decision-making process in a level 1 organization, for there is no formal process for deciding whether the organization is really capable of fulfilling its commitments.

4.3 LEVEL 2—THE REPEATABLE LEVEL

Humphrey describes the second level in the following way:

> The organization has achieved a stable process with a repeatable level of statistical control by initiating rigorous project management of commitments, cost, schedule, and changes.

Thus, the key characteristic of the level 2 organization is that it is stable and under control; it meets its schedules and budgets, within a statistically acceptable variance. But another key characteristic is that the level 2 organization achieves its success not through advanced software engineering methodologies or CASE tools but, rather, through conventional, classical project management.

While the level 1 organization is characterized by utter anarchy, the level 2 organization is characterized by "tribal folklore." Thus, there is a widespread consensus that, "we should all be doing things the same way around here," but nobody has written down the policies or procedures in a formal way. Such an organization may have sent all its professional staff members through training course to learn a common methodology; if the staff members are polled after this training process, most will claim to be following the "spirit" of, say, structured analysis and design, but will also cheerfully admit that they don't follow a set of rigid rules.

Another interesting cultural distinction: while the success of the level 1 organization depends on the skill of its bottom-level technicians, the success of projects within the level 2 organization typically depends on the skill of the project manager. A level 2 company will typically survive the loss of an individual project member (which a level 1 company could not), but if the project manager leaves in the midst of the project, the "team spirit" that he or she created will be lost, and the project may founder.

By way of analogy, Humphrey describes the differences between the levels by comparing different forms of advice that one might get when navigating to an unknown destination, for example, navigating from a downtown hotel in a strange city to an airport at the edge of town. In the level 1 organization, the driver doesn't ask for directions at all, but simply trusts his luck and intuition. The level 2 organization is comparable to the situation where the driver receives verbal instructions, for example, "drive 2 miles until you see a gas station on the right, then take a right and go four traffic lights, then . . . ". The problems with this form of navigation are (1) you don't know that you have made a mistake until it's too late and (2) once you *do* realize you've made a mistake, it's quite difficult to get back on the right path again. The level 3 organization, which we'll discuss next, is comparable to the driver with a road map: the written document not only helps her determine where she is, but also makes possible midcourse corrections.

The level 2 organization may be reasonably successful in its business (as long as there are no major perturbations, such as mergers and acquisitions, major management turnover, or a major change in the *kind* of systems being built). To achieve this stability, the level 2 organization has usually accomplished the following:

- *Software commitment management.* As noted earlier, the organization must have a rational, dispassionate *process* that allows it to say, "No!" when asked to take on a commitment that simply cannot be accomplished. Otherwise, project managers run the risk of being commanded to perform the equivalent of running a 3-minute mile. The level 1 organization responds to such requests without even thinking:

- *Software planning and cost estimation.* The level 2 organization has a more formal and more sophisticated planning and estimation approach than the one typically used in the level 1 company:

- *Configuration management and change control.* This is developed so that modifications to a system, during development as well as ongoing maintenance, can be made in an orderly fashion.
- *Establishment of a software quality assurance organization.* To begin focusing on the *quality* of the delivered system, as well as simple adherence to budgets and schedules.

With these basics in place, what does a level 2 company need in order to improve? The SEI's surveys [3] indicate that the most common weaknesses are these:

88% *Software engineering training.* To transform an informal "tribal folklore" organization into an organization with formal methods, the overwhelming majority of organizations need training for their professional staffs. Ironically, some of this training may have been done years earlier, but it probably has to be repeated.

77% *Regression testing.* While the level 2 company has installed basic configuration management capabilities, it typically needs a formal regression testing process to ensure that modifications to a system perform as intended without damaging previously implemented functionality.

50% *Design error data.* The level 2 organization gathers data about software defects at the coding and testing stage of each project; however, it needs to begin capturing data about defects that are introduced in earlier phases. These defects are typically more serious and more costly to repair if they are not discovered early.

31% *Software process group.* To develop and disseminate a formal software engineering process successfully, it is important to have a group within the organization charged with the task. Many organizations have already assigned this task to a training department or a standards department, but nearly a third of the level 2 organizations have not.

4.4 LEVEL 3—THE DEFINED LEVEL

Humphrey describes the level 3 organization in the following way:

> The organization has *defined* the process, to ensure consistent implementation and provide a basis for better understanding of the process. . . . At this point, advanced technology can usefully be introduced.

The key point about the level 3 organization, then, is that the process has been codified and institutionalized; everyone in the organization can point to "the bible" and say, "This is the way we do things around here."

A key point about the level 3 company: Because it *does* have a formal, written process that everyone follows, process *improvement* is possible. At the end of each project, software engineers and managers will have some ideas on how to do things better next time—so there is an opportunity to *change* the process in order to make it better. To manage this properly, the software engineering process group is an essential component of the level 3 company.

Whether the process is improved, or simply augmented through the use of better tools, a key premise of the SEI process maturity model is that the organization cannot make improvements to the process unless the process is being followed rigorously by everyone. Similarly, attempts to improve productivity by simply telling people to "work harder" generally fail in the level 1 and level 2 companies: people are already working as hard as they can.

What does it take to get to level 3? Here are the key items:

- *Introduction of formal standards*—to distinguish between the informality of level 2 and the formality of level 3.

- *Inspections*—as a means of ensuring that the process is being followed. As a *general* quality-assurance mechanism, the SEI recommends the introduction of formal inspections.

- *More formal testing policies*—the level 2 company has some testing policies in place, the but the level 3 company has added formality, such as a requirement for branch coverage for test cases.

- *More advanced forms of configuration management (SCM)*—the level 2 form of configuration management is typically applied only to the coding and "downstream" activities; the level 3 organization applies SCM to the upstream activities of analysis and design. In addition, the level 3 organization has developed a formal SCM management plan, has installed automated tools, and provides configuration accounting and audits.

- *Formal process models*—it is important to think of the software development process as a *model*, so that it can be treated as a mental abstraction. The more advanced CASE tools, as we will discuss in Chapter 6, incorporate software process models, allowing customization at the organizational level and the project level.

- *Establishment of a software engineering process group*—as noted, such a group is important for the documentation, evolution, and dissemination of the process throughout the organization.

4.5 LEVEL 4—THE MANAGED LEVEL

Humphrey summarizes the characteristics of the level 4 organization as follows:

> The organization has initiated comprehensive process measurements, beyond those of cost and schedule performance. This is when the most significant quality improvements begin.

So the key characteristic of the level 4 organization is that it has initiated a software metrics program, along the lines described in Chapter 7.

The level 1 organization typically has no metrics at all; the level 2 organizations typically have a number of "basic" metrics concerning the ultimate *product* it develops. That is, the level 2 and level 3 organizations measure lines of code or function points to see how big the product is; they measure the number of people and the number of hours, days, or months consumed by the project. All this is necessary to control budgets, schedules, and personnel allocations.

But the level 4 organization is measuring the *process*, too: How much time do we spend on each of the steps in the design phase? How many defects did we have in each step? How much time was required for each of the inspections in each of the steps? How much do the numbers vary from project to project, from week to week, from person to person?

The emphasis in the level 4 organization is gathering metrics to improve the quality of both the product and the process by which the product is built. Thus, the level 4 organization inevitably has a strong, formal software quality assurance group; often, it is this group charged with the task of capturing, analyzing, and reporting the software metrics data.

The emphasis on software quality in the level 4 organization is eloquently described by Humphrey [1] in the following challenge:

> The key question for management is: Do you intend to do anything about software quality? If you do, then your organization must live by four basic quality principles:
> 1. Unless you establish aggressive quality goals, nothing will change.
> 2. If these goals are not numeric, the quality program will remain just talk.
> 3. Without quality plans, only you are committed to quality.
> 4. Quality plans are just talk unless you track and review them.

4.6 LEVEL 5—THE OPTIMIZING LEVEL

In the level 5 organization, the management and "instrumentation" of the organization's process can provide feedback for improvement. As Humphrey describes it,

> The organization now has a foundation for continued improvement and optimization of the process.

So the key characteristic of the level 5 organization is a formal emphasis on continuous, ongoing *process* improvement, based on the metrics captured in level 4.

Thus, the formal process in the level 5 organization must have a mechanism that describes how the process itself is modified. One way of accomplishing this is the "causal analysis" approach described in Chapter 8.

4.7 IMPLICATIONS OF THE SEI MODEL

The summary in the previous sections should give the newcomer a good introduction to the basic process maturity concept. But newcomer and veteran alike need to ponder several important implications of the SEI model:

- You can't skip levels.
- It takes time to move from one level to the next.
- Not many organizations are above level 1.
- Esoteric new technology should be avoided at the lower levels.
- New software organizations are unlikely to start at level 3.
- The levels are already becoming important for software contracts.

4.7.1 You Can't Skip Levels

The organization that finds itself at level 1 often wishes desperately that it could magically skip a few levels and suddenly find itself transported up to level 4 or 5. This is often accompanied by a manic urge to spend large sums of money to solve the problems associated with level 1 and level 2 behavior: "Maybe if we get all our people an expensive CASE tool and bring in object-oriented technology, we can get ourselves up to level 4." Or you might hear a well-meaning manager exclaim, "Well, we'll just run everyone through a training course and update our standards manual; that should do it."

Unfortunately, it's not so easy. Much of the transition from one level to the next is *cultural*. Consequently, one has to go from the stage of anarchy *through* a stage of informal consensus before reaching a stage of formal processes for system development. Untold millions of dollars have been spent on training without changing the culture: the software engineers politely sit through the training course, determined to ignore everything they hear, and then go back to their desks to continue doing whatever they were doing before.[3]

4.7.2 It Takes Time to Move from One Level to the Next

Conceivably, a small software organization with, say, 5 to 10 software engineers could move from level 1 to the higher levels in a matter of weeks or months; on the other hand, the innate culture of the small organization tends to favor the innovative, entrepreneurial anarchy of the level 1 culture.

The real problem is with the large organizations—those with

---

[3] Sometimes the software engineers return from their training courses with all the enthusiasm of a newly converted religious zealot, only to be told by their project manager, "Forget all that crap you learned in class! This is the real world! We have deadlines to meet, and we can't waste time on those fancy theories." Or the software engineer will attend an excellent course on methods for analysis and design of *new* systems and then return to the dreary task of fixing bugs and adding patchwork changes to an old system designed 20 years earlier.

more than 100 software professionals, and especially those with more than 1000. For these organizations, it is reasonable to expect a period of 2 to 3 years between levels, that is, *a decade to go from level 1 to 5!* Humphrey [4] reports that the most difficult transition is from level 1 to level 2:

> By the time an organization invests all the work to get from level 1 to level 2 and writes it down, it often finds that by the time it is "officially" at level 2, it is actually well along the way to level 3. Similarly the move from level 3 to level 4 is easier. However, the move to level 5 is more difficult, because it represents a paradigm shift. The emphasis is on how to prevent problems. Just as organizations have developed procedures for turning in bug reports on a software product, they have to learn to do the same thing for the process. This ultimately means that the people in the organization own the process, rather than the process owning the people.

The possibility of a 10-year effort has struck terror into the hearts of senior management in some software organizations, for they fear that they may be out of business if it takes them until the year 2000 to reach level 4 or 5. In any case, world-class software organizations around the globe are scrambling to get there first.

There is no magic for speeding up the process evolution, though Rubin [5] reports that many organizations are looking for accelerated process improvement ideas. It obviously helps if there is strong commitment and concern for process improvement at every level in the organization; it probably helps if the organization feels that its very survival is threatened, as seems to be the case in a number of manufacturing organizations. But no matter how great the commitment, there is no way to avoid the reality that large organizations have an enormous amount of inertia. Software organizations have the additional inertia represented by the tens of millions of lines of old code that must be maintained.

Note also that organizations can *regress* to lower levels, especially from level 2 to level 1. This could result from mergers or acquisitions at the corporate level, because of turnover in the senior management ranks, or because of extremely high turnover within the technical ranks. Indeed, consultants such as Charles Martin argue that there may even be a form of entropy that causes organizations to regress naturally to lower levels unless there is constant management attention.

4.7.3 Not Many Organizations Are Above Level 1

As of late 1991 [6], the Software Engineering Institute had conducted 59 in-depth on-site assessments of 27 sites and 296 projects, together with some 167 workshop assessments. The in-depth assessments included such organizations as Gunter AFB, the U.S. Space Command, Magnavox, Hughes Aircraft, GTE, JPL, Westinghouse, IBM's SID, Ford Aerospace, McDonnell Douglas, Northrop, Medtronics, TRW, and the Strategic Air Command. The workshop assessments have covered a wider range of companies.

Thus far, the surveys and assessments indicate that approximately 81 percent of the U.S. sites are at level 1; approximately 12 percent are at level 2; approximately 7 percent are at level 3; *and there are no sites at level 4 or 5.* At the project level, 88 percent are at level 1, 5 percent are at level 2, 5 percent are at level 3, and 2 percent are at level 5. Limited surveys suggest that most Japanese and European organizations are also wallowing in the bottom levels of the SEI model, though there is some controversy about the accuracy of the comparisons, because the American sites have been predominantly aerospace, while the European/Japanese sites have not.

Note that these statistics apply to whole *organizations* involved in the development of software, not to individual project teams or midsized departments within the organization. It is quite easy to imagine pockets of excellence within a vast desert of mediocrity, that is, some project managers or department-level managers running their activities with all the characteristics of a level 4 or level 5 organization.[4] But from the perspective of the CEO and the board of directors, it is important that *all* projects and *all* organizations operate at a higher level.

4.7.4 Esoteric New Technology Should Be Avoided at Lower Levels

It should be evident from the foregoing discussion that the key issues for the level 1 and level 2 companies are basic management issues: configuration management, formal budgeting and scheduling, inspections, and so on. So fancy methodologies and CASE tools are not what's needed; indeed, the introduction of esoteric new technology will not only be a waste of money, but could actually set the organiza-

---

[4] For example, SEI concluded in September 1991 that the IBM site involved in software development for the U.S. space shuttle at NASA is indeed operating at level 5 [7].

tion back by pinning everyone's hopes on *technology* solutions rather than *organizational* solutions to the productivity and quality problem.

Does this mean that CASE tools and new software engineering methodologies should be completely banned from an organization until it reaches level 3? No, of course not. Experimentation, pilot projects, and small-scale usage of new technology can continue as it always has in the past. All we are saying is that *the organization should not depend on a massive, expensive, enterprisewide introduction of new technology to solve its problems at level 1 and level 2.*

Paul Jorgensen [8] also makes the important point that tools and software processes are interdependent; thus, an intelligent use of tools could help accelerate the progress of process improvement, and use of new processes will highlight the need for better tools. This interplay between tools and processes is suggested by Figure 4.3; thus, the level 1 organization may only be capable of using the drawing capabilities of many CASE tools. Higher levels of process sophistication are required to take advantage of the analysis and reporting capabilities.

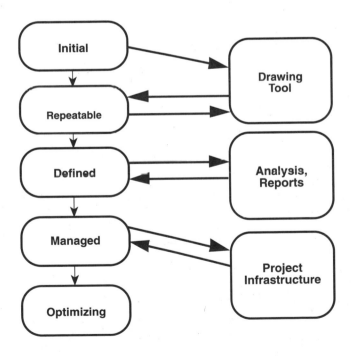

Figure 4.3: Interplay of processes and tools

An important consequence of this idea is that the lower-level organizations should use relatively inexpensive CASE tools that they can afford to throw away as they become more sophisticated. There are a number of simple, useful $500 CASE tools on the market now; one can acquire them for experimentation and learning, and *then* buy the fully integrated $100,000 CASE "environments" after a level 3 process maturity has been achieved. The problem with buying the $100,000 package when the organization is at level 1 is that (1) it may not be used at all, (2) it is likely to be overwhelming in its demand for rigor and formality, and (3) it may ultimately prove to be the wrong product for the organization, but nobody will want to confess that a $100,000 mistake was made. Ergo, it becomes shelfware.

4.7.5 New Software Organizations Are Unlikely to Start at Level 3

The dilemma faced by most software organizations is that the inertia of an existing culture cannot be overcome quickly and easily, no matter how strong the desire of the manager. But what about a new organization? Suppose you were hired as the new MIS manager of a newly formed organization (e.g., one created as the result of a merger or a joint venture) that has *no staff*? Is it possible to hire new people and instantaneously create a level 3 or level 4 organization?

The short answer: it's not impossible, but it is unlikely. Even if the manager is careful to hire people with the proper attitude (i.e., team players rather than solo hotshots), and even if they have prior experience working with the SEI process maturity model, the chances are that the new hires have not worked *together*. Thus, they will need some time to adapt and adjust their former cultural behavior into a new, common culture.

When asked this question about newly formed organizations, Humphrey [3] compared the situation to an "all star" sports team. Even though each of the players might have been the best individual on his or her former team, that doesn't necessarily mean that the individual stars can work together right away.

4.7.6 The SEI Model Is Becoming Important for Software Contractors

Interestingly, some organizations have responded to the statistics mentioned in Section 4.7.3 by saying, "Well, it just shows that we're *all* screwed up, so there's no point getting excited about all this stuff." This is roughly like saying, "We're all sinners, so there's no point in going to church." For some, the absence of a level 4 or level 5 company poses an "existence proof": If you haven't seen any, how do you know they exist?

In general, the skepticism about the SEI model is prevalent among the level 1 companies; the organizations that have gone through the painful bootstrapping process to get to level 2 or 3 are firm believers. It's interesting also that the level 1 companies usually have very few ideas on how to improve their productivity (except "hire more people!"), while the level 2 and level 3 companies have begun accumulating long lists of "action items" for improving their process—improvements that are often rather minor on an individual basis, but quite significant in the aggregate.

Though it may take years for the SEI model to percolate into the business-oriented MIS community, it has already begun to have a major impact within the aerospace and U.S. Defense Department community. For its own internal software development, the DoD has some two dozen "design centers," each of which has between 800 and 2000 professionals. In a 1991 reorganization, these centers have been told that they must "qualify" in order to bid for DoD software development projects, and the qualification process consists of achieving a level 2 SEI certification. And some of the *external* DoD software contractors are being told that they must achieve a level 2 certification in 1991, and a level 3 certification in 1992, in order to bid on U.S. government projects. It should be no surprise, then, that the majority of the companies that have conducted intensive on-site assessments, as indicated in Section 4.7.3, are aerospace and defense contractors.

4.8 STRATEGIC IMPLICATIONS: WHAT SHOULD YOU DO?

As mentioned, organizations in the aerospace and defense sectors have no choice but to pay close attention to the SEI model. Its basic validity has already been confirmed at Hughes Aircraft [9], where substantial cost savings and productivity improvements have been reported. And though there are some criticisms of the model [10], it is also apparent that the SEI is revising its questionnaire and refining the process [11, 6] to make it more suitable; a new "capability maturity model" and associated revised questionnaire are expected to become official by November 1992.

What about MIS organizations, especially in those companies that are not directly associated with, or dependent upon, the U.S. Defense Department? My strong advice is to take advantage of the ongoing work in this area by joining the Software Engineering Institute. Unlike some research consortia whose membership cost millions of dollars per year, affiliation in the SEI program is basically free, and the process maturity project is only one of many important projects it carries on to improve the level of software engineering practice in the United States. Membership is open to all organizations in the United States and Canada. Contact the Software Engineering Institute, Carnegie Mellon University, Pittsburgh, PA 15213 (phone 412-268-7700) for more information about the affiliate program, the software engineering education program, or the SEI quarterly newsletter, *Bridge*.

Of course, one reason to contact the SEI is to arrange for an on-site inhouse assessment of *your* organization's process maturity. But recently, SEI has begun training a number of external organizations in the assessment procedure. As of October 1990, the following companies had been certified by the SEI; more will undoubtedly be added in the future:

- American Management Systems, Inc.
- Arthur D. Little, Inc.
- Booz, Allen & Hamilton, Inc.
- Contel
- Dayton Aerospace Associates, Inc.
- Digital Equipment Corporation
- pragma Systems Corporation
- Software Productivity Consortium
- Technology Applications, Inc.

A number of other organizations have also become involved in the assessment process, using their own questionnaire (such as Capers Jones's Software Productivity Research, Inc.) or a computerized expert system (such as the one developed by Howard Rubin of Rubin Associates, Inc.).

If your management cannot or will not participate in an *external* assessment, then carry out your own internal assessment. The SEI sponsors training programs for organizations wishing to do their own assessment; the training cost is minimal compared to the costs (and benefits!) of the assessment itself. If even this cost is too much, get your librarian to buy a copy of Humphrey's book [1] *and* Roger Pressman's excellent "how-to" book [12].

Bottom line: If you're going to improve your organization, you need to start with an independent, objective technology audit. You need to find out where you are now before you can plan where you're going. And you need a map to guide you from where you are now to where you want to end up. The SEI's process maturity model may have some flaws, but it is a good map and is becoming widely accepted. Until you can find a better map, this one is sure beats wandering through the forest in the dark.

END NOTES

1. Humphrey, Watts. *Managing the Software Process.* Reading, MA: Addison-Wesley, 1989.
2. Rubin, Howard. "How to Become a Software Engineering 'Big Foot,'" *American Programmer*, January 1990.
3. Humphrey, Watts. "Software Process Maturity," *Proceedings of the CASE WORLD Conference.* Andover, MA: Digital Consulting, October 1990.
4. Yourdon, Edward. "An Interview with Watts Humphrey," *American Programmer*, September 1990.
5. Rubin, Howard. "Software Process Maturity," *American Programmer*, January 1991.
6. Bannert, John. "New SEI Maturity Model Targets Key Practices," *IEEE Software*, November 1991.
7. Bush, Marilyn. "Process Assessment in NASA," *Proceedings of the 13th International Conference on Software Engineering*, Austin, TX, IEEE Computer Society Press, May 1991, pp. 299–304.
8. Jorgensen, Paul. "Accelerating Process Maturity with CASE," *American Programmer*, September 1990.
9. Humphrey, Watts, Terry Snyder, and Ronald Willis. "Software Process Improvement at Hughes Aircraft," *IEEE Software*, July 1991.
10. Bollinger, Terry, and Clement McGowan. "A Critical Look at Software Capability Evaluations," *IEEE Software*, July 1991.
11. Humphrey, Watts, and Bill Curtis. "Comment on 'A Critical Look,'" *IEEE Software*, July 1991.
12. Pressman, Roger. *Making Software Engineering Happen.* Englewood Cliffs, NJ: Prentice Hall, 1988.

5

Software Methodologies

> **methodology**. a body of methods, rules, and postulates employed by a discipline: a particular procedure or set of procedures.
>
> *Webster's Ninth New Collegiate Dictionary,* 1988

World-class software organizations are not distinguished by the brand-name methodologies they use. Once you have accepted that reality, everything else in this chapter can be put in proper perspective. There's a lot going on in the methodology field—refinements of structured techniques, successful applications of information engineering, excitement over object-oriented techniques—but an organization that practices an old, tried-and-true methodology rigorously and faithfully will usually beat the pants off an organization using the newest methodology in a sloppy, disorganized fashion.

Let's be optimistic: Let's assume that your organization is practicing its methodology with the formality of a level 3 organization. What should you be looking at in the methodology field? What are the world-class organizations doing with software methodologies? Where is the methodology field heading in the 1990s? Indeed, do methodologies have any more significance in the 1990s than they did in the 1980s or 1970s?

One reason for the importance of methodologies today is that they are rapidly becoming automated. Instead of the textbooks or the 15-volume standards manuals that we struggled with in the 1970s, now we are seeing our methodologies incorporated in dozens of different CASE tools. However, today's CASE tools are typically automating *old* methodologies—that is, methodologies that predate the tools by a decade or more—so we should expect to see a shift in the methodologies themselves over the next few years to take advantage of the capabilities of the tools.

We begin this chapter by looking at the "granddaddy" of methodologies, the *waterfall life cycle.* Then we will examine the salient features of some of the more popular system development methodologies in use today, as well as the emerging *object-oriented* methodology.[1]

---

[1] However, this chapter does not present a detailed description of any of the popular methodologies; to do that would fill several volumes! If you want to learn all the details of a specific methodology, consult the references at the end of this chapter.

Finally, we will look at the phenomenon of methodology paradigm shifts: the process of *changing* a methodology.

5.1 THE WATERFALL LIFE CYCLE AND THE DIFFERENCE BETWEEN "METHOD" AND "METHODOLOGY"

5.1.1 Definition of the Waterfall Life Cycle

Developed in the late 1960s and early 1970s, the "waterfall life cycle" is still the most commonly practiced approach to software development as we move into the 1990s. The waterfall life cycle is illustrated in Figure 5.1.

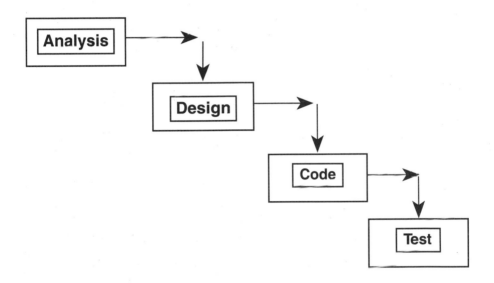

Figure 5.1: The waterfall life cycle

5.1.2 Method vs. Methodology vs. Life Cycle

Now that we have a specific example, we can discuss the differences among a "methodology," a "method," and a "life cycle." Your organization may use these terms differently, and each textbook, CASE vendor, and methodology guru seems to have a different interpretation of the words; unfortunately, as the opening quotation at the beginning of the chapter indicates, dictionaries aren't much help either. Here are my definitions, which you're free to accept or modify:

- *Methodology*—a step-by-step "battle plan," or cookbook, for achieving some desired result. A software methodology usually identifies the major activities—for example, analysis, design, coding, and testing—to be carried out and indicates which people (users, managers, technicians) should be involved in each activity and what role they play. Methodologies often describe "entry" criteria ("these conditions must be satisfied before you can begin the design phase"), exit criteria, and checkpoints for "go/no-go" decisions ("users must decide at the end of analysis if they are willing to continue funding the project").

- *Life cycle*—a synonym for methodology.

- *Method*—a step-by-step *technical* approach for performing one or more of the major activities identified in an overall methodology. Thus, "structured analysis" is a method for carrying out the analysis phase of a project, while object-oriented design is a method for performing the design phase.

In many cases, method and methodology go hand in hand, especially if they were developed by the same organization or are supported by the same CASE tool; conversely, some CASE vendors loudly proclaim that their product is "methodology neutral" or "method independent." And the waterfall life cycle, the grand-daddy of all methodologies, is itself *completely* method independent; it can be used with an information engineering method, a structured analysis/design method, or an object-oriented analysis/design method.

Thus, you must be very careful if your colleagues or your manager tell you, "Oh, we can't use this new object-oriented approach, because we follow a waterfall life cycle." What they *may* be saying is people using an object-oriented approach prefer to do so within the larger context of a methodology/life cycle that permits rapid prototyping and overlapping of various phases of the project. But if they're suggesting that the waterfall life cycle is opposed to object orientation in the same way the Catholic Church is opposed to polygamy, they're wrong.

5.1.3 Problems with the Waterfall Approach

Despite the widespread usage of the waterfall life cycle, there are a number of problems and weaknesses you should be aware of:

- *It's based on paper.* Because of its history, most implementations of the waterfall life cycle are based on paper forms, paper documents, paper diagrams. As my colleague Steve McMenamin once observed when commenting on the weaknesses of early data flow diagrams, "Bubbles don't compile." Written documents are, of course, better than *no* documents, but handwritten documents cannot be subjected to automated error checking and analysis, nor can they be mechanically transformed into executable code.

- *It takes too long to see results: nothing is executable or demonstrable until code is produced.* The results that everyone cares about are in the form of working code; this doesn't occur until several earlier steps have been completed. As we will discuss further shortly, most implementations of the waterfall life cycle insist upon *sequential* phases, which means that months or years may go by before the users sees any tangible evidence of progress.

- *It depends on stable, correct requirements.* In the waterfall life cycle, the quality of the code depends on the quality of the design, and the quality of the design depends on the quality of the analysis effort. If the user's requirements have been misinterpreted or misunderstood, or if the user changes his or her mind about the requirements during the subsequent design and implementation effort, the waterfall life cycle can produce a brilliant solution to the wrong problem. The classical waterfall, as it is traditionally practiced, typically does not have a "configuration management" activity until code has been produced; revisions to the specification are simply disallowed or rebuffed with the comment, "Oh, we'll take care of that during maintenance."

- *It is difficult to trace requirements to code.* The waterfall life cycle is subject to the problems illustrated by the party game of "telephone": as information is passed from analyst to designer to coder, things can be garbled or lost, and the "downstream" person can embellish and add things to the information he or she received from the upstream person. For large systems, it's critical to ensure that there is a one-to-one match between elements of the code and elements of the requirements; this is extremely difficult to do with the waterfall life cycle.

- *It delays the detection of errors until the end.* Error detection in the classical waterfall life cycle is reserved for the formal testing phase of the project. But by then, it's often too late: there is often enormous pressure to put the system into operation with skimpy testing. And it's too late for another reason: if analysis or design errors are detected, they are extremely difficult and expensive to correct. Of course, CASE tools can lessen this problem by detecting logical errors in the specification and design; however, if the analyst fundamentally misunderstood what the user wanted, no CASE tool in the world can spot the error.

- *It does not promote software reuse.* Reuse was not a "hot" concept in the late 1960s and early 1970s. The waterfall life cycle doesn't forbid or preclude reuse; it just doesn't promote or encourage the concept.

- *It does not promote prototyping.* By its very nature, the waterfall approach assumes that the analysis phase can be conducted once, and only once. But as we will discuss in Section 5.2, many people prefer a prototyping approach today, where the user requirements can be ascertained through a process of experimentation and trial and error.

- *It is generally not practiced in a formal fashion.* Because of its bulky, paper-oriented form, most organizations and most software professionals have neither the time nor the stamina to practice a waterfall life cycle in a rigorous, formal fashion; this is compounded by the very culture—typically a level 1 process maturity—in which the life cycle is being practiced. A casual, ad hoc implementation of the waterfall approach typically leads to unpredictable results.

5.1.4 Conservative vs. Radical Life Cycles

Most implementations of the waterfall life cycle presume that one activity must finish before the next begins. But there is nothing written in the Ten Commandments requiring this to be so: indeed, some of the activities could overlap. In the most extreme situation, *all* the activities in the waterfall life cycle could be taking place simultaneously. At the other extreme, the project manager could decide to adopt the sequential approach, finishing *all* of one activity before commencing on the next.

It's useful to have some terminology to help talk about these extremes, as well as about compromises between the two extremes. A *radical* approach to the waterfall life cycle is one in which all activities take place in parallel from the very beginning of the project, that is, coding begins on the first day of the project, and systems analysis continues until the last day of the project. By contrast, in a *conservative* approach to the waterfall life cycle, all of activity N is completed before activity $N + 1$ begins.

Obviously, no manager in his or her right mind would adopt either of these two extremes. The key to recognize is that the radical and conservative extremes defined are the two end points in a range of choices. This is illustrated in Figure 5.2.

Figure 5.2: Radical vs. conservative life cycles

There are an infinite number of choices between the radical and conservative extremes. A project manager might decide to finish 75 percent of the analysis activity, followed by completion of 75 percent of analysis and design, in order to produce a reasonably complete skeleton version of a system whose details could then be refined by a second pass through the entire project life cycle. Or she might decide to finish *all* the analysis activities, followed by completion of 50 percent of design and 50 percent of implementation. The possibilities are truly endless, but how should the project manager decide whether to adopt a radical or conservative approach on her next project? Basically, there is no right answer. The decision is normally based on the following factors:

- How fickle is the user?
- What pressure are you under to produce immediate, tangible results?
- What pressure are you under to produce an accurate schedule, budget, and estimate of personnel and other resources?
- What are the dangers of making a major technical blunder?

None of these questions has a straight black-or-white answer. For example, you can't ask the user of the system, in casual conversation, "By the way, how fickle are you feeling today?" On the other hand, you should be able to assess the situation, based on observation, especially if you're a veteran project manager who has dealt with many users and many upper-level managers before.

If you judge that you're dealing with a fickle user—one whose personality is such that he delays final decisions until he sees how the system is going to work—then you should opt for a more radical approach. The same is true if you're dealing an inexperienced user, who has had very few systems built for her. Why spend years developing an absolutely perfect set of specifications only to discover that the user didn't understand the significance of the specifications?

If, however, you're dealing with a veteran user who is absolutely sure of what she wants—and if she works in a business area that is stable and unlikely to change radically on a month-to-month basis, then you can afford to take a more conservative approach. Of course, there are a lot of in-between situations: The user may be sure of *some* of the business functions to be performed, but may be somewhat unsure of the kinds of reports and management information she would like the system to provide. Or, if she is familiar with batch computer systems, she may be unsure of the impact that an online system will have on her business.

Besides fickleness, there is a second factor to consider: the pressure to produce immediate, tangible results. If, due to politics or other external pressures, you simply *must* get a system up and running by a specific date, then a somewhat radical approach is warranted. You still run the risk that your system will be only 90 percent complete when the deadline arrives, but at least it will be a *working* 90 percent complete skeleton that can be demonstrated and perhaps even put into production. That's generally better than having finished all the systems analysis, all the design, and all the coding—but none of the testing.

Of course, all projects are under some pressure for tangible results—it's simply a question of degree. And it's an issue that can be rather dynamic: a project that begins in a low-key fashion with a comfortable schedule can suddenly become high priority, and the deadline may be advanced six months to a year. In most cases, a "top–down" approach to the various life-cycle activities has the advantage that one can stop an activity at any point and leave the remaining details for subsequent consideration; meanwhile, the top-level analysis that has been completed can be used to begin the top-level design, and so forth.

Yet another factor in project management is the ever-present requirement, in most large organizations, to produce schedules, estimates, budgets, and the like. Sometimes (especially in the level 1 organizations) this is done in a fairly informal fashion, typically because the projects are relatively small and because management feels that any errors in estimating will have an insignificant impact on the whole organization. In such cases, one can adopt a radical approach, even though any attempts at estimating will have to be "gut-level" guesses. By contrast, most large projects require relatively detailed estimates of personnel, computer resources, and so on, and this can only be done after a fairly detailed survey, analysis, and design have been completed. In other words, the more detailed and accurate your estimates have to be, the more likely you are to follow a conservative approach.

Finally, you should consider the danger of making a major technical blunder. For example, suppose that all your past experience as a project manager has been with modest batch-oriented mainframe applications—and now, all of a sudden, you find yourself developing a cooperative processing, client–server management information system with a sophisticated graphical user interface that will process 2 million transactions a day from 5000 terminals scattered around the world. In such a situation, one of the dangers of a radical approach is discovering a major design flaw after a large portion of the top-level skeleton system has been implemented. You may discover, for example, that for your whizbang system to work, a low-level module has to do its job in 19 microseconds—but your programmers suddenly tell you that there is no way on earth to code the module that efficiently—not in COBOL, not in C, not in assembly language, not even in microcode. So, you must be alert to the fact that following the radical approach requires you to pick a "top" to your system relatively early in the game, and there is always the danger of discovering, down toward the bottom, that you picked the wrong top!

However, consider another scenario: you've decided to build a system with new hardware, a new operating system, a new database management system (produced by someone other than the hardware vendor), and a new telecommunications package (produced by yet another vendor). All the vendors have impressive, glossy manuals describing their products—but the vendors have never interfaced their respective hardware and software products together. Who knows if they will work together at all? Who knows if the throughput promised by one vendor will be destroyed by the system resources used by one of the other vendors? Certainly, in a case like this, the project manager might elect a radical approach—so that a skeleton version of the system could be used to explore possible interface problems between the vendors' components.

If you're building a familiar kind of system, such as your 99th payroll system, then you probably have a very good idea of how realistic your goals are. You probably remember, from your last project, what sort of modules you're going to need at the detailed level, and you probably remember very clearly what the top-level structure looked like. In such a case, you may be willing to accept the risks of making a mistake because of the other benefits that the radical approach will give you.

In summary, the radical approach is most suitable for thinly disguised research and development efforts. It is good in environments in which something *must* be working on a specific date and in situations where the user's perception of what he wants the system to do is subject to change. The conservative approach, on the other hand, tends to be used on larger projects, in which massive amounts of money are being spent, and for which careful analysis and design are required to prevent subsequent disasters. However, every project is different and requires its own special blend of radical and conservative top–down implementation. To deal with the individual nature of any project, you should be prepared to modify your approach midstream, if necessary.

5.1.5 Modern Waterfall: Incremental and Spiral Models

The limitations of the waterfall approach have long been known, and have been discussed elsewhere. Barry Boehm, among others, has suggested software development could be managed in a series of "increments": thus, there could be a *series* of waterfall life cycles, one for each increment. DeGrace and Stahl [1] illustrate this as shown in Figure 5.3.

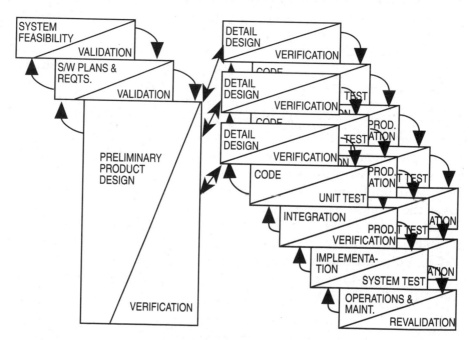

Figure 5.3: The incremental life cycle

Boehm has also suggested [2] that software development could be considered as a series of "spirals." DeGrace and Stahl [1] illustrate the Boehm spiral in Figure 5.4, and point out that it incorporates the use of prototyping, which we will discuss in more detail shortly.

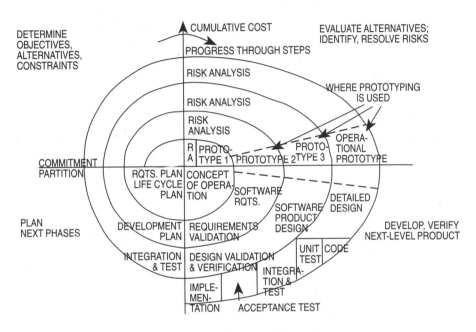

Figure 5.4: The spiral life cycle

5.1.6 Another View of the Modern Waterfall: Automated Transforms of Models

From the preceding discussion, you should be able to see that the waterfall life cycle is not intrinsically evil, but that it has many limitations because of the way it is implemented. With the advent of upper-CASE tools linked to code generators, we are beginning to look at the waterfall life cycle from a new perspective, as suggested by Figure 5.5.

The advantage of this approach, which consultants like Carma McClure [3] refer to as a "transform-based" life cycle, are several:

- *Maintenance can be performed at the specification level.* The projects produced by the classical waterfall life cycle perform all the maintenance activities at the code level, because the analysis and design documents are ponderous paper-based tomes that are impossible to keep up to date. As a result, the analysis and design documents are

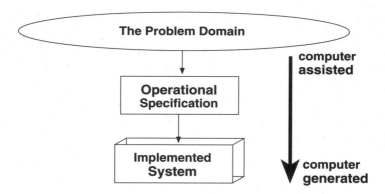

Figure 5.5: The modern interpretation of the waterfall life cycle

virtually guaranteed to be obsolete by the end of the development activity, if not by the end of the very phase in which they were created. By contrast, the transform-based life cycle generates code mechanically, which means that maintenance of the specification level or design level is a viable choice.

- *It enables early checking for errors.* If the requirements and design for the system can be represented as computer-based models, then they can be subjected to error checking and analysis; indeed, this is the major benefit of today's CASE tools. As mentioned earlier in this chapter, the earlier the errors are detected, the easier and cheaper they are to fix. However, consultant Charles Martin correctly observes that CASE tools only spot the "mechanical" errors and that humans are still vital for discovering such errors as the existence of two functions with different names that are actually performing the same thing.

- *It supports requirements tracing.* Because the various models are maintained on a computer, and because each model is derived from the previous one through a series of transformations, it becomes much more practical to *trace* elements of the user requirements through the various models and ensure that they correspond to elements of the delivered code in a one-to-one fashion.

- *It supports software reusability.* As mentioned earlier, the original waterfall life cycle does not prohibit reuse, but there is little opportunity to take advantage of the concept. By thinking of the life cycle as a series of computer-based transformations of models, there is more opportunity to take advantage of existing libraries—not just libraries of code, but also libraries of designs, specifications, and other model components. This concept is discussed further in Chapter 9.

- *It encourages a more problem-oriented specification.* Because the translation into working code is a mechanical process, the modern waterfall life cycle puts more and more emphasis on representing the user requirements in a "problem-oriented" or "application-oriented" fashion. The classical waterfall life cycle offered little guidance in this area, and practitioners often expressed the user requirements in a machine-oriented or language-oriented fashion, since that was the focus of most of their work.

5.2 THE PROTOTYPING LIFE CYCLE

Prototyping has been practiced informally since the first computer program was developed, but it became a sub rosa activity as the waterfall life cycle achieved dominance in the software industry during the 1960s and 1970s; everyone assumed that the "right" way to do things was to analyze rigorously the user requirements *first* and then plunge into the details of design and implementation. Bernard Boar [4] was the first to champion the use of prototyping as a legitimate way of discovering user requirements; Boar's vision of the prototyping life cycle is shown in Figure 5.6.

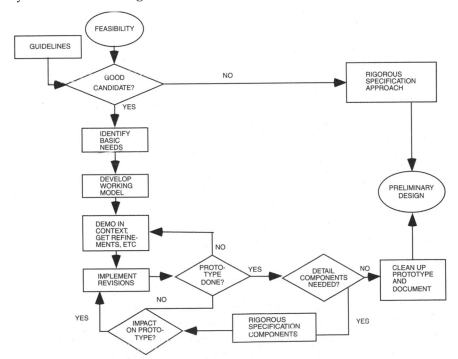

Figure 5.6: The prototyping life cycle

Prototyping is widely praised as an effective way of exploring alternative human interfaces for a system, for example, for exploring different input formats, display screens, and output reports. And it may be the *only* way of eliciting requirements from a user who is unsure of the very nature of the system he or she wants built. However, note that Boar's diagram indicates that some projects may *not* be good candidates for prototyping; one obvious example is the scenario where the system developers lack good prototyping tools.

Also, note that the "radical" form of the waterfall life cycle is, in itself, a form of prototyping. A "skeleton" version of a system can be constructed based on the top levels of design and analysis. If the skeleton proves unacceptable to the user, it can be changed, that is, the specification and design can be changed, and a new skeleton generated. Thus, it is *not* necessary to make a binary choice between a waterfall approach and a prototyping approach; instead, one has to make a choice between a conservative life cycle and a radical life cycle.

Nor is it necessary (or desirable!) to make a choice between the formal rigor associated with a waterfall life cycle and the freewheeling experimentation associated with a prototyping life cycle. One can combine the best features of both. Obviously, the danger of an overly formal waterfall approach is that rigor mortis can set in as each modification to the specification or design is passed through committees and review boards; on the other hand, this should not be used as a justification for "hacking" in the name of prototyping. Connell and Shafer [5] describe an excellent balance between a formal (structured) life cycle and a prototyping approach.

Thus, a key point to remember is that prototyping and waterfall life cycles—or such popular implementations as structured analysis/design and information engineering—can be used together. For example, structured analysis could be used to develop a formal model of the top two or three levels of a system, and prototyping tools could be used to build an initial version of the most interesting (or most important) subsystem. Or information engineering techniques could be used to identify formally the essential entities and relationships in a data model, and prototyping could be used on the same project to concentrate on the human interface issues.

Some organizations experimented with prototyping in the mid-1980s and abandon it because of the additional effort associated with the creation of the prototype. This is because many of the early prototyping tools—high-level interpretive languages, screen painters, and so on—were so inefficient that the prototype had to be thrown away after the user accepted it, and a production version of the system had to be built from scratch using conventional programming languages.[2] But today's more powerful prototyping tools allow for "evolutionary" prototyping, in which the prototype is merely a skeleton of the final system; successive versions of the prototype represent a more fleshed-out version of the initial skeleton.

5.3 POPULAR METHODOLOGIES: AN INTRODUCTION

The most popular methodologies in use today are based on structured techniques or information engineering techniques; the newer object-oriented techniques have attracted a great deal of attention recently and may become the dominant methodology by the end of this decade. Figure 5.7 shows the usage of popular methodologies identified in one recent popularity poll by CASE Research Corporation [6].

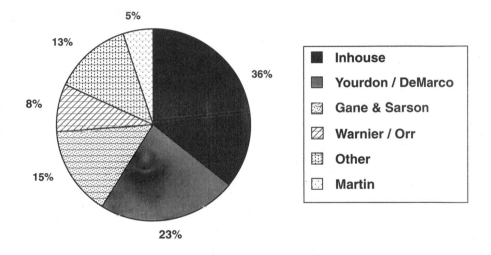

Figure 5.7: Current usage of popular methodologies

The significant thing about this chart is not the popularity of various "brand-name" methodologies, or even the complete absence of object-oriented methodologies, but rather the predominance of "inhouse" methodologies: most organizations pick the best features

---

[2]Early prototyping tools also lacked a number of features that are essential for production systems: security, backup and recovery, and so on.

from several different textbook methodologies and then adapt them to their own needs.

Assuming that an inhouse methodology is practiced in a formal, rigorous fashion, one must still ask whether it is well supported by automated CASE tools. Most commercial tools attempt to support methodologies documented in one or more textbooks; their capability for customization is often quite limited, as we will discuss further shortly.

Another interesting statistic from the CASE Research survey concerns the learning time for popular methodologies, as shown in Figure 5.8.

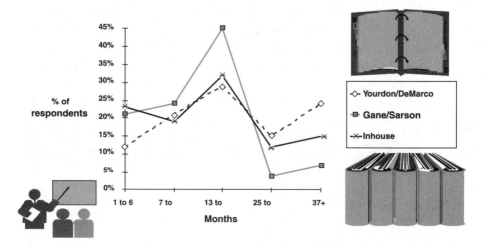

Figure 5.8: Learning time for popular methodologies

There was a time when a methodology could be learned by reading a single book, attending a single three-day seminar, and then practicing for a while. Today's methodologies are often documented in multivolume tomes, such as Martin's treatise on information engineering [7], and supported with multiple classes.[3]

The "bottom line," as Figure 5.8 illustrates, is that the typical software engineer needs 1 to 2 years to become familiar and comfortable with a methodology. An obvious consequence is that organiza-

---

[3] As another example, at the end of 1990, IBM's AD/Cycle, the ultimate CASE environment for carrying out a software engineering methodology, already had 24 manuals! If the trend continues, it will be necessary to start training our future software engineers when they are in kindergarten if they are to ever finish their training!

tions are unlikely to change their methodology at the drop of a hat; having chosen one, they will typically stick with it for 5 to 10 years before choosing a new one. It also suggests that they typical software engineer is unlikely to become proficient in multiple methodologies; learning multiple methodologies is more complex than learning multiple programming languages.

5.4 STRUCTURED METHODOLOGIES

Structured techniques made their first appearance in the late 1960s, with the introduction of structured programming; structured design appeared in the mid-1970s, and structured analysis techniques were documented in the late 1970s. All these methods have been documented in a variety of textbooks [7–14] and articles [15, 16].

Structured analysis and design were originally characterized by two graphical modeling tools—data flow diagrams and structure charts—that emphasized the *functions* performed by a system; additional components of the methodologies included data dictionaries, process specifications, and so forth. More recent forms of the structured analysis methodology [10, 11] have incorporated entity–relationship diagrams and state–transition diagrams to help the software engineer model the *data* and the *time-dependent behavior* of a system. And the *methodology* aspect of the structured techniques, first described by DeMarco [8] as a progression from a "current physical" model to "new logical" model, has also gone through a change, particularly with the emphasis on *essential* models described McMenamin and Palmer [12]. Thus, it is fair to say that the structured analysis/design methodology circa 1989 [11] has undergone a profound evolution from the early writings of DeMarco in 1976 [8].

However, the vintage-1978 forms of structured analysis and design are extremely popular: the textbooks of DeMarco, Yourdon and Constantine, and Gane and Sarson still sell thousands of copies per year in their original, untouched form. Equally important, many of the CASE vendors in the 1990s are basing their automated tools on the methodology described in those early books.[4]

What does this mean about the structured methodology per se? Simply that the methodology itself is quite mature, but that many

---

[4] As an example, many of the CASE tools available in the early 1990s did not include the notion of *events* first described by McMenamin and Palmer in 1984 and described as "event partitioning" in a number of structured analysis/design textbooks.

software engineers are still practicing an old form of the methodology. We will discuss this phenomenon in more detail in Section 5.7. In the meantime, if your organization claims that it is practicing structured techniques, or if your CASE vendor is trying to sell you a tool supposedly based on structured techniques, make sure that it is an up-to-date version.

5.5 INFORMATION ENGINEERING METHODOLOGIES

While modern forms of structured analysis do include entity–relationship diagrams to model the data in a system, there is no doubt that data flow diagrams are the dominant model, and thus, it is fair to say that, *in practice*, structured analysis is more of a function-oriented methodology than a data-oriented methodology.[5]

The information engineering (IE) methodologies reverse the emphasis: *data* plays the dominant role, and functions play a subordinate role. When you ask some organizations to explain what information engineering is, they answer, "Well, it's just the old structured analysis stuff that we learned in the 1970s, except that now we draw the entity–relationship diagrams first and make sure we have agreement on the data model before we draw the DFDs."

But for the purists, IE is more than just drawing ERDs along with the DFDs, and more than just drawing an ERD of the entire enterprise. As promoted by people like James Martin [7], and CASE vendors like Texas Instruments, KnowledgeWare, and others, it also includes business function/ entity-type matrices to show the relationship between business functions within the enterprise and entities they use or modify, entity-type hierarchy diagrams, and a variety of other diagrams.

Perhaps more important than the emphasis on data is the emphasis on the *level* of the model in IE methodologies. While structured methodologies can be, and sometimes are, used to model entire enterprises, in the overwhelming majority of cases they are used to model individual programs or systems. IE, on the other hand, is generally perceived as a higher-level methodology that is intended *first* to model the enterprise and *then* to model the individual systems that constitute

---

[5] This can be seen by looking at the amount of coverage provided by textbooks like [10] to data flow diagrams (DFDs) versus entity–relationship diagrams (ERDs) or by the amount of time spent on DFDs versus ERDs in structured analysis training seminars. Informal customer polls by Yourdon inc. in the mid-1980s indicated that a substantial majority of the companies using structured analysis CASE tools were using the tool to draw DFDs but not ERDs.

it. Thus, IE is becoming gradually more popular as organizations begin committing to "enterprise CASE" and "total methodologies." The chart of popularity in Figure 5.7 indicates that IE is less widely used than SA methodologies as of 1990, but it appears to be the most rapidly growing in popularity.

The emphasis on data versus function, and the emphasis on the *level* of the organization to which the methodology is meant to be implied, is shown in a two-dimensional graph in Figure 5.9.

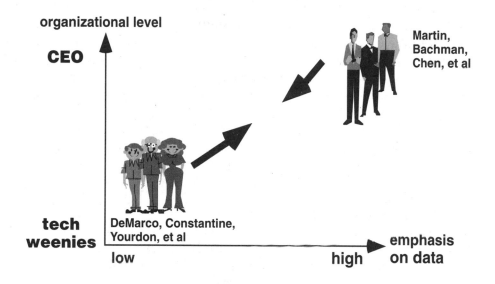

Figure 5.9: Differences between IE and SA

The significant thing is that both "camps" are moving together to a common meeting ground that combines both data and function and appropriate modeling tools for both the tech weenies and the CEO. This suggests that methodologies evolve over time. But as we will see in Section 5.7, the presence of various individuals, consultants, and vendors in Figure 5.9 means that the evolution does not always occur smoothly and gracefully.

5.6 OBJECT-ORIENTED METHODOLOGIES

Though the recent media attention would make it appear that *object-oriented* methodologies have literally sprung into existence overnight, it is in fact a relatively old methodology. Object-oriented programming technologies were first discussed in the late 1960s by the group working on the SIMULA language; by the late 1970s, researchers at Xerox PARC were hard at work developing a language that came to be known as Smalltalk-80. And the first version of the now-popular C++ language was developed by Bjarne Stroustrup at Bell Labs in 1981.

If object-oriented programming could be compared with *structured* programming, then object-oriented design would compare with structured design; as might be expected, it came along somewhat later. The program design methodologies described by Michael Jackson [17] and Jean-Dominique Warnier [18, 19] in the 1970s could be considered somewhat object-oriented in nature, though they did not use those terms. More recent works by Booch [20] and Coad and Yourdon [21] represent the modern flavor of object orientation. Even more recent is the emphasis on object-oriented *analysis*: the first significant book on the subject, by Shlaer and Mellor, appeared in 1988 [22, 23]; additional books [24, 25] have appeared subsequently.

Why the recent shift in interest to an object-oriented approach? In our book on object-oriented analysis [24], Peter Coad and I argue that it is the result of a gradual shift in priorities and technologies:

> Four changes have occurred over the past decade, and are now key factors as we enter the 1990s:
>
> - The underlying concepts of an object-oriented approach have had a decade to mature, and attention has gradually shifted from issues of coding, to issues of design, to issues of analysis. The proponents of functional decomposition spent a decade progressing from structured programming to structured design to structured analysis; we should not be surprised to see the same progression in the object-oriented world.
>
> - The underlying technology for building systems has become much more powerful. Unfortunately, our way of thinking about systems analysis is influenced by our preconceived ideas of how we would design a system to meet its requirements; our ideas about design are influenced by our preconceived ideas about how we would write code; and our ideas about coding are strongly influenced by the programming language we have available. It was difficult to think about structured programming (and thus difficult to think about structured design and analysis) when the languages of choice were assembler, Autocoder and FORTRAN; things became easier with Pascal, PL/1, ALGOL, FORTRAN-77, Structured BASIC, and newer versions of COBOL. Similarly, it was difficult to think about

coding in an object-oriented fashion when the language of choice was COBOL, FORTRAN, or plain-vanilla C; it has become easier with C++, Objective-C, Smalltalk, and Ada.

- The systems we build today are different than they were ten or twenty years ago. In every respect, they are larger and more complex; they are also more volatile and subject to constant change. We will argue in subsequent chapters that an object-oriented approach to analysis (and design) is likely to lead to a more stable system. Also, we find that today's on-line, interactive systems devote much more attention to the *user interface* than the text-oriented batch processing systems of the 1960s and 1970s. Some observers, such as Bill Joy of Sun Microsystems, argue that as much as 75 percent of the code in a modern system may be concerned with the user interface—e.g., manipulating windows, pull-down menus, icons, mouse movements, etc.; this is particularly evident with the graphical user interface available on Apple Macintosh, IBM OS/2 Presentation Manager, and Microsoft Windows. Our experience has been that an object-oriented approach to such systems—from analysis through design and into coding—is a more natural way of dealing with such user-oriented systems.

- Many organizations find that the systems they build today are more "data-oriented" than the systems they built in the 1970s and 1980s. Functional complexity is less of a concern than it was before; modeling the data has become a higher priority.

What does it mean to be object oriented? How does one tell whether the brand X methodology is truly object oriented or whether the adjective is just being used as a marketing term? The purists are still debating this topic, but there seems to be common agreement that there are at least four key characteristics of an object-oriented methodology:

- *Data abstraction*. Instead of functional decomposition, or procedural abstraction, which is the dominant feature of the structured techniques, the object-oriented methodologies emphasize data abstraction. In this sense, then, they are compatible with the data modeling and information engineering methodologies. Data abstraction also includes the concept of superclass and subclass; while these are present in many of the older data modeling methodologies, they are often not as fully developed as, say, the "generalization-specialization" structures and "whole-part" structures described in Coad and Yourdon [24].

- *Encapsulation.* Even the most enlightened and modern forms of structured methodologies and information engineering methodologies view data and function as *separate* items to model; the DFD and ERD are considered separate models and are often created by different people, or even different organizational units. The essence of the object-oriented approach is the concept of tightly packaging, or *encapsulating*, data and function together in such a way that the only means of accessing (or updating) the data is by invoking the associated functions.

- *Inheritance.* The object-oriented methodologies allow an object to "inherit" both data attributes and functions from higher-level "parent" objects. While many of the data modeling methodologies include the concept of superclass and subclass, they often lack the concept of inheritance; similarly, languages like Ada might be considered "object oriented" by some, but its lack of inheritance capabilities rules it out in the opinion of most object-oriented aficionados. Inheritance is a critically important concept, for it helps facilitate reuse; we will discuss this further in Chapter 9.

- *Communication through messages.* In older functional-decomposition methodologies, the communication architecture is based on subroutine-calling mechanisms; thus the overall software architecture is usually based on a synchronous hierarchy of modules or subroutines. In an object-oriented system, the architecture consists of an asynchronous network of objects that communicates by sending *messages* to one another. Many of the would-be object-oriented approaches (e.g., those being promoted by 4GL or relational database vendors hoping to hop on the object-oriented bandwagon) may have powerful data abstraction capabilities, and even some rudimentary encapsulation and inheritance capabilities, but they often lack a message protocol altogether.

Ironically, the object-oriented paradigm is following the same evolutionary path that the structured techniques went through in the 1970s: from coding techniques to design techniques to analysis techniques. In the late 1980s and early 1990s, the vast majority of articles, books, and conference topics appearing under the rubric of "object-oriented" had to do with programming issues, for example, C++ versus Smalltalk, or low-level design issues (e.g., techniques for implementing windows and scroll bars in Microsoft's Windows 3.0 operating system). This suggests that the OO "paradigm" is still relatively immature and will go through a process of increasing sophistication; we discuss this further in the next section.

5.7 METHODOLOGY PARADIGM SHIFTS

5.7.1 The IE–SA Schism and the Three Dimensions of Complexity

While the methodology bigots fight over the relative importance of functions and data or the need to package them together into tightly encapsulated *objects*, it is important to remember that there are actually *three* dimensions of a system that need to be modeled, as indicated in Figure 5.10: functions, data, and time-dependent behavior.

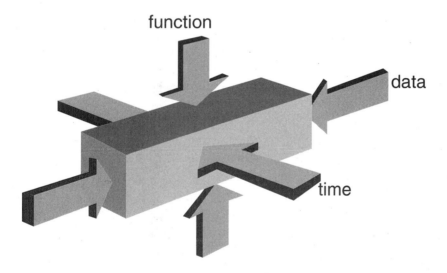

Figure 5.10: The three dimensions of system complexity

The methodologies of the 1970s and 1980s typically focused on only one of these dimensions, because they were intended to be used for special "classes" of systems. As Figure 5.11 suggests, certain types of systems might have only one dimension of system complexity; hence, it would be well served by a methodology that provides rich modeling tools for understanding that dimension.

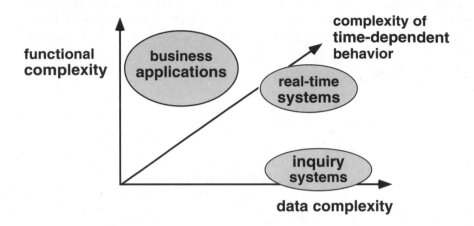

Figure 5.11: Relationship of systems to complexity dimensions

Even today, some systems are complex in only one dimension, for example, data, function, or time; the others may not require significant attention. But more and more systems today are complex in either two, or possibly all three, dimensions. Thus, we are beginning to see process control systems with complex data structures and complex functions in addition to the obvious time-critical interrupt processing, and we are seeing on-line systems (banking, airline, insurance, etc.) whose thousands of terminals and enormous volume of on-line transactions add a critical element of time-dependent behavior to the existing dimensions of data complexity and functional complexity.

Thus, the critical question today is not which dimension to model, but rather which dimension to model *first*. Successful methodologies of the 1990s will incorporate all three dimensions. In the meantime, remember that you can't get out what you don't put in: if a methodology ignores functions (or data, or time) entirely, then it *cannot* claim to provide a complete model of the system's behavior.

5.7.2 The Nature of Paradigm Shifts

Most of the popular software methodologies today are not the result of efforts by IBM or the Defense Department,[6] or large government committees, but were developed and marketed by individual consultants, or by small consulting and training firms. While these

---

[6] It is virtually impossible, for example, to find a practicing software engineer who can tell you that he honestly enjoys following the steps required by DoD-2167A.

small groups passionately believed that their methodology would change the course of Western civilization, none of them could realistically claim that they had the power or the marketing "clout" to impose their methodology upon the industry. They were, in effect, young rebels setting out to revolutionize the industry.

But as Thomas Kuhn observed in a classic study of scientific revolutions [26], there is a typical cycle for such revolutions in *all* fields of science and engineering, including software engineering. If the software engineering methodology created by the young revolutionary succeeds, it displaces the older methodologies because it seen as an effective solution to problems that the older methodologies did not solve. Success not only improves the overall state of the industry, but brings fame and fortune to the consultant who created the methodology. No longer is he called a consultant; now he is a *guru*. He hires disciples to spread the methodology far and wide through the land of savages; he writes books—many books!—to document the methodology in as many ways as he can imagine. He creates CASE tools of his own and blesses the work of other companies whose CASE tools carry his name. And it is all very, very lucrative.

But as the methodology is applied to larger and more complex problems, and as it is applied to a wider range of applications than originally conceived, inevitably it develops problems. Extensions are patched onto the methodology; exceptions and special cases are noted; shortcomings and occasional failures are glossed over, or simply blamed on the inadequacies of the software engineers who used it.

Meanwhile, the guru becomes more and more dependent on the success of his paradigm to pay the rent for his palace and the salaries of his minions. And he becomes less and less willing to listen to the problems and the shortcomings and the exceptions. Even if he has personal doubts about his creation, his sales representatives tell him more and more loudly that it is the *best* methodology in the land, if not the entire world. Anyone who questions or doubts the utter efficacy of the methodology becomes an enemy.

Kuhn points out that in scientific disciplines such as astronomy, this process can continue for centuries until finally the old paradigm collapses under its own weight and is replaced by a new methodology created by a new generation of revolutionary. And the cycle begins anew. In some fields, the cycle does not take centuries, but merely years; José Ortega y Gasset, in *The Revolt of the Masses*, observed that "a revolution only lasts fifteen years, a period which coincides with the effectiveness of a generation." But whether years or centuries, the revolutionary change can be delayed for a surprisingly long time because of politics and the inertia of the institutions using the methodology.

Of course, astronomers dealt with such weighty questions as whether the sun revolves around the earth or the earth revolves around the sun. It's not clear that software engineering methodologies operate on the same cosmic scale; however, the general phenomenon is the same, and the process of change is the same. The software engineering methodologies can be thought of as a series of "technology curves," as shown in Figure 5.12.

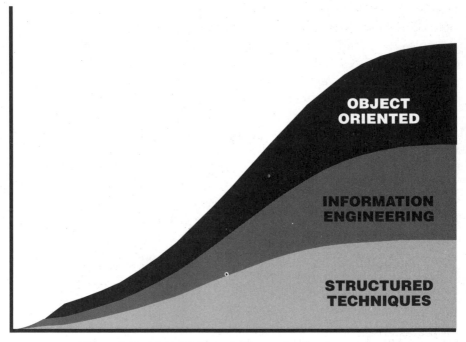

Figure 5.12: Methodologies in terms of technology curves

Thus, the structured techniques began in the early 1970s; went through a period of rapid intellectual growth in the late 1970s, early 1980s, and mid-1980s; and then began to stagnate.[7] Information engineering could be seen as the "next wave" of methodology, which will presumably lead to higher levels of system quality and productivity;

[7] Graduate students in some universities are now being awarded a Master's degree for writing a history of the structured techniques—a sure sign that the movement has stagnated!

object-oriented methodologies are the next wave beyond that. (Note that Figure 5.12 makes no attempt to show the precise point in time when the methodology actually began.)

Everett Rogers [27] describes a series of "stages of adoption" for new technologies, which applies nicely to the adoption of software engineering methodologies:

Stages	Actors	Cumulative % of Actors Adopting
Pioneer	Innovator	0–5%
Early expansion	Early adopters	5–15
Takeoff	Popularizers	15–30
Bandwagon	Followers	30–85
Late	Conservatives	85–95
Terminal	Resistors	95–100

From this perspective, I believe that structured analysis/design methodologies are in the "late" stage of adoption, information engineering is in the "takeoff" stage, and object-oriented methodologies are in the "early expansion" stage.

But this presumes that everyone is using the same form of a methodology, for example, the form of structured analysis documented in 1989 [11]. But this is manifestly not so, as suggested by Figure 5.13. Some organizations are still using an early form of structured techniques, for example, the form first documented by DeMarco and Gane and Sarson; visiting these organizations is like going through a time warp and suddenly finding that the clock has been turned back to 1977; Page-Jones [28] refers to such organizations as operating within "the Realm of Darkness." Others are using an "average" form of the techniques, and some are using a very advanced form of structured techniques.

Why does this matter? Because organizations at the bottom end of one technology curve are unlikely to gain much productivity by jumping off that technology curve and onto the next one, *if they realize where they are on the curve.* Thus, people experiencing difficulties with structured analysis might find it much easier to evolve to a more modern form of that technology than simply abandoning it altogether and adopting information engineering; obviously, the same argument holds true for those thinking of abandoning their primitive use of informa-

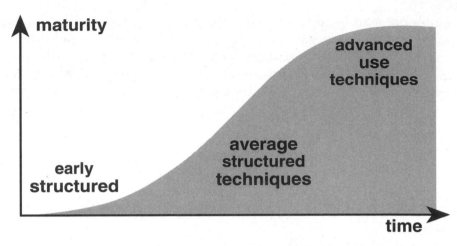

Figure 5.13: Methodology shifts in terms of homogeneity

tion engineering in order to achieve eternal salvation from object-oriented techniques.

Another reason for caution was suggested in Figure 5.14: it takes a long time to learn a new methodology. But while this means that an organization should not be too quick to abandon one methodology and adopt the latest one advertised in *Computerworld*, it also means that some organizations are considering "skipping" a generation of methodologies, for example, leapfrogging over the information engi-

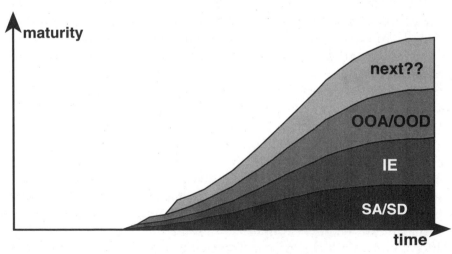

Figure 5.14: Generations of methodologies

neering methodology and going straight from structured techniques to object-oriented techniques.

This is certainly possible, though it must be done with some caution. To make the transition work, it's very important to have a group within the software organization that can focus its attention on the issue of methodologies. This dovetails nicely with the notion of a "software process group"; in Chapter 4, we pointed out that the SEI process maturity model indicates that such a group is a necessary component of a level 3 organization. The main thing this group must keep in mind is that the arguments about SA/SD versus IE versus OO are just *today's* arguments; these methodologies will almost certainly be superseded by new methodologies by the early part of the next millennium.

Whatever the next methodology is, the transition from object-oriented methodologies will not be a smooth one; as noted, the OO gurus and CASE vendors will continue defending their methodology with the same frenzy as a wild animal defending its young.

But there is another group that will hasten the arrival of the next revolution: the current (and future) generation of software engineers. The software field is now old enough that it is quite common to see mothers and daughters, and fathers and sons working together in the field; no doubt there are a few grandparents and grandchildren working side by side in some computer company! But unlike the generation of software engineers who began in the 1960s, today's generation of software engineers has never seen a punched card and has never coded in COBOL. Today's software engineer thinks a 1401 is a World War II bomber; he or she doesn't like mainframes, hates Ada and FORTRAN, and vastly prefers working on Suns and Macintoshes in a language like C++ or Smalltalk.

And just as today's young software engineer thinks his parents' music, clothing, and politics are obsolete, so he also feels that his parents' software engineering methodology is obsolete. Object-oriented aficionados defend their methodology today partly on this "generational" issue: the OO revolutionaries typically argue that the "old" SA/SD approach should be completely abandoned. The older generation typically looks at the object-oriented movement from a "synthesist" perspective: old-timers like Page-Jones [14] and Constantine [13] argue that the best ideas of structured techniques— for example, coupling and cohesion—can be married together with the best concepts of the newer object-oriented paradigm.

Aside from the generational influence, the most common reason for a transition from one methodology to another is simply that the older methodology fails to solve an important class of problems. *Nobody changes methodologies to achieve a 10 percent improvement in productivity.* Even if the expense (training, new standards, new tools, etc.) could be justified, the massive inertia associated with the use of the old methodology would mitigate against the change. But if the marketplace or the user community pushes hard for a kind of system with which the old methodology cannot easily deal, then there may sufficient pressure to switch to a new methodology.

A good example of this in the early 1990s is the fascination with graphic user interfaces (GUIs): everyone wants a system with windows, and pop-up menus, mouses, and scroll bars. The older structured analysis/design and information engineering methodologies were not intended for building systems of this kind, and either fail miserably or offer absolutely no guidance to the system developer. Hence the shift toward object-oriented methodologies, which *do* have useful things to say about windows and scroll bars, mouses, and pop-up menus.

Another force that *could* accelerate the movement to newer generations of methodologies is the underlying technology of languages and tools. The structured methodologies were built around third generation languages like COBOL and FORTRAN; the information engineering methodologies were built around relational database management systems like DB2. But as languages like C++ and Smalltalk become more widely used, and as object-oriented database systems start to proliferate, there is an opportunity to switch to a methodology that takes advantage of the technology.

5.8 METHODOLOGY AND CULTURE

In its simplest form, a software engineering methodology can be regarded as simply a list of rules and guidelines, combined with some graphical notation for modeling the requirements and design of a system. But at a deeper level, a methodology either encourages or requires a certain "mind-set"; thus, its use in an organization tends to create a technology culture that is strikingly different from the culture of an organization using a different methodology.

This is particularly evident today when observing software engineers using an object-oriented methodology. While conducting research for our book on object-oriented design, Pete Coad and I found a number of noteworthy characteristics of the OO camp:

- Teaching by example: the use of pattern languages
- The factors that affect the nature of design work
- Why OOPLers haven't seen the need for graphical models yet
- The nature of the analysis/design "twilight zone" for OOPLers
- The relationship of OOPLs and prototyping
- The importance of reusability
- The difference between SP/SD/SA and OOP/OOD/OOA
- The impact of small, fast OOPL projects on the learning curve

5.8.1 Pattern Languages

Many people working in the object-oriented field referred to *pattern languages* repeatedly, though they may use different terms: metamodels, domain models, and templates were three of the more common synonyms.

The idea of pattern languages has been strongly influenced by the work of Christopher Alexander and his colleagues in a three-volume work [29–31]. Ironically, the work that Larry Constantine and I did in the 1970s in the structured design field was influenced by an earlier Alexander book [32]. Alexander and his colleagues are architects, and the thrust of their work is to help architects design villages and buildings. In *A Pattern Language* [30], he suggests that buildings and towns are naturally designed from combinations of 253 "patterns":

> All 253 patterns together form a language. They create a coherent picture of an entire region, with the power to generate such regions in a million forms, with infinite variety in all the details.

> It is also true that any small sequence of patterns from this language is itself a language for a smaller part of the environment; and this small list of patterns is then capable of generating a million parks, paths, houses, workshops, or gardens.

> For example, consider the following ten patterns:

> PRIVATE TERRACE ON THE STREET (140)
> SUNNY PLACE (161)
> OUTDOOR ROOM (163)
> SIX-FOOT BALCONY (167)
> PATHS AND GOALS (120)

CEILING HEIGHT VARIETY (190)
COLUMNS AT THE CORNERS (212)
FRONT DOOR BENCH (242)
RAISED FLOWERS (245)
DIFFERENT CHAIRS (251)

This short list of patterns is itself a language: it is one of a thousand possible languages for a porch, at the front of a house. One of us chose this small language, to build a porch onto the front of his house.

A common misconception of this concept by the object-oriented community is that we should not try to create designs "from scratch" for each new application. Instead, we should try to find a "pattern" that fits a broad class of problems. Specific applications—for example, the flight simulator for the B-2 bomber—could be designed by looking at the required variations from the generic pattern of flight-simulator systems for new-generation aircraft.

This fits nicely into the concept of "application domain models" that many researchers are currently exploring. It should be possible to provide a handbook to system designers that says, "Look, if you're building a sales order entry system, you should expect to see these 20 basic classes of objects and the following class hierarchies. You may encounter some variations and extensions, but this is the general pattern." It also fits in nicely with the idea of "designware" discussed in Chapter 9.

The big question, of course, is: Where do these domain models come from? Who invents them? Alexander's theme is that patterns evolve naturally because the "right" patterns work, and the wrong patterns simply don't work. This is quite evident in MIS organizations that build the same kind of application over and over again: a tribal folklore develops about the general pattern of the application. (Note, however, that if this were the full extent of the organization's software engineering sophistication, the SEI process maturity model discussed in Chapter 4 would characterize it as only a level 2 "repeatable" organization.)

While an existing pattern can be "stretched" or modified to meet local circumstances, a major change in the scale or complexity of an application can cause serious problems. Inevitably, it will turn out that the old pattern cannot be successfully modified to fit the problem, and a new pattern must be found. Which brings us back to the same question: Where does the new pattern, or metamodel, come from?

There is a simple but crucial cultural difference between the OO community and the SA/SD community in this area: the OO community assumes that a pattern *does* exist, and the job is merely to find it. The SA/SD community, on the other hand, when faced with a problem that no longer fits into an old, familiar pattern, starts from scratch and tries to invent completely new solutions that may or may not fit a pattern.

Why does this happen? Why do OO people and SA/SD people work differently and approach problems differently? Why is their approach to patterns dissimilar? One way of understanding this is to look at some of the other issues affecting design.

5.8.2 The Factors That Affect the Nature of Design Work

There are several key factors affecting the nature of design.

- *The culture and politics of the organization.* The Humphrey process model is one way of characterizing the difference between organizations. But OOPL development organizations have a very different culture from the typical SA/SD organization. Because of the rich library of reusable components, there is a strong cultural tendency to approach new problems by asking: "How can we build this new system from things we already have?" This translates into the technical question: "What existing patterns (objects and class hierarchies) match, or almost match, the requirements of my system?" The SA/SD adherents know that reusability, like other Boy Scout virtues, is a good thing, but it is not a fundamental part of their culture.

- *The available implementation technology.* Culture and technology go hand in hand. The library of reusable components used by the SA/SD community consists of individual, "atomic" modules. Sometimes, as in the case of the Unix library, it is easy to see how modules can be connected and aggregated in useful ways. But this is a bottom–up process, and it runs counter to the conventional wisdom of top–down decomposition.

  The OO community, on the other hand, starts with a reusable library of high-level aggregates (class structures); this approach is typically neither top down nor bottom up but rather "design by exception." The question the OOPLers seem to ask themselves is: "What attributes and methods (services) do I need to extend, or override, or redefine in order to make this general class hierarchy of objects accomplish what I want it to?"

- *The scale of the problem.* There are several key differences between small-scale and large-scale systems. Small-scale systems typically have fewer hardware performance problems so they can take advantage of 4GLs, OOPL technology, and the like. Equally important, they can be implemented by smaller teams, led by one person who can keep the entire "conceptual design" in his or her head. But perhaps most important, the large-scale systems are more likely to be perceived as "one-of-a-kind" systems by their designers. After all, who has ever built a Star Wars system before? What possible existing pattern could it fit? The small- and medium-scale systems are more likely to be the kind of system that has been built before, so it's more likely that successful patterns exist for them.

- *The "distance" between the statement of requirements and the implementation of the requirements.* One of the most difficult technical issues in the SA/SD world has always been the translation of a user-oriented SA model, involving an asynchronous network of DFD bubbles, into a technology-oriented SD model, involving a synchronous hierarchy of modules in a structure chart. This is because the "vocabulary" of a user requirements description is quite different from the "vocabulary" needed to describe the implementation of a system in a conventional 3GL.

For OO people, it appears that if you can describe the problem in a vocabulary that is natural to the users, you have also described the solution in a form that can be directly implemented in an object-oriented programming language. Coad and I have noticed, for example, that OOPLers have found the graphical notation we provided in our *Object-Oriented Analysis* book [24] useful for describing user requirements *and* for describing the design of the system.

5.8.3 Why OOPLers Haven't Seen the Need for Graphical Models Yet

Because languages like Smalltalk and Eiffel are 10 to 100 times more powerful than are the conventional 3GLs, many of the programs and systems developed by OO people are only a few hundred or a few thousand lines of code. Hence, it appears that OOPLers communicate with one another about their design by actually looking at the code and reading it. Diagrams, or graphical models, do not have the mystical aura in the OO community that they have in the SA/SD community.

But I remember that on my first programming projects in the Dark Ages of the 1960s at Digital Equipment Corporation—the math library for a FORTRAN system and the assembler for the PDP-5 minicomputer—I didn't draw any diagrams either. I occasionally drew some cryptic pictures on the back of an envelope, but mostly I conceived of the solution to my problem in terms of my implementation technology (assembly language) and then started coding.

The key point today, I believe, is that the power of object-oriented programming languages (OOPLs) allows a tiny group composed of 2 or 3 people to tackle projects that would require 10 to 100 people and three to five years of effort in a 3GL environment. The tiny group doesn't need any pictures to communicate. But what will happen when the experience of OOPLers on small projects (e.g., 1000 lines of Smalltalk) is scaled up to truly large systems requiring 10,000 to 100,000 lines of code? Sooner or later, noncoding issues will begin to dominate—the problem of precise, unambiguous communication between larger groups of developers and implementors, the problem of communicating with geographically separated users, and so forth. I believe that at this point, if not before, the need for graphical modeling tools will become increasingly apparent.

Christopher Alexander makes some interesting points about precision and diagrams in *The Timeless Way of Building*: [29]

> My experience has shown that many people find it hard to make their design ideas precise. They are willing to express their ideas in loose, general, terms, but are unwilling to express them with the precision needed to make them into patterns. Above all, they are unwilling to express them as abstract spatial relations among well-defined spatial parts. I have also found that people aren't always very good at it; it is hard to do. . . .

> If you can't draw a diagram of it, it isn't a pattern. If you think you have a pattern, you must be able to draw a diagram of it. This is a crude, but vital rule. A pattern defines a field of spatial relations, and it must therefore always be possible to draw a diagram for every pattern. In the diagram, each part will appear as a labeled or colored zone, and the layout of the parts expresses the relation which the pattern specifies. If you can't draw it, it isn't a pattern.

Sooner or later, the OOPL community will have to realize the same truth about large software designs: no matter how powerful Smalltalk may be, if you can't draw a precise picture of the pattern, it doesn't exist. In an OOPL environment, the problem vocabulary and the implementation vocabulary are close enough that we might consider using the same graphical notation for OOA and OOD.

5.8.4 The Nature of the Analysis/Design "Twilight Zone" for OOPLers

For people familiar with structured analysis and structured design, the transition from analysis to design may be difficult, but the distinction between the two is fairly clear. Indeed, the distinction may exist in their minds precisely because the transition *is* so difficult. Conversely, the OOPLers make much less distinction between the two. For them there is implementation, and then there is everything that precedes implementation.

Why the lack of distinction? Primarily because OOPLers mix the activities of analysis and design together. If you listen to OOPLers discuss how they use an object-oriented approach on their typical projects, you'll find that they bounce back and forth between issues that are clearly matters of user-specified requirements and issues that are clearly high-level implementation (design) issues. As previously noted, this is partly because OOPLers use a high-level implementation technology that allows them to think in terms of the user's vocabulary.

But there are other reasons. In some cases, OOPLers are hackers of the worst kind, composing object-oriented code extemporaneously. Perhaps a more charitable way of saying this is that OOPLs come with such a powerful library and (at least in the case of Smalltalk) such a powerful development environment, that prototyping is remarkably easy. If you can build a real prototype just as quickly as you can draw a diagram that represents a formal design of your system, many people would choose the prototyping approach.

This has been further amplified by the small size—at least until now—of OOPL projects. A small project, combined with a very powerful implementation technology, means that one person is often sufficient to do the job. And in any situation where the same person does analysis, design, and coding, it has been difficult to separate the activities.

5.8.5 The Relationship of OOPLs and Prototyping

Why do OOPLers prototype? Because it's there. If you had powerful prototyping tools in your environment, wouldn't you use them? The more interesting question is: What use do OOPLers make of prototyping? The straightforward answer is the same use that SA/SD developers do: they use it to build a working demonstration quickly in order to get feedback from the users. It gives them something to play with, something more real and tangible than a bunch of bubbles and boxes on a piece of paper.

Veteran OOPLers go beyond this. They build prototypes to discover early where the hard parts of the system will be. OO veteran Jeff McKenna, developer of the OOATool CASE tool, has observed, "I try to find out what I don't know, because I know that I can design and code what I *do* know." This suggests that object-oriented techniques may have been more successful than SA/SD on projects with ambiguous requirements, where it's very difficult to write a formal, precise statement of user requirements.

There is a more significant question: How does OOD help developers discover more quickly what they really know about the problem and what they don't? It may just be that OOPL environments provide faster and more powerful prototyping facilities than a 4GL does. Or it may be something more profound: by getting users and developers to think about the encapsulated combination of data and functions, it's possible that difficult, ambiguous aspects will come to the surface more quickly.

5.8.6 The Importance of Reusability

Reusability seems to be the golden word in the OO community, much as cohesion was the buzzword with structured design and essential (logical) model was a buzzword with structured analysis. All OOPLers talk about the benefit of reusability, and, to their credit, they seem to take advantage of the concept with a vengeance. But reusability is a subtle and complex concept, and more research is needed to understand how OOPLers use reusability differently from SA/SD people.

For instance, how does the OO community justify spending more time on a project to create new reusable components for a library? In an OO project, an automobile could be defined as an instance of class VEHICLE. Alternatively, one could define a new subclass AUTOMOBILE of class VEHICLE, with additional subclass attributes such as OPERATING-COST-PER-MILE. Whether it is easier to do this in an OO environment than in an SA/SD environment is not the issue; the issue is whether the developer will spend the time thinking about the potential value of having a new subclass called AUTOMOBILE.

It's also not clear how the OO community solves the configuration management problem associated with a reusable library. For example, suppose the high-level VEHICLE class has an attribute of weight. The inheritance concept means that any subclass below AUTOMOBILE also has an attribute of weight unless it has been overridden or redefined. Now suppose I decide to change the definition of weight from pounds to kilograms. Is it any easier to gauge the impact of this change on all the subclasses of VEHICLE than it would be to gauge the impact of a similar change to a system developed with SA/SD techniques?

5.8.7 The Difference Between SA/SD and OOA/OOD

What, then, is the difference between the way "structured" people develop systems and the way "object" people develop systems? The differences are greater than some would suggest and less than others would believe. Many OO purists, for example, complain that some prominent members of the SA/SD community are trying to "objectify" their designs by first drawing data flow diagrams and then gathering a bunch of bubbles around a common data store and calling each assembled bubble bunch an object.

"The problem is that they first think about the problem in functional terms and then make a cosmetic effort to change the model to make it look like it's object oriented!" the OO purists exclaim. "So they really look at the problem from a very different perspective than we do."

The OO community is equally critical of data modelers, whose ERD models describe objects and relationships but say nothing about the processing functions/methods/services that are to be carried out.

Yet when OOPLers are asked how they develop a design of their applications, the diagrams they draw to explain their work often turn out to be thinly disguised data flow diagrams! Why bother arguing about design notation? Because notation—drawings—is one of the three major components of a typical methodology; the other two are criteria for evaluating the goodness or badness of a design and "cookbook" strategies for creating designs.

The nature of a diagram has a strong influence on how one looks at a problem. Thus, the OOPLers argue that most SA/SD developers use data flow diagrams or structure charts as their major modeling tool and inevitably view the systems they build from a functional point of view.

But SA and SD are more than just diagramming techniques. A major component of SD, for example, is a collection of guidelines and criteria for evaluating different candidate designs for a system. This presupposes that there is more than one possible design to correctly implement some well-defined problem. Is this also true in the OO world? "Well, yes, of course," the OOPLers will reply. "There are many different ways to design a system in Smalltalk or C++ to solve a problem." So whether one works in an SA/SD world or an OOA/ OOD world, one must eventually deal with the same question: How do you tell the good designs from the bad designs?

SA/SD practitioners are familiar with the concepts of coupling and cohesion as a way of evaluating intermodule and intramodule connections. They know that the guidelines of "span of control" and "scope of effect/scope of control" are useful ways of evaluating the morphology, or shape, or a hierarchy of modules.

Lo and behold! There are highly analogous criteria for evaluating an OOD design! Coupling and cohesion, span of control, and various other guidelines are just as meaningful, but there may be more "dimensions" to consider than in the SA/SD world: methods, classes, inheritance, messages, and collaboration among objects. Many of these guidelines are discussed in [21].

5.8.8 The Impact of Small, Fast OOPL Projects on the Learning Curve

The rapid prototyping and high-productivity aspects of an OOPL like Smalltalk mean that a typical OOPLer works on 10 to 12 projects a year. This is in stark contrast to the experience of a typical SA/SD developer, who often works on the same project for two or three years.

The result is that the OOPLers' experiences are amplified. If they try a design approach that works, they're likely to repeat that experience a dozen times in a year. If they try something that basically doesn't work, they'll have that experience repeated several times within a matter of months. It's a lot easier to remember what you did on the last project.

Perhaps this is one reason OOPLers are more comfortable with the concept of looking for an existing pattern from which to generate new systems. If you only build three payroll systems in the course of a decade, each one at a different company, it's easy to treat each project as a unique experience. For OOPLers, the third project occurs within the first year, and by then you've got it right. After that, it's merely a matter of repetition.

END NOTES

1. DeGrace, Peter, and Leslie Hulet Stahl. *Wicked Problems, Righteous Solutions: A Catalogue of Modern Software Engineering Paradigms.* Englewood Cliffs, NJ: Yourdon Press/Prentice Hall, 1990.
2. Boehm, Barry. "A Spiral Model of Software Development and

Enhancement," *Proceedings of an International Workshop on the Software Process and Software Environments*, Coto de Caza, Trabuco Canyon, California, 1985.

3. McClure, Carma. "Software Automation in the 1990s and Beyond," *Proceedings of Fall 1989 CASE Symposium*. Andover, MA: Digital Consulting, September 1989.

4. Boar, Bernard. *Application Prototyping*. Reading, MA: Addison-Wesley, 1984.

5. Connell, John, and Linda Bryce Shafer. *Structured Rapid Prototyping*. Englewood Cliffs, NJ: Yourdon Press/Prentice Hall, 1988.

6. Boone, Gregory H., Vaughan P. Merlyn, and Roger E. Dobratz. *The Second Annual Report on CASE*. Bellevue, WA: CASE Research Corporation, 1990.

7. Martin, James. *Information Engineering*, Vols. 1–3. Englewood Cliffs, NJ: Prentice Hall, 1990.

8. DeMarco, Tom. *Structured Analysis and System Specification*. Englewood Cliffs, NJ: Yourdon Press/Prentice Hall, 1978.

9. Gane, Chris, and Trish Sarson. *Structured Systems Analysis: Tools and Techniques*. Englewood Cliffs, NJ: Prentice Hall, 1977.

10. Ward, Paul, and Stephen J. Mellor. *Structured Systems Development for Real-Time Systems*, Vols. 1–3. Englewood Cliffs, NJ: Yourdon Press/Prentice Hall, 1986.

11. Yourdon, Edward. *Modern Structured Analysis*. Englewood Cliffs, NJ: Yourdon Press/Prentice Hall, 1989.

12. McMenamin, Steven, and John Palmer. *Essential Systems Analysis*. Englewood Cliffs, NJ: Yourdon Press/Prentice Hall, 1984.

13. Yourdon, Edward, and Larry L. Constantine. *Structured Design*. Englewood Cliffs, NJ: Yourdon Press/Prentice Hall, 1979.

14. Page-Jones, Meilir. *The Practical Guide to Structured Systems Design*, 2nd ed. Englewood Cliffs, NJ: Yourdon Press/Prentice Hall, 1988.

15. Yourdon, Edward. "Sayonara, Once Again, Structured Stuff," *American Programmer*, November 1991.

16. Stevens, Wayne. "Structured Design, Structured Analysis, and Structured Programming," *American Programmer*, November 1991.

17. Jackson, Michael. *Principles of Program Design*. New York: Academic Press, 1975.

18. Warnier, Jean-Dominique. *Logical Construction of Programs*. New York: Van Nostrand Reinhold, 1974.

19. Warnier, Jean-Dominique. *Logical Construction of Systems*. New York: Van Nostrand Reinhold, 1981.

20. Booch, Grady. *Object-Oriented Design with Applications*. Redwood City, CA: Benjamin Cummings, 1991.
21. Coad, Peter, and Edward Yourdon. *Object-Oriented Design*. Englewood Cliffs, N J: Yourdon Press/Prentice Hall, 1991.
22. Shlaer, Sally, and Stephen Mellor. *Object-Oriented Systems Analysis: Modeling the World in Data*. Englewood Cliffs, NJ: Yourdon Press/Prentice Hall, 1988.
23. Shlaer, Sally, and Stephen Mellor. *Object Lifecycles: Modeling the World in States*. Englewood Cliffs, NJ: Yourdon Press/Prentice Hall, 1992.
24. Coad, Peter, and Edward Yourdon. *Object-Oriented Analysis*, 2nd ed. Englewood Cliffs, NJ: Yourdon Press/Prentice Hall, 1991.
25. Rumbaugh, James, Michael Blaha, William Premerlani, Frederick Eddy, and William Lorensen. *Object-Oriented Modeling and Design*. Englewood Cliffs, NJ: Prentice Hall, 1991.
26. Kuhn, Thomas. *The Structure of Scientific Revolutions*. Chicago: The University of Chicago Press, 1970.
27. Rogers, Everett. *Diffusion of Innovations*, 3rd ed. New York: Free Press, 1982.
28. Page-Jones, Meilir. "Structured Methods Are Dead. Long Live Structured Methods!" *American Programmer*, November 1991.
29. Alexander, Christopher. *The Timeless Way of Building*. New York: Oxford University Press, 1979.
30. Alexander, Christopher. *A Pattern Language*. New York: Oxford University Press, 1977.
31. Alexander, Christopher, Sara Ishikawa, and Murray Silverstein, with Max Jacobson, Ingrid Fiksdahl-King, and Shlomo Angel. *The Oregon Experiment*. New York: Oxford University Press, 1975.
32. Alexander, Christopher. *Notes on the Synthesis of Form*, 2nd ed. Cambridge, MA: Harvard University Press, 1971.

6

Case Technology

Virtually all world-class software organizations are using CASE technology, but not all organizations using CASE are world-class software organizations. CASE—computer-aided software engineering—is the most important of all the technological advances that have occurred in the software engineering field in the past decade—but many organizations are wasting millions of dollars in the illusion that putting a fancy workstation on everyone's desk will turn ugly ducklings into swans. Other organizations are playing a "wait-and-see" game, not yet convinced that CASE technology has advanced to the stage of "industrial-strength" tools.

My purpose in this chapter is to survey the broad field of CASE technology, to offer suggestions for acquiring CASE technology, and to forecast future developments in the technology. To become or remain a world-class player in the software game will require a good understanding of this important and fast-moving technology.[1]

6.1 A BRIEF HISTORY OF CASE TECHNOLOGY

Some will argue that we have had CASE tools since the first assembler, editor, and debugging package; indeed, all the mainframe-based software development tools are "CASE" in the strict sense of the word. Today, most of the mainframe-based CASE products fall into the category of "lower-CASE" tools, for they provide support for the "downstream" activities of coding, testing, debugging, and maintenance.

The *real* CASE movement began with the advent of personal computers and the development of "upper-CASE" tools to help automate the upstream activities of systems analysis and design. The very

[1] However, if you have been living in a cave for the past five years and have never heard of CASE, this chapter is *not* intended as an introduction to the subject. For background reading, consult the reference books [1–4] listed at the end of the chapter. For an ongoing update of current CASE trends, the three best newsletters I can recommend are *CASE Trends* (P.O. Box 294-MO, Shrewsbury, MA 01545-0294); *CASE Outlook* (11830 S.W. Kear Parkway, Suite 315, Lake Oswego, OR 97035), and *CASE Strategies* (Cutter Information Corp., 1100 Massachusetts Ave., Arlington, MA 02174).

first PCs, which appeared in the 1979–1981 period, were not powerful enough for much beyond computer games and tiny BASIC programs, but within a few years, 10-megabyte hard disks were added to the repertoire of the standard PC, and the CASE revolution was born.

Thus far, there have been three "generations" of CASE technology, roughly characterized as follows:

- *First generation* (1984–1986)—simple drawing tools implemented on PC/XT-class machines. These were stand-alone tools used on an individual basis.

- *Second generation* (1987–1989)—tools implemented on 80286-class PC/AT machines, but still limited to 640K, MS-DOS, and 20–40 megabyte hard disks; better graphics capabilities, early code generation, and "bilateral" interfaces to other tools. At this stage, we first began to see groups of 10–12 PCs used at a project-level of integration.

- *Third generation* (1990–??)—tools implemented on 80386 machines with up to 16 megabytes of memory and 100-megabyte hard disks, using OS/2, Windows 3.0, or Unix. Multitool integration through a shared repository; beginning of attempts to create enterprise-level of CASE usage.

The early CASE tools, those of the first and second generations, had a number of limitations. Indeed, the limitations listed next seemed adequate justification for some companies *not* to make a major investment in CASE throughout the 1980s:

- *Sluggish technology.* The early XT-class machines lacked the computational power for creation, error checking, and manipulation of complex system models at a reasonable speed.

- *Stand-alone products.* Little or no integration was provided between tools. Some software development organizations developed their own interface programs to convert the output produced by one tool into a format acceptable to another tool; others simply reentered data on a manual basis.

- *Primitive dictionary/repository.* Early CASE tools had simple dictionaries, often implemented in a PC-based DBMS like dBASE-III, to store data definitions. There was no underlying metamodel to describe the nature of information being stored.

- *Limited graphics capability.* Because the early PCs had crude graphics, the early CASE tools were equally primitive. Diagrams were often created with character-based graphics rather than bit-mapped graphics.

- *Little or no flexibility for change.* The idea of customizing the graphics or the underlying semantic rules imposed by the CASE tool either had not occurred to early CASE developers or was too difficult to implement. What the salesperson showed you was what you got. Period.

- *Limited life cycle support.* Most of the early CASE tools would support only one or two activities, for example, creation of structured analysis data flow diagrams. And because there was no integration with other tools, it was virtually impossible to have CASE support through the entire life cycle.

- *Limited error checking.* While the early CASE tools did provide *some* error checking, it was typically quite limited. More important, the error-checking features were not customizable or extensible.

- *Limited methodology support.* The tool might support the Yourdon–DeMarco brand of structured analysis, but not the Gane–Sarson variant, or vice versa. In any case, if the tool supported structured analysis, it often did not support data modeling with entity–relationship diagrams, or vice versa.

- *Implementation on only one vendor platform.* The tool would operate on DOS-based PC-compatible platform, *or* a Unix-based platform, *or* a Macintosh platform—but not all three. The concept of open systems was unknown to the CASE community in the early days.

Thus, for people fascinated with technology, these limitations seemed like a good excuse for not acquiring CASE tools through most of the mid- and late-1980s. On the other hand, the current generation of software engineers often forgets that we put a man on the moon in 1969 with second generation IBM-7094 technology. In any case, even if the early CASE tools were primitive, *technology is not the real limitation in today's CASE tools.*

A 1989 survey conducted by Robert Binder Associates in Chicago highlights the fact that the 1980s were a time for "onesy-twosy" purchases of CASE tools for smallish projects, implemented primarily with MS-DOS on stand-alone PCs.[2] Binder's survey, which was conducted before the introduction of the popular Windows 3.0 operating

---

[2] A more recent survey by Binder [5] shows the results of three surveys conducted in 1988 and 1990. The latter surveys also provide interesting information about the level of maturity and training of people using CASE tools.

system, showed that 83 percent of CASE users were running their tool in an MS-DOS environment; Unix, OS/2, and VMS (the operating system for DEC's VAX machines) each accounted for only 3 percent. It's reasonable to expect that in the 1990s, CASE users will rapidly move from MS-DOS to Windows 3.0, and probably more slowly toward to the trouble-plagued OS/2 operating system environment.

Binder's survey also showed that 60 percent the vintage-1989 CASE user community had *no* connection between their CASE workstations, or at best a manual file exchange; 23 percent had a LAN-based CASE environment; and 17 percent had a multiuser single system.

Most interesting were Binder's figures on the number of copies of CASE tools installed in organizations, shown in Table 6.1, and the size of the CASE projects, shown in Table 6.2.

Table 6.1: Number of CASE Copies Installed

23.3%	0–1 copies
40.0	2–10 copies
6.7	11–20 copies
13.3	21–50 copies
16.7	> 50 copies

Table 6.2: Size of CASE Projects

13.3%	< 1 person-year
26.7	1–2
30.0	2–5
16.7	5–10
3.3	10–25
3.3	25–50
6.7	> 100

6.2 CHARACTERISTICS OF CURRENT CASE TECHNOLOGY

Today's CASE technology is now more than five years old and is approaching its first decade. It's more mature and is becoming "industrial-strength" in nature. And the tools are becoming more integrated and addressing a larger segment of the systems development life cycle. As a result, a significant fraction of the systems development organizations in the United States have begun to feel, in the early 1990s, that the time has come to "get serious" about CASE—even if it takes them another three to five years to implement their plans.

This means more than just buying five copies of brand X CASE tool; there were lots of companies in the late 1980s who did just that, and the five copies ended up as "shelfware," because nobody could use them. Today, getting serious about CASE means *enterprise* CASE: *everyone* in the systems development organizations—as well as the end users who become involved in systems development projects—has his or her own CASE tool. From this perspective, CASE tools are like a toothbrush: they are not meant to be shared.

6.2.1 General Features

What has happened to the underlying technology to spark this movement toward enterprise CASE? The CASE tools of the 1990s provide support for all this:

- Creating a model of user requirements in a graphical form, for example, data flow diagrams, entity–relationship diagrams
- Creating software design models for both the data and the procedural code
- Error checking, consistency checking, analysis, and cross-referencing of all system information
- Building prototypes of systems and enabling a simulation of the system
- Enforcing organizational standards for specification, design, and implementation activities in the system development life cycle
- Generating code directly from the design models
- Providing automated support for testing and validation
- Providing support for reusable software components—in the form of designs, code modules, data elements, and so on
- Providing interfaces to external dictionaries and databases
- Reengineering, restructuring, and reverse engineering of existing systems
- Storing, managing, and reporting system-related information and project management information

Any CASE vendor you talk to will invariably tell you that his or her product has all these features, and more. But in this field, as in so many other walks of life, everyone lies; it's just a question of when they lie, where they lie, and how much they lie. *You* have to see how good a job the CASE vendor does in these areas; typical weak areas in the early 1990s for many CASE vendors are testing, reuse, and reengineering. Additional checklists later in this chapter can be used to evaluate vendors in some specific areas of CASE technology, such as graphics capability and repository technology.[3]

The single most important technological development in the CASE industry at the beginning of the decade was the development of advanced, integrated repositories; indeed, industry spokesmen like George Schussel of Digital Consulting suggested that the year 1990 could be labeled as "the year of the repository," and industry guru Ken Orr suggests that repositories are the "soul" of the CASE movement [6]. As suggested by Figure 6.1, today's CASE environment could be regarded as a number of tools clustered around the repository; it is the emergence of repository technology that truly identifies and characterizes the third generation of CASE technology. We will discuss repository technology in more detail shortly.

Figure 6.1: The central role of repository technology

[3] As Capers Jones points out, a CASE vendor who tells you that his tool provides "full life cycle support" should be challenged in several areas: finding and fixing bugs, paperwork support, project management, security, virus protection, configuration control, and so forth.

6.2.2 Diagramming Capabilities of CASE Tools

From the beginning of the PC-based CASE revolution in the mid-1980s, diagramming capabilities have played an important role, especially for the upper-CASE tools that help automate the activities of analysis, design, and information engineering. What new things should we expect from the CASE tools of the 1990s?

One thing is already apparent: the CASE vendors are getting carried away and are beginning to deluge the software engineer with too many different kinds of diagrams. When performing systems analysis, the CASE user typically has the ability to produce data flow diagrams, dependency diagrams, control flow diagrams, decomposition diagrams, Hatley–Pirbhai diagrams, decision tables, and decision trees. The designer can create structure charts, Warnier–Orr diagrams, Jackson diagrams, action diagrams, flowcharts(!), state–transition diagrams, screen layouts, decision tables, and dialogue flow diagrams. And the database designer can create Bachman diagrams, Chen-style entity–relationship diagrams, Coad–Yourdon object diagrams, Booch diagrams, logical record diagrams, and data structure diagrams.

The plethora of diagrams is dazzling, but perhaps overwhelming for many software engineers. By analogy, it's nice to know that Howard Johnson's has 28 flavors of ice cream, but nobody wants to eat them all at the same time; indeed, nobody can remember all 28 flavors, and most of us are content with vanilla, chocolate, and strawberry. We should not fault the CASE vendors for providing so many different diagrams, but it will be important for software organizations to settle on a reasonable subset that they intend to use on their projects.[4]

Since the mid-1980s, it has been evident that the creation of diagrams on a CASE tool is a mixed blessing. It takes almost as long to create a diagram initially with a CASE tool as it would take to draw the diagram by hand. But revisions and corrections—which are crucially important—can typically be done 10 times faster with a CASE tool. Because of this, software engineers should feel encouraged to revise, refine, and continually improve their system models—just as someone using a modern word processing system feels no hesitation about drafting and redrafting a document dozens of times to make it as good as it can possibly be.

---

[4] Note that if it's difficult for the professional software engineers to remember the semantics of 28 flavors of diagrams, it's even more confusing for the end users. One or two diagram types is about all we should try to foist upon them.

But the tedious nature of creating the diagrams in the first place is gradually being recognized as a serious problem. In many organizations, for example, CASE tools are banned from JAD sessions, because they slow down and distract the rapid-fire discussions between user and technicians; instead, an "electronic whiteboard" is used to scribble diagrams, which are then printed in a hard-copy form and passed on to mindless drones to be carefully entered into a sophisticated CASE tool.

But if the diagrams are tedious to enter in the first place, does this suggest that the very nature of the CASE tool's user interface is awkward? It is important to remember that the graphic diagramming capability is what the user (software engineer) sees; it *is* the user interface. Because graphical models have become the new paradigm for thinking about systems (instead of textual code), the diagramming capability *is* the system. Thus, it is of paramount importance. If we expect our software engineers to sit all day in front of a "boob tube" like the one shown in Figure 6.2, it should be pleasant to use; unfortunately, most CASE environments are *not* pleasant to use.

Figure 6.2: The typical CASE environment

There are a number of questions to ask about the graphic capabilities of a CASE tool, perhaps more than the average software engineer would be aware of at first glance. And these are issues about which the *purchaser* of CASE tools—for example, the manager who signs the purchase order—may be completely oblivious. But like the companies that bought office automation systems in the 1970s and discovered that the secretaries hated the choice that had been made on their behalf by a benevolent dictatorship, so many software organizations today will find that their software engineers hate the CASE tools that have been imposed upon them if they don't pay careful attention to the graphics issues summarized here:

- *How quickly can the diagrams be changed and redrawn?* Ideally, the CASE tool should be allow the software engineer to modify diagrams and have those modifications reflected on the display monitor in "real time." If the user has to stop and wait 30 to 60 seconds for the CASE tool to recompose the diagram, element by element, the tool will be seen as an intolerable nuisance.

- *How easily can the diagram be saved and retrieved?* Saving and retrieving of diagrams is the analog of saving and retrieving a document in a word processing system; the user understands that this might take a few seconds, but it should not be long enough to justify taking a coffee break. Anything longer than 30 seconds is grounds for criticism; anything longer than 60 seconds should be regarded as intolerable.

- *How many objects can be placed on the diagram?* Early CASE tool often limited the user to a dozen objects—for example, bubbles on a data flow diagram—or to as many objects as could be created in an 8-inch-by-11-inch drawing space. Modern CASE tools should give the user a "virtual" drawing space of, say, 10 feet by 10 feet, with a capability of placing hundreds, if not *thousands*, of objects on the diagram. Indeed, the number of objects should be limited only by the amount of available hard disk space.

- *How many **different** diagrams can be on the screen at the same time, for example, in different windows? Does the tool support a variety of large screens and all normal variations on VGA/EGA display technologies?* In many cases, the software engineer will want to display a data flow diagram *and* an entity–relationship diagram, *and* a state–transition diagram, all at the same time. The first question to ask, of course, is whether the CASE tool permits this at all; the second question is whether it can be accomplished in a practical manner. Because of the limited size of most display monitors—typically 13 inches or less—it is often useless to attempt displaying several windows of information on one monitor. Most CASE tools will take advantage of larger display screens if the user is lucky enough to have one, but another practical alternative—which the CASE tools often do *not* support—is multiple display monitors connected to the same PC.

- *What capabilities exist of panning, zooming, and other graphical manipulations?* Virtually all CASE tools have *some* capabilities for zooming in to take a close-up look at a portion of the diagram or zooming out to see a large, complex diagram in a reduced format; the question is how user-friendly those features are. The early CASE tools were often developed by organizations that had little or no experience building graphics-oriented programs, and the results showed. The best thing to do here is "test drive" the various CASE products to get a comparative feel, and remember that this is the environment that the software engineer will be subjected to eight hours a day, five days a week.

- *What about "free-form" drawings or annotations on a "formal" diagram?* In addition to the formal graphical constructs of a data flow diagram, or entity–relationship diagram, many software engineers want the ability to incorporate notes or comments on their diagrams; or they may wish to add some graphic "clip art" objects to the diagram to represent external organizations, users, or computer equipment. The CASE tool should allow for this.

- *Can users create their own customized icons? Can they modify the standard ones?* Here is a simple test: ask the CASE vendor if you can modify the data flow diagrams so that functions/processes normally represented by "bubbles" will be represented instead by triangles. Some vendors will tell you that the religion of structured analysis does not permit triangles; others will tell you that this is a major change, and will require six months and $100,000 (i.e., the same thing *you* tell *your* users when they ask for a seemingly simple change!); and a few vendors will make the modification on the spot, while you are talking with them.

- *Can the user control **when** the error checking is done?* As discussed shortly, one of the valuable features of a CASE tool is that it analyzes the models created by a software engineer for completeness and consistency; the question is *when* the error checking should be done.

Imagine a new generation of word processing system, for example, that insists on spell checking each word as soon as you typed it in. To some, this would be a boon, but to others (like me) it would be a nightmare; not having the freedom to "turn off" such a feature would be simply unacceptable to the marketplace.

- *Does the CASE tool support color? Can the user customize the use of color?* The vast majority of PC-based tools support color today, though many Unix-based tools have not yet escaped from the monochrome world of black and white. The real question here is one of customization: Can users decide for themselves if data flows should be red and entities should be green? Can they change the colors?

- *What kind of mouse support does the tool provide?* Will it support left-handed people as well as the mainstream "righties"? Will it support alternatives to a mouse, for example, keyboard cursor control, or pen/tablet input?

- *If the tool supports "leveling" of diagrams, how does the user move from level to level? Is it easy to show two levels at the same time?* A number of popular software development methodologies use "decomposition" diagrams, for example, leveled data flow diagrams. CASE users often want to see the "parent" diagram and the "child" diagram side by side on their screen. And they want to traverse levels of the diagram quickly and easily, with a minimum of keystrokes and mouse movements. It should be possible, for example, to double click on a bubble in a data flow diagram and *automatically* be shown the child diagram associated with that bubble.

- *Can the user "toggle" between one dialect of diagram and another?* A typical example is the Yourdon–DeMarco dialect of data flow diagram, versus the Gane–Sarson dialect, or the Bachman versus Chen forms of entity–relationship diagrams; the difference in diagramming notation is minor, and the user should be able to toggle back and forth quickly and easily.

- *Can the user create his own type of diagram, with its own rules and notation?* This is much more than just turning blue data flow bubbles into green triangles; the question is whether the CASE tool is extensible enough that it will support the creation of a graphical modeling notation that the vendor did not create by himself. The critical technology that permits this is the repository, which we discuss shortly; however, the graphical support is also critical. The user needs a way to describe the graphical shape and form of a desired icon, as well as the graphical details of connections between icons. While such information obviously has to be stored in a repository, it also requires a reasonable amount of sophistication in the graphics component of the tool.

- *What control does the user have over the size, font, and placement of text in diagrams?* Many current CASE tools evolved from the older character-based display technology, where *everything* was displayed in 10-point Courier font. With today's graphics technology, this is simply unacceptable: the user should be able to control the size, font, and placement of textual information associated with *each* object on the diagram. This is particularly important today, because many of the documents produced by CASE tools are being incorporated into desktop publishing systems and published as external documents for customers, regulatory agencies, news media, and so on.

- *Can the user control the "rubber banding" of arrows between objects?* Many CASE vendors seem to think that all arrows from one object to another should be drawn with horizontal or vertical lines; others will use arcs or Bezier curves constructed by some algorithm within the tool—but will not give the user any flexibility to stretch, or bend, the arrows. Boo! Hiss!!

- *What control does the user have over the placement of arrows at the edge of an object, and for the shape of the arrowheads themselves?* These may seem like "picky" points, but they can be a source of extreme annoyance and frustration. If a CASE user draws an arrow connected to some object, she should be able to determine *where* on the object the connection is made, and she should be able to choose from a variety of arrowhead shapes, as well as determining whether the arrowhead is filled (with black ink) or empty.

- *How closely does the diagram approximate WYSIWYG?* Sometimes the problem here is that the screen resolution is not the same as the printer resolution; for example, Macintosh computers typically display information on the screen at a resolution of 72 dots per inch, but print at 300 dots per inch. This can lead to some minor, but annoying, discrepancies between the diagram one sees on the screen and the diagram produced on the laser printer. Far more annoying is the CASE tool that uses entirely different internal logic for displaying and printing; in this case, there may be little or no resemblance between the displayed diagram and the printed document.

In addition to the graphics capabilities, the *error-checking* capabilities of modern CASE tools is crucial. Indeed, without this, CASE is little more than a "PC-draw" program that can be acquired at a far lower cost. The value of the error checking is well known: studies have shown that it if a defect is introduced into the system in phase N of the project, it is 10 times cheaper to detect it and correct it while still in phase N than to allow it to "leak" into phase $N + 1$. An example of error checking of a data flow diagram is shown in Figure 6.3:

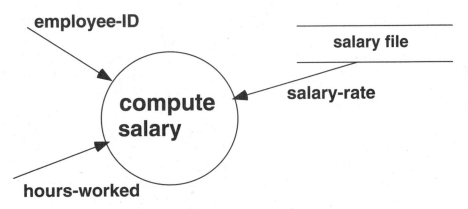

Figure 6.3: Error checking of a data flow diagram

This is an example of a "black hole"—the salary computation bubble receives lots of input but produces no output. Obviously, an error like this is easy to spot on a small diagram, but it can be overlooked if buried in the middle of a huge system. Modern CASE tools have dozens of similar error-checking rules to ensure that the software engineer produces a high-quality specification and design. Among the categories of error checking are

• Syntax checks
• Consistency checks
• Completeness checks
• Traceability checks from analysis to design, and so on
• Functional decomposition checks
• Cross-checks between levels of a diagram (sometimes called "vertical balancing") and between different types of diagrams (sometimes called "horizontal balancing")

6.3 CASE REPOSITORIES

As noted earlier, a major component of today's CASE environment is the *repository*. This is the place where all the system information is kept, and it is far more than the simple dictionaries associated with the early CASE tools of the mid-1980s. However, the term "repository" is more a marketing term than anything else; the term "dictionary" or "encyclopedia" would have been just as appropriate, but since they were used to describe older products, most CASE vendors have adopted the *au courant* term of "repository."

Whatever its name, the modern repository contains everything the software organization needs to know in order to create, modify, maintain, and evolve a system. Thus, it should contain information about

- The application (problem) domain
- Models of the implementation/solution
- Information about the methodology being used
- Project history, resources, schedules, budget, and so on
- The organizational context—organization charts, strategic plans, critical success factors, and so on

Some repositories still include only the first two items in the list; and many contain information about a software development methodology that has, for all practical purposes, been locked into code within the CASE tool. Some CASE tools lack the project management items, and many lack the organizational information. However, the clear trend is toward a comprehensive repository that contains all this information, for a full repository provides the basis for

- Project management and control
- Software reusability
- Code generation
- Integration of different CASE toolsets
- Sharing of information about the system
- Integrity among all model components

Each of these capabilities is beneficial in its own right, but it is the *combination* that is so important.

6.3.1 Contents and Definition of the Repository

Each item in the repository is described in great detail; a typical list of descriptive attributes would include the following:

- Identification (a unique name)
- Definition (meaning)
- Type
- Alias
- Composition (subcomponents)
- Parents (objects in which this object is a component)
- Rules for using the object
- Who/when created it
- Who/when last updated it
- Whether/by whom it can be updated
- Status
- Version number
- Where it is stored (e.g., physical file name)

Note the emphasis on configuration management issues in this list; many of the current CASE tools are still somewhat weak in this area.

Also note that much of this information could be considered as *rules* describing what can be put in the repository; such rules are part of what is often called a "metamodel" of the repository; the contents of the repository are often called "metadata" or "data about data." These rules provide change control, version control, security control, as well as access privileges and auditing.

Because the metamodel describes the very essence of the repository itself, it is attracting more and more attention today. As Jack Nelson [7] describes it,

> The model establishes "data standards" for the metadata we manage in application development and support. In this role, the model helps us find our way through the semantic jungle surrounding CASE metadata. A single definition for what we mean by each metafact helps add rigor to the application development process and helps tool vendors and users understand how to build and use CASE tools.

The scope of the metamodel is broader than many imagine; Nelson portrays it as shown in Figure 6.4.

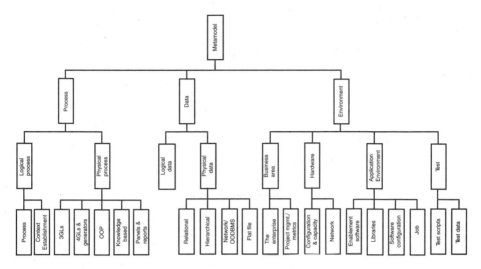

Figure 6.4: The scope of the repository metamodel

Most repository metamodels are described, or documented, in terms of an entity–relationship diagrams; thus, as we will discuss further, one way of evaluating a vendor's repository is to examine the metamodel documentation. A number of standards organizations around the world, including IRDS and PCTE, are working to standardize repository metamodels; McClure and Follman [8] summarize the status of the standards efforts as of late 1990.

6.3.2 Implementation of the Repository

In the early 1990s, the majority of commercial repositories were implemented on top of a conventional relational database, for example, DB2, Oracle, or IDMS. Repository products such as IBM's Repository Manager/MVS or DEC's CDD/Repository provide facilities to upload/download (or check-in/check-out) repository data between a central master repository (located on a mainframe or server) and individual workstation repositories. Commercial repositories also provide a means for exploring of repository definitions to other external dictionaries, as well as automatic "populating" of repositories from external dictionaries and/or diagrams.

When evaluating the implementation of a CASE vendor's repository, here are some critical questions to ask:[5]

---

[5] A different perspective on evaluation of CASE vendor repositories is suggested by KnowledgeWare's Pete Privateer [9].

- *Can the vendor **show** you the metamodel for his or her repository?* CASE marketing representatives, clever snake-oil salesmen that they are, know that it's a good idea to tell innocent customers that, "yes, of *course* we have a metamodel for our repository." But if they can't put an official document in your hands (typically in the form of an entity–relationship model) that describes that repository, it doesn't exist. In the 1990–91 time period, it has become quite fashionable to critique IBM's metamodel, but at least it exists. Other well-known vendors claim to have a much more advanced repository metamodel, but at the time this book was written, it was only vaporware.

- *Does the repository require a mainframe host computer?* Because some vendors have chosen a mainframe-based DBMS like DB2 as the underlying "engine" for their repository, they are stuck with a technology that *requires* a mainframe. This may be acceptable to many large software organizations that have already placed most of their other information resources on a mainframe host, but it is entirely unacceptable to others. Beware the CASE vendor who gives you some kind of "religious" argument in this area; for example, "God intended that repositories always reside on mainframes, because a repository will always be too big and require too much number crunching to ever fit on a file server or workstation."

- *Is the repository centralized, or can it be distributed?* The vendor who opts for the mainframe technology solution has usually opted for centralization as well, and even the repository vendors who place their product on a workstation or file server often assume that their repository must be physically located in one place. For the software development organization that has centralized its work force, this is quite acceptable. But for the organization that has some of its software engineers in New York, others in Los Angeles, and still others in Manila or Paris, the notion of a *distributed* repository is preferable. Some vendors, like DEC and Softlab, offer a fully distributed repository; others try to "fake" it by suggesting that a batch-mode check-in/check-out capability will facilitate distributed software development. Bah! Humbug!

- *Is the repository based on a relational DBMS or object-oriented DBMS?* The typical repository of the early 1990s is based on an ER diagram metamodel, implemented on a relational DBMS; some, like DEC's CDD/Repository, are based on an object-oriented metamodel (with single inheritance) implemented on a relational DBMS. By the mid-1990s, I expect to see fully object-oriented metamodels (with *multiple* inheritance) implemented on object-oriented database management systems. For the first generation of repositories that organizations build, today's relational technology is adequate. But relational technology was intended primarily for *structured* data, particularly data consisting of numbers and text. As organizations become more ambitious about storing *all* their metadata in a repository, they will inevitably wish to store larger and larger amounts of *unstructured* data; in particular, they will want to store images, voice data, and graphics as well as numbers and text,[6] which are better suited to object-oriented database management systems than relational architectures.

- *Can the repository be customized? Can it be extended?* Having a metamodel for one's repository is not enough; there must be a facility for *extending* the metamodel and/or changing some of its contents to suit the needs of the organization. When asked this question, some vendors will give you a blank look and mumble something unintelligible about plans for a future release. Others will proudly tell you that their metamodel has been implemented in 130,000 lines of Prolog (thus allowing them to claim their repository has artificial intelligence) and that they would be happy to send an army of repository engineers into your organization to modify the metamodel for you at an unspecified cost. And a few—only a few— will show you how *you* can extend the metamodel in the privacy of your own DP shop. Since the metamodel effectively embodies the organization's software development methodology, and since we saw in Chapter 5 that some 36 percent of U.S. software organizations use a customized methodology, it follows that this is an important capability to look for in a repository.

- *What kind of reports are provided? Can the reports be customized and extended? Are online, interactive browsing and searching capabilities included?* Obviously, any repository product will have extensive reporting capabilities, with cross-reference listings, "where-used" reports, lists of objects defined but not used in any of the system models, and so on. The key issue here is extensibility and customization, since any individual organization will inevitably find that the standard vendor reports aren't quite adequate for its

---

[6] An example: Tom DeMarco has suggested that software review/inspections could be videotaped and the entire session could be stored on optical disk for subsequent retrieval. Today's storage technology makes this possible, albeit still somewhat expensive and clumsy. But today's repositories are not adequate for *managing* this kind of data.

needs. Since, as mentioned, most repositories are implemented with a conventional relational DBMS, it should be possible to take advantage of the report generation and ad hoc query facilities of the DBMS to provide customized reports. But in addition to *batch* reports, online, interactive queries will become more and more important as repositories gradually become the central "warehouse" of organizational metadata. To find a reusable component, nobody wants to search through a 3000-page batch report; browsing and searching capabilities are essential.

- *Are the diagrams produced by the CASE tool stored internally based on what was drawn, or are they drawn automatically based on information in the repository?* Clearly, no repository is going to store bit-map images of screen drawings; the logical contents of the diagram ("this bubble is connected by a two-headed arrow to that box . . .") are stored instead. Thus, when something is changed in the repository—for example, the definition of one of the data elements—all the affected objects and diagrams can be changed automatically. But this still leaves the question of how the drawing is generated. In addition to the "logical contents" information, the *topological* information is crucial: if I draw a data flow "bubble" in the top left-hand corner of my screen when composing the diagram, I want it to show up in the same place whenever the CASE tool regenerates the diagram from the information stored in the repository. Many CASE tools today lose the topological information somewhere in the process of saving and retrieving diagrams.[7]

6.3.3 Repository Wars

Simple CASE tool repositories have existed for a number of years; however, it is only with the current vintage-1990 generation of repositories that we are beginning to see different vendors store their metadata in a common repository. As Chikofsky [10], points out,

> With an open, shared architecture, a repository offers all sorts of opportunities for vendors who put their own self-interest ahead of the common good. . . .

---

[7]On the other hand, consultant Charles Martin points out that a good CASE tool should let the user enter the components of the diagram in quick tabular data entry form and then create a diagram automatically as a time-saving "first cut" for the user. Such "autodraw" capabilities can be found on tools like the Bachman product, but are not widespread. Such autodraw capabilities could be even further enhanced using the "shape recognition" capabilities of the pen-based computers discussed in Chapter 11.

A shared repository brings a culture shock for many CASE vendors. For the first time, their tool is not alone with its data. . . .

Any vendor must use defensive programming to protect its tool against data changes that the tool may not be able to understand. What we need are rules of etiquette. . . .

Chikofsky argues that we will have to suffer through a period of "repository wars" while the vendors learn the "rules of etiquette" that are necessary for peaceful coexistence. Examples of the "dirty tricks" that Chikofsky foresees during these repository wars are as follows:

1. Cooperate incompletely. Only share part of the data collected by your tool. (inevitable until the AD/Cycle Information Model is finished!)
2. Hide information. Store values for attributes in description text fields.
3. Always make changes. Even if you are only reading data, be sure to change something. That way, your competitor will have to search to find what changed, slowing it down . . .
4. Operate off a different copy. This is sort of like keeping two sets of accounting records . . .
5. Retain locks on everything. Lock everything in sight . . .
6. Undo changes. Reinstate what other tools have changed.
7. Use encryption. Put your data in the repository in a way no other tool can understand.
8. Sow disinformation. Choose an attribute value that your tool doesn't use, but your competitor does. Then plant extraneous instances all through the repository. These should make the other tool gag . . .

6.4 CATEGORIZING CASE VENDORS

For an organization about to select a CASE product, it's a good idea to understand the nature of CASE vendors. Andrew Topper [11] points out that, as of 1991, there are some 300 CASE vendors in the U.S. market; however, they can be grouped easily into a few common categories:

- Hardware vendors
- DBMS vendors
- CASE toolmakers
- Methodology vendors
- Consultants and educators

Of course, some vendors will claim that they cover more than one of these categories. And the categories are becoming somewhat more blurred because of the collaborations and joint ventures that are forming between vendors like DEC and Texas Instruments, Intersolv (née Index Technology) and Deloitte, and so on. However, a wolf in sheep's clothing is still a wolf; one can still determine the basic nature of most CASE vendors today. And each category has its strengths and weaknesses, as summarized next.

6.4.1 Hardware Vendors

This category includes such obvious examples as IBM, DEC, Sun, Hewlett-Packard, Apple, Unisys, and Bull. Because of their history and culture, the hardware vendors tend to be more oriented toward the lower-CASE tools—for example, code generators, programming aids, and testing aids. Some have suggested that it makes sense for the hardware vendors to "own" the lower-CASE technology, but the subindustry of CASE code generators, compiler-writers, and other related companies would fiercely disagree.

Similarly, there is a tendency to cede the repository technology to the mainframe vendors, since they also have a history of dominance in the database area. It is no surprise that the two most widely watched repository products in the United States in the early 1990s are the ones developed by IBM and DEC. However, it is not necessarily the advanced technology or elegant implementation that makes these repositories attractive, but rather the fact that IBM and DEC have the size and "clout" to encourage other CASE vendors to standardize on their repository metamodel. This size and clout brings one other major advantage to those companies considering massive CASE purchases: worldwide support. For medium-sized software development organizations located entirely in the United States, this may not be an issue; for but large organizations with far-flung international locations, it is important indeed.

The strength in lower-CASE technology suggests a corresponding weakness for the mainframe vendors: a lack of real understanding of methodologies and upper-CASE issues and a lack of appreciation for the importance of workstations and LAN networks for CASE environments.[8] In the United States, IBM's decision to form business

---

[8] A good example of the problems caused by the mainframe orientation of hardware vendors is the apparent lack of success of the Japanese SIGMA CASE effort, described in the May 1990 issue of *Nikkei Computer* as a "$200 million failure." SIGMA was begun in 1985 as a $200 million MITI-sponsored CASE initiative, but its activities were dominated by the Japanese mainframe vendors who tended to overemphasize the development of mainframe-based lower-CASE tools and deemphasized workstation-based upper-CASE tools.

partnerships with upper-CASE vendors Bachman Information Systems, KnowledgeWare, and Intersolv suggest a lack of expertise in upper-CASE technology, and DEC's efforts at building upper-CASE tools have also been criticized [10, 12].

6.4.2 DBMS Vendors

Typical examples of this category are vendors like Software AG, Informix, and Oracle. In earlier days, one might have been concerned that the DBMS product was tied to one hardware platform, but all the successful DBMS vendors today support a variety of platforms.

As one would imagine, the DBMS vendors have a good background in data modeling and information engineering; this is evidenced by the well-thought-out metamodel that the vendors have developed for their repository. And while the majority of large DBMS vendors today are tied to an underlying *relational* technology, most are actively exploring object-oriented extensions. Thus, it is reasonable to expect that these vendors will support an object-oriented repository by the middle of the 1990s.

The major concern with the DBMS vendors is that they tend to be fairly weak in other methodologies besides information engineering, for example, structured analysis and design. However, the organizations seriously considering the DBMS vendors for their CASE tools have typically *already* made a commitment to the vendor for the DBMS package itself and have generally taken advantage of the 4GL languages that accompany the package. Indeed, such organizations may have already made an intellectual commitment to information engineering and may not find the lack of a strong function-oriented component to the methodology something to worry about.

6.4.3 CASE Toolmakers

This is the largest category of vendors. It includes not only the large organizations like KnowledgeWare, Cadre, Intersolv, and Interactive Development Environments but also hundreds of smaller vendors with "niche" products.

A major question to ask here concerns the relationship between the tool and the software development methodology selected by the organization. Is the CASE tool a methodology "companion" or a methodology "copycat," or is it "methodology neutral"? There is nothing wrong with any of these categories, as long as one knows what one is buying, and as long as the vendor accurately describes its wares.

A tool that is "methodology neutral" generally provides rich graphics capabilities and may provide powerful repository capabilities but typically does not impose any methodological rules upon the user; these must be filled in by the software development organization, though the obvious place to put such rules is in the repository itself. A "methodology companion" is a CASE tool that provides an informal implementation of a textbook methodology; for the organization that wishes to capture the "flavor" of a methodology, but not enforce hard, rigid rules, this might be the preferable choice.[9] The "methodology copycat" is, of course, the likely choice of the organization that is whole-heartedly committed to a particular brand-name methodology.

The major concern with the toolmakers is their relatively small size, their limited marketing ability, and their limited support facilities. On the other hand, for initial experimentation with CASE, one advantage is that the spectrum of toolmakers is broad enough that one can find almost any niche. In particular, vendors like Popkin Software, Computer Systems Advisors, and Visible Analyst provide surprisingly useful tools at a modest cost typically 5 to 10 times below the cost of the "full-featured" tools.

6.4.4 Methodology Vendors

Typical examples of the methodology vendors are James Martin Associates, Michael Jackson Systems Ltd., and Learmonth-Burchett (LBMS). While these vendors may also have tools to sell, their obvious strength lies in their expertise with a specific methodology. If one wants a CASE tool based on the brand X methodology, there is a good argument for talking to the company that created the brand X methodology.

However, it's important to see whether the vendor is flexible and is willing to modify the details of the methodology. It's also important to see if the vendor has any willingness and/or ability to support multiple methodologies, since a large organization is almost certain to find multiple methodologies in use for various projects. Unfortunately, many of the methodology vendors are religious fanatics about their work and are unwilling to concede that other methodologies might have a place in the world. Hence, if you accept their CASE tool and their methodology, you have accepted their religion and foresworn all others.

---

[9] In terms of the process maturity model described in Chapter 4, this almost guarantees that the organization is operating at level 1 or level 2.

6.4.5 Consultants

The last category is the consultants; typical examples are Andersen Consulting, Computer Sciences´Corporation, EDS, and American Management Systems.

The most common benefit of working with these vendors is that they have *lots* of practical, real-world experiences "in the trenches" using and applying CASE.[10] Similarly, these vendors are the ones most likely to provide real assistance in the development of *designware* (discussed further in Chapter 9) and reengineering of existing systems (discussed further in Chapter 10).

On the other hand, the consultants often have only secondhand or thirdhand understanding of the underlying methodology on which the CASE tools are based; their strength is in the application of CASE tools and the actual building of systems, not in teaching the methodology. Thus, if an organization is selecting a CASE vendor partly on the basis of the vendor's ability to train its own staff, then consultants may not be the best choice.

6.5 SELECTING A CASE PRODUCT

The question, "Which CASE tool should I buy?" is about as easy to answer as the questions, "Which car should I buy?" or "Which personal computer should I buy?" Just as there are over 100 manufacturers of IBM-compatible PC-clones, there are over 300 manufacturers of CASE products. Selecting the best CASE tool is not easy. The answer to the questions just posed is: "It depends . . .".

6.5.1 Price and Vendor Stability as Major Issues

Because organizations are now making large-scale CASE acquisitions—hundreds of copies of workstation-based products, at a total cost of millions of dollars—the criteria for selecting a CASE tool are

---

[10] By contrast, many of the other CASE vendors will admit that they don't use their own tools for their own work. Or they may use the tools to develop their payroll system, but not for the specification, design, and construction of their own tool. A good test is the following challenge: "Show me the data flow diagrams and entity–relationship diagrams, *produced by your own CASE tool,* that you used to design and implement your tool; or at least show me how you used your CASE tool to produce the second release of your product." This is particularly appropriate in the early 1990s, when many of the CASE vendors are loudly proclaiming that the newest version of their tool has been built with an object-oriented approach. However, this rarely involves any automated support from their own tool, which supports information engineering and/or structured techniques. Thus, the claim about object orientation usually means only that their latest release was coded in C++. Big bloody deal.

becoming the same as those for selecting any other major software product. Thus, some organizations will look closely at the price of the product, reasoning that discounts should be available if they make large-volume purchases. Others look closely at the stability of the vendors, reasoning that it's better to buy a higher-priced product from a company that will be around for a while than an inexpensive product from a company that will be out of business next year.

For those concerned about the price issue, it's worth remembering that the price of standard CASE products is likely to drop substantially over the next several years. When a new technology is introduced to a relatively small market, the vendors often have to charge a high price to recoup their development costs; it's interesting, for example, that mainframe-based COBOL and FORTRAN compilers often had a $10,000 price tag as recently as the late 1970s. But if the market expands tremendously and the vendors are able to produce large volumes of their product at a relatively low unit cost (i.e., the cost of duplicating a manual and a few floppy disks), then the price can come down dramatically. We are already seeing a number of vendors with $500 CASE products whose functionality is surprisingly close to that of the $5000 products; this trend will continue.

At the same time, the issue of vendor stability will also continue to be important. Given the enormous number of vendors in the marketplace, a major shakeout in the CASE industry is inevitable; indeed, the 1991 merger between Index Technology and Sage Computer Systems suggests that it is already underway. When the dust settles, we will have a three-tiered industry: at the top will be a few billion-dollar companies like IBM and DEC; below that will a dozen or so $100 million players like KnowledgeWare, MicroFocus, and Softlab; and at the bottom will be literally hundreds of niche players with revenues of $1 million to $10 million. If your organization is only buying one or two copies of a CASE product to play with, vendor stability is not a major concern; however, if you are buying hundreds of copies, it will become increasingly important in the future to avoid the bottom layer of the industry and stick with vendors in the top two layers.

6.5.2 The Risk of CASE Failure

Of course, *selecting* the CASE tool is just one of the steps in the "game plan" to acquire and deploy CASE technology. Regardless of which vendor is chosen, the risk of failure is ever present: it is quite possible to spend millions of dollars on CASE tools, and then discover a few years later that it had no impact whatsoever on productivity or quality. But as Carma McClure [4] points out, the causes of CASE failures are numerous:

- No methodology or standards in place
- Ignoring the importance of management
- Too much emphasis on CASE as the "silver bullet" solution
- Confusion about what the CASE tool does
- Misuse of the tool
- Perception of CASE as a risk
- Unwillingness to change current methods
- Uncertainty (or lack of consensus) about what problem the CASE tool is trying to solve: productivity? quality? speed of development of new systems?
- Poor integration of the tools
- Inadequate functionality
- Poor documentation or training

Thus, technical issues such as missing functionality or poor tool integration cold be a cause of failure, but most of the items on the list are cultural or managerial in nature.

Avoiding these problems requires three fundamental things:

- *Senior management support, with reasonable expectations.* CASE won't produce overnight miracles, and senior management must understand this.
- *A moderate level of sophistication in the software development organization.* Uneducated hackers won't make good use of CASE.
- *A plan for implementing CASE.* The plan should allow for starting slowly, with pilot projects, before inundating the organization with CASE. And the plan must ensure that the right tools are chosen for the job: upper-CASE tools, for example, could be a waste of money in a purely maintenance-oriented shop.

6.6 CASE IMPLEMENTATION STEPS

Detailed plans for implementation of CASE technology are readily available; Roger Pressman [13] offers an action plan that is comprehensive in its technical and organizational detail; Barbara Bouldin [14] offers detailed advice that focuses on the cultural and political aspects of technology transfer. But *any* plan for installing CASE technology must include these steps:

- A software engineering "audit" to determine organizational readiness
- Selling the concept of CASE to various levels of management and workers in the organization
- Education of the software engineers and project managers *before* the installation of CASE
- Selection of the appropriate CASE tools
- Installation of the tools
- Postinstallation evaluation

Each of these activities is discussed in greater detail in the paragraphs that follow.

6.6.1 The Software Engineering Audit

As we discussed in Chapter 4, it is useless to install new technology if the organization is not ready for it; this is particularly true of CASE, which changes the very nature of how software engineers do their day-to-day job. *If CASE is introduced in a massive way into a level 1 organization, it will probably fail.*

There is nothing wrong with a primitive organization experimenting with CASE tools, and a level 1 organization can probably get some benefit from lower-CASE tools such as workstation-based "programmer's workbench" products. But a tightly integrated set of upper-CASE and lower-CASE tools, grouped around a centralized repository, will only work if the organization is at level 2 and seriously on its way to level 3.

Thus, one of the first steps in planning for CASE must be a technical audit of the organization's process maturity. As discussed in Chapter 4, there are a number of organizations that are now certified to conduct an SEI process assessment; in addition, a number of consulting organizations have their own assessment procedures that are similar in spirit, if not in detail. If an external audit is not possible, a self-audit is better than nothing; books by Humphrey [15] and Pressman [13] can help provide the necessary questionnaires.

Such an audit may indicate that the organization has no formal software engineering life cycle or methodology. If this is the case, then the methodology should be introduced *before* the CASE tool. In turn, this implies that the software engineers should be trained in the use of the methodology before the CASE tools arrive; the issue of education will be discussed further in Section 6.6.3.

6.6.2 Selling the Concept of CASE

It is naive to expect that everyone in a software development organization will be enthusiastically in favor of acquiring CASE technology. Senior management may feel it's too expensive, project-level managers may feel that it's a fad that will just interfere with getting the job done, and software engineers may feel that it's a devious plot to eliminate their jobs. Any plan to implement CASE will include a significant selling effort, and the world-class organizations devote as much effort to this task as they do to the task of choosing their CASE vendor.

In most cases, a different "sales pitch" has to be constructed for senior management, middle-level management, and the technicians. Each has different interests and priorities, and CASE evangelists will take these into account as they develop their sales pitch.

6.6.2.1 Senior Management

Members of senior management, for example, generally see software as just one of many crises to be dealt with; on the same day they listen to a multimillion-dollar CASE proposals, they may also be considering a proposal to build a new factory, worrying about a hostile takeover, and negotiating to avoid a union strike. Senior managements—particularly those entirely outside or above the software development organization—typically have little or no emotional involvement in the CASE decision; as suggested by Figure 6.5, they are interested primarily in an economic justification.

Figure 6.5: Selling CASE to senior management

In Europe and Asia, planning for CASE is typically done in a top–down organizational fashion, so senior management may become involved in the planning for CASE from the very beginning. By contrast, U.S. organizations typically implement CASE in a bottom–up fashion: first experimenting with one or two units, then trying the technology at the project level, and then finally seeking senior management approval. Each approach has its advantages and disadvantages, and the CASE evangelist must know how the decision making process operates in his organization.

To say that senior management is swayed by economic arguments is fairly obvious and provides little advice to the CASE evangelist. The real question is: *What kind of economic argument?* An important survey by Paul Radding [16] indicates that "strategic vision" arguments are used by about 40 percent of the companies acquiring CASE, and "value-added" arguments are used by another 40 percent; "cost displacement" and/or "cost avoidance" justifications are used by the remaining 20 percent. Radding reports that the most successful CASE implementation projects are sponsored by senior managements who feel that CASE provides them with a strategic competitive advantage in the marketplace, for example, by being able to bring new products into the marketplace much faster than their competitors. The "value-added arguments—the argument that benefits will exceed costs—is commonly used, but is more subjective and runs the risk of rejection from financially astute senior managers. A good summary of the economic issues associated with CASE is provided by Capers Jones [17].

As Richard Barton [18] points out, the strategic objective argument and value-added argument are typically used by innovators and industry leaders. When a technology becomes mature, conservative organizations can make a "cost avoidance" justification: spending money today avoids greater costs in the future. A good example of this today is the justification of workstation-based programmer workbench lower-CASE tools to avoid the larger expensive of mainframe upgrades in the future. As the technology nears the end of its useful life, the industry laggards use the "technology imperative" argument: "if we don't start using this technology now, we'll be forever left behind." These stages are illustrated in Figure 6.6. In a recent article [12], I suggested that this could begin occurring as early as 1992 with software engineers rejecting prospective employers who have not installed CASE; however, many of my colleagues feel that this phenomenon won't become common until the mid-1990s.

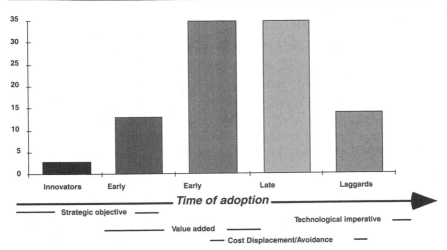

Figure 6.6: Cost justification used by leaders and laggards

6.6.2.2 Middle Management

Selling CASE to a middle management—especially to the project-level manager pictured in Figure 6.7—is often far more difficult than the job of convincing senior-level management to make a large financial investment.

Figure 6.7: Selling CASE to middle management

Why should this be so? Because middle managers are much more emotionally involved in the CASE decision: their careers are on the line. And they are much more involved in the technical issues, since they themselves are former technicians with some vague memories of what it was like to program in the good old days. They may be favorably disposed to the *concept* of CASE, but they will want to be involved in the technical details of the decision-making process. And their favorable disposition is balanced by a wary skepticism of "silver bullet" promises made by the snake-oil CASE salesman.

The most common concern that middle-level managers have is that the introduction of new CASE tools may cause a *short-term* productivity problem that will impact their current project. This is a healthy concern, as most organizations have found that productivity typically declines for the first 3 to 6 months after the introduction of CASE tools, and sometimes by as much as 25 percent during the first year; net productivity increases may not be visible for 18 to 24 months. This may be acceptable to the organization that has a 5-year perspective on productivity improvement, but it is of great concern to the project manager struggling with a politically important deadline on his next project.

The other common reason for resistance from middle managers is more subtle, more insidious, and more difficult to counter: fear of the impact of organizational change, loss of power and control, and so forth. As noted in Chapter 4, a successful level 2 organization depends on the skill of its project managers, who impose their own personal style of management on each project. Installation of CASE may remove much of this personal power, and many middle-level managers may be uncomfortable with the thought.

There is no easy solution to this political problem, though Bouldin [14] offers a number of excellent ideas. One common approach is to demonstrate the validity of the CASE concept with one or more pilot projects. Pilot projects have long been considered an excellent way to introduce and justify new technology; in an earlier book [19], for example, I recommended the use of pilot projects for introducing structured techniques. The characteristics of a good pilot project for CASE technology are the same as for any other new technology:

- It should be a medium-sized project, not too big and not too small.
- It should be important and visible, not one whose failure would bankrupt the organization.
- It should be staffed by enthusiastic volunteers, not by people who feel a gun is being held to their heads.

- The pilot project team should be well trained and supported by external consultants (e.g., from the CASE vendor).
- The pilot project should be carefully measured.
- Success stories should be advertised to help promote the new technology.

If this is all standard advice, are CASE users following it? Radding's survey [16] suggests that many are ignoring it. While some 60 percent of the organizations considering CASE use pilot projects to justify and sell the technology, some 40 percent sell the idea of CASE with critical projects.[11] Radding reports that some users bypass the entire pilot project phase and that others have short pilot projects of three months or less; indeed, the pilot project is often the first version of a critically important production system. *Thus, in many organizations, management is sold on the critical project first, and CASE second.*

6.6.2.3 Technicians

What about the technicians? As suggested by Figure 6.8, technicians come in a variety of sizes, shapes, colors, and ages. The technician's reaction to CASE may be based on a number of factors, but years of experience seems to be the most common differentiator.

Figure 6.8: Selling CASE to the technicians

Senior technicians with 5 to 10 years or more of experience often react in the same fashion as middle managers. They too are wary of

---

[11] Note that this is compatible with the idea of using a "strategic advantage" argument, as discussed earlier.

silver bullet promises, and they may have a number of technical objections to the features of the tools proposed by the CASE evangelist. But more than anything else, they tend to worry about the impact of the tool on their status, prestige, and creative freedom. Pilot projects will convince some of the merits of CASE, but some will continue to resist. In general, the safe assumption is that 10 percent of the senior technicians will *immediately* adopt CASE tools; 10 percent will *never* adopt the tools; and the remaining 80 percent will muddle along and slowly, over a period of two or three years, incorporating the tools into their day-to-day work.

Junior technicians—those with one to three years of experience—are generally willing and anxious to change; the danger is that their work habits may be so deeply ingrained that it is difficult for them to change. This is not so much of a problem when using the "methodology-neutral" or "methodology-companion" CASE tools discussed earlier, for they do not make any rigid demands upon the software engineer. However, a "methodology-copycat" tool that rigidly imposes a formal methodology will represent a severe culture shock to the software engineer.

The novices, fresh out of school with their computer science degree and a burning passion to write yet another compiler for an organization that wants only payroll systems, may not be aware that a "CASE revolution" is underway. If they were lucky enough to attend a top-notch university, they have already been exposed to workstations and CASE. They may assume that everyone in industry already has a personal workstation, plus another one at home. They have no culture to unlearn; they will wonder only why the organization moves so slowly.

One last point about the technicians, especially those with 5 to 10 years of experience: *they don't trust senior management.* Their general assumption is that senior management has no idea of what's going on "down in the trenches" where the software gets built, and their strong suspicion is that senior management is interested only in speeding things up to push more mediocre software out the door more quickly. Management's desire to speed up the delivery of software is understandable, particularly when it is seen as a strategic competitive advantage, but the jaded software engineers who have been in the business for a decade are firmly convinced that management is perfectly willing to sacrifice quality—and anything else—in order to speed things up. Whether this is true, and whether it really represents senior management's opinion, it nevertheless represents a deep, pervasive "gut-level" suspicion on the part of the technicians. In such an atmosphere of distrust—and in many organizations, utter disgust with senior management—it's unlikely that CASE will achieve long-term benefits.

6.6.3 Education of Software Engineers

As mentioned earlier, a technology audit may point out that the organization needs to install a formal methodology before selecting CASE tools. In any case, there is a high likelihood that the software engineers will require some training in the selected methodology. The key question here is one of timing: should the education take place before the tools are installed, during the tool installation process, or after the software engineers have had a few months to play with the tools?

I am a firm believer in pragmatism: whatever works is fine. But in most organizations, attempts to educate the software engineers during or after the installation of the CASE tools is a disaster; prior education is strongly advised. The issue here is similar to that of allowing children to use electronic calculators before they have learned to do multiplication and long division by hand. If they don't understand how the process works, they have no idea whether the calculator has produced a plausibly correct answer; the reason children should learn arithmetic by hand is so that they will know whether their subsequent calculator-generated answers have the decimal point in the right position. The same is true with CASE. Period.[12]

6.6.4 Selecting the Appropriate Tools

Selection and detailed evaluation of CASE tools is a tedious, time-consuming job. It is beyond the scope of this book to provide a detailed checklist of criteria to consider or questions to ask. Some guidance may be found in basic books on the subject [2–4] as well as a recent article by Andrew Topper [11]; a checklist of CASE criteria used by Pacific Bell Telephone for a 2000-unit CASE acquisition is discussed in [20]. And, of course, this is an area where a number of consulting firms are happy to offer their advice and guidance.

[12] On the other hand, many of today's CASE tools are so complex that it is virtually impossible to expect the novice user to remember all the features at the end of a training class. There may be a need for what consultant Charles Martin calls "just-in-time" training to coordinate tool and methodology training with the corresponding phase of the systems development project.

6.6.5 Installation and Postinstallation Evaluation

Part of the CASE plan should include details on how the tools will be deployed through the organization. In most cases, it is utterly unrealistic to assume that everyone in the organization can be given a suite of CASE tools on the same day; Pacific Bell, for example, plans to deploy its 2000 CASE tools over a seven-year period. The most common strategies are to deploy the CASE tools on a project-by-project basis or a department-by-department basis.

The plan should also include a postinstallation assessment, perhaps two to three years after the tools have been deployed. Senior managers and auditors may insist on this, but in any case, the software development organization has a responsibility to gather measurements to ascertain the impact of the CASE tools. Indeed, this should be part of an overall metrics program, as discussed in Chapter 7.

6.7 CASE FUTURES

What should we expect from the CASE industry over the next 5 to 10 years? How will it impact the future of software development? Much of what we are likely to see is simple evolution of today's features. But the major change will be a shift from individual tools to groupware tools, as discussed shortly.

6.7.1 Ongoing Evolution of Today's Features

Most of the major CASE vendors have another three to five years of development work just evolving what they have now. While writing this chapter in the summer of 1991, for example, I received a public relations memo from Texas Instruments announcing its intention to provide an Ada code generator for its IEF product in June 1992. Similarly, Andersen Consulting has announced that it will port its FOUNDATION product to the DEC environment. Other CASE vendors are busily porting their products to Unix or Windows 3.0 or to new hardware platforms.

Perhaps the most significant evolution will be the transition to AD/Cycle and the support for shared repositories. Critical assessments of AD/Cycle [7, 11] suggest that it may be 1994 or 1995 before we see a fully implemented version of the IBM and DEC repository environments, with a full suite of integrated tools from heterogeneous CASE vendors. This is all part of a move toward "open systems" in the CASE community: it will gradually become possible to create a CASE environment that mixes together different hardware platforms (PCs, Macs, Sun workstations, VAX workstations, etc.), different operating systems (Unix, MS-DOS, Windows 3, OS/2, etc.), and different DBMSs (DB2, Oracle, DEC's Rdb, etc.) for repository storage. Today's CASE environment is characterized by *homogeneous* hardware/software platforms; the environment of the mid-1990s will be much more heterogeneous.

Meanwhile, most CASE users have another three to five years of work getting their organizations to use *existing* technology effectively. If the CASE vendors froze their products tomorrow, most organizations wouldn't notice the difference for another few years.

6.7.2 Changing the Culture

Perhaps the most significant part of CASE evolution will be a gradual change in the culture of the software engineering organization. CASE-driven software development will be a specification-driven process rather than a code-driven process; it will emphasize building of systems from reusable parts, with continual automated checking. The software engineer will work in a responsive, interactive environment, with a human interface far more sophisticated than that associated with today's tools. And, as discussed shortly, the CASE environment will incorporate expert system technology in such areas as methodology selection and usage.

Carma McClure [4] characterizes the cultural change in terms of a "pre-CASE' and "post-CASE" environment:

Pre-CASE	Post-CASE
Emphasis on coding, test	Emphasis on analysis, design
Paper models	Rapid prototyping
Manual coding	Automated code generation
Manual documentation	Automatic documentation
Testing of code	Testing of specs and design
Maintaining code	Maintaining specs and design

The world-class software organizations are keenly aware of the differences between these two environments and are working hard to move from the former to the latter. Of course, most organizations would agree, philosophically, that the post-CASE environment is preferable, but here is a good test to determine whether this is just philosophical bullshit or a *real* change: tell your programmers that they can no longer make any changes to source code (just like you told them 10 to 20 years ago that they could no longer patch binary object code); *any* change must be accomplished by changing the specification or the design model and regenerating the code.

6.7.3 Understanding How Software Engineers Work

McClure [4] also argues that the culture change will be accompanied by a dramatically improved environment for software engineers:

Current environment	Post-CASE *Intelligent* Environment
User-friendly interface	*Customized* interface
Diagnostic	Corrective
Supportive	Directive
Helpful	Teaching
Responsive when queried	Reacts to events it detects

Such a transition is technologically exciting, but it presumes that we know much more about how software engineers work than we really do. Indeed, CASE tools may prove to be useless if they don't fit comfortably with the way people work—unless, of course, we can change the way people work. The most difficult task of the software organization will be that of striking a balance between adapting tools to the way people work and adapting people's work habits to the constraints and capabilities of the tool.

In the extreme case, it has often been observed that "if your only tool is a hammer, then every problem looks like a nail." The problem of tool inadequacy is usually not so severe with CASE technology, but most software engineers and software managers have given little thought to the question of how software people really work—because the work has typically been internalized within each individual. A good example is the tribal folklore concerning "top–down" software development: most textbooks extol it as a virtue, and many believe that it is the "natural" way to work; as a result, many CASE tools encourage, or even *insist* on, top–down development.[13]

However, recent work by Raymonde Guindon [21, 22] at MCC suggests that the natural inclination of many software engineers is *not* a purely top-down approach, but rather a mixture of top–down and

---

[13] Here is a simple test for a structured analysis CASE tool: Can you *first* create a low-level diagram and *then* create its parent? Is there some way to "double-click" on an entire diagram and say, "Please create a higher-level bubble that represents this diagram"? Many CASE tools require that the parent be created first; the double-clicking activity creates a new "child" diagram as a decomposition of the selected bubble.

bottom–up. A video recording of the activities of a software engineer working on a real-time elevator (lift) control system, for example, showed the behavior exhibited in Figure 6.9.

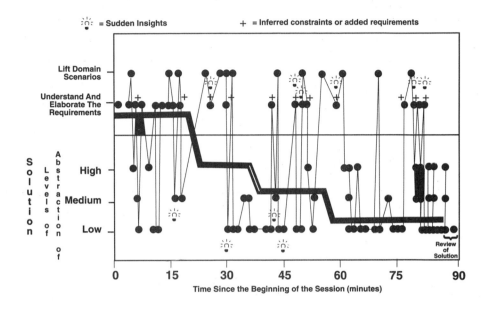

Figure 6.9: How software engineers really work

Thus, one of the likely developments of the next decade, as CASE tools begin to proliferate and profoundly impact the way people work, is more research and study on just that topic.[14]

6.7.4 Groupware CASE Tools

Building small systems is less and less of a problem today; CASE tools, fourth generation languages, and a variety of the other "silver bullet" solutions discussed in Chapter 2 are gradually improving the productivity of systems that are intrinsically small enough to be developed by individuals or small groups of people.

But as Figure 6.10 suggests, the enormous number of tiny systems will be offset by a smaller number of *huge* systems, for which a very

---

[14] Ironically, MCC's Human Interface Lab, which sponsored much of the research by people like Guindon and Curtis, was closed down at the end of 1990 and the remainder of the MCC Software Technology Program was effectively disbanded at the end of 1991. There remain many other research centers, of course, but the loss of MCC's activities is discouraging.

different category of CASE tool will be needed. Examples of such big systems are the flight control software for the Boeing 777 aircraft, which consists of 2+ million lines of code; the next generation FAA air traffic control system, estimated at 12 million lines of code; NASA's space station, estimated at 40 million lines of code; and the Strategic Defense Initiative "Star Wars" system, estimated to require 60 to 100 million lines of code.

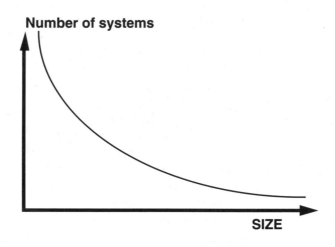

Figure 6.10: Big systems versus small systems

As Curtis, Krasner, and Iscoe [23] point out, the CASE tools requirements for projects of this size are fundamentally different from those for small projects:

> ... software tools and practices conceived to aid individual activities often do not provide benefits that scale up on large projects to overcome the impact of team and organizational factors that affect the design process.

As a result, it is quite likely that the most significant development of the mid- to late-1990s (after the current generation of integrated-repository CASE tools have been fully developed) is a new generation of *groupware* CASE tools. As the term implies, these tools will be more concerned with the activities of groups of people rather than focusing on the development needs of the individual.

As an example of the difference between today's generation of CASE tools and the groupware tools of the future, consider the prototype CASE tools called gIBIS (an acronym for "graphical issue-based information system") developed by Conklin and Begeman at MCC [24].

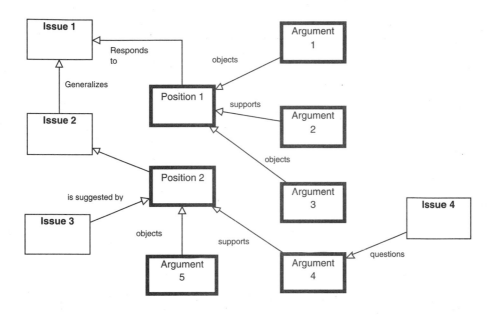

Figure 6.11: The gIBIS CASE tool

Such a tool helps project managers and software engineers keep track of important "issues" in a project (e.g., "which operating system shall we use?" "which software design methodology shall we use?"), "positions" on those issues, and arguments in favor of, or opposed to, the various positions. Tools like gIBIS can help organizations document *why* things are done, as well as the more traditional activities of documenting *what* has to be done (i.e., requirements models) and *how* it is to be done (i.e., design models)

Groupware CASE tools will become more and more important on large projects, where members of the project team are physically separated—in different buildings, different cities, or even different countries. Groupware tools will also be important to senior managers, because they are essential for enabling concurrent activities in a project—and concurrency is essential if "speed to market" remains an important issue. In addition, groupware tools help remedy failures of coordination and communication, and can enhance group performance by enabling computer-assisted reviews and inspections. Finally, groupware tools can help enhance the workplace "quality of life," by making it possible for project team members to communicate about personal and social events through the medium of electronic mail.

As Kashdan [25] points out, researchers are exploring a number of different mechanisms for groupware in experimental settings like MIT's Project Athena and at Xerox PARC. These mechanisms include different approaches for message sending and group communication, as well as group decision support. And, on the razzle-dazzle technology side, a number of researchers are exploring shared displays, shared pointing devices, and a variety of "in-room" versus "separated" facilities; it will probably be at least middecade before many of these devices become commercially feasible, though modest examples are already available.[15]

Many of the most useful groupware CASE tools will be simple derivatives of familiar office automation (OA) tools, such as

- Electronic mail
- Online calendars
- Facilities scheduling (reserving of conference rooms)
- Document preparation and online comments
- Project planning and control
- Shared databases/files and access controls
- Automatic message sending protocols

The important point here is that many of these OA already exist and do not need to be invented anew by the CASE community. Instead, they need to be integrated into the CASE environment; thus, if a CASE vendor tells you, as one recently told me, that electronic mail is "orthogonal" to his product (meaning that it involves a different "dimension" of software), you should find yourself a different vendor.

In addition to the classical OA groupware mechanisms, there are a number that can be applied specifically to software. We should expect to see the following capabilities of the groupware-CASE generation of the mid- to late-1990s:[16]

[15] One such modest example, having nothing to do with CASE per se, is the class of groupware product that allows several people on a network to mark up a shared copy of a text document.

[16] Many of these capabilities were suggested by Sam Redwine, who led a groupware workshop at the Fourth International Workshop on CASE, held in Irvine, California, in December 1990.

- Software configuration management (including notification of changes)
- Trouble reporting and change tracking
- Software project oriented planning and control systems
- A "contract" model for coordination between tasks
- Tools that can act as an effective group member
- Support for concurrent activities
- Tools to support new people on a project (training, group history, summary of group decisions, etc.)
- Assessment (metrics) of the group process itself.

6.7.5 Expert System Technology in CASE

The possible applications of artificial intelligence and expert system technology to CASE are legion. The most obvious examples are in the areas of

- Debugging
- Maintenance and impact analysis of proposed changes to code
- Systems analysis
- Configuring software packages
- Transforming analysis models into design models
- Assistance in partitioning and leveling of models
- Application-specific "domain models"
- Advice on which methodology to use

It is reasonable to expect that fifth generation AI/expert system technology will gradually become a part of CASE, particularly as the CASE market grows large enough to support the massive R&D efforts that will be required.[17] Tutoring systems, diagnostic systems, and "analyst's helper" tools will gradually become part of CASE; today's methodologies already take one to two years for the average software engineer to learn, as we saw in Chapter 5, and the methodologies of the mid-1990s will undoubtedly be even more complex. More sophisticated user interfaces, made possible by AI and expert system technology, will also creep into the CASE environment, though CASE will not be the driving force to create such interfaces; however, as the rest of the

---

[17] Paul Harmon [26] has recently an even broader trend: a growing convergence of CASE, object-oriented methodologies, and expert system technology.

computer community receives natural language processing, voice recognition, handwriting recognition, and voice output, so will the CASE community.

6.7.6 Multimedia CASE

Today's CASE tools make straightforward use of graphics and relatively primitive use of sound and color. Far more sophisticated technology is already available, and we can expect next generation CASE tools to take advantage of digitized voice recording, video recording, hypertext, and animation. As mentioned earlier, this might facilitate video/sound recording of design reviews, with the results stored in a repository, and available for recall on a software engineer's CASE tool.

More exotic examples involve the use of smell, sound, touch-sensitive screens, and virtual reality to provide the "ultimate" in multimedia CASE. Whether or not this happens depends to some extent on the future of display technology. MCC's visionary Project Leonardo [22] focused, among other things, on a "project team blackboard" predicated on the feasibility of wall-size display screens in the future; an alternative approach at Xerox PARC is described by Clarkson [27], who suggests that we may find ourselves continuing to suffer with miserably small 15-inch display screens for the next decade. In this case, according to the Xerox PARC researchers, the issue will be how to squeeze ever more information onto a fixed-sized screen; one approach being explored is that of three-dimensional visualizations of informations (e.g., using "rooms" instead of mere "windows") onto a two-dimensional surface.

END NOTES

1. Boone, Gregory H., Vaughan P. Merlyn, and Roger R. Dobratz. *The Second Annual Report on CASE*. Bellevue, WA: CASE Research Corporation, 1990.
2. Fisher, Alan S. *CASE: Using Software Development Tools*. New York: John Wiley & Sons, 1990.
3. Gane, Chris. *Computer Aided Software Engineering*. Englewood Cliffs, NJ: Prentice Hall, 1989.
4. McClure, Carma. *CASE Is Software Automation*. Englewood Cliffs, NJ: Prentice Hall, 1988.
5. Binder, Robert V., and Judith E. Phillips. "Trends in CASE Users and Usage," *American Programmer*, July 1991.

6. Orr, Ken. "The Repository: The Soul of a New Technology?" *American Programmer*, December 1990.

7. Nelson, Jack. "Assessing the AD Information Model," *American Programmer*, July 1991.

8. McClure, Carma, with Jeanne Follman. "Repository Standards: A Must for CASE Tool Integration," *American Programmer*, December 1990.

9. Privateer, Peter. "How to Evaluate a Vendor's Repository Enablement," *American Programmer*, December 1990.

10. Chikofsky, Elliot. "Repository Wars: Can We Make a Repository Foster Cooperation?" *American Programmer*, December 1990.

11. Topper, Andrew. "Evaluating CASE Tools: Guidelines for Comparison," *American Programmer*, July 1991.

12. Yourdon, Edward. "A CASE of the Blahs," *American Programmer*, July 1991.

13. Pressman, Roger. *Making Software Engineering Happen.* Englewood Cliffs, NJ: Prentice Hall, 1988.

14. Bouldin, Barbara. *Agents of Change.* Englewood Cliffs, NJ: Yourdon Press/Prentice Hall, 1989.

15. Humphrey, Watts. *Managing the Software Process.* Reading, MA: Addison-Wesley, 1989.

16. Radding, Paul. "A Survey of Organizational CASE Strategies," *Proceedings of the Fall 1990 CASE World Conference.* Andover, MA: Digital Consulting, October 1990.

17. Jones, T. Capers. "Why Choose CASE?" *American Programmer*, January 1990.

18. Barton, Richard. "Justifying CASE," *CASE Trends*, May–June, 1990.

19. Yourdon, Edward. *Managing the Structured Techniques*, 4th ed. Englewood Cliffs, NJ: Yourdon Press/Prentice Hall, 1989.

20. Yourdon, Edward. "Pacific Bell," *American Programmer*, September 1989.

21. Guindon, Raymonde. "The Process of Knowledge Discovery in System Design," *Proceedings of HCI '89 International.* New York: Elsevier, 1989.

22. Guindon, Raymonde, and Bill Curtis. "Control of Cognitive Process During Design: What Tools Would Support Software Designers?" *Proceedings of CHI '88.* New York: ACM Press, 1988.

23. Curtis, Bill, Herb Krasner, and Neil Iscoe. "A Field Study of the Software Design Process for Large Systems," *Communications of the ACM*, November 1988, pp. 1268–1287.

24. Conklin, Jeff, and Michael L. Begeman. "gIBIS: A Hypertext Tool for Exploratory Policy Discussion," MCC Technical Report Number STP-082-88. Austin, TX: MCC, 1988.
25. Kashdan, Norman R. "CASE and Distributed Computing Environments," *American Programmer*, July 1991.
26. Harmon, Paul. "CASE, Object-Oriented Programming, and Expert Systems," *American Programmer*, October 1990.
27. Clarkson, Mark. "An Easier Interface," *Byte*, February 1991.

7

SOFTWARE METRICS

The Mets have a record of 10 wins and only 1 loss so far this year for games on Tuesday night. . . . but they have won only 4 out of 25 games where they were behind in the eighth inning.

TV announcer Ralph Kiner, commenting on the Mets-Expos game on Tuesday, June 25, 1991.

Where do they get those crazy numbers? I keep asking myself. At a moment's notice, the announcers can tell you Gregg Jeffries's batting average as a left hander during the last 10 games or as a right hander when there were more than two people on base. And it's a pretty safe bet that the players and the managers know the numbers, too. Baseball, the informal, knockabout game of summer I played as a boy, has become a game of numbers. *Why don't we run our software projects this way?*[1]

The Software Engineering Institute's process maturity model suggests that the introduction of metrics comes toward the end of the process improvement process, that is, that only the most sophisticated organizations have implemented a metrics initiative. But it is hard to imagine an organization making *any* improvement if it doesn't measure what it is doing. A phrase from Tom DeMarco's *Controlling Software Projects* [1] has often been repeated in this regard, "You can't control what you can't measure."

Unfortunately, it is abundantly evident that hardly any DP shop measures anything at all about the way it develops its primary work product. Don't take my word for it: look around you. Ask questions. Look for some numbers: What's the average number of defects per thousand lines of source code in your organization? What is the productivity rate in your shop (in function points) for the analysis phase, the design phase, and the testing phase of your projects? If you're going to be a world-class software shop and subject yourself to the kind of scrutiny that my beloved Mets suffer every day, you should even know what your productivity rate is on Tuesdays. And you

---

[1] Though the Mets were behind 5 to 4 in the bottom of the ninth on this particular evening, they beat the odds and won the game when Kevin McReynolds hit a grand slam home run with two outs, two balls, and two strikes.

should know what the odds are of finishing a project on time when you're behind schedule in the eighth inning.

Why? Why measure anything about software? That is the first topic addressed in this chapter. Next, we'll discuss *what* to measure: time, effort, and defects. And finally, we'll review some guidelines on *how* to measure software phenomena—specifically, how to institute a software metrics initiative.

7.1 WHY MEASURE?

Why indeed? For the individual software engineer, there may be very little motivation to indulge in software metrics. If I think of myself as a good, professional programmer, why should I care how many lines of code I wrote today? I worked hard, wrote as many lines of code as I could, until I got tired/bored/hungry. Tomorrow, I'll write another bunch of code, and some more the next day—until one day I'll be done. Of course, management always wants to know how much progress I've made, and when I'll be finished, but that's just because management is typically anal compulsive and doesn't understand how the process works. Anyone who has written code knows that you start at the beginning and proceed one instruction at a time until you get to the end of the program. When you get to the end, you're done.

If baseball players had the same attitude, it would be a very different game. Indeed, maybe ballplayers *do* have this same kind of attitude: I go up to the plate every chance I get, and I swing at every ball that looks as if it's over the plate. Some of them I hit, some I miss. Who knows how many hits I'm going to get in a season? We'll know at the end of the season. Maybe it's only the TV announcers who have the obsession for keeping track of the number of hits that a switch-hitter has when batting right-handed in night games—but it's a sure bet that the players and the managers are aware of the relevant statistics. And it's a sure bet that the players and the managers have more than an academic interest in *improving* their statistics—so they can win the World Series, negotiate a more lucrative contract next year, get elected to the All-Star Team and ultimately to the Hall of Fame, and maybe even become a movie star or head of a software company (after all, it happens in football, so why not in baseball?).

This is at the heart of the argument for capturing software metrics: *The desire to improve.* If we were all basically satisfied with what we were doing, there would be no need to measure, no need to keep track. For some 20 years, it has been blindingly obvious that our senior management and our end users aren't satisfied with what we're doing, but that hasn't seemed to matter very much: *we* have been satisfied, or at least reasonably confident that we were doing as well as could be reasonably expected. So why bother measuring?

Today, the world-class software company knows that it cannot be satisfied with what it's doing—even if its current performance is pretty damn good. The reasons were discussed in Chapter 1: software is now a global industry, and a lot of hungry people around the world are aching to eat your lunch. Even if you're good, they aim to be better. To stay in business, *you* have to be better—better than you were last year, better than you were yesterday. *But you can't improve if you don't know your current situation.*

This, then, is the fundamental argument for investing time, money, effort, and people in the business of capturing, analyzing, reviewing, disseminating, and ultimately *acting* on software metrics: the desire to learn more about the process by which your organization develops software, so that you can improve it. For example, Capers Jones argues that productivity is a function of project size, and, as shown in Figure 7.1, the distribution of effort on common software-related activities varies considerably as a function of project size. Is this true of your projects and your organizations? You won't know if you don't have a metrics program that provides such information.

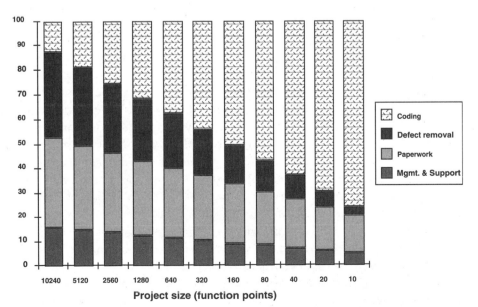

Figure 7.1: Distribution of project activities as a function of project size

But there are two other, related reasons:

- Metrics are needed to validate and calibrate "generic" models of software productivity, reliability, and so on.
- Investments in productivity tools, techniques, methodologies, and so on can't be justified without good metrics.

To illustrate the first point, consider the extent of "tribal folklore" that has developed about software numbers:

- At least 50 percent of our software resources is spent on maintenance (or is it 60 percent? or 80 percent?).
- The average programmer produces 10 to 15 lines of code per day (or is it 5? or does it matter?).
- Only 10 to 15 percent of a development project is devoted to coding, but 50 percent is devoted to testing.
- A module should not be more than 50 lines of source code in a well-modularized program.
- A module's "span of control"—the number of immediate subordinate modules that it calls—should be approximately 7± 2.

Some of these "eternal constants" are believed simply because they have been repeated so often and published in so many books; others are believed because they are uttered with great solemnity by famous gurus. It's like saying, *Nobody ever hit more than four home runs in a game. It can't be done.*

The widely published "eternal constants" may be good yardsticks in the software development business, but they need to be validated and calibrated to suit the idiosyncrasies of each organization. An excellent example of this calibration can be found in David Card's *Measuring Design Quality* [2], which tests the accuracy and relevancy of a number of widely accepted software "truths" for a sample of approximately 500,000 lines of FORTRAN code for a group of satellite tracking systems. The conclusions Card reaches about his software may not apply to your software (e.g., if you have 500,000 lines of COBOL for a group of financial systems), but you'll never know if you don't capture your own software metrics.

Another reason for metrics: you'll never be able to justify major investments in CASE tools, reengineering, reusability, methodologies, or other "big-ticket" technology-oriented solutions to the productivity problem if you don't have some metrics to back you up.[2]

7.2 WHAT TO MEASURE?

The aspiring world-class software organization, intent on setting up an exemplary software metrics initiative, has to decide *what* to measure. On the one hand, you can't measure everything; indeed, you can't even measure everything that looks interesting—it would cost too much, take too much time, and generally inundate everyone in the organization with a deluge of numbers. On the other hand, you should be wary of measuring too little: don't pin your hopes on only one productivity metric, such as lines of code per person per day. Metrics guru Howard Rubin argues that the high mortality rate of metrics initiatives—nearly 80 percent in the first 18 months of activity—is primarily due to this reason: the metrics team picks one or two "magic numbers" to measure, only to learn (when they go back for more money) that management sees no relevance in the numbers they have been so carefully capturing.

More advice: avoid making your measurements too narrow. As Paul Strassmann [3], points out, "Productivity claims can be made faster through clever rearrangement of accounting costs than through any other means." A typical example of this is the organization that installs very detailed metrics for its *development* activities, but ignores maintenance. The result of this lopsided scrutiny? Suddenly people begin finding all sorts of excuses for classifying work as maintenance that previously got done under the rubric of development.

Another piece of advice: beware of measuring only the *product* of software development (i.e., the code) and not the *process* by which the software product is developed. Measures of the product—how many lines of code were written, how many defects they contained, and so on—is like telling the baseball player at the end of the year how many hits he had and how many times he struck out. Without information about the *process*, there's not much chance that the statistics next season

---

[2] Unfortunately, some evidence collected by Paul Radding suggests that this may not be true if the technology itself is relatively new and untested. His survey of the justification process for introducing CASE tools showed that a substantial number of senior managers were convinced by an argument that CASE would give them a "strategic edge" over the competition—an emotionally appealing argument that may not require any hard numbers about costs and productivity benefits. For more discussion of this, see Chapter 6.

will be any better. The baseball player needs to know some things about his own process; for example, 82 percent of the time he swings at a curve ball, he misses, while 73 percent of the times he goes after a fast ball, he gets on base. And software engineers need information about *their* process in order to learn how to change, how to improve.

David Card [4] suggests that the following criteria should be used to judge the usefulness of proposed metrics for a software organization:

- *Understandable.* If software engineers and project managers fundamentally don't understand the meaning or derivation of the metric, its usefulness is diminished. This is probably the single most important reason why the "lines-of-code" metric continues to be used, despite the obvious technical merits of a function point metric.

- *Field-tested.* A metric proposed by a researcher may have great intuitive appeal and a sound theoretical basis, but until it has been confirmed in practice, it should be regarded with caution. Perhaps the best example of this is the well-known Halstead "volume" metric, which has only recently been thoroughly debunked in field tests.

- *Economical.* It should be relatively easy to capture and/or compute the metric. It is particularly important that the metric-capturing activity *not* interfere with the actual work of software development; otherwise, we suffer a form of the well-known Heisenberg uncertainty principle. In the best case, the metrics should be captured as a natural by-product of the work itself.

- *High leverage.* It doesn't help much to gather voluminous metrics in an attempt to find ways of improving productivity by 0.005 percent. A good metric will help pinpoint those parts of the software development process in which minor changes will cause significant improvements.

- *Timely.* Delivering the metrics six months after the completion of a project is of no interest to the project team, though it may be relevant to researchers and historians. For the benefit of the software engineers and the project managers, the metrics should be available on a real-time basis. Many interesting metrics, for example, are captured during walkthroughs/inspections of the design or specification of a system; the resultant metrics should be available to the project team within 24 hours after the conclusion of the inspection meeting.

So what does all this mean? For starters, it says we should focus on measuring the basics: software size, software defects, and software effort. Additional metrics—for example, customer responsiveness metrics—can be added later, if they can be related to business objectives that are important to managers and users. The truly world-class software organizations are building a "chart of accounts" for collecting metrics data; for an excellent discussion of the chart of accounts and the concept of economic productivity in software, see Jones [5].

7.2.1 Measuring Software Size

Perhaps the most important thing for an organization to measure is the *size* of its software efforts, for example, the amount of code written and tested, the number of pages of functional specifications, or the number of diagrams in the design model. The reason it's so crucial is that most of the "political" metrics—budgets, schedules, and personnel allocation—are based on estimates of the amount of work to be done.

Here's another way to look at it: the item identified by the Software Engineering Institute as the most common deficiency of level 1 organizations is the ability to estimate software size. If you underestimate the size of your software task by a factor of 10, then it really doesn't matter what tools, languages, or methodologies are used on the project: the budget, schedule, and manpower allocation will be so inadequate that the project will almost certainly fail.

Since the final deliverable of most software projects is working *code*, it follows that the size metric in many organizations is a code-oriented metric such as "lines of code" or "source statements." Over the past decade, there has been a gradual movement toward *function points* as a more appropriate software metric, and enthusiasts like Capers Jones argue that by the mid-1990s, it will become the dominant metric.

For those unfamiliar with function points, a good description can be found in Jones [5], Albrecht [6], or DeMarco [1]; more information can also be obtained from the International Function Point User's Group (IFPUG) [7]. The number of function points for a computer program (or module, subroutine, procedure, etc.) is based on an algorithm that computes a weighted sum of inputs, outputs, inquiries, master files, and interfaces to other programs; as one might expect, the algorithm is contained in software metrics packages and is now even part of some commercial CASE tools. Table 7.1, based on the work of Capers Jones [5], shows a rough comparison between function points and lines of code in familiar languages.

Table 7.1: The relationship between function points and lines of code

Assembler	320
C	150
COBOL	106
FORTRAN	106
Pascal	91
PL/I	80
Ada	71
Prolog	64
APL	32
Smalltalk	21
Spreadsheet languages	6

Not everyone is convinced the function points are an appropriate metric; organizations working with real-time systems often complain that function points are not relevant for their work, and while a modified metric called *feature points* has been developed for the real-time community, many of these people prefer to continue working with the old familiar metric of lines of code.

The fundamental weakness of the lines-of-code metric has been known for decades; among these weaknesses are the obvious bias it creates against high-level languages and the implicit motivation for the programmer to write more lines of code to accomplish the same amount of work. Nevertheless, these weaknesses may not be fatal if, for example, the programming language has already been chosen for the project, and if the metrics are used at an aggregate level rather than being used to compare the efforts of individual programmers on a day-to-day basis. Whether you use function points or lines of code, *by far the most important thing is to measure **consistently** across all projects.*

This means, for example, that you must decide whether blank lines and comments count in your measure of lines of code; do "declarative" statements count, or only executable statements? Do reused lines of code—for example, those that have been copied into the source code with an INCLUDE or COPY statement—count each time they are invoked, or only once? Whatever the answer to these questions, make sure it's the same answer for all projects. The easiest way to accomplish this, of course, is to use a computerized measuring package to examine code that has already been written; however, it's important that everyone use the same assumptions to estimate the amount of code that has not yet been written in a project.

Of course, there are other deliverables in a software development project besides code: designs, specifications, test cases, users manuals, and various forms of documentation. Most of these work-products can't be measured in units resembling lines of code, but they have all been expressed in units of function points [5]. Since many (if not all) of the ancillary work-products are intrinsically textual, or are components of published documents, some organizations measure them in units of "formatted output pages" produced by their text editor or document publishing system; others measure more "atomic" units such as words and diagrams. Again, consistency is the key issue.

7.2.2 Measuring Defects

The notion of counting bugs hardly needs to be explained; however, a comprehensive metrics program will also keep track of the nature of the defects, the source of the defects, the severity of the defect, and the time when it was discovered.

Categorizing the severity of a software bug is something I normally advise companies to avoid when they are first implementing a software metrics program; things tend to degenerate when you have a 10-level grading system covering everything from nuclear war to irrelevant glitches in a system. If you must make a distinction between different levels of severity, keep it simple: three levels should be enough. Thus, a "severe" error might be one that prevents a user from getting any work done at all; a "moderate" error might be one the requires a substantial amount of extra work for the user to "work around"; and a "minor" error might be one that is noticeable to the user, but that does not substantially interfere with his or her work. Again, consistency is important: you'll have to decide in advance whether to count a defect only once or whether to count it additionally each time it occurs; similarly, does a defect get counted only once, no matter how many users it affects, or does it get counted once per user? If in doubt, ask the users: they will have a more realistic (and more politically important) perspective than the programmers on the project.

More important than severity is a categorization of the "taxonomy" of the software defects. For example, at the coding level, the defect might be any of the following categories:

- A reference to an uninitialized variable
- A subscript range error
- An "off-by-one" loop control (going through a loop once too many time, or once too few)
- A program error caused by an incomplete edit: garbage input was allowed into the system.
- Incorrect parameters passed to a module
- And so on.

It may be time consuming and tedious to collect this information, and it may lead to some arguments among the programmers, but it is nevertheless enormously useful information. In many organizations, a few categories of software defects dominate all others; one study at AT&T Bell Labs, for example, indicated that nearly 40 percent of the errors in a large group of "C" programs were module interface errors. Discoveries like this can highlight the need for better training, better tools, better languages, or other improvements in the software development environment.

Identifying the *source* of the defect—that is, whose bug is it?—is also tremendously important, though it is rarely done in the United States. Schulmeyer [8] introduces the concept of a "net-negative producer": someone who introduces so many defects into the software he or she develops that he lowers the productivity of the entire project team. If such a metric could be introduced in the proper cultural environment, the discovery of the "negative producer" could point the way to additional training and assistance, or it might indicate that the person is better suited to an activity other than writing code. Some companies attempt to turn this into a positive experience by identifying the "zero-defect" producer, that is, the one (or few) producers who have no defects at all in their work products. While this is commendable, it's not clear that it helps us do a better job with all the people and all the work that is *not* defect free.[3]

Finally, identifying *when* the defect occurred is important. Unfortunately, it is much easier to document the date and time when a software bug was discovered than to document when it was actually

---

[3] Of course, another possibility would be to capture the data (during walkthroughs, reviews, or inspections) and make it available to the producer *without* making it visible to the manager. Aggregate team-level defect statistics might be published and reported to the boss in order to ensure that attention was being focused on the number of defects.

caused; however, the people who discover the bug can often determine whether it was caused during the current "phase" of the project, for example, the coding phase, or whether it "leaked" into the current phase from a previous phase, for example, the analysis phase or the design phase. Again, this requires some effort, and it may lead to some arguments, but it is enormously valuable. The folklore of the software engineering field says that a substantial percentage—often as high as 50 percent—of the software errors that are ultimately discovered in a production system can be traced by to errors made in the systems analysis phase of the project.[4]

Here are some additional examples of defect-related metrics that could be captured in a software organization:

- Defect rate by hour, day, week, or month.
- Defect rate per function point, or similar attempts to measure defects at the analysis/design stage of the project.
- Mean time between failures (MTBF).
- Mean time to repair a defect (MTTR).
- Defect backlog.
- MTBF as a function of the load on an online system.
- Tests passed on first attempt, clean compilations on first attempt, error-free design/analysis inspections on first attempt.
- Error "leakage": analysis errors that slip through to the design phase, design errors that slip through to the coding phase, and so on.
- Cumulative software defects discovered during each "version" or "release" of a system.
- Defects discovered per person-hour of review effort (normalized by system size, e.g., by function point).
- Impact of management decisions (e.g., changing the project schedule or manpower allocation above or below optimal levels) on defects. For a fascinating discussion of the impact of such "crunch-mode" management decisions on software reliability, see Putnam and Myers [11].

---

[4] Not only are such errors common, they are also extremely expensive. Boehm [9] argues that the cost of error correction increases 10-fold if the error leaks from one phase to the next. And Martin [10] argues that as much as 75 percent of the total cost of error correction can be attributed to errors found in the analysis phase of the project—many of which are not discovered until much further downstream.

7.2.3 Measuring Effort

For the organization that has no software metrics program, the most politically difficult thing to measure is the effort expended by the people on the project. Software engineers are prone to argue vehemently that because they are "professionals," they should not be required to punch a clock and keep detailed records of what they do all day long. They complain (justly) that since nobody keeps track of their overtime hours, any effort to measure their 9-to-5 hours is a farce. They worry that someone in Accounting will decide they are spending too much time at lunch and that their trips to the bathroom may even be monitored. They worry that their hard-hearted boss will bust their chops for working 38 hours last week and won't even notice that they worked 88 hours the week before that.

Whether or not this is what the organization intended, it's often what the software engineers feel, and if they feel this way, there is a significant danger that the time sheets will be completely fictitious. My strong advice to companies whose software professionals suffer from such paranoia is that they begin with "anonymous" time sheets: the detailed work-activities should be filled in, but the name of the individual should be left out.

When you measure the effort expended by people in the software organization, make sure that you include the overtime hours, regardless of whether the employee is paid for them. If you don't count overtime hours, you run the risk of perpetuating a management approach that DeMarco and Lister [12] describe as the "Spanish theory of value," that is, assuming that any schedule problem can be solved through the simple expedient of unpaid overtime.[5] Indeed, some organizations have experienced unexpected management backlashes after the introduction of CASE tools or other productivity aids: the productivity improvements resulted in fewer hours of unpaid overtime, which the employees loved, but which provided no financial benefit to management.

Consistency is also important when it comes to measuring effort. It's fairly obvious that expended effort should be measured for people *directly* involved in activities that are *directly* associated with the software product, for example, programmers involved in the act of programming, designers involved in the act of systems design. But what about "indirect" activities such as training? What about the idle time

[5] For more on the Spanish theory of value, see my review of *Peopleware* in Appendix B. Better yet, read their book!

experienced by the "direct" people between assignments? And most important, what about all the "indirect" people—managers, assistants, co-op students, librarians, accountants, trainers, receptionists, secretaries, and the host of others—who make it possible for the software engineers to get their work done? My strong recommendation is to include the effort of everyone who is even remotely involved in the development of software in your organization—including the janitor, the night watchman, and every level of management.

This is not an academic issue: depending on what activities and which people are included in your measurements, the productivity figures can vary by *a factor of 100*. If you measure only the coding activity of a single programmer for one day, and then "annualize" the results (i.e., multiply by the number of working days in the year), it's easy to conclude that your people are turning out as much as 25,000 lines of code per person-year. However, if you measure the total software effort by the entire software organization for a full year, including the canceled projects, the nonproductive activities, as well as all development, maintenance, and enhancement of old systems, you are more likely to conclude that your people (including the janitors) are producing only 250 lines of code per person-year.

7.2.4 Customer Responsiveness Metrics

The software systems and software products that we develop are meant to be *used*—used by people we sometimes call "users," but who might be better thought of as customers. Many of the world-class software organizations are now capturing metrics describing the interactions between their software product and the customer, especially in those cases where the customer has a question, complaint, or problem with the system. Whether the customer is an external customer whom we never see, or an internal "user" in the marketing department or accounting department, the interactions are usually logged in the form of phone calls, trouble reports, e-mail messages, and so on.

The most obvious interaction with a customer, of course, is the software defect: virtually every metrics initiative will have the good sense to capture the number of software defects, as discussed earlier. But not every customer contact is an indication of a bug; many may be questions about how to use feature X in the system, how they can order an extra copy of the user manual, when the next version of the system is scheduled for release, and so on.

Regardless of its nature, every customer inquiry deserves a response, and in the best of all worlds, everything the customer perceives as a problem deserves a solution. Thus, the metrics group should consider keeping measurements of the following:

- *Timeliness of responses to customer problems.* How quickly does the software organization answer the phone, respond to written inquiries, or answer its e-mail? Some organizations might want to see how many times their "hot line" phone service subjects customers to 30 minutes of Lawrence Welk Muzak; other organizations might want to see if written trouble reports are answered in less than a week, and so on.

- *Quality of responses to customers.* In some cases, the response might be, "We got your message and we'll look into it," and in others it might be, "we got the printout showing the problem you had, and we'll have a fix to the problem within five business days," and in still others it might be, "we can't answer your question because you didn't give us your customer-support registration number." Thus, the initial response often does *not* provide a solution to the customer, but *does* give the customer an idea whether his problem will ever be solved. Naturally, information about the quality of the responses would have to be determined through interviews, surveys, or questionnaires involving the users themselves, *not* by talking to the people receiving the trouble reports.

- *Timeliness of solutions to customers.* How quickly is the customer's problem resolved? Of course, in the best of cases, the problem is resolved at the same instant the customer describes it, but for serious problems, the resolution may come hours, days, or even weeks after it was first reported.

- *Quality of solutions.* If the solution is a message like, "Yeah, we know about that problem and we'll fix it in the next release; meantime, what you gotta do is X and Y and Z . . . ", the customer may not regard the solution as "acceptable." In other cases, the solution may consist of a software patch or revision to the software. And, of course, the trouble report may not have been caused by a software bug, but rather confusion about how to use some feature of the software. In any case, the quality of the solution offered to the customer should be evaluated through questionnaires or surveys.

7.2.5 Miscellaneous Metrics

What else should one consider measuring? This will depend, of course, on the organization and its priorities. However, here are a few possibilities:

- *Reusability.* How many components are in the reusable library? How often is each component used? What is the quality (in terms of defects, etc.) of the reusable components compared to that of "ordinary" components? How much more (or less) time and effort is required to develop reusable components than ordinary components? What is the cost, per component, to maintain and manage the reusable library? What percentage of each new system is composed of reusable components, and how is that figure changing over time?

- *Reengineering.* All the metrics described should be applied to *existing* systems as well as new systems under development; however, the problems involved in this effort are discussed in the next section . In any case, if a reengineering effort of the nature described in Chapter 10 is implemented, metrics should be used to keep track of the time and effort involved in restructuring, reengineering, or reverse engineering old software.

- *CASE tools.* If the organization decides to bring in CASE tools, a wealth of metrics should be gathered before and after the tools arrive. What is the average cost, per software engineer, of the tools? What is the average learning time? How many hours per day (or what percentage of overall work time) are the tools being used? How many problems *with the tools themselves* are being reported? Naturally, the time, effort, and defects associated with tool-built systems need to be carefully measured in order to see whether the tools have indeed brought about an improvement in productivity and quality.

- *Software methodology metrics.* It may be useful to gather metrics to confirm or reject the guidelines or "heuristics" associated with various software engineering methodologies. Some of the most fascinating metrics of this type were reported by Card [2] for structured design, using a sample of 500,000 lines of FORTRAN in eight large scientific systems. His data indicated, for example, that standards that arbitrarily limit module size (e.g., "thou shalt not create any module larger than 50 statements!") are ill advised; that common coupling (e.g., sharing data through FORTRAN COMMON) is not as bad as we thought; that module fan-out should *not* be limited to 7 ± 2, but a smaller number like 2 or 3; and that unreferenced variables are a good indicator of trouble.

7.3 HOW TO MEASURE—SETTING UP A METRICS PROGRAM

All the metrics described are important, but they will be useless if captured on a piecemeal, helter-skelter basis; indeed, even when captured faithfully on an individual project, they are of limited value. The best situation is a companywide metrics program, where *every* project is measured and *every* software engineer (as well as his or her managers, administrative assistants, etc.) are measured.

We saw in Chapter 4 that a fully implemented software metrics program is associated with level 4 companies; thus, very few organizations have really gone about this in an aggressive way. Japanese software organizations, like Hitachi Software Engineering, have long gathered metrics on a companywide basis, and a few exemplary U.S. organizations, like Hewlett-Packard, have made some notable progress. The "bible" for setting up a companywide metrics effort has been written by two Hewlett-Packard employees, Bob Grady and Debbie Caswell [13]; it should be considered required reading for anyone contemplating such an effort.

Grady and Caswell offer the following basic guidelines for instituting a software metrics initiative:

1. *Define company/project objectives for the program.* If it is perceived that the software metrics effort is just a research project or yet another crazy idea from the standards department, it will fade away within a few months. The metrics program will cost money, will require the full-time efforts of one or more people and the part-time effort of almost everyone in the organization, and will create a certain amount of fear, resistance, and resentment. Thus, it won't survive unless there is a clear objective, eloquently articulated from senior levels of management, for capturing the metrics; for example, "we intend to have the highest quality of any organization in the Widget industry, and we can't do that unless we measure what we're doing and *how* we're doing it."

2. *Assign responsibility.* A metrics program doesn't just happen; nothing useful will result from a request that everyone gather data about his or her time, effort, and software defects. A person, or group of people, must be given the responsibility for capturing the data, collecting it, storing it, analyzing it, and

disseminating it throughout the organization. For a small organization, this may be a part-time responsibility; for a large organization of several hundred people, it will typically require the full-time effort of two to five people. In some organizations, the metrics group may be considered part of the quality assurance organization; however, I strongly advise that you do *not* appoint the training organization or the standards organization, since these groups have about as much political credibility as Kurt Waldheim.

3. *Do research.* It may sound rather simple to collect a bunch of numbers and then produce a bunch of charts and graphs showing trends, averages, and standard deviations. But there is a great deal of activity in the software metrics field, and it is a good idea for the newly formed metrics group to carry out some research to make sure they are aware of the latest developments. What's the latest research on the applicability of function points? Is there a better way to represent the complexity of a program than McCabe's cyclomatic complexity metric, which typically applied *after* code has been written? And what tools are now available to help capture and analyze the metrics data?

4. *Define initial metrics to collect.* There is an ugly dilemma here: if you capture too much data, you'll be swamped and nobody will have the faintest idea of what the numbers mean. But if you capture too little data, *and if it turns out to be data that nobody cares about*, the metrics initiative will die a premature death.[6] The basic metrics of size, effort, and defects just described should be sufficient, but it is *imperative* that the metrics group relate these metrics to business-oriented metrics—profitability, earnings per share, market share, new customers brought into the fold, and so on—that senior management cares about.

5. *Sell the initial collection of these metrics.* Reaction to the metrics program in general, and to the specific metric categories that have been identified, will range from neutral to passionately negative. A "sales" effort is needed to convince project-level managers that the time, effort, and cost of capturing the metrics will be worthwhile, and a sales effort will be needed to convince working-level software engineers that the metrics won't be used to punish them. And that, in turn, usually requires a sales effort, strongly supported by senior management, to convince project-level managers *not* to use the metrics in a negative, punitive fashion. This issue is discussed further.

---

[6] Howard Rubin argues that this is the reason for the high mortality rate for most software metrics initiatives: 80 percent of the initiatives collapse or fade away within the first 18 months.

6. *Get tools for automatic data collection and analysis.* The more work that has to be done by hand, the more the entire metrics effort will be seen as disruptive; indeed, it runs the risk of invoking the Heisenberg uncertainty principle: by measuring the phenomenon, you run the risk of *changing* the phenomenon. The best scenario is one where most of the work done on a day-to-day basis by the software engineers is *automatically* available to a software metrics program; if the software engineers work in a highly automated CASE environment, this should be feasible. Equally important is the database for storing the data; it should be highly flexible so that new and different combinations of data can be extracted and manipulated. The normal CASE repository may not be adequate for this; companies that are really serious about software metrics, like AG Communication Systems in Phoenix, have developed their own relational database for their metrics data.

7. *Establish a training program in software metrics.* Working-level practitioners will need some training to learn how to capture the required metrics about their day-to-day work, and project managers will undoubtedly need some training to learn how to interpret and act on the various metrics reports that are produced by the metrics group.

8. *Publicize success stories and encourage the exchange of ideas.* It's important to communicate the notion that software metrics are not *passive*, but rather are a tool for *action*. Thus, metrics can be used to help spot things going wrong in a project before serious trouble develops; in general, metrics can be used to see how various parts of the software development process can be improved. When this is done, and when positive results can be seen, it needs to be publicized. This is more than just a simple call for "PR" activity: veterans of the software metrics wars point out that a metrics initiative is *always* under attack from other parts of the organization that consider it expensive overhead, even when its value has been demonstrated. Why? For the same reason intelligent people question the need for a savings program in good economic times or the value of vitamins when they are feeling healthy.

Though a comprehensive software metrics program may be associated with level 4 organizations, this does not mean that level 1 and level 2 organizations can or should ignore the issue of metrics altogether. As Marilyn Bush [14] points out, such organizations should begin by capturing some "baseline" measurements to learn what their current productivity and software quality is; in most cases, the level 1 organizations have no idea, and the level 2 organizations have focused all their measurements on accounting-oriented data like budgets and head counts. Bush also points out that it may be difficult to establish an accurate baseline, because much of the important data about previous projects will have been irrevocably lost, or was never measured in the first place; however, even a crude baseline is better than no baseline at all.

Note also that the level 1 and level 2 organizations will typically focus all their measurements on the *product* itself and will not measure anything about the process. This is because the level-one organization has no process that is applied consistently from one project to the next, and in the level 2 organization, the process is often broken only into macro-level steps like "analysis" and "design," with little attention to the hundreds of micro-level subactivities. Also, the level 2 organization may impose rigid accounting-oriented procedures on such activities as systems analysis, but may not offer any guidance on *how* to carry out the analysis activity; thus, one project may choose to use information engineering to carry out its systems analysis, while another project may choose to use structured analysis.

But metrics of the product are a beginning, and as the organization captures more and more data about the product, it will begin to have more and more interest in the process by which that product was developed. Thus, just as tools and processes are interdependent—a point we observed in Chapter 4—so metrics and processes are interdependent. Introducing basic metrics in the level 1 organization can help it on its way to achieving higher levels of process maturity.

7.4 SOME FINAL OBSERVATIONS ABOUT METRICS

From the foregoing comments, it follows that tool support is critical for efficient capturing of data. Thus, the organizations that are doing good work in software metrics are typically those that have already invested in some form of CASE technology for their workers. However, if the CASE tools are of the "lower-CASE" variety, then the metrics will tend to be slanted toward code-level metrics; perhaps this also explains why many of the industry-accepted metrics like function points and software defects have typically been applied to the product of the coding phase of the project. As design-level and analysis-level CASE tools become more prevalent, we should expect to see more interesting design-level and analysis-level metrics being published and discussed.

Linking the technical metrics to *business* metrics is the key issue for getting a metrics initiative accepted by senior management. Rubin [15] argues that while the metrics "currency" in MIS organizations may be function points and lines of code, the MIS organization must be able to translate its technical currency into business currency; for example, "an increase in productivity of x function points per year will increase corporate profits by y dollars per share."

However, acceptance of the software metrics initiative by project management and working-level technicians is just as important; if, for example, project managers feel that the metrics effort is just a nuisance that interferes with the *real* work of the project, they will ignore it or sabotage it. This means that the software metrics must be designed so that they help the manager *during* the project rather than providing an interesting postmortem after the project is over. While this may seem obvious, it is not always easy to accomplish, and it may require some unusual management decisions; managers at AG Communication Systems [16] report that the first people in the 900-person software organization to receive advanced workstations were the members of the software metrics group—so they would have the tools to analyze metrics data and produce metrics report in "real time" for the benefit of the project managers.

If the right cultural environment exists, the concept of software metrics will be perceived by the technical staff as a positive, not a negative, phenomenon; however, as mentioned earlier, it has to be clear from the very beginning that the objective of the metrics effort is not to catch the underperformers and punish the people with software defects, but rather to learn and improve the process. Depending on the morale in the organization, there may be some skepticism that management is really serious about this, and the first time a project manager misuses software metrics to reprimand someone who underperformed, cooperation from the troops in the trenches will disappear.

A final note: you should never be completely satisfied with the metrics you are capturing. Some will eventually prove irrelevant, and there will always be a need for new ones. Thus, the investment of people, tools, and other resources for software metrics should be regarded as an ongoing cost of doing business—just as the overall business regards the accountants who provide the P&L statement, balance sheet, and annual report as an ongoing cost of doing business.

END NOTES

1. DeMarco, Tom. *Controlling Software Projects*. Englewood Cliffs, NJ: Yourdon Press/Prentice Hall, 1982.
2. Card, David. *Measuring Design Quality*. Englewood Cliffs, NJ: Prentice Hall, 1990.
3. Strassmann, Paul. *Information Economics*. New York: Free Press/Macmillan, 1985.
4. Card, David. "What Makes a Software Measure Successful," *American Programmer*, September 1991.
5. Jones, Capers. *Applied Software Measurement*. New York: McGraw-Hill, 1991.
6. Albrecht, Alan J. "Measuring Application Development Productivity," *Proceedings of the Joint IBM SHARE/GUIDE Application Development Symposium*. Chicago: GUIDE International Corp., October 1979.
7. International Function Point User's Group, 5008 Pine Creek Drive, Westerville, OH 43081-4899. Phone 614-895-7130, fax 614-895-3466.
8. Schulmeyer, G. Gordon. *Zero Defect Software*. New York: McGraw-Hill, 1990.
9. Boehm, Barry. *Software Engineering Economics*. Englewood Cliffs, NJ: Prentice Hall, 1981.
10. Martin, James. *An Information Systems Manifesto*. Englewood Cliffs, NJ: Prentice Hall, 1983.
11. Putnam, Larry, and Ware Myers. *Measures for Excellence: Reliable Software on Time, Within Budget*. Englewood Cliffs, NJ: Yourdon Press/Prentice Hall, 1992.
12. DeMarco, Tom, and Timothy R. Lister. *Peopleware*. New York: Dorset House, 1987.
13. Grady, Robert, and Deborah Caswell. *Software Metrics: Establishing a Company-Wide Program*. Englewood Cliffs, NJ: Prentice Hall, 1988.
14. Bush, Marilyn. "Getting Started on Metrics—Jet Propulsion Laboratory Productivity and Quality," *Proceedings of the 12th International Conference on Software Engineering*, Nice, France, March 1990.
15. Rubin, Howard. "Measuring 'Rigor' and Putting Measurement into Action," *American Programmer*, September 1991.
16. Clay, Bud, Susan Webber, George Grzybowski, and Ed Yourdon. "The Software Metrics Program at AG Communication Systems," *American Programmer*, September 1991.

8

Software Quality Assurance

> There is a central quality which is the root criterion of life and spirit in a man, a town, a building, or a wilderness. This quality is objective and precise, but it cannot be named.

> The search which we make for this quality, in our own lives, is the central search of any person, and the crux of any individual person's story. It is the search for those moments and situations when we are most alive.
>
> Christopher Alexander
> *The Timeless Way of Building*

Everyone talks quality today. It's fashionable. It's what everyone wants to hear. *But less than 10 percent of U.S. software organizations are taking a world-class approach to software quality.*

One indication of the current popularity of quality is the rash of testimonials from chief executives of computer companies. Consider these two comments from IBM and Hewlett-Packard:

> In today's competitive environment, ignoring the quality issue is tantamount to corporate suicide.
>
> John Young
> CEO, Hewlett-Packard

> We believe quality improvements will reduce quality costs 50 percent over the years. For us that translates into billions of dollars of added potential profit.
>
> John Akers
> President and CEO, IBM

We begin this chapter by asking the metaphysical question, "What *is* software quality?" Then we will examine various approaches to achieving higher levels of software quality: creation of a software quality assurance (SQA) organization, causal analysis, and cultural approaches.

8.1 WHAT IS SOFTWARE QUALITY?

There is no point spending millions of dollars trying to improve software quality if we don't have a common agreement about what it *is*. Here are some common definitions of software quality:

- Absence of defects (no bugs)
- The difference between a "plain vanilla" and a luxury version of the product, for example, the difference between a VW and a Mercedes
- Fitness for use (as suggested by J. M. Juran)
- Something that meets specifications (as suggested by Phil Crosby)
- Adherence to ISO 9000 quality standards, which will become a general European quality standard in 1992

Dunn [1, 2] suggests that we look at the notion of software quality from a more pragmatic view by asking what we *see* when we look at a high-quality software product. In Dunn's view, what we see are a number of "ilities":

- Reliability
- Usability (and usefulness)
- Maintainability
- Salability (if management is going to pay more for quality, it ought to be assured that it is going to get a return on its investment)

One popular characterization of quality today is 6Σ *quality*, where Σ is the symbol for "standard deviation." In terms of software, this translates into a defect rate of approximately three to four defects per *million* lines of code; by contrast, the typical software product produced by the average software organization in the United States has three to four defects per *thousand* lines of code.[1]

Average companies are content to operate at a 99.98 percent level of quality, but that translates only to approximately 4Σ quality; by contrast, 6Σ is equivalent to a 99.9999998 percent level of quality. Improving from 3Σ to 4Σ requires a 10-fold improvement or (if quality is measured only by the absence of defects), a 10-fold reduction in bugs. A 30-fold improvement is required to go from 4Σ to 5Σ, and a 70-fold improvement is required to go from 5Σ to 6Σ.

Does this matter? In other industries, the best-in-class companies are typically at a 6Σ level of quality and they dominate their markets. And in some industries, customers have come to depend on this level of quality: the airline industry, for example, operates at 6.4Σ level of

---

[1] For function point fanatics, this means that the average organization has approximately 3 to 4 defects for every 10 function points, if they are using a conventional third generation programming language. The 6Σ level of quality is approximately 3 to 4 defects per 10,000 function points.

quality. In a typical year, the odds are approximately 2.5 million to one that an airplane journey will be something other than uneventful.

Does this matter in software? Ask the folks at Bell Labs who are concerned with the reliability of their switching system software. Until 1990, they thought that a defect rate of three to four defects per 100,000 lines of code was adequate; after all, it's a hundred times better than the average software organization. But a nationwide telephone outage on January 14, 1990—caused, of course, by a software error—made it evident that a higher level of quality was needed.[2]

8.2 WHAT IS SOFTWARE QUALITY ASSURANCE?

In many organizations, SQA is just a fancy name for testing. And testing is what programmers do to find bugs in their programs. Unfortunately, there are a number of problems with this classical view:

- *It assumes that people test their own programs.* And while it makes sense for people to participate in reviews of their programs, and perhaps even do some initial testing of their own, it has long been known that people cannot be expected to find all their own bugs.[3]

- *It assumes that bugs are an independent life form.* It is interesting that Americans typically use the term "bug" to describe a software defect; in the vocabulary of many software organizations, there are "live" bugs and "dead" bugs, big bugs and small bugs, killer bugs and sleeping bugs. But if they are treated as independent life forms, then there is no effort to associate the insertion of the bug into the program with something that the programmer did. By contrast, Japanese software organizations typically refer to defects as "spoilage."[4]

---

[2] Subsequent incidents of telephone outage in June 1991 have just emphasized this point. In the 1991 incidents, it appears that the problem was caused by inadequate testing of what was thought to be a "minor" modification to an existing system.

[3] Programmers are likely to suffer the same logic error(s) in creating test cases that they suffered when writing the code in the first place. And some would argue that programmers are psychologically disinclined to find bugs: they are more interested in demonstrating to the world that it *works*, not that it *breaks*.

[4] Mikio Ikoma, who works as chief of staff of the Inspection Department at the Software Works of Hitachi, Ltd., suggests that the cultural differences between American software and Japanese software may be deeper than just the characterization of defects as "bugs" or "spoilage." In a recent paper [3], he suggests that the heterogeneous culture of the United States may have led to an assumption that software bugs are heterogeneous (and can thus be modeled with software reliability models based on a Poisson arrival rate); the Japanese society, being more homogeneous, may have unconsciously assumed that the software defects it creates will also be homogeneous: if one bug is found in a program, the Japanese assume that it will have brothers and sisters, aunts and uncles clustered around it.

- *It assumes that testing is done only once, at the end of the development phase.* But world-class organizations know that testing, or perhaps more appropriately *defect prevention*, must be done in the earlier phases of systems development, for example, in analysis and design. If testing is delayed until the end of coding, it's too late. You can't test quality into a software product if it's not there to begin with.

- *It assumes that testing deals only with the **product**, not with the **process** by which the product was built.* As we have emphasized in earlier chapters of this book, the most significant improvements in quality and productivity come from improvements to the *process* of systems development, but as we saw in Chapter 4, this can occur only when everyone is following the same process in a standardized fashion.

Dunn [2] suggests a better definition of SQA and the role of the SQA organization:

> The job of SQA is to assure people that every effort has been made to ensure that software products have the desired "ilities."

Thus, in Dunn's view, a useful SQA program should concern itself with the following issues:

- Minimizing the number of defects in delivered software
- Creating mechanisms for controlling software development and maintenance so that schedules and costs are not impaired
- Making certain that the product can be used in its intended marketplace
- Improving the quality of future releases and future products

The important thing to realize here is that an SQA organization does not ensure quality by itself. *It cannot.* If your company has slapped a newly created SQA group onto the side of its existing software development organization, in the hopes that it will magically introduce quality into the delivered products, it might as well ask the SQA group, in its spare time, to transmute lead into gold.

Software quality is built into a software product, from the beginning, through the caliber of the people who create it, from the technology used to create it, and by means of a management discipline that oversees the process. An SQA group is part of this last component, management discipline. And an SQA group can ensure the planning and execution of a quality program involving all three elements: good people, good technology, and good management discipline.

Approximately 75 percent of U.S. software development organizations have an independent SQA group. However, a recent survey by the American Society of Quality Control [4] indicates that the state of the practice of SQA is abysmal. The survey found the following depressing statistics:

- Most SQA personnel have no formal training in quality.
- Less than 25 percent of SQA personnel have professional SQA certifications.
- Most SQA groups do not use a statistical approach to quality control.
- Only 12 percent of U.S. companies use hard indicators to quantify quality.
- Only 10 percent use a Pareto analysis.
- Only 6 percent use an "error-prone" analysis to identify high-risk software components.[5]
- Very few companies use commercial SQA tools.
- Only 4 percent use software reliability models (e.g., those developed by Littlewood, Shooman, Musa, et al.).
- Only 7 percent use software complexity models (e.g., those developed by McCabe or Halstead).
- Only 13 percent formally quantify the cost of their SQA program in order to determine a "cost of quality."

8.3 HOW DO COMPANIES PURSUE SOFTWARE QUALITY?

A recent CASE survey [5] provided some additional depressing statistics on the method(s) organizations used to pursue quality; the results are summarized in Figure 8.1.

Obviously, for 42 percent of the organizations, *anything* would be better than what they are doing now. Or, to put it another way, if a company simply announces that it is in favor of quality, but doesn't do anything about it, nothing will happen.

---

[5] Most organizations that *do* perform such an analysis find that 5 percent of the code is responsible for 50 percent of the defects, and 10 percent of the code is responsible for 90 percent of the defects. The key, of course, is to identify *which* 10 percent is high risk.

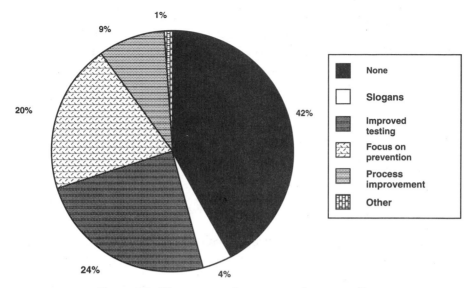

Figure 8.1: How companies pursue software quality

A small percentage of companies rely on slogans, for example, "Quality Is Job Number One" or similar mindless phrases. This makes great television commercials, but is unlikely to have an impact on the actual work being performed. Unless it is combined with some positive management action, nothing will happen. Indeed, even an increased emphasis on testing, an approach favored by 24 percent of the respondents, is not likely to have a dramatic effect on software quality; as Capers Jones points out, most forms of testing are less than 30 percent efficient in finding defects.[6]

A formal SQA organization is needed, but simply creating the organization isn't enough. *The culture of the organization must change.* An example of an organizational approach that focuses on defect prevention and process improvement—the remaining two categories shown in Figure 8.1—is discussed in Section 8.5.

While the statistics shown are depressing, they also offer enormous opportunities for organizations that want to be world-class competitors: it would be much tougher if everyone were doing a good job at software quality! The optimistic thing to remember is that there

---

[6] An organization determined to use testing as its form of quality assurance should at least couple it with Fagan-style inspections. Michael Fagan's original work at IBM was published in 1976 [6, 7]. Another good source is Freedman and Weinberg's book on inspections [8].

are software complexity models [9] and there *are* software reliability models, in the form of commercially available products, that can be used to predict mean time between failures (MTBF) for software systems as well as predict the number of undiscovered defects in a system about to be released to the user community.

Indeed, there are now management models showing the impact of "crunch-mode" project management on software quality and defects. In the past, managers have typically only grappled with the trade-offs between time, people, and functionality when political pressure is applied on a project to "hurry up" the schedule. But Putnam's research [10] can be used to show senior management the expected (probabilistic) number of defects remaining in a system at all states of development, and what it will cost them to put a "buggy" system into operation prematurely. Putnam's model can be used to predict when the number of software defects will fall to a level where the system can be said to have reached "operational capability." An example is shown in Figure 8.2.

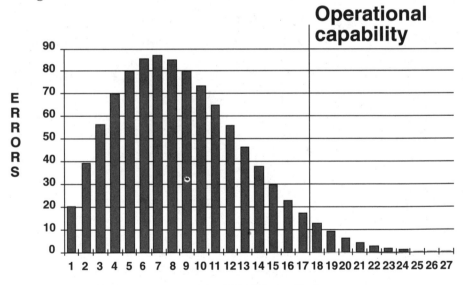

Figure 8.2: Putnam's software reliability model

8.4 CULTURAL APPROACHES TO SOFTWARE QUALITY

Zultner [11] argues that a cultural approach is necessary to instill higher levels of quality. Drawing on Deming's "14 points," Zultner recommends the following 14 steps for creating a quality culture in a software development organization:

1. Create constancy of purpose for the *improvement* of systems and service.
2. Adopt the new philosophy of quality.
3. Cease dependence on mass inspection (especially testing) to achieve quality.
4. End the practice of awarding business on price alone. *Minimize total cost.*
5. Constantly and forever improve the systems development process.
6. Institute training on the job.
7. Institute leadership.
8. Drive out fear so that everyone may work effectively.
9. Break down barriers between areas. *People must work as a team.*
10. Eliminate slogans, exhortations, and targets that ask for zero defects and new levels of productivity. (Slogans do not build quality systems.)
11. Eliminate numerical quotas and goals. *Substitute leadership.*
12. Remove barriers to pride of workmanship.
13. Institute a vigorous program of education and self-improvement for *everyone.*
14. Put *everyone* to work to accomplish the transformation.

8.5 CAUSAL ANALYSIS

One of the most effective organizational "techniques" for improving software quality is an approach known as *causal analysis.* It is a defect prevention process and a systematic method for identifying problem areas. Causal analysis is part of the development process; it emphasizes not just the discovery of defects, but also an evaluation of what caused the defect to occur. Though a team problem-solving process, software engineers evaluate their own defects. Most important, the causal analysis approach provides feedback that can improve the use of tools, improve the training and education provided to software engineers, and improve the overall development process itself.

As practiced at AG Communication Systems [12], causal analysis takes the form shown in Figure 8.3. A variation is suggested by Tom Gilb [13], as shown in Figure 8.4.

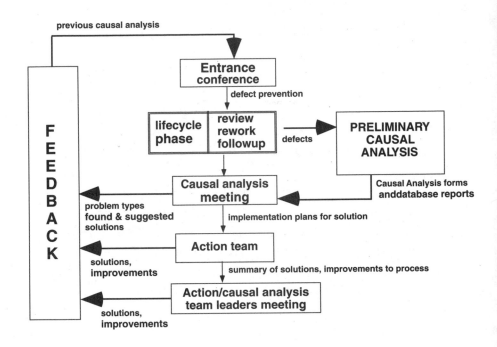

Figure 8.3: The AGCS causal analysis process

At the beginning of each life-cycle phase (analysis, design, coding, etc.), an "entrance conference" is held to review deliverables from the previous phase, review process/methodology guidelines, review appropriate checklists, and set team quality goals. These activities serve as a *defect prevention* process, since they focus the team's attention on the process-oriented details of the project activity they are about to begin.

During the life-cycle phase itself, the organization schedules normal reviews (also known as inspections, walkthroughs, etc.) to review each work-product; if defects are discovered, some "rework" may be required, with follow-up reviews. But most important, as indicated in Figure 8.3, the defects themselves are subjected to a preliminary causal analysis activity.

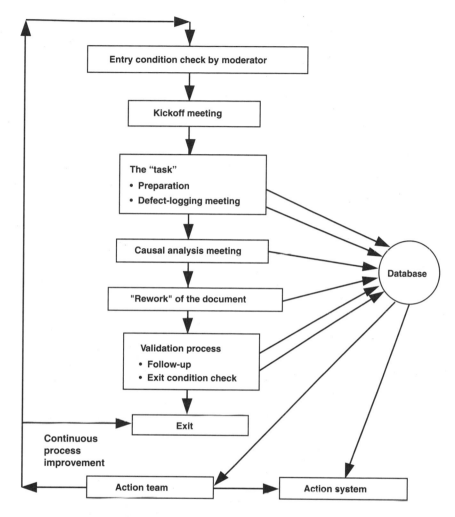

Figure 8.4: Gilb's view of causal analysis

The causal analysis meetings emphasize *individual* analysis of problems. As Gilb [13] describes it,

A sample of defects logged is sufficient. Somewhere between a few and 20 defects are discussed. These defects are taken as samples of current reality. Their cause is assumed to be faults in the process (which then cause individuals to make errors). The primary purpose here is not deep analysis but rather putting the problem on the agenda. It appears that about three minutes per "action item" is sufficient. Any additional time for serious analysis should be spent by the action team . . . .

First, the selected defect is noted—usually a severe defect—so that all participants can find it on their documentation set. Then, a category is guessed at, primarily to aid discussion—for example, education, omission, transcription, or oversight. Then, generic defect causes are listed, using a minute of time and key phrases like "programmer training" or "no inspections of the source." Finally, a minute is given to brainstorming potential actions that participants believe might remove the problem category from the process in the future and that they personally might find acceptable.

An important part of the causal analysis activity is the addition of defect items to a database. Each database entry should contain a description of the defect, a description of how the defect was resolved, and a preliminary analysis of the cause of the defect.

At the end of the life-cycle phase, the AGCS causal analysis approach calls for another meeting. This meeting consists of another brainstorming session to analyze the cause of defects, an evaluation of results versus the goals that had been established in the entry conference, and a list of suggested process improvements.

An action team then responds to the improvement suggestions. In the AGCS approach, this team is led by a manager and includes people from the tools group, the training department, and the process group, but Gilb [13] describes the action team in a more general fashion:

> The action team consists of anyone who evaluates the action items and other related data in the database. It is responsible for improving the process. There are at least two different variations:
>
> *Local.* In a local team, the inspection participants themselves take responsibility for doing some further analysis and process improvement work.
>
> Typically, one individual takes responsibility (with a formal indication to the moderator) to follow up the action items within a week, involving perhaps two hours of work. However, some of the best resulting process changes occur when a small group of about three actually works out a useful practical and economic solution.
>
> As IBM found, the disadvantage of the local group is that its members are typically already members of project teams and that their project manager tends not to permit them to work on future process improvements at the expense of the short-term deadline pressure.

Global. IBM's reported action teams are "offline" to the project groups and inspectors doing the causal analysis. They are separately managed and budgeted, and they are specially trained to do process analysis and correction. They may do it themselves or employ other groups to do it (e.g., consultants or quality circles), but they maintain primary responsibility for selecting the problems to be solved and for reporting progress on solutions.

Generally, the action team should be responsible for the following:

- Prioritization of action items
- Status tracking of action items
- Implementation of action items
- Dissemination of feedback
- Administration of the causal analysis database
- Generic analysis
- Visibility of success stories

8.6 A PASSION FOR QUALITY

If everyone is in favor of software quality, why aren't more organizations doing something about it? Why is it that some 42 percent of software organizations indicate that they are in favor of quality, but don't do anything about it? Zultner [11] suggests that a number of cultural obstacles are to blame:

1. Lack of constancy of purpose.
2. Emphasis on short-term schedules.
3. Evaluation of performance, merit rating, and annual reviews.
4. Mobility of software professionals and managers.
5. Managing by "visible figures" alone.
6. Excessive personnel costs.
7. Excessive maintenance costs.

Perhaps there is a simpler explanation for many organizations: *a lack of passion.* To illustrate this, consider the following question:

If you are competing against another company for a software project, do you think that cost or quality or development schedule will be most important?

In the overwhelming majority of U.S. software organizations, the answer would be "cost" or "schedule." But listen to the response from Tomoo Matsubara at Hitachi Software Engineering:

> Quality is first! *Always* first! If we deliver bad quality to the customer, the customer will complain many times, over and over. But if we are late, he will complain only once—and then maybe he will forget. And if we have underestimated the cost, the customer will not complain at all—for he will not know we have made the mistake. We will bear the burden of the cost mistake.

This is the voice of the world-class software organization. This is the answer I received consistently when I visited all the major software organizations in Japan [14].

As another example of a passion for quality, consider NEC's software organization, which holds internal semiannual software quality conferences for its professional staff. NEC software engineers are asked to submit technical papers to be presented at the conference; Figure 8.5 shows the number of papers submitted over a six-year period ending in 1988.[7]

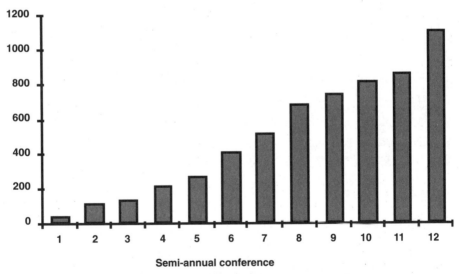

Semi-annual conference

Figure 8.5: Technical papers submitted at NEC's semiannual software quality conferences

[7] A colleague tells me that the chairman of NEC opens the conference and then sits in the center of the front row throughout the entire two-day conference. The story is apocryphal, but may well be true.

By contrast, a report in *The Wall Street Journal* of October 4, 1990 reported on a Gallup survey for the American Society of Quality Control, in which over half of 1,237 corporate employees said their companies claimed that quality is a top priority; however, only 14 percent said their company followed through with effective programs, and only 1 in 7 felt that his or her company offered a chance to participate in quality decisions.

8.7 STRATEGIC IMPLICATIONS

What can senior management do to improve the software quality situation in their organization? Creating a formal SQA group is necessary, of course, and an investment in tools and techniques that will lead to higher-quality systems is a prerequisite. But most of all, management must make a demonstrable commitment to quality.

Quality should be defined in specific, quantifiable terms that all the players in the organization can understand. The organizational structure should be realigned, if necessary, so that those responsible for quality have the authority to provide input at a senior level in the organization. There should be a clearly understood reward system for quality—otherwise, why will anyone bother? And the trade-offs between quality and other constraints (budgets, schedules, etc.) should be clearly articulated.[8]

And what if management doesn't listen? One possibility is to change the culture without changing the management structure. The "quiet revolution" espoused by DeMarco and Lister [15] suggests that the software engineer should improve quality for his or her own personal satisfaction, even if the organization doesn't know about it, care about it, or approve of it. And indeed there are a thousand minor day-to-day decisions that senior management doesn't know about; the software engineer might well take the attitude, *what they don't know won't hurt them, and might even help them.*

But I recommend open revolution; at the very least, I suggest that you try Apple Computer's notion of "empowerment." *Push back.* If management tells you, implicitly or explicitly, to do something that clearly and irrevocably destroys quality, *just say "no!"* Here are some examples:

---

[8]However, note that this is a typical American perspective. Ikoma [3] suggests that in Japan, there is no trade off.

- If they ask you to "speed up testing," *just say "no!"*
- If they say, "don't worry about a few bugs . . .," *just say "no!"*
- If they say, "we'll pin down the specifications later, just start coding," *just say "no!"*
- If they say, "don't worry, this is just a beta test version, so it doesn't matter if it has bugs in it," *just say "no!"*
- If they say, "I don't care if there *are* bugs, we gotta get this system delivered by January 1," *just say "no!"*

None of this will make you popular. Indeed, you need to be prepared to vote with your feet. But wouldn't it be more fun to work for a company that cares about quality as much as you do?

END NOTES

1. Dunn, Robert. "SQA: A Management Perspective," *American Programmer*, November 1990.
2. Dunn, Robert. *Software Quality: Concepts and Plans*. Englewood Cliffs, NJ: Prentice Hall, 1990.
3. Ikoma, Mikio. "Japan–United States Structural Impediments in Software Quality Assurance," *American Programmer*, November 1990.
4. Gruman, Galen. "Management Cited in Bleak SQA Survey," *IEEE Softwar*, Vol. 5, no. 3, May 1988, pp. 102–103.
5. Boone, Gregory H., Vaughan P. Merlyn, and Roger R. Dobratz. *The Second Annual Report on CASE*. Bellevue, WA: CASE Research Corporation, 1990.
6. Fagan, Michael E., "Advances in Software Inspection," *IEEE Transactions on Software Engineering*, Vol. SE-12, no. 7, July 1986.
7. Fagan, Michael E. "Design and Code Inspections to Reduce Errors in Program Development," *IBM Systems Journal*, Vol. 15, no. 3, 1976.
8. Freedman, Daniel P., and Gerald M. Weinberg. *Handbook of Walkthroughs, Inspections, and Technical Reviews*, 3rd ed. New York: Dorset House, 1990.
9. DeMarco, Tom. *Controlling Software Projects*. Englewood Cliffs, NJ: Yourdon Press/Prentice Hall, 1982.
10. Putnam, Larry, and Ware Myers. *Measures for Excellence: Reliable Software on Time, Within Budget*. Englewood Cliffs, NJ: Yourdon Press/Prentice Hall, 1991.

11. Zultner, Richard E. "Software Quality Engineering: The Deming Way," *American Programmer*, June 1989.
12. Clay, Bud, George Grzybowski, Susan Webber, and Edward Yourdon. "Quality Metrics at AG Communication Systems," *American Programmer*, September 1991.
13. Gilb, Tom. "Advanced Defect Prevention Using Inspection, Testing, and Field Data as a Base," *American Programmer*, May 1991.
14. Yourdon, Edward. "The Two Faces of Japanese Software," *American Programmer*, December 1988.
15. DeMarco, Tom, and Timothy R. Lister. *Peopleware*. New York: Dorset House, 1987.

9

Software Reusability

9.0 INTRODUCTION

Software reusability will go down in history as one of the major technical contributors to software productivity and quality in the 1990s. Even though we have talked about reusability since the 1960s (or before), we have rarely practiced it effectively in most organizations. But the DP organizations that survive the decade of the 1990s will be those that have achieved high levels of reusability; if your organization doesn't have plans to capitalize on this technology, it, and you, are in trouble.

In this chapter, we first examine why software reusability is so important. Then we look at the reasons why reusability is *not* being practiced in many organizations. Next, we take a closer look at the definition of "reusability" and see that it can mean many different things: there are many "levels" of reusability. Finally, we examine the technological and organizational means of achieving higher levels of reusability; while the technological solutions are important, the organizational solutions are far more important.

9.1 WHY DOES IT MATTER?

Software reusability has been glorified as a Boy Scout virtue since I first learned how to write a computer program in 1963, and probably for many years before that. Like loyalty, thrift, and bravery, software reusability is something that everyone believes in, and that most people try to practice from time to time. A few digital Gandhis have managed to achieve high levels of software reusability, but most of us software sinners have not even made a serious attempt—all we do is talk about it.

What do we mean by "high level of software reusability"? Here is a simple rule of thumb: the best DP organizations are achieving reusability levels of 70 to 80 percent, while the typical shop achieves levels more on the order of 20 to 30 percent. Thus, when faced with the task of building a system requiring 100,000 lines of code, the good shop writes 20,000–30,000 lines of new code and reuses 70,000–80,000 lines of code from a library of reusable components. The bad shop treats the

100,000-line system as an intellectual exercise never before tackled by the human race and writes 70,000–80,000 lines of new code, with only 20,000–30,000 lines taken from a library. To make matters worse, the bad shop has little or no control over the manner in which the code is reused; the typical approach is to make a physical copy of the code to be reused and then make slight alterations as needed.

The primary benefit of software reusability is, of course, higher productivity. In a superficial sense, the DP shop that achieves 80 percent reusability is four times as productive as the DP shop with 20 percent reusability. However, the savings are rarely this great, because the benefits of reusability require

- An investment to create the reusable components in the first place. This "capital investment" is then amortized over the number of new systems or programs that can make use of those components. Obviously, the more often the components can be reused, the less onerous the initial capital investment.

- An investment to perform higher levels of testing and quality assurance than would normally be expected for unique software components. Higher levels of testing and QA are required by, and justified by, the higher levels of usage. Most organizations find that they need two to four times as much testing for reusable components as for unique components.

- An investment to maintain libraries, browsers, and other facilities so that software engineers can *find* the reusable components when they need them. This can range from a simple index of available components to an online, interactive expert system search facility based on keywords, and so on.

Nevertheless, it is not unusual to see DP shops achieving productivity increases of 50 to 200 percent from serious, deliberate use of software reusability.

There is another reason to emphasize reusability: *increased quality*. As mentioned, a reusable software component always requires more testing and quality assurance than its nonreusable brethren—simply because the consequences of an error are that much more serious. But if this is the bad news, the good news is that modules with heavy reuse will, by definition, have higher quality than ordinary modules; in simple parlance, the bugs are shaken out much more quickly and thoroughly. Thus, building a new system with a large percentage of reusable modules means that we are using modules with the "Good

Housekeeping Seal of Approval"; while we may still suffer from problems of poor specifications or bad designs, at least the basic software building blocks will be solid.

There is another benefit that is often overlooked: reusability can provide a mechanism for *prototyping;* as several researchers at the Software Productivity Consortium point out, "Reusability and prototyping are two sides of the same coin." Many current approaches to prototyping depend on high-level languages and/or screen-painting tools to build a quick-and-dirty "skeleton" version of a system; the problem is that while the external facade of the system may look impressive to the user, there is nothing behind the facade—no functionality that the user can exercise to see if the prototype is actually doing something useful. A prototype built from reusable components, on the other hand, can provide full functionality, since it is built from fully coded and fully tested components, and because the components already exist, the prototype should be just as easy and quick to build as any other form of prototype.

9.2 WHY AREN'T WE DOING IT?

If reusability is such a good thing, why aren't we doing more of it? There are four major reasons:

- Software engineering textbooks teach new practitioners to build systems from "first principles"; reusability is not promoted or even discussed.

- The "not invented here" (NIH) syndrome, and the intellectual challenge of solving an interesting software problem in one's own unique way, prevents the reuse of someone else's software component.

- Unsuccessful experiences with software reusability in the past have convinced many practitioners and DP managers that the concept is not practical.

- Most organizations provide no reward for reusability. Productivity is measured in terms of *new* lines of code written, and reused lines of code are typically discounted by 50 percent or more.

Let's examine each of these problems in more detail.

9.2.1 Software Textbooks Don't Teach Reusability

Almost every textbook and every university course in programming, systems design, systems analysis, or software engineering teaches the student how to solve problems, design systems, and write code "from scratch." In a few rare cases, the student might be taught a form of "bottom–up" design, in which she begins with existing library modules and composes larger aggregates to solve the desired problem. But in most cases, the student is given a blank sheet of paper (or an empty CASE workstation) and is instructed to analyze/design/code "top–down"—for example, by identifying major functions and decomposing them into smaller subfunctions. Nowhere is the student told that the problem she is solving has probably been solved hundreds of times before and that the most practical approach is to find an *existing* approximate solution and refine it to meet her special needs. Indeed, most universities would consider this a form of plagiarism and would penalize the student heavily for such "unethical" behavior!

Not surprisingly, this educational bias becomes deeply ingrained and stays with the student when she joins the work force. No wonder so many junior programmers experience severe culture shock when they learn that their first job (possibly for several years!) will be to maintain musty old programs written by previous generations of programmers.

9.2.2 The NIH Syndrome

The NIH syndrome is pervasive in American industry; it is certainly not confined to software development! In every field of business, science, and engineering, people have an innate urge to reinvent the wheel, solving age-old problems over and over again.

The NIH syndrome is particularly acute in software development, perhaps because each design problem appears to the novice software engineer to be such a novel puzzle. And as we know, any software problem—no matter how small—has myriad possible solutions. Some solutions are faster, some are slower; some are larger, some are smaller; some are more elegant, some less so; indeed, some solutions are more reusable, and others are less reusable. But all the solutions can be correct; like a game of chess, there are an infinite number of ways to play the game and win.

The important thing to realize is that the novice software engineer derives great intellectual pleasure from solving familiar problems—whether it is a binary sort, a missile trajectory calculation, or a FICA tax calculation—on her own, with the possibility of *possibly* finding a better solution.

In most cases, software engineers eventually grow tired of reinventing solutions to problems *they themselves* have already solved;

sooner or later, the novelty and excitement wanes. The journeyman software engineer gradually builds his own personal library of previously solved problems, through which he rummages whenever faced with a new problem that has familiar overtones.

We should not fault the curiosity of fledgling software engineers, or their desire to find a better solution to age-old software problems; after all, this is how progress is made. In any case, it is human nature.

However, it is important for a DP shop to provide the appropriate encouragement, incentive, and education so that the software engineer can begin focusing his intellectual energy on problems that have *not* been solved, while reusing existing solutions to problems that *have* been solved. As we will see shortly, this encouragement is often lacking.

9.2.3 Unsuccessful Experiences with Reusability

Obviously, the notion of software reusability is not a new concept—and it would be unfair and inaccurate to suggest that no one has tried to accomplish it. Indeed, many DP shops did try to implement reusable libraries in the 1960s and 1970s; however, the results were often so unimpressive that the effort was abandoned.

Why have previous results been unsuccessful, and what can we learn from the failures? In my experience, the difficulties with software reusability have either been pure management failures, pure technical failures, or a combination of the two. The most common causes were the following:

Management Failures

- *Inadequate resources or investment.* Reusability doesn't happen merely as a result of management slogans and exhortations. The resources required to build, maintain, and manage a reusable library obviously depends on a number of factors, but the dollar investment can be quite high: one division of Motorola estimated the cost at $1 million (but was easily able to justify the cost with a return-on-investment calculation).

- *Not creating a separate group to create reusable software components.* As discussed shortly, it is unrealistic to assume that software engineers will have the time, energy, and foresight to create reusable software components while trying to develop software for a specific project. A separate group of reusable component producers is needed.

- *Not rewarding software engineers for reusability.* This is discussed in more detail in Section 9.2.4.

Management/Technical Failures

- *Inadequate configuration control.* If the organization can't keep track of which version of which reusable components are currently used in which systems, the reusability effort will get out of control and eventually collapse.

- *Inadequate searching/browsing/lookup mechanisms.* If you don't know where the reusable components are, or if you can't find one that meets your needs, you won't use it. Developing an adequate searching mechanism is partly a technical problem and a potentially non-trivial problem: some have suggested the need for expert system AI technology to match the needs of a component user with the features of library components. But it's also a management problem: if management doesn't invest resources to build a library retrieval mechanism, it will never get built.

- *Too little control over what gets put into the library.* The result is often an enormous amount of low-quality junk, with overlapping functionality, undocumented features, and so on. As an example, Tom DeMarco (former president of the U.S. Modula-2 User's Group) recently described the Modula-2 library: "It has 30,000 procedures and is virtually useless."

Technical Failures

- *Including software components that are too large and/or have too many side effects.* This was one of the most common problems with reusable libraries in the 1960s: there was a tendency to create "general-purpose" components that attempted to do all things for all people under all conditions. The result typically was that the component didn't do anything terribly well for anyone, and often had disastrous, and totally unacceptable, side effects (such as clearing a CRT screen before displaying some desired text). A better example of reusable components—indeed, the *ideal* example, in my opinion—is the Unix library, whose components are tiny (often less than 10 lines of code), and with no side effects.

- *Undocumented interfaces.* If the software engineer can't figure out what input parameters are required, and what output parameters are produced, by the reusable software component, it's virtually impossible to use.

- *No facility for exceptions and overrides.* In many cases, the software engineer will say, "I need something like module X in the library . . .

but just a little bit different." The "little bit different" may involve slightly more or slightly less functionality, different data parameters, a different calling sequence, and so on. Traditional software development techniques couldn't deal with this: one had to use all the reusable module or none of it, and consequently, the software engineer often decided not to use any of it. With today's workstation environments and Macintosh-like graphical user interfaces, the programmer can, in the most primitive case, use a "cut and paste" approach to scavenge (and thus partially reuse) source code from a library; a far better approach is provided by many object-oriented programming environments, which allow the software engineer to create subclasses of standard objects in order to create the needed overrides and exceptions.

- *Software overhead required to compile, link, and execute the reusable module.* If a reusable module could be found in the 1960s and 1970s, it often imposed an unacceptable overhead of CPU cycles and/or memory for compilation, link editing, and execution. While the overhead still exists today, it is much easier to tolerate with multimegabyte memory space and processors that are typically 10 to 100 times faster than predecessor machines.

9.2.4 No Rewards for Software Reusability

Many DP shops *do* emphasize productivity today. Indeed, productivity—whether measured in lines of code or function points—has been one of the most important measures of a DP shop's effectiveness for three decades or more.

But the sad fact is that almost all DP shops measure productivity in terms of *new* code written by the software engineer; no credit is given for modules or software components that have been reused. No reward or recognition is offered the software engineer who has a higher level of reusability in his code than his peers.

Some organizations *do* count reused code, but with only a fraction the value of new code. Thus, a system consisting of 100,000 lines of new code and 100,000 lines of code taken from a reusable library will be given the same productivity value as 150,000 lines of new code. What the organization *should* be doing is measuring the productivity of *delivered* functionality to the end user, not the number of lines of newly invented code that frequently repeats the intellectual effort done by dozens of previous software engineers.

Within reasonable limits, software engineers behave just like Pavlov's dogs: if they are rewarded for writing new code, they will write more new code; if their efforts to reuse existing code are effectively penalized, then they will avoid making the effort.

Sometimes the problem is more insidious. The DP shop may promote the benefits of reusability, and may even give full credit to the software engineer who reuses existing code in lieu of writing new code. But there is still a problem: Where does the reusable code come from in the first place? As mentioned earlier, additional effort—over and above what one would expect for a "normal" software component—is required to design, code, test, and perform quality assurance on a software component that is intended *from the outset* to be reusable; a good rule of thumb is that such reusable components will take twice the effort of a "one-shot" component. For the software engineer and the DP manager working to finish a specific project on time and within budget, the question is: Where is the time, and the budget to invest in the creation of reusable software components? This is more than an academic question, for without such an investment, there may be no library of reusable components, and without a library, there will be no reusability.

The problem is typically the result of the *focus* of productivity efforts in most DP shops. Most DP organizations tend to concentrate on *individual* productivity improvements through tools, techniques, training, and so on. A few focus on *project-level* productivity, using networked CASE tools, JAD sessions, and so on. But software reusability should be aimed at *enterprise* productivity, and the DP organization must treat it as a capital investment rather than hoping each software engineer will have the inspiration, dedication, and energy to create reusable software components for the good of the enterprise in his or her spare time.

Indeed, this strongly suggests that the DP shop should have a separate group of software engineers devoted to the development of highly reusable software components. We will discuss this in more detail in Section 9.5.

9.3 LEVELS OF REUSABILITY

Much of the foregoing discussion implied that the major "asset" to be reused in a software development organization is *code*, that is, executable statements in C, Pascal, COBOL, or FORTRAN (or even, shudder, assembly language!). As we will see, reusability involves much more than just code . . . but since code is what everyone talks about, let's start with code.

9.3.1 Reusing Code

What's involved in reusing code? The phrase "code reuse" usually conjures up images of making a subroutine call to a module in a library, but it can take any of the forms listed here:

- *Cut and paste of source code.* This has been taking place since programs were first written on punched cards and stone tablets. In some cases, the code is reused in exactly the same form as the original; in other cases, as mentioned, it may be modified to suit slightly different circumstances. Obviously, this approach is better than no reuse at all, but it is the most primitive of all forms of reuse. In earlier days, there was a significant clerical cost associated with transcribing the code to be reused, but that has largely disappeared with today's cut and paste text editors; nevertheless, the software engineer runs the risk of introducing errors during the copying (and modification) of the original code. Worse is the configuration management problem: it is generally impossible for the DP manager to keep track of the multiple mutated uses of the original "chunk" of code. Nevertheless, this is probably the most commonly practiced form of reuse today.

- *Source-level "includes."* Most high-level programming languages contain a mechanism for copying, or "including," source program text from a library. In COBOL, for example, the COPY statement is used for this purpose; in C, the INCLUDE statement does the same job. In some languages, the specified library file is copied verbatim; in others, parameter substitution can be used to accomplish a minor amount of customization. Most often, the "include" facility is used to copy standard data definitions or parameter values, which we will discuss further in Section 9.3.2; however, it can also be used to copy executable program statements. In the latter case, a disadvantage of the "include" facility is that a copy of the specified statements is made *each* time the include statement is invoked; thus, it tends to be used primarily for "tiny" macros or functions that involve only two or three executable statements.

- *Binary links.* Most programming languages also provide for "external" calls to subroutines, procedures, or functions contained in a library. These external functions have already been compiled or assembled, but they must still be incorporated into the program that invokes them; this is usually done during a "load" or "link-edit" step after compilation of the main program. The primary advantage of this form of reuse is that only one physical copy of the reused component needs to be included, regardless of the number of times it is invoked; the linkage is accomplished through subroutine calls or function invocations.

* *Execution time invocation.* The problem with all three forms of source code reuse mentioned is that programmers must know, at the time they write their code, *which* component they wish to reuse; the "binding" of the reused component takes place at coding time, compile time, or link-edit time. In some cases, though, programmers may need the flexibility to allow their program to determine, *at execution time,* which component should be invoked. Some programming languages facilitate this by allowing the definition of *dynamic* functions/procedures, the identity (or address) of which will be resolved at runtime.

9.3.2 Reusing Data

As mentioned, source code "include" or "copy" mechanisms are typically used by programmers to reuse data declarations, for example, table layouts, record definitions, and "global" parameter assignments. When I was a novice programmer, one of my mentors passed on the advice, "The only literal constants you should ever have in a program are zero and one—and I'm not even sure about those!" That's still good advice in the 1990s—even for "natural" constants like 3.14159, which should *always* be defined with a symbolic parameter in a separate parameter file and "include-d" in any program that needs the value.

With the advent of CASE technology, the obvious manifestation of reusable data is the CASE repository. This will make possible not only reusable data declarations, but also reusable declarations of all kinds: data flow diagrams, entity–relationship diagrams, physical database designs, structure charts, and the like. The most trivial form of reuse facilitated by a CASE repository is code reuse and parameter-definition reuse that the programmer is concerned with; the more important forms are *design* reuse and *analysis* reuse, discussed shortly.

9.3.3 Reusing Designs

The major problem with any form of code reuse is that coding takes place after the hard part is done in a project: analysis and design.

For years, we have known that coding consumes only 10 to 15 percent of the time and effort of a project, so any attempt to increase coding productivity—whether through reuse, higher-level languages, or pure black magic—can only have a limited impact on overall project productivity. Nevertheless, almost all the historical attempts at implementing reuse were focused on code-level components.

Today, the world-class software organizations realize that much more significant results can be achieved through reuse at the design or specification level. As Biggerstaff and Lubars [1] point out, code reuse typically occurs only at the bottom levels of a system design hierarchy; design reuse, though, typically results in whole "branches" of the tree structure being reused. This is illustrated in Figure 9.1.

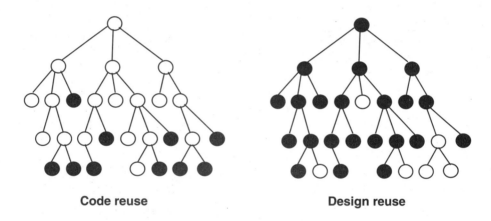

Code reuse   **Design reuse**

Figure 9.1: Code reuse versus design reuse

9.3.4 Reusing Specifications

If design reuse is good, then analysis reuse—the reuse of specifications—is even better, for it allows us to eliminate completely the effort involved in designing, coding, and testing an implementation of that specification. In the 1970s, specification-level reuse was virtually impossible, as most software organizations depended on textual "Victorian novel" documents to describe user requirements. By the 1990s, with the advent of graphical techniques such as structured analysis, specification-level reuse was an interesting concept—but still largely impractical, since the specifications were typically developed as paper documents and generally not kept up to date.

In the 1990s, though, we will see the world-class software organizations moving aggressively toward specification-level reuse, because the specification "models"—data flow diagrams, entity–relationship diagrams, state–transition diagrams, "structured English" process specifications, and so on—are maintained in CASE repositories. Thus, during the analysis phase of a project, the systems analyst should be able to browse through a corporate repository of previously completed projects, looking for similar specifications that could be used as the starting point for the next new project. One of the more exciting forms of specification-level reuse will be *designware*, discussed in Section 9.4.3.

9.3.5 Miscellaneous Examples of Reuse

While code, data, designs, and specifications are the most obvious candidates for reuse, they are not the only ones. World-class software organizations are looking at *all* work-products in a system development project to see if they can be captured and stored in a form for subsequent reuse. Some of the possible candidates are

- Cost–benefit calculations and estimates
- User documentation
- Feasibility studies
- Test data sets

Finally, consider one component that *cannot* be stored in a repository: the people who make up the project team. The experience, infrastructure, and camaraderie formed by a project team during one project should be carried over—that is, reused—in the next project wherever possible. While this may seem to be common sense, it is not common in the typical software shop: teams are busted apart at the end of the project, and the individuals are scattered to the wind and reassigned to other projects. As we pointed out in Chapter 4, *peopleware* approaches to software productivity often achieve results several times greater than technical approaches; this applies to reuse, too.

9.4 TECHNOLOGICAL APPROACHES TO REUSABILITY

From a technical perspective, software reusability can be accomplished by any of the following mechanisms:

- Component libraries
- Object-oriented development techniques
- Designware
- Design recovery

Each of these is discussed next.

9.4.1 Component Libraries

The foregoing discussion suggests that modern CASE repositories will gradually become the "storehouse" of reusable software components. But, today, most organizations equate reusability with "libraries"—typically source code libraries of functions, subroutines, or (in the case of object-oriented programming languages) *classes*. "Parameter files," COPY libraries, and libraries of file layouts and record definitions are also common examples.

Thus, if I wanted to verify that a software development organization was "serious" about reusability, I would look closely at its existing library. How well documented are the library components? What kind of configuration management is used to keep track of current and previous versions of the library components? How well tested are the components?[1] What kind of browsing and searching mechanisms are available to help software engineers find useful components? Who is allowed to insert new components into the library? Without satisfactory answers to these questions, the mere existence of a "reusable library" is hardly noteworthy.

If the organization is emphasizing code-level reuse, then it is also interesting to ask these questions: How many components are in the library, and how big are they? Successful organizations typically have libraries with 200 to 400 components; an organization with more than 1000 components is likely to have very little usage of its components. This strongly suggests that the real-world mechanism for effective reuse is that the software engineers gradually "internalize" the identity and basic features of those 200 to 400 components; they may not remember all the technical details (e.g., the calling sequence or the

---

[1] To see how serious an organization is in this area, check to see if it distinguishes between different *levels* of testing for its library components. Some components may be completely untested; others may have been informally tested by the developer; some may have been tested by a separate quality-control group that can certify that a formal inspection of the component was conducted, or that a complete "branch coverage" was performed with test cases. If none of this information is available, the appropriate documentation for the user of the software component is caveat emptor.

detailed behavior), but when faced with the need for a module to carry out function X, they will remember, "Oh, yeah, there's some module in the library that does something like X—the whatchamacallit module, I can't remember the exact name, but I know it's there . . .". With 1000 or more components, there is no hope that the average software engineer will *ever* remember what's in the library.

Successful code-level libraries also typically contain *small* components; in the case of the Smalltalk class library and the Unix library, the components are typically only 5 to 10 statements in the source program language. Small components typically carry out one well-defined, functionally cohesive task, typically without imposing unreasonable performance or memory overhead. On the other hand, a library with gargantuan components—each consisting of 100,000 lines of code that attempt to do everything for everyone—is less successful. Software engineers will typically argue that they can't afford the overhead of the gargantuan component, nor can they tolerate the various side effects it may have.

9.4.2 Object-Oriented Development Techniques

One of the most attractive promises made by proponents of object-oriented development methodologies is that of greater reuse. In addition to the benefits of encapsulation of data and functions into an integrated whole, the object-oriented approach uses *inheritance* to facilitate reuse: a newly created object can be defined as a "subclass" of an existing object and automatically inherit the attributes and functions (or methods) of its parent.

This feature is found in many of the object-oriented programming languages (e.g., C++, Eiffel, and Smalltalk—but not Ada), but it won't be of much help to the COBOL community until the appearance of an object-oriented COBOL language.[2] In the meantime, various object-oriented analysis and design methodologies [2, 3] are emerging to help software engineers focus on the benefits of inheritance at an earlier stage in the software development life cycle.

And there are alternative approaches to achieving the inheritance benefits usually associated with object orientation. One of the most attractive is the Bassett frame technology approach developed by Paul

[2] The CODASYL Committee formed an Object-Oriented COBOL Task Group in November, 1989 and a draft standard of a new COBOL language is expected to emerge in the 1993–94 time frame. In the meantime, it is likely that we will see "unofficial" versions of OO-COBOL (or COBOL++) from one or more compiler vendors even before the draft standard emerges.

Bassett at Netron, Inc. [4]. While the conventional object-oriented approach uses only a "same-as, *plus*" inheritance metaphor (i.e., the subclass is the same as the parent, *plus* additional specialized attributes and functions), the Bassett approach also uses a "same as, *except*" metaphor. Indeed, this is exactly what a software engineer wants when he considers reusing a component in a library: "Gee, this component does exactly what I need, *except* that it also does X and Y, which I don't want . . .".

9.4.3 CASE Tools and Designware

As mentioned earlier, CASE tools will be an important component of software reusability technology in the 1990s; far more important than the drawing tools and error-checking features of the PC-based tools is the concept of a common *repository* for storing a wide variety of analysis, design, code, and data elements.

While this much is obvious, there is an interesting corollary: we may begin to see *reusable application programs* provided to the marketplace in the form of fully loaded CASE repositories; at least one vendor has begun referring to such a class of products as *designware*.[3] This is an exciting development for the software industry, because it promises a higher-level, more aggressive form of reuse—and it offers an alternative to the customary approach of buying commercial software packages and attempting to customize the package at the source program level.

If I want a common class of generic application program—a payroll system, for example, or an inventory control system—it is often more economical to buy a commercial package than develop it myself. But to tailor the package to my organization's specific needs, I either have to hope that the vendor has provided a great deal of flexibility through parameterization, or (shudder) I have to resort to modification of the vendor's source code. But instead of buying the source code, why not buy a repository full of data flow diagrams, entity–relationship diagrams, and data declarations? It's quite likely that 90 percent of the specification and design of the generic application will be satisfactory, but the 10 percent that must be modified should be modified at the analysis and design level, and then— through the use of a code generator attached to the CASE product—I should be able to generate a fully customized version of the package for my own use.

[3] Ken Orr refers to such an approach as *RAM*, or *reusable application model(s)*.

CASE vendors that are also in the service or consulting business—for example, Andersen Consulting—have an obvious opportunity to create such designware products. For less rational reasons—that is, the obsessive decision not to provide COBOL code generation—some of the DBMS vendors have also begun providing designware products. During the 1990s, we should expect to see a number of additional "players" in this business (though not the CASE vendors who are strictly "toolmakers" in nature) and ultimately the package vendors themselves will find it necessary to follow this trend.

9.4.4 Design Recovery *à la* MCC

For the organization that wants to focus its efforts on software reuse, one of the immediate problems to be faced is that the library of reusable components is initially empty. Where do the components come from? How long does it take to fill the library with enough components to provide a meaningful contribution to the organization?

The idea of a Software Parts Department—a group whose only job is to create reusable components—is discussed shortly. But regardless of which people create the components, a common assumption is that the components cannot be created until *after* the organization has decided to "get serious" about reuse. A different approach is being pursued by researchers at MCC, and it warrants serious attention if you want a "jump start" on creating a reusable library: consider your existing portfolio of old software—which, in most organizations, consists of tens of millions of lines of code—as a source of reusable components. This approach, which has a different focus and objective than the software reengineering techniques discussed in Chapter 10, is described by Biggerstaff and Lubars [4] as *design recovery*. Two research projects, DESIRE and ROSE, are underway to develop tools and techniques for finding and extracting nuggets of reusable gold from the oceans of old code.

An interesting point is that the lack of documentation for old software means that expert system technology will probably be necessary to help us find useful patterns for reuse. MCC's expert systems look at variable names, comments in the code, and even the formatting of source code to obtain clues to the behavior of alien code. Of course, *your* organization may have sufficient documentation that this may not be necessary, but the basic idea remains the same: harvest your old software in order to populate the empty library of reusable components.

9.5 ORGANIZATIONAL APPROACHES TO REUSABILITY

While technological approaches are obviously important, the key ingredient for achieving high levels of software reusability in organizations is *management*. There are three things that management must do:

- Provide a reward mechanism to instill a greater awareness of the desirability of reusability
- Provide "proactive" leadership at the beginning of system development projects to encourage reusability
- Change the DP organization to create a group whose sole job is to create reusable modules

Each of these topics is discussed in more detail now.

9.5.1 Providing a Reward System

As mentioned earlier, software engineers will not be motivated to seek opportunities for reusability if they see no benefit in such action; management must provide some recognition and reward to encourage a greater awareness. At the very least, lines of code (or function points) taken from a reusable library should be given the same value, when measuring the work done by a software engineer, as lines of new code. Since it will, it is hoped, be somewhat easier to find a reusable module in a library than to create a new one from scratch, this should encourage the software engineer in the right direction.

Slogans, commendations, letters of praise, and other such public recognition of individual reusability efforts may also be useful, though the first reaction on the part of the typical software engineer is likely to be one of mild suspicion. The important thing is to ensure that the software engineers understand and believe that this is not a short-term management "fad," to be forgotten when the next budget crunch occurs, but rather a long-term, deeply felt part of the overall DP culture. In the best case, the software engineer will gradually begin to feel guilty every time he writes a new module of his own, and will wonder why he couldn't find an appropriate candidate in the library of reusable components.

Several DP shops around the world are now experimenting with the idea of direct financial rewards—usually in the form of royalties—to software engineers to encourage them to create reusable software components.[4] Of course, this may open a Pandora's box of manage-

---

[4] The extent of the royalties would presumably be based on the number of times the reusable components was accessed. This suggests that perhaps some compensation should be provided to people who aggressively *use* components in the library as well as those who *create* components for the library.

ment problems—in the case of one software shop in Germany, it even created an outcry from the company's labor union—but it could also show that management is serious about recognizing the value of creating reusable software assets. If your company provides recognition and reward for patentable inventions, or other forms of intellectual property that are trademarked and copyrighted, it should consider doing the same for software components.

9.5.2 Provide a Proactive Management Approach

Most software development organizations exhibit a very passive attitude toward reusability: aside from occasional management slogans and exhortations, nobody pays much attention to the concept until the end of a development project. Then—and only then—someone might ask, "Hmmm, I wonder how much reusability we achieved on this project?" If anyone bothers to take a close look at the finished system, the answer might be, "Gee! What a surprise! This time we achieved a level of 34 percent reusability! I wonder how we did that?"

After the reusability concept has been practiced for a few years in an organization, it might be appropriate to set an overall organizational goal of, say, 50 percent or 60 percent for *all* projects. But in the early days, this is clearly not appropriate. In any case, the practical thing is to estimate consciously, deliberately, the likely and desirable level of reusability for each project *at the beginning of the project.* That is, the project manager and the senior software engineers involved in the early stages of analysis and design should be able to say, "Hmmm . . . this looks like another inventory control system, almost the same as the last inventory control system we built. We should be able to achieve a level of 80–85 percent reusability on this project."

How do we know that this is a serious estimate and not just fanciful dreaming? By building the reusability estimate into the project schedule and budget! If 80–85 percent of the code in the new system can be obtained from a reusable library, then the time required to design, code, and test new modules should be reduced considerably—and the project schedule and budget should reflect that.[5]

Obviously, the initial estimates of reusability have to be tracked as part of an overall program of software metrics in the organization (see Chapter 7 for more discussion of this). Project management should compare the *actual* level of reusability at the end of the project against

[5] I must admit that I did not think of this clever idea myself. It was described to me during a visit to Toshiba Company's Software Factory in October 1988. I don't know if *every* Japanese software company uses this approach, but it was common among the half-dozen large software companies I visited in Tokyo.

the original estimates and should keep track of the overall trend of reusability across all projects on an ongoing basis.

9.5.3 Change the Organization to Create a Group of Component Producers

As mentioned earlier, it is unreasonable to expect that software engineers will have the time, energy, or foresight to create general-purpose reusable modules while working under the normal project pressures of schedules, deadlines, and budgets. Anything created in this environment will have been *first* created as a special purpose and then, if time permits, revised in some fashion to make it more general.

A far better approach—and the only one that is likely to create a stable, useful library of reusable parts—is to create a separate group whose only job is to create reusable parts. This will typically be a small group—perhaps only 2 or 3 software engineers in an organization of 100–300 professional staff—but there should be more than one in order to create some flexibility, personnel backup, and a sense of shared enterprise. These software parts producers should be part of an overall "Software Parts Department," whose organizational structure might look like this:

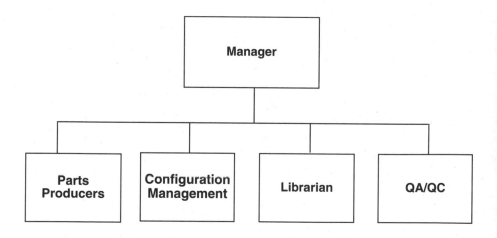

This does not mean that the Software Parts Department would refuse to consider submissions from the rest of the organization; however, such submissions would be carefully examined to see whether they are appropriate candidates for inclusion in the library and carefully checked for completeness, correctness, and overall quality. It is highly likely that any software components submitted by other parts of the DP organization would be considered a "rough draft" for the official reusable parts producers to revise, rewrite, and/or improve.

How would the Reusability Parts Department know what kind of reusable components to produce? One obvious way would be to respond to requests from other parts of the organization that see (or anticipate) the need for such components. But an equally important source would be the initiative of the Parts Department itself, *based on its ongoing analysis of "normal" modules developed by the rest of the organization.* Of course, this implies that *all* software developed throughout the organization is maintained in a central library or CASE repository and is available for review and analysis by a central group. If appropriate, the Software Parts Department could create new reusable components and suggest that other software engineers replace their specialized modules with the newly developed reusable ones.

9.6 STRATEGIC IMPLICATIONS

Everyone is in favor of software reuse, but the world-class companies are beginning to invest the time, effort, and money to make it work. That's what you need to do, too. Here are some questions to consider, along with the ideas presented in this chapter:

- What is the typical investment required to build and support a reusable library? Can it be expressed in percentage or ratio terms? Is it a function of the degree of reusability that one wants to achieve? As a simple case, suppose one has a DP shop with 100 people and a goal of 50 percent reusability in the next three years: How many people and how much money will it take?

- Does a DP shop have to be of a particular size to justify an investment in reusability? With a 20-person shop, does it make sense to dedicate one person to be a "component builder"?

- Are there any commercial configuration management packages that can help manage the use of reusable components (e.g., taking care of updates whenever a reusable component is modified)?

- What does reusability mean in a maintenance environment? Code can be salvaged from old code to be used in new development projects, but is it useful for "normal" maintenance?

END NOTES

1. Biggerstaff, Ted J., and Mitchell D. Lubars. "Recovering and Reusing Software Designs: Getting More Mileage from Your Software Assets," *American Programmer*, March 1991. Biggerstaff and Lubars have been actively involved in software reuse and design recovery at MCC. For information on the DESIRE and ROSE research projects, contact the authors at Microelectronics and Computer Technology Corp., P.O. Box 200195, Austin TX 78720; phone 512-343-0978, fax 512-338-3899.
2. Coad, Peter, and Edward Yourdon. *Object-Oriented Analysis*, 2nd ed. Englewood Cliffs, NJ: Prentice Hall, 1991.
3. Coad, Peter, and Edward Yourdon. *Object-Oriented Design*. Englewood Cliffs, NJ: Prentice Hall, 1991.
4. Bassett, Paul G. "Engineering Software for Softness," *American Programmer*, March 1991. The Bassett frame technology concept has been widely applied in conventional third generation languages like COBOL. Additional information can be obtained from Netron, Inc., at 99 St. Regis Crescent North, Downsview, Ontario M3J 1Y9 Canada, phone 416-636-8333, fax 416-636-4847.

Not reference

1. Reifer, Don. "Software Reuse: Myth or Reality," *American Programmer*, March 1991.

10

Software Reengineering

Software organizations all over the world are spending at least half their budget maintaining existing systems, but the world-class organizations are working to optimize that expenditure through the use of restructuring, reengineering, and reverse engineering tools.

Is CASE automating the right system development life cycle? Do the popular methodologies—structured analysis, information engineering, object-oriented analysis—really address the crucial issues that face most organizations today? If they do nothing but tell us how to build new systems, then they leave unanswered the question of how to cope with systems built 20 years ago. The issue can be seen visually by examining the classical system development life cycle portrayed by Connell and Shafer [1], as shown in Figure 10.1.

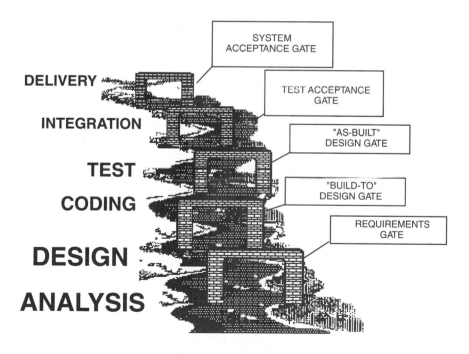

Figure 10.1: The classical life cycle

A more modern version of the life cycle, which includes rapid analysis and prototyping, is portrayed by Connell and Shafer in Figure 10.2.

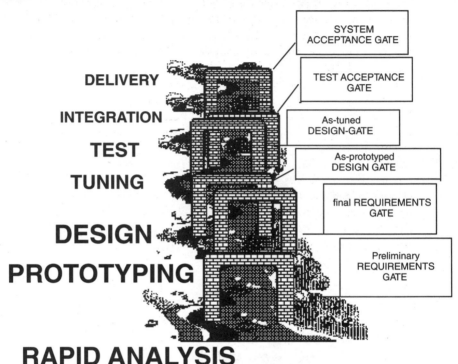

Figure 10.2: The rapid prototyping life cycle

But notice that both these models portray systems development as a straight-line process, culminating in delivery of the system to the customer. Nothing is said about maintenance, enhancement, fixing of bugs in the field, etc. This is not intended as a criticism of Mr. Connell and Ms. Shafer, whose book is filled with excellent advice and guidelines; it is endemic to the entire field, as it focuses its attention on the problems of building new systems.

A different perspective on the life-cycle issue is suggested by Eric Bush, former chairman of Language Technology, Inc. [2]:

> One reason that we as an industry . . . still today direct our automation efforts at the 20% problem instead of the 80% problem is that we describe our own activities with incorrect models. We still use models that were conceived in the 1950s. We have not updated them as the events that they were invented to describe

clearly panned out differently than anyone anticipated. There is a spooky analogy here with traditional specification-based development. The specification for the software life cycle was written at the beginning of programming, before we had sufficient experience to anticipate what it would be like. What we ended up needing as users is very different from what we said we needed when the spec was drawn up. But we stuck to the original specification, and thirty years later we have delivered a CASE industry behind time, over budget, and not responsive to the problem at hand. What we clearly need is a CASE for existing systems, tools that automate the tasks that programmers actually perform. It is telling that "CASE for existing systems" sounds like an oxymoron. It sounds strange because we are still under the influence of a false model, a model that says the business of software engineering is to create new programs, so computer aided software engineering should be the automation of creating new programs. What is the gain in automating lubrication and bug fixing? If instead we say that the business of software engineering is to adapt existing systems, then the automation of system adaptation is the natural domain of CASE.

Bush suggests that it would be more appropriate to think of the systems development life cycle as a true *cycle*, as shown in Figure 10.3.

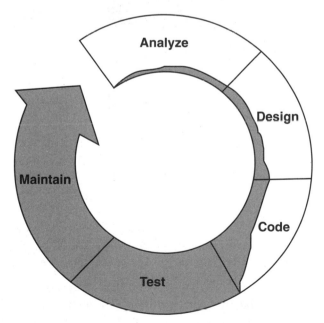

Figure 10.3: Eric Bush's conception of the system life cycle

From this perspective, what software engineers would normally call "new development" is just radical maintenance. Software becomes seen, in Bush's term, as an "immortal asset" of the organization, outliving generation upon generation of software engineer as it traverses its endless cycle.

Another term commonly heard in software maintenance today is that of a *legacy system.* As Dietrich, Nackman, and Gracer [3] describe it

> Developers of application software systems must often work with "legacy systems." These are systems that have evolved over many years and are considered irreplaceable, either because re-implementing their function is considered to be too expensive, or because they are trusted by users. Because of their age, such systems are likely to have been implemented in a conventional procedural language with limited use of data abstraction or encapsulation. The lack of abstraction complicates adding new applications to such a system and the lack of encapsulation impedes modifying the system itself because applications come to depend on system internals. We describe in this paper our experience in providing and using an object-oriented programmer's interface to a legacy system.

Thus, many systems today are taking the form shown in Figure 10.4, with a "wrapper" of code around the original software. Gradually, the wrapper becomes more and more robust, and the original legacy code can slowly wither away.

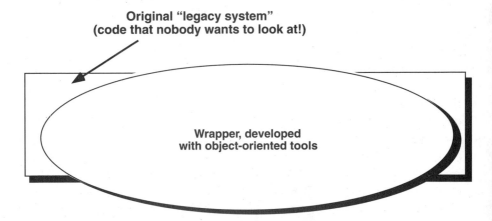

Figure 10.4: Wrappers and legacies

10.1 PLEASANT MYTHS WE HAVE BEEN FORCED TO ABANDON

Many software organizations are not yet looking at their existing installed base of software as an immortal asset or as a collection of legacy systems. They continue to believe that these old clunkers can be patched with minimal effort and that most of the energy and resources should be devoted to the development of new systems.

To operate this way, though, requires that we believe in three important premises—premises that the world-class organizations have acknowledged as myths, and have abandoned. These myths are

- *We can always afford to scrap our old systems and replace them with new systems, as long as we can demonstrate to users and management that the new system will be better.* One major telecommunications company discovered that this premise is no longer true when it tried to justify the redevelopment of an old payroll system. The old version required 40 full-time maintenance programmers, and everyone was convinced that a new version—developed with modern tools and methodologies—would be considerably easier to maintain. The problem: the company estimated it would take an additional 40 people to develop the new system, and the development schedule was seven years. *Seven years!* In these turbulent times, governments come and go, empires are born and destroyed, careers flourish and wither in seven years. And even for a large company, who has 40 people sitting around with nothing to do? The capital budget required to redevelop many of the old-generation legacy systems is simply too large to justify scrapping them, even if a new system was better.

- *We can be absolutely, positively, totally confident that a new replacement system would be much, much, **much** better than the old one.* Oh yeah? That's what we told management last time, and the time before that . . . and it wasn't always true. A common problem in this area is that the software development group uses the newest language, the newest tools, and/or the newest methodology *for the first time* on the redevelopment project; because of the learning curve, the project ends up taking much longer than had been anticipated. In other cases, redeveloped systems using new tools and techniques surprise everyone by consuming far more hardware resources than had been planned; the old system may have been highly optimized to conserve memory, CPU cycles, or disk accesses; and the project team building the new version may have failed to take this into account.

- *We can always figure out what the old system is doing and translate it into a new implementation.* In the mid-1980s, one organization within the U.S. Defense Department found itself maintaining a system that had been developed during the early years of the Vietnam war; the system consisted of 600,000 lines of COBOL, and it had no documentation. When redevelopment of the system was considered, management finally had to face the fact that not only were the original programmers long gone, but also the original users. The system was now being maintained by third generation maintenance programmers who communicated with third generation users; nobody had the slightest idea of *what* the system was originally intended to do, let alone *how* the system was accomplishing whatever it was supposed to do. Perhaps this situation is a little more extreme than the typical maintenance project, but to a greater or lesser extent, this characterizes what most maintenance programmers face: lack of knowledge about what the old system is doing.

Because of these three myths, more and more organizations are realizing that their existing portfolio of old software has to be reconsidered as a potentially valuable asset. Rather than throwing old systems away, or simply patching them until they collapse, the world-class organizations are investing money to refurbish the old systems. The technologies used to accomplish this are known by various names: restructuring, reengineering, and reverse engineering. We will examine all three.

10.2 RESTRUCTURING

Restructuring is a technology that transforms unstructured ("rat's nest" or "spaghetti bowl") code into functionally equivalent structured code. While this does not necessarily turn bad code into good code, it does tend to dramatically reduce the complexity of the program by reorganizing the logic flow so that the programmer can read the program listing in a straight-line fashion.

The usefulness of restructuring is based on the premise that the restructured code is functionally equivalent to the original program: given the same inputs, it will produce the same outputs. While the theoretical proof of this functional equivalency dates back to the original "proof" of structured programming [4], most maintenance programmers would want the insurance of a formal regression test.

But this suspicion—a natural character trait of maintenance programmers—actually provides a hidden benefit to the restructuring concept. It encourages the organization to develop a formal regression testing policy, which many organizations lack.[1] Regression testing can be, and should be, applied on *all* maintenance changes, independent of the decision to restructure the code. Many maintenance programmers have developed their own "private" regression test suite, often consisting of vast quantities of life production data; such tests are often wasteful of computer resources, and they often perform a woefully inadequate job of testing the code.

Thus, one of the interesting side benefits of an organizational decision to restructure old programs is a decision to develop a standardized regression testing procedure, to be applied whenever any change is made to existing software. As a result, *all* regression testing becomes more formal, more effective (in terms of test coverage), and more efficient.

As mentioned earlier, the theory of restructuring dates back to 1966; the first experimental restructuring product (which operated on FORTRAN programs) appeared in 1975, and COBOL-oriented commercial products began to appear in the marketplace in the mid-1980s. There are now several commercial products and services available, though the overwhelming majority of them are aimed at COBOL applications; organizations with vast libraries of software in FORTRAN, C, assembler, or other languages have little or nothing available to them.

The restructuring products typically add approximately 10 percent to the size and runtime of the original program, though optimizing compilers may offset some of this overhead. While an additional 10 percent overhead for hardware resources might be intolerable for some applications, it is usually negligible; in any case, it can usually be cost justified by the maintenance savings of 10 to 30 percent reported by most organizations.

Is restructuring a panacea? Obviously not: it may be a good long-term strategy for improving the quality (and decreasing the maintenance costs) of existing systems, but it is unlikely to solve short-term maintenance crises. And it does not turn lead into gold: if the original

---

[1] As mentioned in Chapter 4, one of the characteristics of a level 1 company (on the SEI scale of process maturity) is the lack of a configuration management process. Regression testing is one facet of configuration management.

program was intrinsically rotten to begin with, it will simply be transformed into a structured rotten program. Most important, if the original program did not provide the functionality required by the end user, restructuring will not add any of that desired functionality; all it can do is provide a better organized "base" program to which new functionality might be more easily added.

An interesting commentary on the market acceptance of restructuring was provided by Ulrich [5]: of the approximately 5000 IBM MVS mainframe shops in the United States, only about 500 had installed restructuring packages by 1990. Thus, approximately 10 percent of the potential market has accepted this technology; the rest are either ignoring it or are focusing their attention on other aspects of reengineering and reverse engineering.

10.3 REENGINEERING

The basic idea of reengineering is to clean up gradually an old mess. Every time the maintenance programmer touches an old program, it should become a little bit better than it was before; at the very least, it should not become any worse!

The objective of reengineering technologies is not to change the underlying functionality of the software—that is, the external behavior of the software, as seen by the user—but to modify the internal *technology* (implementation) of the software, in order to ease the maintenance burden. Another way to think of it is that reengineering simplifies the user interface *as seen by the maintenance programmer* required to make changes to the system. Another objective is to clean up the old software and make it ready for reverse engineering, which we will discuss in the next section.

Another interesting benefit of reengineering is that old software can be more easily "farmed out" to contract programmers, even though they may be perceived as less loyal than full-time staff programmers.[2] As we will discuss shortly, the "static analysis" capabilities of reengineering tools can be used to compare "before-and-after" ver-

---

[2] The issue of loyalty is usually an illusion, especially if the maintenance work is contracted to a "cottage industry" individual, who is happy to receive above-average fees to conduct maintenance programming work from his or her home. While it's true that some staff programmers may make a lifetime career out of maintaining some rotten old software, many others will leave at the first opportunity: they are no more and no less loyal than the programmers who work in a "body shop" consulting firm because "it's a job."

sions of modified software, in order to ensure that maintenance changes do not degrade the quality of the software.

Two of the key questions when investigating restructuring or reengineering are: *Which programs should be reengineered first?* and *When is reengineering a waste of time?* We will discuss these questions in Section 10.5.

Reengineering activities usually fall into three categories:

- Cleaning up old code and data
- Static analysis of existing code and data
- Dynamic analysis of existing code and data

The separate activities involving code and data are shown in Figure 10.5. The first step, an "environmental analysis," typically consists of an examination of job control (JCL) statements, file declarations, intermediate files, overlay structures, and so on. Since these components may have been developed 10 to 20 years ago for a more primitive hardware environment, some relatively simple changes (e.g., eliminating intermediate files and overlays and simply running all the programs together in a virtual memory environment) can often save vast amounts of computer time and resources.

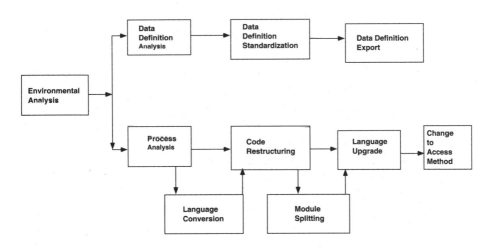

Figure 10.5: Reengineering activities

Data definition analysis and standardization generally involves scanning the source code of old programs to locate the DATA DIVI-

SION of the COBOL programs or equivalent data declaration components of other programs. Synonyms—for example, the 25 different names that have been chosen for the common data element CUS-TOMER—are standardized. And, as Figure 10.5 indicates, the standardized data names are then exported. This last step, which was the subject of great "hoopla" product announcements from many traditional CASE vendors in the 1990–91 time period, will be discussed shortly.

On the code side, reengineering may include a variety of "clean-up" activities, including reformatting of source code, restructuring of code logic (as discussed earlier), conversion or upgrading of the language in which the original programs were written, and splitting of "humongous" modules into more appropriate bite-size pieces.

A key technology for reengineering is the *repository*, which we discussed in Chapter 6. Many of the software reengineering products have, as their objective, the gradual consolidation of most or all of the components of the original software into a CASE repository. This process is illustrated in Figure 10.6.

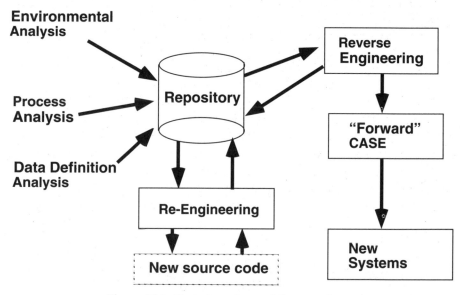

Figure 10.6: Reengineering and the repository

Many of the reengineering tools are not concerned with *changing* the existing software, but merely facilitating a better *understanding* of the existing software. Studies by IBM have suggested that the typical maintenance programmer spends approximately 47 percent of his time analyzing code, simply trying to understand it. In situations like this, sometimes reading a program listing is not enough: the maintenance programmer needs a great deal of information that can be gleaned from a static analysis of the program, and sometimes he needs to *watch* the program as it executes.

Here are some examples of the kind of static analysis that can be useful for better understanding of the behavior of "alien" code, that is, software written by a generation of programmers long since departed:

- The number of lines of code, function points, and so on
- The number of IF statements, GOTO statements, and/or other difficult or dangerous types of program constructs
- Location of all the PERFORM or CALL statements in the program as well as all program EXITs
- The amount of "dead" code—code that can never be reached by any logic path and that can therefore never be executed
- The number of unreferenced variables[3]
- The percentage of "unstructured" code
- The percentage of uncommented code
- McCabe cyclomatic complexity metric or other measures of program quality/complexity

While these reports and statistics may give the maintenance programmer a better feeling for the overall nature and quality of the program, it may not be sufficient for understanding its behavior in specific circumstances—for example, when trying to track down a bug. In this case, *dynamic* analysis of the program's behavior—using such products as ViaInsight from VIASOFT Corporation or MicroFocus Workbench from MicroFocus Ltd—could help answer questions like these:

- *What are all the possible paths to a particular statement in my program?* This question comes to mind when the maintenance programmer knows that his program has "crashed" at a particular location—but he doesn't know how the program arrived at that location. "How did I get here?" is the question that needs to be answered.

[3] As we saw in Chapter 7, David Card reports in *Measuring Design Quality* that there may be a high correlation between programs with unreferenced variables and high numbers of defects and maintenance problems.

- *What are all the statements that access or modify a specified data item, including aliases, subfields, and so on?* This question is important when the maintenance programmer knows that his or her program has "crashed" because a certain variable or data element was clobbered. The question is: "Who did this?" Thus, the programmer might want to find all references to the field ZIP-CODE or all fields indirectly affected by (or related to) ZIP-CODE.

- *What will happen to the behavior of my program if I change variable X?* Because the overall behavior of the program is *not* well understood, the maintenance programmer may need to perform some experiments: change the value of a parameter and execute a small portion of the program to see what happens. Purists may object to this, arguing that it leads to sloppy programming and extemporaneous patching of programs. And of course, there is the danger that the limited experiments conducted by the maintenance programmer may not exhibit all the side effects of a proposed change; however, a static analysis tool could assist by providing an "impact analysis" report of all portions of the program affected by a proposed change. But during the heat of the debugging effort—when an online system has crashed and hundreds of users are screaming at the top of their lungs—the *discovery* process facilitated by the dynamic analysis tools can be a life-saver.

10.4 REVERSE ENGINEERING

The basic idea of reverse engineering is to "uncover" or "rediscover" the design, and/or the specification, from the existing code. A number of "low-level" products exists today; such products can produce low-level process specifications from source code, or structure charts from source code, or data dictionary (repository) entries from a COBOL DATA DIVISION. However, the high-level translation of code into leveled data flow diagrams or data declaration statements into an entity–relationship diagrams is a far more difficult job, and usually requires an artificial intelligence approach. High-level "data-oriented" reverse engineering products are available from a few companies like Bachman Information Systems, but "process-oriented" products were fundamentally unavailable when this book was written.

However, research and development is currently underway in a number of CASE vendor organizations to build process-oriented reverse engineering tools, and it is likely that we will see some credible products by the mid-1990s. Meanwhile, some organizations are investigating reverse engineering of code into *objects* [6]. But lost forever are the *assumption* and *alternatives* that went into the analysis and design of the software; as Figure 10.7 illustrates, the assumptions and alternatives affect every stage of the development of a system; however, they are rarely documented, and there is no earthly way for a reverse engineering tool to reconstruct them.

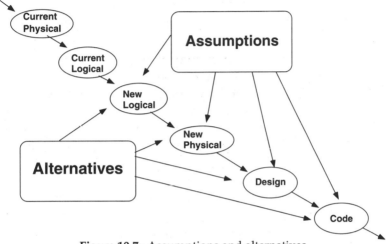

Figure 10.7: Assumptions and alternatives

As illustrated in Figure 10.8, reverse engineering of existing *code* may lead to a variety of textual or graphical documents. But the textual information is often little more than a one-for-one reformatted version of the original source code, as illustrated by Table 10.1.

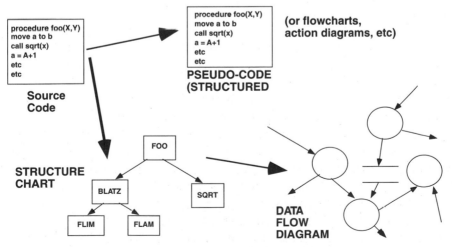

Figure 10.8: Reverse engineering of code

Table 10.1: Before-and-After Reverse Engineering of Code

COBOL CODE	PROCESS DEFINITION STATEMENT

Program-ID. Payroll.
  Author. J-Hacker.
  Date-Written. JA-01-90.
	Define Process Payroll;
	  RPD is J-Hacker
	  Attribute Date-Written 'JA-01-90';

FD Master-File
  01 Master-Record
 	
  05 Acct-No-Master PIC X(5)
	Define Set Master-File;
	Define Entity Master-Record;
	  Attribute level-number 01;
	Define Element Acct-No-Master;
	  Attribute level-number 05;
	  Attribute PIC 'X(5)';

Control-Paragraph.
 	
Open I-O Master-File
Perform Read-Transaction
...
Read-Transaction.
  Move Acct-No-In to Acct-No-Out
	Define Process Control-Paragraph.
	  Part of Payroll;
	  Updates Master-File;
	  Utilizes Read-Transaction;
	...
	Define Process
	Uses Acct-No-In to Derive Acct-No-Out;

On the data side, reverse engineering is illustrated by Figure 10.9; the major product is a populated repository of data element definitions and/or various graphical diagrams describing the logical organization of the data.

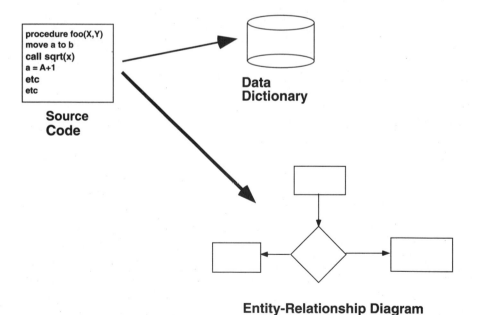

Entity-Relationship Diagram

Figure 10.9: Reverse engineering of data

Recently several of the "forward" CASE vendors— KnowledgeWare, Texas Instruments, Intersolv, Andersen Consulting, Cadre, and so on—have announced "backward" or reverse-engineering tools. While the current product offerings are relatively unexciting, because they operate at a fairly low level, there is still a significant benefit: existing code and data are "imported" into a CASE repository, allowing subsequent reengineering and "forward" maintenance activity to take place in a much more productive environment.

10.5 A REENGINEERING STRATEGY

Because the portfolio of existing systems is so massive in most organizations, any decision to restructure, reengineer, or reverse engineer that software can be a momentous decision. Not only does it affect tens of millions of lines of old code, but it affects the day-to-day work of up to half (or more) of the software professionals in the organization.

Thus, one of the important decisions that an organization must make if it decides to adopt restructuring technologies is just how it will go about the technologies. Typical strategies are these:

- A top–down edict from senior management
- The "sheep dip" approach
- Bottom–up "socializing"

Each of these is discussed in more detail now.

10.5.1 The Top–Down Edict

The managerial *dictum* is a favorite of many top-level managers, and it has been attempted on several occasions in companies implementing reengineering. While it may be applicable to the imposition of new tools and methodologies for *new* development work, it is usually impractical as a means of implementing reengineering.

Why is this so? Partly because of inertia: the application portfolio is too large to change overnight, no matter what senior management might say. If it took 20 years to accumulate the mountain of crap that the organization is trying to maintain, all the edicts in the world will not change it overnight. It might be possible for a large organization to reengineer its application portfolio in a 5-year period, but 10 years is more realistic.

As we have seen throughout this book, most of the major "sea changes" in an organization are likely to be 5- to 10-year efforts. In the case of reengineering, not only is there a massive amount of old software to convert, but also a major culture change to effect. Many maintenance programmers have been doing the same job, with the same tools, upon the same old code, for a decade or more; expecting them to change overnight is naive and foolish.

There is another problem with the senior management edict: while the initial edict may be relatively simple—for example, "rejuvenate the old payroll system, and cut maintenance costs by 25 percent"—there is a common problem of "expectation slippage" during the reengineering project, as Berlinger [7] points out. In the midst of the reengineering project, a revised edict will say, "by the way, while you're at it, we could use a graphical user interface front end . . . ," and a few weeks later, another edict will say, " . . . and it wouldn't be a bad idea to modify the database to capture the new human resource data that the government is requiring." Naturally, the budget, schedule, and work force allocation for the project stays as it was originally estimated, but the creeping escalation of features is likely to swamp what was originally described as a straightforward reengineering project.

10.5.2 The "Sheep Dip" Approach

The basic approach here is to "dunk" all the software engineers in a "bath" of new technology and expect them to become overnight experts in the new technology.[4]

While the sheep dip approach may minimize short-term training costs, it has generally been ineffective wherever it has been attempted—because the staff cannot use the new tools, methods, or techniques instantaneously and the details of the training are lost. It is not an approach recommended for introducing technology for the development of new systems, and it is certainly not recommended as a technique for implementing reengineering technologies.

10.5.3 Bottom–Up Socializing

Some organizations feel that the best way to introduce reengineering is on a voluntary basis. Thus, a "reengineering technology" group might set itself up as a "center of excellence" and broadcast

---

[4] The term "sheep dip" was suggested by Gerald Weinberg, author of the classic textbook *The Psychology of Computer Programming*. The term recalls the approach used by farmers to rid their sheep of termites or fleas, or whatever other strange parasites sheep pick up in the course of their miserable lives.

its existence to other project teams within the organization. Then, on a voluntary basis, they would lend advice and guidance to those groups that wanted it.

There are some obvious disadvantages to this approach: some hard-core resisters might never ask for help, and it would be difficult to predict the pace at which the reengineering technology could be spread through even the more forward-thinking part of the organization. But as an initial strategy, it has its merits: it allows a new, possibly threatening, technology to be introduced in a nonthreatening way.[5]

10.5.4 A Reengineering "Life-Cycle" Plan

Of course, reengineering or reverse engineering of one or two systems can always be done on an ad hoc basis. But an enterprise-level commitment to reengineering is a *major* commitment and will take years to accomplish. More important, reengineering tools and techniques change the way system developers and maintainers "do business," just as any other automated system changes the way its "users" do business.

Thus, implementation of restructuring, reengineering, and/or reverse engineering on a large scale should be regarded as a systems development project and should be planned with the same life-cycle activities of analysis, design, implementation, and testing that you would use on any other project.

As part of this life-cycle plan, you should look for resistance to change. It's unrealistic to assume that everyone will enthusiastically support the implementation of reengineering, or any other new technology. As we saw in Chapter 6 when we discussed the introduction of CASE tools, a *sales* effort is necessary to convince senior management, project-level management, and technicians of the merits of the new technology. The selling effort is needed before, during, and after the implementation of the CASE tools.

If this is true of CASE in general, it is doubly true of reengineering-oriented CASE tools. You should expect resistance, *anticipate* it, and accept it as natural and normal. In Section 10.5.7, we will discuss one practical manifestation of this resistance to change, a strategy known as "windows of opportunity."

If you haven't experienced this resistance before, it can take you by surprise—both in terms of the nature of the resistance and the

[5] A good example of an organization that used just this strategy to introduce reengineering is Pacific Bell [8].

vehemence with which it is expressed. Here are some examples of the objections you're likely to hear from maintenance programmers when you suggest that they should begin using new reengineering tools:

- *I don't need any help.* Many maintenance programmers are perfectly satisfied with the level of work they are doing and are sincerely convinced that they are as productive as could be reasonably expected. The suggestion that they should begin using new tools carries an implicit suggestion that management isn't satisfied with the level of work they have been doing.

- *Don't you dare touch my program.* It doesn't take long for maintenance programmers to feel a sense of personal ownership of the program they have been maintaining; and if it has been their sole assignment for the past seven years, this reaction is quite understandable. Viewed from a constructive perspective, one could say that maintenance programmers feel personally responsible for anything that might go wrong with the programs they are maintaining, and if the program is "mission-critical," they may feel that pressure very strongly. From a negative perspective, we might argue that the program represents job security; the introduction of reengineering tools carries with it the implied threat that others will become familiar with the program, and the job security may be lost.

- *The old ways are better.* This is, of course, a standard reaction to any form of new technology. Again, there is a positive and a negative interpretation of such a reaction. The positive interpretation is that maintenance programmers have built a set of homegrown tools and techniques for maintaining their program, and they fear that the new reengineering tools will invalidate their own tools and won't work as well. From a negative perspective, this reaction suggests a feeling of insecurity and fear of obsolescence: the old ways are better because maintenance programmers aren't sure they'll be able to learn the new ways.

- *OmyGod—one more thing I have to learn!* This comment comes from the maintenance programmer who is already overworked, besieged with crises, and generally frazzled beyond all reasonable redemption. Programmers tiptoe past the office of this poor lost soul, fearful of disturbing him as he frantically tries to keep up with the barrage of trouble reports, memory dumps, user demands, and abuse from management. Reengineering tools?—it's the last thing this person wants. But all this is the symptom of the indispensable programmer—and as we will discuss in Section 10.5.7, some organizations feel that it's best to "bite the bullet" before the indispensable person becomes any more indispensable.

- *I don't like PCs—I want to do all my work on the good old mainframe.* The PC is a threat, simply because many of the new reengineering tools come packaged with a PC. And the poor maintenance programmers, raised on mainframe technology of the 1960s and 1970s, have never even learned how to use the text editor on a PC. They're nervous about all this "windows stuff"; they find MS-DOS intolerably primitive and OS/2 unbearably piggish. They want their mainframe tools and utilities; they want their trusty 3270 terminal. They want to be left alone. Who can blame them?

10.5.5 Which Systems Get Reengineered First?

Assuming that one has managed to overcome the resistance to change with at least some portion of the software engineering staff, there remains a major question of prioritization: *Which systems should be reengineered first?* There are several possibilities:

- All the systems could be reengineered at the same time. (This approach is sometimes called the "big-bang" or "nuclear warfare" approach, for obvious reasons.)
- The oldest systems could be reengineered first, on the theory that they are the ones most in need of rejuvenation.
- The newest, or most recently developed systems, could be reengineered first, on the theory that they are the most salvageable.
- The buggiest systems could be reengineered first, on the grounds that they are the ones causing the most havoc within the user organization.
- The most critical systems could be reengineered first, on the grounds that they will have the most visible payoff. (Alternatively, one might argue that this strategy is attractive only to masochists and those with a strong death wish!)

Actually, *none* of the strategies listed is recommended. Instead, an approach known as "portfolio analysis," discussed in Section 10.5.6, should be used to identify potential *candidates* for restructuring, reengineering, and/or reverse engineering.

But this has to be done within a framework: those involved with reengineering must have a good understanding of management's "vision" of the organization's hardware/software architecture. Is the organization committed to its current mainframe architecture for the foreseeable future, or is it moving toward a "downsized" architecture of PCs and LANs? Is it planning to update its database architecture from a flat-file approach to a relational approach in the next several years, or is it moving from relational to object-oriented databases? Is it moving from batch to online, from centralized to distributed, cooperative, client–server architectures?

On a larger scale, the reengineering architect must have a good understanding of the enterprise's "business vision" for the next several years. What's the point of reengineering all the software for a bank if the bank plans to turn itself into a discotheque? Why reengineer software for a division that is about to be shut down or sold off?

Once the long-term strategy is understood—particularly in terms of the long-term target technology architecture—the reengineering evangelist can analyze existing systems for conformance to the long-term vision. And—politically quite important!—he or she can look for short-term payoffs within the long-term strategy. While the complete reengineering effort may take 5 to 10 years, it's important to be able to show some positive results within a politically appropriate time scale, usually 12 to 18 months.

Depending on the nature of the organization's target technology and its current systems, the reengineering effort will take one of the forms suggested by Figure 10.10.

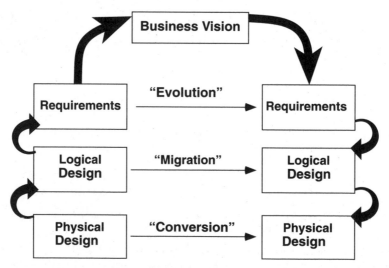

Figure 10.10: Evolving existing systems to the future

In the simplest case, existing systems may merely require "conversion" to a different hardware environment or operating system; in this case, restructuring and reengineering, as described earlier in this chapter, may be appropriate, but full-scale reverse engineering may not be. But if the new environment is sufficiently different from the current one, it may be necessary to recover the "logical design" of the original system; this can be migrated to a logical design for the new architecture. A more drastic change—for example, the change from a batch to an online architecture or a flat-file to a relational database environment—might require reverse engineering up to the requirements level before "evolving" the system to the new environment. And of course, if the business itself is going to change, then the original requirements must be modified or extended before the new system can be developed.

10.5.6 Portfolio Analysis

The portfolio analysis approach was described by Language Technology [9, 10] as a strategy for prioritizing possible candidate systems for reengineering and reverse engineering; the strategy described here is a specific application of a more general strategy used by such organizations as ITT, Boston Consulting Group, and other firms for prioritizing various decision-making opportunities.[6]

The portfolio analysis strategy is illustrated by Figure 10.11. Note that the diagram has a horizontal axis and a vertical axis and that it partitions the x-y space into four quadrants.

The horizontal axis in Figure 10.11 represents user satisfaction, or the degree of importance the user community attaches to the various systems it uses. This can usually be determined though surveys, interviews, questionnaires, and so on.

The vertical axis of Figure 10.11 represents the technical quality of the various systems. This can be measured using the McCabe complexity metric, the Halstead metric, statistics about defect rates, and data about past maintenance costs. However it is measured, the technical quality metric should correlate well with ease of maintenance.

Each system currently being maintained is then evaluated and placed in the appropriate place in the grid; in Figure 10.11, the size of each "bubble" represents the size (in lines of code, function points, etc.) of the system.

---

[6] Independently of the issue of reengineering, this is a useful exercise to go through on a periodic basis. Many software organizations have little or no idea of what their users think of the systems they have been maintaining for the past several years.

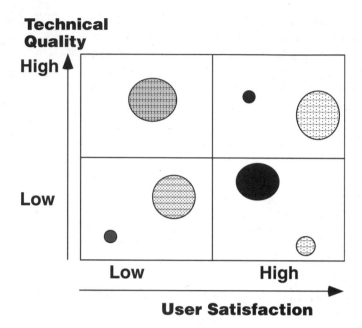

Figure 10.11: The portfolio analysis strategy

Within this framework, each quadrant suggests a different strategy for reengineering and/or reverse engineering. For example, the systems in the upper right quadrant could be considered the "winners"—the systems everyone loves. The high score on the user scale suggests that the users are happy with the existing system, and they consider it relevant to their needs. And the high score on the technical scale suggests that the maintenance programmers find it relatively easy to keep the systems going. In short, these are the *last* systems that need to be tampered with; in a world full of problems, these systems can be left alone.

The systems in the bottom right quadrant of Figure 10.11 are ideal candidates for restructuring and/or reengineering, but *not* for reverse engineering. The high user rating suggests that the systems are acceptable to the user, so they are presumably providing most or all of the required functionality. On the other hand, the low technical rating suggests that the systems are driving the maintenance programmers crazy; these systems are probably good examples of periodic miracles by which the maintenance programmers work through the night, or through the weekend, in order to produce the reports desired by the user after an insidious bug has destroyed the entire database. But since the *functionality* of the systems is acceptable, reverse engineering is not needed; what's needed is reengineering in order to fix the rotten code.

The systems in the top left quadrant are, in a sense, irrelevant: the maintenance programmers love them, but the users hate them. Restructuring or reengineering is probably unnecessary, since the high technical quality suggests ease of maintenance, but in any case, it would not make the users any happier. If anything is to be done with the systems in this quadrant, reverse engineering is the technology to use.

Finally, the systems in the bottom left quadrant: these are the losers, the ones everyone hates. These systems are the ones that should be scrapped and rewritten if anything is to be done with them. If this is not possible, then restructuring and reengineering is probably needed first, just to clean up the existing functionality. Following that, a reverse engineering effort can be used to uncover the latent design and specifications and add the functionality required to satisfy the users. Within each of these quadrants, a number of additional questions can be asked:

- *What is the strategic importance of the system to the organization?* Strategically important systems do not make good examples of pilot projects, as discussed in Chapter 6, but once the reengineering technology has been proven, high-importance systems would normally take priority over the low-importance systems.

- *What is the current reliability of the system?* Some systems may be ugly inside and virtually impossible to change or modify, but the functionality that exists may be solid as a rock. Other systems may be so fragile that they crash and collapse on a regular basis; no matter how elegant the functionality, the frequent occurrences of defects will probably give these systems a higher priority for reengineering effort than the stable systems.

- *What is the frequency of current maintenance activities?* Some systems may have a low technical quality, but may not be subject to frequent requests from the user community for new features; others may be quite volatile because of rapidly changing business conditions, government regulations, or plain old whimsy on the part of the user community. Again, we would expect that stagnant systems would be left alone and the reengineering efforts would be applied to the systems that, by their very nature, require frequent updates and revisions.

For organizations wishing to carry out a more detailed and sophisticated analysis, a Kiviat graph display can be used to portray as many as eight attributes of systems under maintenance.

10.5.7 Windows of Opportunity

Suppose that all the existing systems have been prioritized: the software manager knows exactly which systems should be restructured, which ones would be improved through the use of static/dynamic analysis tools, and which ones should be reverse engineered to produce structure charts, data flow diagrams, and entity–relationship diagrams. What next?

The simple approach of starting with the highest-priority system ignores one problem: the human element. As discussed earlier, it is quite possible that the maintenance programmer(s) assigned to high-priority projects might violently resist the introduction of reengineering tools, or the very thought that their precious system might be subjected to some kind of automated analysis and/or transformation. What then?

Many organizations have found that they must wait for a "window of opportunity"—a brief period during which the reengineering technology has a chance of being applied successfully before the resistance sets in again. Here are some examples of windows of opportunity:

- *The day that the "sole living expert" maintenance programmer retires or quits.* At this point, the organization will normally assign a new programmer the responsibility of looking after the code so jealously guarded by the dearly departed sole living expert. For a period of, typically, two to three months, the new maintenance programmer will complain loudly about the low quality of the program, the stupidity and low standards of the former programmer, and various other injustices associated with his miscrable fate. This is a good time—a window of opportunity—for introducing some reengineering technology to help improve the maintainability of the software. But the critical point to remember is this: *after two or three months, the new programmer has attached his own ego to the program.* The window of opportunity has closed. As John Johns of AT&T points out, "No amount of argument will convince the programmer that the program can be improved once the ego commitment is made."

- *Before major enhancements are made or the system is completely rewritten.* If a major disruption threatens the peace and stability of the maintenance programmer (who may have thrown up his hands in defeat), and if everything else is going to change, why not add the extra change of reengineering technology? However, at the end of the enhancement project, the window closes again.

- *When exceedingly difficult bugs exist in the system and the maintenance programmer has given up attempting to find the bug.* This happens quite often with online or real-time systems, where the bug pops up rarely and in unpredictable situations. After several weeks or months or searching for the bug, the maintenance programmer may have to admit defeat. Assuming that the bug is serious, and *must* be fixed, the maintenance programmer may have no choice but to accept some new technology that he might have preferred to avoid.

- *When the organization decides to "bite the bullet" and fire a recalcitrant "sole living expert."* This is never easy or pleasant to do, and most organizations will put it off as long as they can. But if the organization is held hostage to the whims of a single "indispensable" person who resists all reasonable efforts to accept new reengineering technology—assuming, of course, that management has decided that such technology is essential—then there may be no choice but to remove the maintenance programmer from the job. Again, a window of opportunity opens when the new person is assigned; it closes again after a period of a few months.

10.6 THE REENGINEERING PROJECT

With the guidelines and advice from the previous section, you should be ready to start a reengineering project. Here are the steps you should consider:

- Define the scope of the project; get organized.
- Collect the source materials and tools.
- Validate the source materials.
- Analyze the source code and data.
- Produce new documentation.

Each of these steps is discussed in more detail now.

10.6.1 Define Project Scope

There are big reengineering projects, and there are small reengineering projects; sometimes management has rather modest objectives, and sometimes it is looking for a complete revolution. Here are the kind of questions you should ask—and for which you had better get some definitive answers!—before you launch your reengineering project:

- *What is the scope of the project?* Which program(s) or systems(s) does it include? Is the effort associated with only a small, localized project or an entire user organization? It's a good idea to draw a structured analysis context diagram to ensure that you, the users, and management agree on the boundaries of your project.

- *Do we need to rearchitect the data structures?* Restructuring the data can be a massive exercise for many organizations, because it requires physically reorganizing the data itself, and this very same data must continue to be used by the old version of the software while the conversion takes place. The exercise has been described by some as being akin to changing a tire on an automobile while it is barreling along a Los Angeles freeway at 60 mph.

- *Do we need to carry the reengineering effort up to the level of an enterprise model?* If so, it will probably affect a number of other existing systems, as well as most current and future systems.

- *Do we need to save the business rules?* In some cases, the organization may decide that the only thing worth saving is the data; the business rules that operate upon the data are embedded in the procedural code of old systems, and the organization may have decided that since the rules are obsolete (or about to be changed), they may as well be thrown away. As noted earlier, reverse engineering tools are currently rather weak on the process side, so a decision of this kind would be a boon to the reengineering project team.

- *How big/small an improvement do we need to make?* As mentioned earlier, the extent of management's expectations can have a dramatic impact on the nature of the reengineering project. A 10 percent improvement can often be achieved with nothing more than the "environmental analysis" shown in Figure 10.5, but a 50 percent or 100 percent improvement may require radical reorganization of the old software. And a dictum that "software defects must be reduced by a factor of 10" can suggest that stern measures indeed are required.

Once these questions are answered, the initial phase of the reengineering project will normally involve such administrative things as developing a project plan and defining the team's responsibilities. But another major activity is the collecting of source materials.

10.6.2 Collect Source Materials and Tools

Often the biggest problem with a restructuring or reengineering effort is simply finding the source code and associated materials; attempts to reengineer with nothing more than compiled object code are rather hopeless. Thus, the project team normally has to gather together items such as

- COBOL source code
- COPY members, or INCLUDEd parameter files
- Cataloged procedures, or other job control statements, SQL procedures, and so on
- Databases (IMS DBDs, IDMS schemas, etc.)
- Data views (IMS PSBs, IDMS subschemas, etc.)

All this may be captured on a PC or a mainframe, depending on the nature of the tools and the size of the system to be reengineered. An even more important factor is the location of the CASE repository used by the organization, since this may be the physical place where the data is stored.

10.6.3 Validate the Source Materials

Simply gathering the source materials into one large pile is often not enough: it's often important to validate carefully the source materials to ensure that they correspond correctly to the production version of the system. Thus, the reengineering team must look at operator-run books, inventory lists, and other documents to confirm that all the source materials have been obtained. This can often be assisted by producing a high-level system flowchart (tools may be available to produce this directly from JCL statements) to ensure that everyone knows exactly which programs, databases, and intermediate files are involved.

The project team must produce a list of missing source code and then take steps to track it down; data dictionary lists and appropriate summary documentation should also be produced.

10.6.4 Analyze Source Code and Data

Obviously, this is where the reengineering and restructuring tools described in this chapter would be used. Wherever possible, of course, automated tools should be used for this effort; and in most cases, it makes sense to use standard commercial tools.

However, keep in mind that *manual* scanning of source files will also be necessary. Standard text retrieval tools and editors—the ViaInsight product, MicroFocus Workbench, and so on—can be used to look through the source code to see where reports are created, how display screens are used, and how the existing software modules access the databases.

In short, reengineering CASE tools can provide a great deal of automated assistance, and in the case of restructuring, the process can be entirely automated; however, it is virtually impossible to remove the human element from most reengineering projects.

10.6.5 Produce Documentation

Finally, after all the code has been cleaned up, restructured, and reorganized, it is important to produce a complete documentation set for the new version of the software—something that may have never existed for the old software!

Thus, the software team should be prepared to clean up the textual documentation (if any) from the old system, produce manuals, print diagrams, and produce a collated document of text and diagrams.

10.7 CONCLUSION

The fundamental message of this chapter is that the software life cycle of the 1990s must emphasize maintenance and ongoing evolution of systems; the capital investment in old software over the past 35 years is simply too great to throw it away.

But while reengineering technologies can help save this investment, it must be used intelligently. The portfolio analysis approach discussed earlier is one way of prioritizing the effort; no doubt there are other strategies as well.

At the time this book was written, the most useful of the technologies is that of *reengineering*. Restructuring, by itself, is a useful technology, but it can bring about only a marginal improvement in maintainability of old systems: it reorganizes the procedural code, but does nothing for the data. Reverse engineering may well be the promising technology of the 1990s, but it has not arrived yet—and probably won't amount to much more than a simple accumulation of data element definitions into a CASE repository until the mid-1990s.

END NOTES

1. Connell, John, and Linda Bryce Shafer. *Structured Rapid Prototyping: An Evolutionary Approach to Software Development.* Englewood Cliffs, NJ: Yourdon Press/Prentice Hall, 1989.
2. Bush, Eric. "A CASE for Existing Systems," Technical Report. Salem, MA: Language Technology, Inc., 1989.
3. Dietrich, Walter, Lee Nackman, and Franklin Gracer. "Saving a Legacy with Objects," *Proceedings of the OOPSLA 1989 Conference,* pp. 77–83.
4. Böhm, C., and G. Jacopini. "Flow Diagrams, Turing Machines, and Languages with Only Two Formation Rules," *Communications of the ACM,* May 1966, pp. 366–371. Also reprinted in Edward Yourdon, ed., *Classics in Software Engineering.* Englewood Cliffs, NJ: Yourdon Press/Prentice Hall, 1979.
5. Ulrich, William M. "The Evolutionary Growth of Software Reengineering and the Decade Ahead," *American Programmer,* October 1990.
6. Yourdon, Edward. "Japan Update," *American Programmer,* February 1991.
7. Berlinger, Scott. "Reengineering: Leveraging Your CASE Investment," *American Programmer,* October 1990.
8. Yourdon, Edward. "Pacific Bell," *American Programmer,* September 1989.
9. Yourdon, Edward. "RE-3." Part 1: "Reengineering, Restructuring, Reverse Engineering," *American Programmer,* April 1989.
10. Yourdon, Edward. "RE-3." Part 2, *American Programmer,* June 1989.

11

Future Trends

While many of the technologies discussed in this book have a patina of newness about them, they are, in fact, not so new. CASE technology, metrics, reusability, and reengineering technologies date back to the 1980s, 1970s, or even the 1960s. So what new things should we expect in the 1990s?

The fundamental message of this chapter is that technology changes more rapidly than predicted, but people change more slowly. Given new technology, people tend to do the same old thing they were doing before—just a little cheaper and faster. It takes people a long time to find new applications for new technology.[1]

Perhaps this is because true revolutions are few and far between; most of what we see in our field, or any other field of technology, is evolution. The future developments we will discuss in this chapter primarily fall into the category of evolutionary developments that we can expect to see gradually creeping into practice during this decade— not the revolutionary discontinuities that may or may not happen during the decade.

To give you the flavor of what is revolutionary and what is evolutionary in the computer field, a report in the October 15, 1990 issue of *Computerworld* indicated that many esoteric technologies such as foreign language translation, pattern-matching technology, and neural networks have not even reached the stage of tentative investigation in most organizations. The level of interest in various technologies is shown in Figure 11.1.

But whether it takes the form of revolution or evolution, change is a given in our industry. The purpose of this chapter is to describe some of the characteristics of technology evolution and to provide some advice on how to prepare for it. For those interested in the *general* study of technology evolution, a number of textbooks [1–4] are recommended.

---

[1] When they do begin using technology to do new things, it gradually changes life-styles and work-styles; the new life-styles and work-styles change society, which eventually changes technology again. A good example of this during the past few years is the impact of the fax machine, which is now being used to send orders to delicatessens, to request songs to be played at radio stations, and to enhance life-style in ways that were probably never anticipated by the technologists.

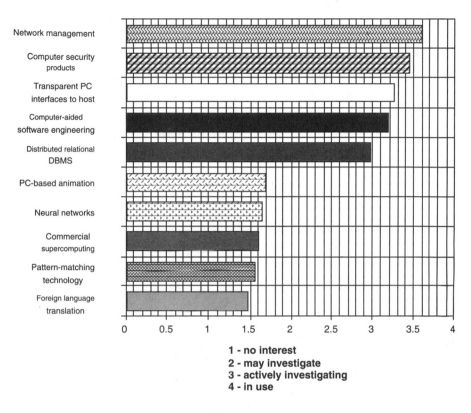

Network management	
Computer security products	
Transparent PC interfaces to host	
Computer-aided software engineering	
Distributed relational DBMS	
PC-based animation	
Neural networks	
Commercial supercomputing	
Pattern-matching technology	
Foreign language translation	

0   0.5   1   1.5   2   2.5   3   3.5   4

1 - no interest
2 - may investigate
3 - actively investigating
4 - in use

Figure 11.1: Levels of interest in technology

11.1 WHY DOES TECHNOLOGY EVOLUTION OCCUR?

If we are going to plan and prepare for technology evolution, we should have some understanding of how and why it occurs. Basalla [1] offers this explanation:

> ... if evolutionary change is to occur, then novelty must find a way to assert itself in the midst of the continuous ... the argument that economic incentives were the driving force behind the invention and patenting of a majority of novel artifacts is not persuasive. Although many inventors were motivated by the unrealistic belief that their particular gadgets would earn them a fortune, others pursued novelty for the psychic rewards it brought. In neither instance, however, do we find inventors working to supply pressing human needs or carefully appraising economic conditions, calculating precisely what innovations are most likely to bring the higher financial returns. For this reason, many patent holders

belong in the company of the technological dreamers who repeatedly, enthusiastically, and ingeniously provide solutions to problems that are mainly of concern to themselves.

Another interesting characteristic of technology evolution is that the immediate use, and even the potential long-term use, of a new invention is difficult to determine. And *the inventor himself is often the worst spokesperson for its potential uses*. Thomas Edison, for example, published an article in 1878 describing 10 ways that the phonograph might prove useful to the public:

- Taking dictation without the aid of a stenographer
- Providing "talking books" for the blind
- Teaching public speaking
- Reproducing music
- Preserving important family sayings, reminiscences, and the last words of the dying
- Creating new sounds for music boxes and musical toys
- Preserving the exact pronunciation of foreign languages
- Teaching spelling and other rote material
- Recording telephone calls

Notice that "taking dictation" was first on the list, but musical reproduction was only fourth; many of the other suggested applications look ludicrous to us a century later. As Basalla [1] reports, "even a decade later, Edison resisted efforts to market the phonograph as a musical instrument and concentrated on selling it as a dictating machine." This is something that venture capitalists and technology-lovers should keep in mind when listening to proposals from technology-dreamers: the technology may be terrific, but it will probably be used for something other than for what it was intended.

Can *anyone* predict how new technology will be used, or how it will evolve? Noted science fiction writer and eminent scientist Arthur C. Clarke thinks not [2]:

> All attempts to predict the future in any detail will appear ludicrous in a few years. . . .
>
> This book . . . does not try to describe *the* future, but to define the boundaries within which possible futures must lie.

If we regard the ages that stretch ahead of us as an unmapped and unexplored country, what I am trying to do is to survey its frontiers and to get some idea of its extent.

The detailed geography of the interior must remain unknown—until we reach it.

Clarke also provides three "laws" to help put discussions about new inventions into proper perspective. These are wonderful aphorisms and should be etched onto the foreheads of all technology dreamers and technology skeptics:

Clarke's First Law

Whenever a distinguished but elderly scientist says that something is possible, he is almost certainly right. When he states that something is impossible, he is very probably wrong.

Clarke's Second Law

The only way to discover the limits is to venture a little way past them into the impossible.

Clarke's Third Law

Any sufficiently advanced technology is indistinguishable from magic.

For jaded veterans of the computer field, "magic" is something that evokes the "Wow!" reaction. The original Macintosh computer elicited that response; Steve Jobs's NeXT machine drew a somewhat muted "wow." But most of the PC hardware and software today produces a "ho-hum" from observers: yes, it's a little faster and a little cheaper, but so what?

In 1991, when this book was being written, demonstrations of pen-based software from GO Corporation and Microsoft and pen-based laptops from NCR, GRiD, and Momenta drew loud "Wow's!" from crowds at computer conferences. Conference delegates behaved with the wanton abandon of priests at a religious conference suddenly being told that celibacy was no longer required. Grown men and women could be seen sitting on the floor in their business suits, huddled over notebook-size pen-based machines, playing furiously with their toys with the same intense concentration today's youngsters reserve for their Teenage Mutant Ninja Turtle toys.

But why does this matter? Why not wait until leading-edge technology has become well established to make plans? For any new technology, a number of harried managers can be heard to mutter under their breath, "Maybe if we wait long enough, all these fads will have disappeared . . .". The main problem with this wait-and-see attitude is that it takes most organizations a long time to adapt to new technology, indeed, a long time to change its culture in any respect, as we saw in Chapter 4 and Chapter 6.

Studies of the software industry indicate that it takes 10 to 15 years for new technology to become widely used. Evidence of this can be seen in the slow deployment of CASE tools through the industry, the long period of time required to promulgate new versions of CO-BOL, and the fact that most organizations still don't have an enterprise data model, even though the idea has been discussed for some 20 years. So if you see a new technology that looks promising, there's a good reason to get started using it *now* if you want to have it well deployed in your organization by the beginning of the next millennium.

11.2 THE IMPACT OF HARDWARE ON TECHNOLOGY EVOLUTION IN THE SOFTWARE FIELD

There is no question that advances in software technology are intimately associated with corresponding advances in hardware. And throughout the career, if not the entire lifetime, of everyone in the software field, hardware technology has improved by a steady 20 to 30 percent annually, *compounded*. Will this continue for the rest of this decade?

A recent study by Al Cutaia [5] suggests that hardware technology will not only continue to advance, but the cumulative results will be staggering. Cutaia summarizes his predictions by stating that

> the results obtained by technology mapping showed that the 1987 system and its parts may be expected to change as follows from 1987 to 2000.
>
> • cost reduction: factor of 145
>
> • capacity increase: factor of 90
>
> • reliability improvement: factor of 2 to 225
>
> • performance improvement: factor of 56
>
> • size reduction: factor of 250

These predictions are based on a careful technology, illustrated in Figure 11.2, as well as projections of technology improvements in such areas as memory capacity and memory costs, shown in Figures 11.3 and 11.4.

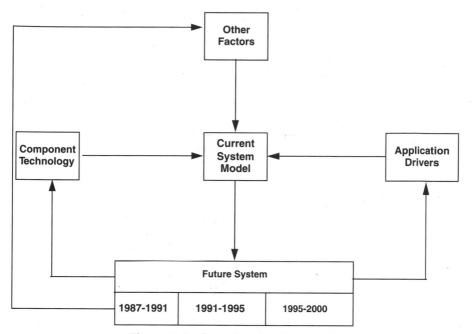

Figure 11.2: Cutaia's technology model

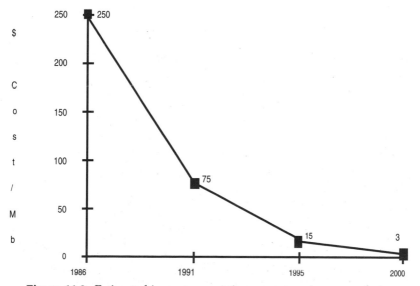

Figure 11.3: Estimated improvements in memory cost per megabyte

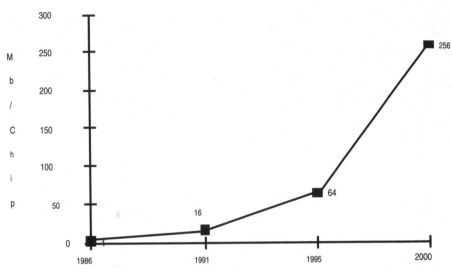

Figure 11.4: Estimated improvements in memory capacity

On top of this, Cutaia predicts that parallel processing architectures will add a performance improvement of between 444:1 and 1038:1 by the end of the decade.

On a more informal basis, two prominent scientists, Gordon Bell and Kenneth Wilson, argued about the likely improvements in computer technology at the 1987 Fall Joint Computer Conference. Bell, who was instrumental in developing much of DEC's early generations of hardware, and who has been involved in supercomputer start-up companies, predicted that hardware technology would advance 10-fold over the next five years (by 1992); this would be followed by another (compounded) 10-fold advance during the next five years; and that, in turn, would be followed by yet another 10-fold improvement in the five years culminating in the year 2002.

Kenneth Wilson, a Nobel laureate physicist, and director of the supercomputer center at Cornell University, had a more ambitious prediction: he argues that computer hardware technology will advance by a factor of 100 over the next five years, then another factor of 100, and by yet another 100-fold advance.

Bell thus predicts that the hardware technology of 2002 will be 1000 times more powerful than that of 1987; Wilson argues that our technology will be 1 *million* times more powerful. Regardless of whose predictions—Cutaia's, Bell's, or Wilson's—are more accurate, there is no question that the hardware of the mid-1990s and late-1990s will be *qualitatively* more powerful, not just a mere quantity of 20 or 30 percent. How would today's system development activities be influenced by hardware a thousand times or a million times more powerful than today's?

The technology for software developers is likely to be the main concern of those reading this book, but it is important to note one of the "drivers" in Cutaia's model shown in Figure 11.2: *the user.* The prospect of dramatically more powerful hardware affects the very nature of the application, as well as the tools and languages we software weenies use to develop the system. *Hardware enables new kinds of applications, which may drive new software technologies.* The following projections from Cutaia illustrate this dramatically:

- In 1980, 100 percent of the transactions in a typical system were simple text, requiring an average of 600 bytes of storage each.

- In 1987, 24 percent of transactions were "office automation" transactions, requiring an average of 2000 bytes each.

- In 1995, only 5 percent will be conventional business-oriented transactions of the kind we built systems for in 1980. Thirty percent will be voice-data transactions, requiring 42,000 bytes; 10 percent will be mixed text and graphics, requiring 5000 to 10,000 bytes; and up to 40 percent will be image-based transactions, requiring 20,000 to 50,000 bytes each.

Remember also that hardware improvements do not occur in just one dimension. The 1995 mix of transactions mentioned is made possible partly by the improved storage capabilities of hard disk and optical disk storage and partly by hardware-based compression algorithms that allow complex images and graphics to be stored even on small-memory machines. As illustrated by Figure 11.5, we will see improvements in size, cost, and speed—in addition to the various other categories indicated by Cutaia.

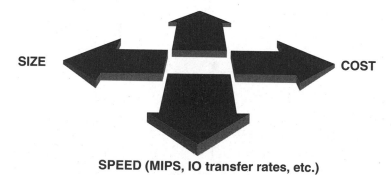

SPEED (MIPS, IO transfer rates, etc.)

Figure 11.5: The dimensions of hardware improvement

Today's example of "hot" new technology is pen-based computing, but we can only barely imagine what form computing will take by the end of the decade. Today's notebook machines—patterned after the ubiquitous "form factor" of the 8.5- by 11-inch piece of paper—will appear in a dazzling variety of sizes and shapes, from credit card size to wall size. We will have disposable computers, so cheap that they can be thrown away after one use, and they will be so small that they can be attached to every pig, chicken, and cow in the farmyard, implanted in every potato and ear of corn in the fields, and buried in the packaging in which we buy our milk and cereal.

What will software developers do with this new hardware power? One might expect to hear fewer complaints about the inefficiencies of fourth generation languages, code generators, object-oriented programming languages, and so on; indeed, one might hope that a 1000-fold improvement in hardware technology would forevermore banish the use of assembly language and low-level languages like C from the repertoire of the professional programmer. But my experience of the past 25 years—experience that probably qualifies me as one of Clarke's "elderly scientists"—suggests otherwise. People will still be programming in assembler and C for a long time. Sigh.

But it *is* reasonable to expect that *every* software developer will have his or her own personal workstation, hundreds of times more powerful than the terminals and low-grade PCs found on most programmers' desks today. Nobody would refuse a programmer a calculator or a telephone or a wastebasket today; we are only a few years from treating superpowerful CASE tools in a similar vein. In general, we can assume that the IPSE/APSE CASE tools currently being developed by research groups around the world will be practical commodities by the middle to late part of this decade; this is in stark contrast to today's CASE tools, in which it often takes a full 48-hour weekend of computer time to "consolidate" workstation-based local dictionaries into a central repository. In short, development tools will be able to afford much more compute-bound activity; recompiling a 750,000-line Ada program (which takes a week of computer time on a DEC VAX computer today) will not be seen as a major problem. Similarly, arguments about inefficiency in the resulting application program may also disappear.

Will more powerful hardware bring more thorough testing? If *quality* of testing can be associated with quantity, then there is reason for hope; however, we have long known that even with nearly infinite computing capacity, we could not provide complete, exhaustive testing of large, complex systems. So careful selection of test cases, analysis of branch coverage, and all the other components of "smart" testing today will probably continue to be important. On the other hand, if the testing of complex real-time systems evolves in the direction of *simulation*, as Morrison [6] suggests, then more powerful hardware will indeed be necessary. It is probably no accident that the simulation models for the Strategic Defense Initiative's "Star Wars" program operate on Cray computers.

From the statistics provided by Cutaia, and from current developments in the computer field, it seems likely that the major thing that will "suck up" all the CPU cycles provided by next generation hardware will be *human interface* technology. "The 1990s," says Bill Curtis of the Software Engineering Institute, "will be the decade of the human interface" [7].

We will certainly see a proliferation of handwriting-based computer technology; early models are already beginning to appear, and the next generation may well be able to accomplish real-time *cursive* handwriting recognition. Digitized voice input and voice output will be combined with video, optical disk, and perhaps speech recognition—together with wireless communications and the lightweight portable machines that we can carry with us. As mentioned in Chapter 6, this technology is being driven by the consumer marketplace (or what the technology dreamers assume the consumer marketplace wants). In turn, this will demand new technologies from the software developers, of which *pencentric* systems—systems that are fundamentally based on the *pen* as the major input device, rather than the keyboard—will be the first.

11.3 LIKELY DEVELOPMENTS IN THE SOFTWARE AREA

As suggested, hardware technology is likely to be the key driver for next generation software—not only in terms of the tools and languages made possible by faster hardware, but also indirectly in terms of the new kinds of applications the users will want to use on their new hardware.

What other software developments are we likely to see? One probable development is continued advancement in the area of code generators and application generators: it is reasonable to expect that by the end of this decade, if not sooner, we will be able to generate code directly from specifications for 90 percent of the normal applications, in contrast to 5 to 10 percent today. Thus, organizations ignoring CASE technology today because it does not provide full code generation should realize that they run the risk of being left behind by developing technology—*and it will be too late to grab the technology by 1995.*

Similarly, it is reasonable to expect that we will have full reverse engineering of old code—both on the data side and on the process side—by the end of the 1990s, probably with massive use of expert system technology. As discussed in Chapter 10, the reverse engineering technology of 1990–91 is still relatively primitive, and many organizations have chosen to ignore it. But remember: technology advances faster than we think, and people change more slowly.

Ironically, the systems being reverse engineered by the end of this decade are likely to be the tens of thousands of small, undocumented 4GL programs that are being written at this very moment.[2] But COBOL programs will still be written in the year 2000, even though COBOL itself may not look very much like the current COBOL-85. And despite the occasional predictions that assembly language will be outlawed by the U.S. government sometime this decade, it is likely that someone who is absolutely *determined* to sink to the lowest level of programming languages will be able to find an employer who will indulge his base instincts.

What about methodology improvements? Will we ever see a "unified field theory" of software development methodologies? Some consultants and gurus have been predicting this for well over a decade, but it has not happened yet; today, there is activity underway to combine the best elements of structured analysis, information engineering, and object-oriented methodologies; one such effort is known as "Euromethod." But it is much like trying to combine the world's religions into one: even if Catholicism, Buddhism, Judaism, and Moslem religions are compatible, there is little reason to think that the 1990s will offer any more compelling reasons for them to join together than in past decades.[3] In our field, computer hardware advances are more likely to lead to *new* methodologies—for example, "pencentric systems methodology"—than an ecumenical marriage of the existing methodologies.

---

[2] A contrary opinion: Tom DeMarco [8] argues that, in surveys he has conducted, only 0.5 percent of production application programs today are coded in a 4GL. That's one-half of 1 percent.

[3] Tim Lister has an interesting insight here: if the marketplace wanted such a marriage to take place, he argues, it would have happened already.

In any case, it *is* likely that the successful methodologies of the 1990s will do a much better job of providing step-by-step guidance, together with automated support, for *all* the activities in the life cycle, from womb to tomb.

Another area of software development technology is sure to improve in the 1990s, though it has little to do with advances in hardware technology: ongoing creation of massive database of previously completed software projects to provide *metrics* for widespread, accurate estimates. Today, there are a handful of commercial organizations—Howard Rubin Associates and Capers Jones's Software Productivity Research probably the most notable among them—that have databases of 10,000 projects or more. By the end of the 1990s, we should have databases of 100,000 projects, available for public access.

11.4 CONTEXT ISSUES: FOR WHOM ARE WE DEVELOPING OUR SYSTEMS?

A current emphasis for many software developers is that of extending the range of computer applications to include white-collar and blue-collar workers who have no previous experience with computers; for example, the initial applications for many of the pen-based computer systems will be aimed at truck drivers and insurance claims adjusters.

However, much of the work that goes on here is based on the assumption that the vast majority of the human race is still computer illiterate, if not computer phobic. The phobia is not restricted to computer systems; it extends to cameras, VCRs, automated teller machines, dishwashers, and a wide range of electronic equipment. In most cases, as Curtis [7] suggests, the problem is in the design of the user interface, but many software developers make the implicit assumption that an even larger part of the problem is that the users are somehow mentally deficient. And while it is a gross oversimplification, there is also a tendency to associate computer phobia with the generation of people over 40, for example, one's mother or father, or Aunt Matilda or Uncle George, who can never seem to figure out how to program the VCR to record the late-night Humphrey Bogart movie.

Regardless of whether this is a fair accusation, it's nevertheless evident to everyone that the generation of children has *no* trouble operating today's electronic gadgets, regardless of whether they come with instructions in English, Japanese, or Sanskrit. And this is a key point for today's software developers to remember: *today's children will eventually grow up and become tomorrow's generation of users.*

Tomorrow's users will be much more computer literate: an American child born in 1980 will write an average of 10,000 lines of code before finishing high school. While most of this code will be meaningless jumbles of BASIC and LOGO, there is no doubt that the user of the mid-1990s and late-1990s will have a much better understanding of how to interact with computers than will the generation of users who grew up in the 1950s, 1960s, and 1970s. Our image of the truck driver-as-user may be a useful mental model today, but will be useless by the end of the decade.

This is only part of the "context" question to which software developers must give a great deal of thought as they plan for tomorrow's systems. Some additional questions include the following:

- What will the world be like in the year 2000?
- What will your company be like?
- What kind of systems and applications will be built?
- What will hardware be like?
- What will programming languages, database management systems, and software tools be like?

Of course, it is entirely beyond the scope of this book to forecast what the world will be like in the year 2000 (or any other year). But for some companies, this will become a major activity. During the 1970s and 1980s, we have seen the emphasis shift from issues of programming (e.g., structured programming) to issues of design, to issues of analysis. During the 1990s, many organizations are attempting to concentrate on *enterprise modeling* before they even begin to worry about specifying the requirements for an individual system. And if this is true, it is quite possible that the world-class organizations of the next decade will be doing *global* modeling, which will influence their enterprise models, which will influence their business plans, and which will ultimately influence the analysis, design, and implementation of individual systems.

When thinking about context, remember also that today's new system will be tomorrow's maintenance problem: the system built in 1980 will be 20 years old by the end of this decade. And today's organization, which currently spends 50 percent of its budget on maintenance and enhancement, is likely to be spending 90 percent of its time on these activities by the end of the decade. On the other hand, today's complex systems will seem trivial tomorrow, just as the systems that seemed complex to us in the 1970s (e.g., involving 100,000 lines of code) now seem rather mundane.

11.5 CONCLUSIONS: WHAT TO DO?

One of the themes running throughout this book is that change occurs slowly. If you are to accomplish any of the changes suggested in this book, and if you are to prepare for the next wave of hardware and software technology, you need to sell your senior management on the notion of a 10-year horizon.

You also need to remember that the biggest problem will be that of inertia. Don't worry about technology: it will change faster than you think. *People* issues will be the most significant of all.

To put it another way, *technology transfer* will be the biggest problem with new system development technologies in the year 2000, just as they were in 1990 and in 1980. To deal with the technology transfer problem, you can read books [9], join research consortia (MCC, SEI, ESPRIT, etc.), attend conferences like the annual International Conference on Software Engineering, and set up internal groups within your company to focus on technology transfer issues. *But you have to get started now.*

Is "now" too late? No! At a 1983 conference on the use of computers in education and training in New Delhi, an Indian government minister, Vikram Sarabhai, made the following observation:

> Our initial backwardness, our late arrival on the scene, and the small investments we made in the past need not remain as our handicaps but can be turned into our most valuable advantages if we make the right decisions now, order judicious investments and march forward with determination.

This observation was true in the 1980s, and it remains true in the 1990s. Now it's up to you to march forward with determination. You'll be marching beside a number of other organizations around the world who are determined to be among the best, and therefore among the survivors, as the software industry moves inexorably into the twenty-first century.

END NOTES

1. Basalla, George. *The Evolution of Technology.* New York: Cambridge University Press, 1988.

2. Kuhn, Thomas. *The Structure of Scientific Revolutions*. Chicago: The University of Chicago Press, 1962.
3. Clarke, Arthur C. *Profiles of the Future*, 2nd ed. New York: Holt, Rinehart and Winston, 1984.
4. O'Neill, Gerard K. 2001: *A Hopeful View of the Future*. New York: Simon & Schuster, 1983.
5. Cutaia, Al. *Technology Projection Modeling of Future Computer Systems*. Englewood Cliffs, NJ: Yourdon Press/Prentice Hall, 1990.
6. Morrison, John. "A Wicked Problem—Software Testing in Large-Scale Systems," *American Programmer*, April 1991.
7. Curtis, Bill. "Usability: The Quality Issue of the 1990s," *American Programmer*, February 1991.
8. DeMarco, Tom. "The Second Pastist Pronouncement," *American Programmer*, March 1989.
9. Bouldin, Barbara. *Agents of Change*. Englewood Cliffs, NJ: Yourdon Press/Prentice Hall, 1989.

Appendix A

Software Technology in India

DELHI—"India is like a snake," explained Rajendra Pawar shortly after I arrived on a sweltering, humid day in mid-August. "The head is moving into the twenty-first century, but the tail is still in the seventeenth century. Our problem is keeping the head moving forward while not forgetting about the body and the tail."

This proved to be an apt metaphor, and one that stood me in good stead during a two-week tour of Delhi, Madras, Bombay, and Calcutta. Another metaphor: Delhi is the Washington of India, the center of government and home to international embassies. Madras is like Boston, known for its rich academic heritage (now I know the origin of the term "Boston Brahmin"; Madras's Brahmin sect is considered the most intellectual, most reverent, and closest to God). Bombay is New York and Chicago rolled into one. And Calcutta . . . well, no one offered an analogy for Calcutta. Calcutta is Calcutta, unlike any other city, utterly overwhelming to a first-time Western visitor.

My trip was organized and sponsored by the National Institute of Information Technology (NIIT), India's largest and most prestigious computer education company. NIIT's managing director, Rajendra Pawar, is an old friend with whom I began doing business in 1982, when I ran my own training and consulting firm. After years of sending consultants and instructors to lecture on structured systems development techniques, I finally accepted a long-standing invitation to visit India myself.

Why? Not to see the Taj Mahal or sample the curry, but to investigate the global software scene. India is a massive country of 850 million people, with an educational system and an official business language inherited from 250 years of British colonial rule. The Indian people—many of whom I have met in colleges, companies, and research labs around the United States—are obviously bright, energetic, and ambitious. Their salaries, I assumed, were far below the bloated wages we pay our software people. I had read about Texas Instruments' software development group in Bangalore, about Tata's software work in England and about negotiations to establish a satellite link for software development work between India and Massachusetts. I decided it was time for a firsthand look at what was going on and what the implications might be for our software industry.

Through seminars, informal luncheons and dinners, and meetings at government agencies, professional computer societies, and private sector companies, I had a chance to talk with over 300 software engineers and DP managers, as well as with dozens of senior executives and government officials. I also gathered valuable information on the Indian computer industry from *Dataquest*, *Computers Today*, and *Computers and Communications*, three of India's surprisingly numerous computer publications. And I was given an excellent summary of India's future software plans by NASSCOM, a newly formed National Association of Software and Service Companies.

As I found during my visit to Japan, there is more to the popular stories and myths about Indian software and Indian programmers— and less. India has more indigenous manufacturers of PC clones than I had realized (about 40), but far fewer mainframes; IBM, which left India in 1976, still led all manufacturers in 1988 Indian computer revenues as a result of selling a mere six mainframes. There is far more Unix expertise than I had anticipated, but far less experience managing large, complex software development projects. Relational databases and 4GLs are widely used, but CASE technology is virtually unknown, and no one seems to have heard of software reengineering.

Advanced AI projects are going on in some parts of the country, but large segments of the business community still labor under the vintage-1960s illusion that software is free and should take no time to develop. Some 25-MHz 80386 machines are available, but many of the larger companies only got rid of their 1401s two or three years ago. In a land of cheap labor—a programmer typically earns 3000 rupees (US$180) a month, and full-time household help can be hired for 150 rupees a month—India is accustomed to overwhelming any problem with a "Chinese army" approach. Yet the Indian software engineering labor force is 20 times smaller than ours. India, the snake.

Notwithstanding these contradictions, I returned home convinced that India has an opportunity to become a major force in the global software marketplace by the end of this century. There are no guarantees, of course, and India may well prove to be its own worst enemy as it strives to build its software industry to the level of North America and Europe. We have yet to see whether a country with a stifling bureaucracy and a socialist economy, dominated by government-owned "public sector" companies, can nourish the entrepreneurial spirit of a Silicon Valley or a Route 128. India does have huge, successful, highly competitive industrial conglomerates such as Tata, but Tata's much touted software subsidiary, Tata Consultancy Services (TCS), is only a $30 million operation. It remains to be seen whether it can grow to the size of a Computer Sciences or an EDS or if its heavy-industry manufacturing parent company will spawn the kind of massive software factories I saw at Toshiba, Hitachi, Fujitsu, and NEC.

Still, it would be folly for anyone seriously interested in the software industry to ignore India. If you're in the CASE business, you should be watching the developments of TCS's CASEPAC and TELCO's (another Tata company) Turbo-Analyst product, in addition to all the American and European products. If you're in the software services and consulting industry, you should consider establishing a strategic alliance with one of the Indian software houses (but stop the shortsighted practice of importing cheap Indian programmers on one-year assignments, as if they were some kind of high-tech migrant workers; I'll explain why shortly).

If you're a computer hardware manufacturer, consider following Texas Instruments' lead and establish a software development group for your operating systems and compilers in Bangalore. If you run a DP operation at a bank or financial services organization, and you're looking for good, cheap applications software, contact the people at Citicorp Overseas Software Limited (COSL) in Bombay (or contact their U.S. marketing office, listed under Section A.5, "Resources," at the end of the chapter). If you don't fall into any of these categories, if you're just an ordinary software developer who wants to know whence cometh the next wave of competition, consider subscribing to one of the Indian computer journals (see Section A.5, "Resources").

A.1 A BRIEF RETROSPECTIVE

Before examining India's current computer scene in detail, a brief look at how it got its start might be helpful. I didn't ask when the first computer appeared in India, but the consensus is that computerization began—primarily in the government sector—in the early 1960s. IBM had the lion's share of the market: the IBM 1401 was the most common "big machine" in the country for nearly two decades. Because of India's ties to England, ICL was also well represented, and Univac and Burroughs had both established presences.

The most significant event in India's early computer history was a 1976 government law restricting foreign ownership in India-based corporations to 40 percent; majority ownership had to be held by Indians. IBM and Coca-Cola, among others, refused to accept the new situation and moved their operations out of the country. (I'm not sure which departure was more significant. How can anyone imagine writing software without clutching a bottle of Coke?) In any case, IBM retreated to Australia where it has continued to service the Indian market. But for all practical purposes, the 360/370/308X mainframe period of the 1960s through the early 1980s passed India by. Imagine! A country without IBM mainframes! It's almost as mind-boggling as the notion of a country without Coca-Cola and McDonald's (an indigenous company ripped off the Coke logo and bottle design and began producing "Campa Cola," but I can report from personal experience that it's not the real thing!).

It is not only politics that explains the slow growth in computer usage. It's also India's general status as a struggling Third World country, far more concerned with hunger, disease, illiteracy, and poverty than with the luxuries of online banking systems and management information systems. Before this decade, there were some computers in use, but the overall level of computerization was about what you would expect of the Soviet Union.

All this changed dramatically in the mid-1980s. There were two reasons: First and most important was the PC revolution, which suddenly brought the price of computing power down to a level the country could afford. The PC revolution probably began in India two or three years later than it did in the United States, and it is by no means as widespread or impressive numerically. But after five years, India is caught up in almost the same level of PC euphoria the United States has enjoyed for the last decade.

The second change occurred when Rajiv Gandhi assumed leadership of the country after the assassination of his mother, Indira Gandhi, in 1984. A manager and technocrat, Gandhi was determined to lead the head and body and tail of India into the twenty-first century. To accomplish this, he identified telecommunications and information technology as a "core sector" industry, along with such traditional industries as steel, power generation, oil, and automobiles. He actively encouraged the growth of a local information technology (IT) industry and loosened the government stranglehold on imports of foreign hardware and software. Sadly (for the computer industry), Gandhi lost power and was voted out of office before he could implement fully all these changes. More tragically, he, like his mother before him, was assassinated, in May 1991.

But Rajiv Gandhi's influence on the Indian computer industry was significant. Import duties, for example, are still high—typically 107 percent of the base price—but there are legal mechanisms for avoiding the duty in some cases. You can now find DEC and HP, Sun, and even Macintosh computers in India. And, yes, there are a few IBM mainframes, though IBM has not yet moved back into the country. But you probably won't find any true-blue IBM PCs or PS/2s, due to the numerous indigenous PC-clone manufacturers. XT-class, 286-class, and 386-class machines are everywhere, manufactured by companies such as Hindustan Computers Limited, Wipro Information Technology, Pertech Computers, and Zenith.

In summary, the history of the Indian computer industry can be neatly divided into two phases: a stagnant, IBM-less, pre-PC period and a new, thriving era that began with the introduction of the PC and Gandhi's push for modernization of the IT sector.

A.2 INDIA'S COMPUTER INDUSTRY TODAY

There are three ways of looking at the Indian computer industry: by reviewing industry statistics on computer hardware and software, by looking at the kind of computer projects undertaken by Indian organizations, and by assessing the level of sophistication of its technology. The industry statistics are useful, of course, and provide an overall glimpse at both the hardware and software components; financial figures are reported in rupees, "Rs. crores" (a crore is 1 million rupees, a commonly used figure in Indian business discussions) and "Rs. lakhs" (hundreds of thousands of rupees), at an exchange rate of approximately 17 rupees to the U.S. dollar. The second and third categories are more subjective, based on my conversations with DP professionals and others during my visit.

A.2.1 Industry Statistics

The July 1989 issue of *Computers and Communications*, a leading Indian computer magazine, reported that the annual information technology industry revenues for the year ending March 31, 1989 were Rs. 1,095.26 crores. By comparison, the output of the Japanese IT industry is approximately Rs. 10,000 crores, and the Hong Kong IT industry is approximately Rs. 825 crores. The overall composition of the Indian IT industry is summarized in Figure A.1.

Although tiny by U.S. or Japanese standards, the Indian IT industry is growing at a rapid pace of approximately 59 percent annually. This compares with a 12 percent growth rate for the IT industry in the United States. As indicated earlier, India's governmental authorities play a large role in determining the future of the IT industry. Thus, a first glance at Figure A.2 would seem to indicate an interesting irony: the government is not a major computer user when compared with the private sector. This is partly the result of strong and widespread antipathy toward computers by many clerical and administrative workers, who fear that management is introducing automation to reduce staff. This attitude largely disappeared in the United States in the mid-1960s; now we worry more about the dehumanizing aspects of computers and other "soft" issues. In India, however, the feeling is so strong that one state government recently announced it had decided not to automate its administrative functions.

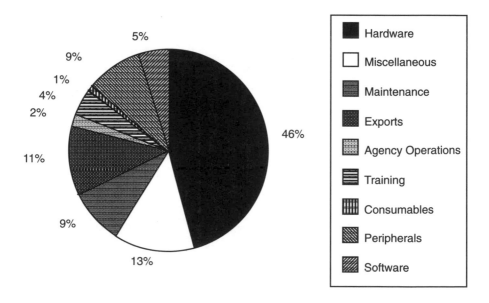

Figure A.1: Composition of the Indian IT industry

When looking at Figure A.2, be aware that the "public sector" category represents government-owned companies in the "core sector" industries of oil, steel, automobiles, airlines, and so forth. And the defense category is clearly a component of government; indeed, so is education, since educational policies and expenditures are more centrally controlled than in our highly decentralized situation. Thus, directly or indirectly, the Indian government does control slightly over 60 percent of the IT industry.

As Figure A.1 shows, the hardware and peripherals sectors represent approximately 55 percent of the overall IT industry. To help put this in a different perspective, look at Table A.1 which shows the revenues and growth rate of the top 20 Indian IT companies for the year ending March 31, 1989, as reported by *Computers and Communications*. Thus, the largest computer company in India generates approximately US$71 million in annual revenues; annual revenues of approximately $7 million are sufficient to earn one a place on the top 20 list.

Obviously, most of the companies are engaged in a combination of hardware, software, consultancy, and other ventures. It is also interesting to see the revenues of the top 20 software vendors in India, shown in Table A.2.

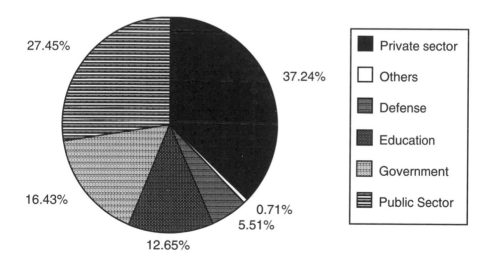

Figure A.2: Indian IT industry by market segment

Finally, since India is so interested in the possibility of expanding its software export industry, it is instructive to look at the leading software export companies, as reported in the July 1989 issue of *Dataquest*; these are shown in Table A.3.

Table A.1: India's leading software export companies

Company	Revenues (Rs. crores)	Growth Rate in %
Hindustan Computers Ltd. (HCL)	121.02	100.90
CMC Ltd.	102.07	36.82
Wipro Information Technology (WITL)	93.95	72.83
Electronics Corp. of India Ltd. (ECIL)	75.93	63.29
Sterling Electronics	53.83	49.36
Tata Consultancy Services (TCS)	43.83	51.14
ICIM Ltd. (estimated)	42.00	–6.67
Pertech (PCL)	40.00	515.38
Essen	30.85	173.74
Tata Unisys Ltd. (estimated)	29.00	31.82
DCM Data Products	23.85	28.86
Hinditron	27.40	17.55
ESPL (estimated)	25.00	19.05
Zenith	20.54	28.46
OMC Computers	17.02	36.71
Computer Point	17.00	15.41
ORG	15.82	41.12
IDM	13.94	–26.05
Minicomp	13.40	106.15
CMS Computers	12.37	23.70

To put this in a global perspective, International Data Corp. (IDC) estimates that worldwide revenues in the software market for 1990 will be approximately US$128.3 billion; by the year 2000, worldwide software revenues are projected to be US$300 billion. This means that India's software exporters will represent approximately one-twentieth of 1 percent of the worldwide software market. Hardly enough to attract attention.

Of course, India's software industry could double or quadruple (with significant revenues and benefits within the country) and still not represent enough of a threat for anyone to notice. Thus, India's hopes of increasing software exports from today's level of Rs. 100 crores to Rs. 1500 crores by 1995 may be an ambitious goal, but it can certainly be accomplished without provoking a severe counterattack from overseas competition.

And we should not expect that all India's computer exports will be aimed at the U.S. and Western European markets. Indeed, *Comput-*

ers and Communications, in its annual survey of the IT industry, observed that a "major share" of 1988–89 exports had actually gone to the USSR. While there are limits on the extent of high-tech hardware that can be exported to Eastern bloc countries, India can always export turnkey software products and customized software services. Japan, too, is a potential market, with the advantage of being much closer than the United States.

Table A.2: Top 20 Indian Software Companies

Company	Revenues (in Rs. lakhs)
Tata Consultancy Services (TCS)	1,035
HCL Limited	695
Wipro Information Technology (WITL)	463
Computer Point	299
WSL	219
Hinditron	150
Godrej & Boyce	118
ORG	104
NIIT	100
PCL	96
Softek	92
Infosys	91
Meera Computers	62
Mastek	52
Digital Equipment	44
IDM	31
Aurelec	24
Advanced Micronic	23
A. K. Saxena	22
Indotronix	22

Table A.3: Leading Software Export Companies

Company	Revenues (Rs. crores)	% of total revenues	% of total exports
Tata Consultancy Services (TCS)	32.0	74	32.0
Tata Unisys (TUL)	27.5	93	27.5
Citicorp Overseas Software (COSL)	5.5	100	5.5
Datamatics	4.86	88	4.86
Texas Instruments	4.5	100	4.5
Total of leaders	74.36		74.36
Other companies	25.64		25.64
Industry total	100.0		100.0

Dataquest also provided some figures on the "contribution factor"—annual revenues generated by each employee—in the different segments of the Indian IT industry. The figures tell an interesting story:

	Employee Contribution Rs. lakhs/person/annum
Hardware vendors	6.35
Peripherals	4.96
Software companies	1.95

Dataquest went on to remark that if major software exporters like Tata Consultancy, Tata Unisys, Citicorp Overseas Software, and Infosys were taken out, the remaining software firms would show an average contribution of Rs. 0.68 lakhs per employee per year—or about US$4000 per year.

Clearly, it's the export of software products that is responsible for the major component of employee contribution in the software industry, not the delivery of software "services" (otherwise known as "body shop" labor). But even at the higher level of Rs. 1.95 lakhs per employee per year, the software industry is obviously operating at a much lower level than the hardware and peripherals companies. Perhaps this is one reason why several Indian software firms are operating at break-even or even at a loss.

One widely acknowledged reason for India's software industry woes is rampant piracy. Independent surveys by Tata Unisys and Wipro indicate that almost 80 percent of computer users in the country use some pirated software. NASSCOM has made its own estimates of software piracy by looking at India's domestic hardware sales and estimating what software revenues should be—assuming, for example, that software expenditures for micros are approximately 20 percent of the hardware cost, and so forth. NASSCOM concluded that India should have generated Rs. 130 crores in the year ending March 31, 1989, but actual software revenues were only Rs. 75 crores.

Piracy is obviously a major problem: in addition to international friction (India, for example, is one of eight countries on the U.S. "priority watch list" because of its alleged failure to protect U.S. intellectual property rights), it damages the domestic software industry by creating the widespread mind-set that software is free.

NASSCOM also has some intriguing figures on the overall computer industry and the software sector. One of its most interesting reports is a projection of national computer expenditures (hardware and software combined) as a percentage of gross national product (GNP):

Year	Computers as a % of GNP
1985	0.07
1987	0.13
1990	0.25
1995	0.65
2000	1.00

Thus, computer expenditures are not estimated to reach the 1 percent level for another 10 years. By contrast, most developed countries spend between 3 and 5 percent of their GNP on computers. I believe this is a terribly significant statistic: to build a viable export industry, India must have a strong domestic computer industry as a foundation—computers must be part of every business, part of the culture, part of the social infrastructure. At a level of one quarter of 1 percent of the overall GNP in 1990, India's computer industry is barely visible.

What can we conclude from all this? Obviously, India's IT industry is tiny when compared numerically with that of Japan, Europe, or the United States. Not only are its revenues much lower, but its contribution to the country's GNP is roughly 10 times lower than in the more developed countries. And the industry "infrastructure" is still fairly fragile. While it may seem impressive that there are 40 companies manufacturing PC-clone computers, it's nothing when you realize that the United States has some 500 computer hardware manufacturers (not counting peripherals), some 4000 service companies, and some 8000 software companies.

On the other hand, the Indian computer industry is growing rapidly. As indicated, we could see several more years of compounded 50 percent annual growth before other countries begin to regard India as a serious threat. By then, a strong domestic industry may be sufficiently healthy to compete in the world marketplace and continue its growth. To achieve this, India must have a carefully conceived 5-year and 10-year plan, and it must have active encouragement and investment from the government (I'll discuss my thoughts on this shortly).

A.2.2 The Nature of Systems Projects in India

Investment and encouragement by the government may not be enough to create the kind of growth that everyone is hoping for in India. I am concerned that the primary obstacle to major growth in the IT industry may turn out to be limited experience and expertise. As noted, India is basically a land without IBM mainframes. And, while many of its programmers are familiar with COBOL, there is an almost total lack of experience in the alphabet soup of IBM operating systems, telecommunications packages, and database management systems: MVS, VM, CICS, DB2, JES3, IDMS, SAA, SNA, . . . ad nauseum.

India is primarily a country of micros and minis. Thus, there is a wealth of experience with MS-DOS, Unix, and DEC's VMS operating systems; with Intel-based 80x86 micros, Motorola-based 680x0 workstations, and VAX minicomputers; and with such relational database packages as ORACLE, UNIFY, and SYBASE. Much of the programming is done in C, some in BASIC, and some (typically on the larger machines) in COBOL. In addition, many software development organizations—probably far more than in the United States—are using such fourth generation programming languages as Focus and Mapper.

Herein lies an advantage and a disadvantage. Because most Indian organizations had no computers at all until a few years ago, they don't have the 30-year legacy of RPG, COBOL, and assembly language programs that plague so many American organizations. Transaction volumes are still relatively low, and databases are still relatively small, so most Indian organizations can begin their automation efforts with 4GLs and relational databases—and, in a sense, leapfrog over generations of technology that we're stuck with.

On the other hand, the story of the past 30 years of information systems in the United States is more than just a story of generations of hardware technology and the evolution of programming languages. It is also a story of growing sophistication on the part of two generations of end users, some of whom now occupy the highest levels of management and government in the country. It is also a story of growing sophistication on the part of two generations of computer professionals who have gradually learned how to let the users' business needs dictate computer strategies, not the reverse.

This has not yet happened in India. As I heard story after story of the travails of my Indian colleagues attempting to bring computers into an organization for the first time, I thought the clock had been turned back 30 years. "Our management doesn't understand the importance of software," I heard repeatedly. "They don't see why they should have to pay for it, and they don't understand why it takes any time to develop. They keep hearing that their children are learning to program in school, so they assume it's all trivial. And they don't know how to describe their requirements accurately enough so that we can build the right system . . . ."

Thus, while it could be argued that the Indian software industry has the technical expertise to program new systems (as long as it's not on IBM mainframes), there is less evidence that it knows how to design large, complex online distributed processing systems or that it is capable of analyzing the requirements of an end user's business system. In the short term, this may limit the software export industry to body shop operations.

Another aspect of Indian systems development projects is their size: most are tiny by U.S. standards. The vast majority of projects I heard about involved 2 or 3 people for 4 to 6 months; the entire DP organization often consists of only 5 to 10 people. These are legitimate projects, to be sure, and they result in useful systems, but in a typical U.S. organization, such projects would hardly merit any formal project management and would probably gravitate out of the DP organization and into the end-user organization.

As discussed in an article concerning Pacific Bell (*American Programmer*, September 1989), the emphasis in U.S. DP organizations is shifting to "programming in the large," and the larger shops typically have well over a thousand DP professionals. While India has a few large DP organizations and a few large projects, the general scale of things is about a hundred times smaller.

So what? U.S. DP organizations are not necessarily better because they're larger, nor are large projects necessarily more sophisticated (indeed, they tend to be riskier and have a greater chance of outright failure). But I think these issues of size and complexity color India's plans to build a large software industry. India could continue simply to rent out programmers to work on big U.S. projects, but it is evident that kind of "industry" has the lowest per employee revenue contribution. Higher-revenue contributions come from the "value-added" activities of delivering turnkey systems and building complete software products.

If India decides to build turnkey systems or software products for micros and midsized minicomputers, it has a reasonable chance of competing; experience gained from providing these services and products for the domestic marketplace should prove helpful for competing abroad. But the more aggressive and dedicated software professionals with whom I spoke seem to have larger ambitions: they hope to build an Indian-style EDS or Computer Sciences and to produce the kind of large, sophisticated software products that we expect from Computer Associates, McCormack and Dodge, ADP, and others.

I simply don't see any realistic way for this to happen in the next decade. The problem is that when it comes to big projects, big systems, managing big DP organizations, and dealing with sophisticated telecommunications networks, distributed systems, and the like, India is already 10 years behind most of the developed countries. As long as these technologies continue to advance, and as long as the end-user community continues to grow in sophistication, it is more likely that India will continue to lag 10 years behind.

There is another dimension of technology lag: India's woefully inadequate telecommunications network. After learning that my flight from Madras to Bombay would be delayed for four hours, I spent another hour with an NIIT manager trying to call the Bombay office to advise them of the delay. It was fruitless: we could not get a connection. Indians are accustomed to this, and have even accepted the fact that if they make an advance deposit of 5000 rupees, it may still take four years to get a new phone installed. Shrugging, they smile and say, "Actually, it's much better now than it was before—and it's getting better all the time." Two years ago, direct-dial long-distance calling was possible in only 20 cities; today, it's up to 200 cities.

The poor telecommunications technology makes it almost impossible to build a decent online or distributed system. Data transmission speeds are typically limited to 1200 baud, though they are occasionally as high as 2400 baud. However, major satellite-based public sector networks—with such exotic names as SAILNET, COALNET, RAILNET, BANKNET, and OILCOMNET—are under development and should be in place within the next year. It's quite possible that India may have a decent telecommunications network within five years, but I believe it is a major obstacle for the development of large systems today.

Obviously, many in the Indian computer industry hope my gloomy prognosis is wrong, and it's certainly possible. Indeed, a thoughtful DP manager from CMC (one of the largest public sector software development firms) offered the following comment: "We're perfectly happy to 'track' some four or five years behind the United States. By the time we get around to doing the things you did five years ago, the hardware and software technology will have improved so much that we will accomplish with 10 people what you accomplished with 100."

On a broader scale, we have certainly seen examples of countries rising from the ashes to become major economic powers, postwar Japan and Germany being the two most obviously examples. I am not competent to judge whether India has the drive and determination to achieve such an economic transformation. But it does seem that it would take a miracle for the country's tiny IT industry to catch up with the United States, Europe, or Japan in the foreseeable future.

A.2.3 The Level of Indian Technology

Some might suggest that India's lack of experience with large, complex software systems is not the key issue, but rather it is India's ability to stay abreast of the latest technological developments. One might argue it's less important to have the most expertise with 1000-person systems development projects than it is to be in the forefront of research and development in AI, neural net computers, natural language processing, supercomputers, and the like.

There is some leading-edge work going on in India, though I didn't have the time or opportunity to see it. India has ordered at least one Cray supercomputer, though, as I write this, the United States is still debating the merits of allowing such a transaction. And the government has recently allocated seed money of approximately Rs. 16 crores for the development of an indigenous fifth generation computer by 1993. The task has been assigned to four scientific institutes in the country: the Tata Institute of Fundamental Research in Bombay, the Indian Statistical Institute in Calcutta, the National Center for Software Technology at the Indian Institute of Technology (IIT) in Madras, and the Indian Institute of Science in Bangalore.

On a more mundane level, it's fair to say that India is generally aware of most current software technology developments, but these aren't being put to widespread use. Several people I met said they had begun experimenting with expert systems; given that expert system shells are widely available on PCs, it's logical that Indians would be aware of the technology. But when it comes to practical use and experience, again it appears India is 5 to 10 years behind us.

The same seems to be true of software engineering and CASE. My former company, Yourdon Inc., has conducted seminars on structured analysis and design in India since 1982, and NIIT's college-level DP curriculum incorporates the same material on structured techniques that I've seen in U.S. universities. But are these techniques actually used on a widespread basis? From the feedback I got in my conferences, I think not. The reasons I typically heard were (1) our users and managers don't appreciate the need to spend a lot of time on systems analysis; (2) our projects aren't really large enough to warrant such formal techniques; (3) we have relational databases and 4GLs, so we don't need any of that structured stuff; and (4) we don't have automated support, and we got tired of drawing all those diagrams by hand.

The lack of automated support was a big problem in the United States, too, prior to the introduction of CASE technology. People in India are aware of CASE, but again, the level of experience and familiarity is far lower. To drive this point home, consider that 50,000 to 70,000 CASE products have been installed in the United States; from my discussions with CASE vendors and DP professionals, I estimate there are only approximately 200 in India. Tata, for example, developed CASEPAC, which is marketed by OnLine Systems in the United States, but there are no CASEPAC installations in India (aside from Tata itself) because of the paucity of IBM mainframes.

Why are there so few CASE products in India? The first answer, of course, is that there are fewer software engineers: the United States has approximately 20 times as many programmers and analysts. But the real answer has to do with economics: if you were a DP manager, could you justify a $10,000 CASE product when your programmers were earning roughly $2400 a year? To make matters worse, foreign CASE products typically have an import duty of 107 percent—so the least expensive of the American CASE products still represents more than a year's salary, and the more popular high-priced products would cost over US$20,000. From this perspective, it's a wonder there are any imported CASE products in the country. And indeed, there are very, very few: only 80 of the 200 CASE products in use are imported. The rest are indigenous products, available (without import duty, of course!) at a price of approximately US$1000.

The typical Indian DP situation—small systems, microcomputers, naive end users—has some interesting consequences in terms of software engineering technologies. When I raised the subject of software reengineering and reverse engineering in my lectures, my audience consistently responded with a blank look. They considered the ideas intellectually interesting but utterly irrelevant. When I suggested they would eventually have to cope with software maintenance problems and to begin thinking of their software as an "immortal asset"—

and yes, I did tell them it was Eric Bush of Language Technology who coined this delightful phrase—they guffawed.

I told them we had spent most of the 1970s and 1980s fervently believing we could use a host of "silver bullets" (CASE, structured programming, chief programmer teams, Ada, etc.) to replace gradually bad systems, written in prehistoric times, with perfect new systems. I said we were only now coming to realize we were wrong on two counts: first, none of the silver bullets has yet really generated perfectly maintainable systems, and second, many of those bad old systems could never be replaced because they were too expensive and because nobody had the slightest idea of what the system requirements were. For a nation just embarking on the development of new systems, a nation currently facing no software maintenance problems, such a message was not only unpopular, it was unfathomable.

I got the same reaction to several other software engineering technologies. Software metrics is largely an unknown concept, though one local organization is trying to popularize some of the tools and techniques of Larry Putnam, developer of the highly respected SLIM estimating model. Over and over again, people quizzically said to me, "What do you mean by software metrics? What is it that we would want to measure?" Similarly, software reliability models are largely unexplored. And software reusability is considered an interesting concept but not a high priority.

When micros first appeared in the United States in the early 1980s, a new community of semiprofessional programmers, hackers, and end users suddenly appeared and busily set to work coding an endless variety of applications in BASIC, assembler, and C. Battle-scarred mainframe veterans watched with some amusement, knowing that those trivial initial systems would eventually grow to large, complex monstrosities and that a new generation would have to relearn the lessons learned so painfully on mainframes in the 1960s and 1970s. That, in a nutshell, is what's happening in India today.

A.3 THE FUTURE OF INDIAN SOFTWARE

India's goal for its software export industry is ambitious: the plan is to expand an export industry currently valued at approximately $10 to $15 million to approximately $100 million by 1995. Some of the more aggressive government ministers have challenged the software industry to set even higher goals. "Why not aim for $500 million in exports by 1995?" they ask.

This sounds highly unreasonable: even though most parts of the Indian computer industry have been growing at the rate of 40 or 50 percent, or more, for the last few years, it would require an annual compounded growth rate of 60 percent to achieve a 10-fold increase by 1995. We have learned all too well in the United States that it's difficult, if not impossible, to maintain near-explosive growth rates forever. As Prem Shivdasani, president of India's NASSCOM, told me in Bombay, "We're going to have to make some fundamental changes in order to achieve the kinds of numbers the government wants from us."

NASSCOM has already made its own estimates of how the Indian software export industry will change over the next five years. Its estimates of the current composition of software exports, and the estimated composition for 1995, are shown in Table A.4.

A.3.1 The Need for People

One of the first questions that has to be addressed when looking at such ambitious plans is where India proposes to get enough people to develop all this software. A 1985 study, entitled "Report of Working Group on Evolving Strategy for Teachers' Training for Implementing Computer Education Programs," estimated that by 1990—just three months from now!—India would need an additional 440 Ph.D. computer scientists, 6375 master's graduates, 3480 B.S. graduates, and 10,600 "others" for a total of 20,895 people. This is considerable growth for a country that at the moment only has about 50,000 programmers.

More significantly, current projections for 1995 (based on an estimated installed base of 1 million PCs and several thousand minis) indicate a need for an additional 225,000 professional programmers—just to satisfy the domestic demand. To achieve an export target of Rs. 3500 crores, NASSCOM estimates that an additional 185,000 professionals will be needed.

Where are all these people going to come from? Roughly 150 universities, a handful of regional engineering colleges, and other educational institutions in India are presently turning out about 10,000 new graduates each year—of whom probably only half could be considered "world-class" professionals, because of the lack of well-trained faculty, a shortage of computer facilities, and so forth. Even with an output of 10,000 new people a year, the 1995 labor supply (including the most optimistic estimate of an existing force of 80,000 people) would only reach about 140,000—far short of the required number.

Though the quality of Indian universities is generally high, the likelihood that they will be able to gear up to produce a large number of people in a short period of time is fairly remote. Indian universities are just too slow to change—slower, even, than American universities.

It seems the only solution is a massive growth in the privately sponsored industry training of software professionals. Dozens of companies, of which NIIT is the largest, offer a wide range of PC-related courses in Lotus, dBase-III, and BASIC. But the number of legitimate graduates of two- or three-year programs who have had professional software engineering training is much smaller.

NASSCOM has made a number of recommendations for dealing with this shortage, including

- On-the-job training of people in various industries
- Exchange of faculty and industry personnel—using people in industry as visiting faculty, and exposing academic faculty members to the real-world requirements in industry
- Courses designed in cooperation with companies who need the software engineers and conducted by educational institutions
- Using retired industry personnel as faculty members
- Utilizing schemes such as the U.S.–India Cooperative Science Program to get people from U.S. industry or academic institutions as faculty members for some period of time

These are all terrific ideas, but they take time to implement and require strong commitment and enthusiastic support. One of the advantages of a country like India, with its highly centralized planning and governmental activities, is that the federal government could, if it chose, set up specific programs and provide substantial financial assistance to help create an army of software engineers.

While I personally doubt this will happen as quickly as the Indian government and the computer industry would like—because institutions and bureaucracies move slowly, especially in India—it's important to keep these numbers in the proper perspective: finding another 200,000 software engineers may not be such an awesome task when one considers that India's total population is 850 million people.

A.3.2 The Brain Drain

The personnel shortage is worse than it might appear from these numbers, for a steady flow of the best Indian software engineers emigrate each year to Australia, England, Canada, and the United

States. A study by the IIT in Madras found emigration of its graduating class was at the 20 percent level through most of the 1960s and 1970s, but rose to 27 percent in the 1978–82 period, and to 35 percent in the 1983–87 period. Even more dramatic is the figure for graduates in computer science and engineering, a degree program instituted in 1982: of the first batches of graduates in 1986–87, 58.5 percent emigrated. What's the point of training 100,000 new software engineers if they're all going to move away in search of higher salaries?

India's emigration is, of course, our immigration: the influx of Indian engineering and computer talent is just part of the larger influx of foreign talent. Many Indian students come to the United States to pursue graduate degrees (possible, in most cases, only if they can get a scholarship or teaching grant) and then stay on in the country after graduation. Others are recruited in India by ordinary American firms, or by American firms run by Indian expatriates, or by local Indian firms whose notion of export software is exporting warm bodies who can write code for cheap prices.

The effect of the brain drain is not entirely obvious within India; indeed many Indians seem to feel they are pulling off some kind of minor coup. "We have good, cheap, well-educated, hardworking people," they say. "Look how successful we have been sending them to other countries."

But the long-term consequences are devastating. It's typically the best and the brightest who go, leaving behind the less talented to build India's indigenous industry. Despite fairly tight visa regulations, most who go to the United States (or Europe) to study or carry out short-term assignments find some way of staying; they resist any effort from their original Indian employer to cajole them into coming back. Those who get left behind in India resent their company for not sending them.

If the country had millions of highly qualified software engineers—as it did, for example, in the case of construction workers who migrated to Saudi Arabia during the oil boom—the brain drain would not be a problem. But India would have difficulty building its software industry even if there were no brain drain.

This problem has to be addressed, but no one I met discussed it—aside from a general wringing of hands and agreement that it was a concern. A trivial solution would be for the government to clamp down on emigration, à la the Soviet Union's treatment of Jews. But aside from the odious moral and ethical aspects of such an approach, I seriously doubt it would be practical: India has a centuries-old tradition of sending its students abroad, dating back to the early days of British rule. Unless India wants to become a closed society and suffer the stagnation so apparent in the USSR, a heavy-handed effort to prevent emigration is unlikely to succeed.

But if a stick won't work, maybe a carrot would. Perhaps the government could offer a bounty or bonus for returning emigrants. Or it could form a venture capital pool to attract the brighter and more entrepreneurial emigrants back into the country to start their own fledgling businesses. These solutions might raise political problems in a country where there are so many other urgent needs to be addressed—but someone within the government or the computer industry needs to come up with some creative ideas in this area. At the very least, India should stop congratulating itself on the short-term revenues it earns when it exports one of its precious software engineers.

A.3.3 The Stages of Growth

Notwithstanding the previous comments, it's evident that India is basing a significant portion of its current export industry on the simple notion of exporting cheap labor. Despite the long-term disadvantages, there is a short-term advantage that needs to be understood: it creates an "entree" for Indian software firms that might otherwise never be noticed in foreign markets. Who in New York has even heard of Bangalore? Who wants to do business with a Unix shop 10,000 miles away, in a city where the slightest rainfall often renders the telephone system totally inoperable? But a company that can offer its services (or its products) at one-half or one-third the local price commands attention. Quite simply, it's a way of getting a foot in the door.

But if body shop programming is not a good long-term strategy, what is? I believe India will go through the following stages over the next 5 to 10 years:

1. Building a reputation by providing cheap programming services on site at the customer's location

2. Shifting the programming services back to India, with well-specified programs and systems delivered via telecommunications link to the overseas customer

3. Gradually shifting the emphasis and focus from low-cost services to high-quality services

4. Shifting from a service industry to a product industry by finding market niches or by providing higher-quality, lower-cost clone products

5. Finding a true value-added software-intensive product in some application area that encapsulates India's own unique expertise

Several of these stages may overlap, and different parts of the Indian computer industry may be operating in different stages at the same time.

A.3.3.1 Stage 1

Stage 1, which represents approximately 80 percent of India's 1989 software exports, has a further disadvantage to the ones already discussed: by uprooting a programmer from India and moving him or her to the United States (or Europe, Australia, etc.) to perform services on site, the costs escalate substantially. A typical Indian programmer with three years' experience might earn $200 in India—approximately 10 times less than his or her American counterpart in New York, Boston, or Silicon Valley. But by the time we pay the plane fare from India to New York, plus the cost of housing, food, and transportation, much of the cost differential—that is, the cost advantage the Indian company would normally enjoy—disappears. Instead of a bargain 10 percent, the customer ends up paying perhaps 50 percent of the standard American price for an Indian programmer.

Some Indian software companies have identified another potential problem: the probability that it will become increasingly difficult to obtain work permits in foreign countries. This is less likely to be a problem in Commonwealth nations (though a recent article [1] argues that some English companies show a bias against using Indian software companies), but it could well become an obstacle in the United States and other countries. In a larger sense, the political climate is always a potential problem when a country tries to export its labor force in order to make money.

Despite these possible pitfalls, there is no question that on-site services will continue to be India's primary software export strategy for the next few years. One of its advantages—of tremendous concern to small start-up software companies—is the lack of major capital requirements for product development. Some marketing costs are necessary to promote the concept of on-site services, but these are minimal compared to the cost of marketing software products.

There is a final reason why stage 1 is an important—even necessary—short-term strategy: it helps build credibility that can lead to turnkey systems development projects in India.

A.3.3.2 Stage 2

In stage 2, the bulk of the work is done on Indian soil; this is precisely what Citicorp's COSL operation and Texas Instruments'

Bangalore software group are all about. To make this work requires a good international telecommunications facility, which India must work hard to improve. I'm not convinced that a dedicated satellite link is needed today to make stage 2 work, but a combination of fax, electronic mail, and data communications at a minimum of 9600 baud is necessary. And if stage 2 is going to operate on a large scale within 5 to 10 years, then a high-speed satellite link will be necessary.

Another important ingredient for true off-shore software development of a customized system for an end-user application is a good, solid software engineering methodology for specifying the requirements and design of a system. As mentioned, India has been exposed to some software engineering methodologies—especially the structured systems development techniques—but it has very little experience in the advanced technologies of CASE tools, reengineering, software reusability, and so forth. The country also has very little experience in the development of large, complex, distributed IBM mainframe systems. And it lacks the project management experience associated with any large project.

Hence the most likely entree for turnkey projects will be the small to medium-sized Unix and mini/micro projects. "Porting" Unix or a C compiler to a new machine is one area where Indian software companies could do an excellent job, and coding well-defined user applications in a 4GL/RDMS environment is another.

NASSCOM has made the interesting observation that India itself will gradually need more and more big, complex systems. Indian end-user organizations today have a tendency to look to overseas software companies; however, NASSCOM recommends a policy be adopted of awarding such large contracts to the most competent country "with the express condition that 90 percent of the project team be derived from India and that the [contract] winner pass on the technology to the Indian participant." It will take several years for such a strategy to provide "technology transfer" of large-project experience, but it's a clever idea, and I think it should be followed.

NASSCOM also points out that India has a trade deficit with several industrialized countries and that perhaps the Indian government should insist on Indian software personnel being included as project team members in large projects within the host country. While this would have obvious advantages to India, the political objections within the host country might be overwhelming. I could only imagine this strategy working as part of a larger bilateral trade arrangement, for instance, as part of the sale of several military aircraft to India. As a bargaining chip by itself, I think it would be useless.

Perhaps the biggest obstacles confronting the stage 2 software export industry are the difficulty and expense involved in marketing. Though reasonably well known in the United Kingdom, Indian software companies are virtually unknown in the United States—and potential clients are likely to have a great deal of concern about the risk of contracting with any organization so far away. This may be why the better known examples of turnkey software development projects are done by "captive" organizations, such as TI's Bangalore operation. Citicorp's operation began this way, too, but now roughly half of COSL's business comes from non-Citicorp clients.

Tata's P. V. L. N. Rao explained to me that the foreign client's concern takes some interesting forms. American clients, he said, are beginning to ask for more and more quantitative evidence that software developed overseas has been thoroughly tested; ironically, they often don't ask for such assurances from domestic software organizations. And since one of the major reasons for contracting with an Indian software organization is the expectation of higher productivity and lower costs, American clients are likely to be more demanding about firm estimates of budgets and schedules at an early stage in a project. For example, the client will say, "We want to know how much more productive and inexpensive you will be on this project."

NASSCOM is aware that it may have to deal with the issue of credibility by providing insurance and legal protection on software development contracts. It has recommended that a comprehensive insurance policy be developed and that the issue of software product liability be studied more carefully.

There is one additional issue that poses an obstacle for Indian companies at the stage 2 level and beyond: the government's stringent controls and stiff import duties on imported computer hardware and software (and just about everything else that has to be paid for in a hard currency!) However, this is more a problem for the domestic software industry: companies that can demonstrate that imported computer equipment will generate export revenues can avoid import duties.

Indeed, many of India's newer software organizations, including COSL, are located in a suburb of Bombay known as the Santa Cruz Electronics Export Processing Zone (SEEPZ), which provides duty-free import facilities to companies operating export businesses. This makes it possible to acquire the badly needed foreign hardware for the turnkey systems projects. Even without import duties, computer hardware is an expensive, precious commodity. Indian software organizations find it difficult to compete against their international counterparts who glibly place a Sun workstation on every software engineer's desk.

A.3.3.3 Stages 3 and 4

Sooner or later, if India really does want to be a serious "player" in the global software marketplace, it will have to shift its focus from a low-cost service orientation to a high-quality service orientation, and ultimately to a product orientation. India is well aware that product development is an area capable of exponential growth and that it is the area exhibiting the fastest growth in the world marketplace. Equally important, the Indian software industry recognizes that the stage 4 product-based industry has the opportunity of providing a much higher return on investment and higher employee "contribution," as the incremental cost of making another copy of a software product on a floppy disk is trivial.

On the other hand, a product-based industry virtually demands a significant amount of venture capital and that is in short supply. One obvious source of financing is the government, and a recent report [2] noted that India's Export-Import Bank had budgeted Rs. 14.9 crores for software export ventures in the year ending March 31, 1989. A variety of financing schemes, at levels far above the US$1 million level represented by the ExIm Bank's current funding, will be necessary for stage 4 to become a reality.

NASSCOM has also recommended that the Indian software industry be more aggressive about joint ventures, in India as well as abroad, in order to build up a software product industry more quickly. There is nothing to prevent Indian companies from acquiring overseas software firms and software publishers; Japan, Korea, and Taiwan are already involved in buyouts of U.S. software companies. India's biggest problem in this area is simply one of capital.

Ironically, India's greatest asset in stages 1 and 2—highly productive, inexpensive software engineers—may prove to be largely irrelevant in stages 3 and 4, at least in the short term. Several studies of global software trends have observed that the cost of marketing a software product is much higher than the cost of developing the product. Indeed, marketing costs are often as much as 80 percent of the list price of a software product. How is India going to cope with this? Again, significant venture capital investments are going to be necessary.

NASSCOM has spotted another area where India will have difficulty dealing with the marketing costs of software products. High marketing costs drive most software distributors, agents, and publishers to insist on high sales commission rates—commissions of 40 and 50 percent are not uncommon. India, on the other hand, is reluctant to consider commissions above 15 percent; with such an attitude, U.S. software marketing organizations simply won't be interested.

To make matters worse, the Indian government does not permit foreign distributors of Indian software packages to retain their marketing fees and commissions in their own country. I don't know what bureaucratic genius came up with this, but it has to be one of the stupidest regulations I've ever encountered: no foreign distributor is going to have the slightest interest in working with Indian software firms under such conditions.

In addition to spending a lot of money on marketing and advertising, I believe any marketing "pitch" will have to emphasize the high quality of Indian software. This is one area where India's stage 2 emphasis on product insurance and product liability could prove a long-term advantage. U.S. software developers, particularly in the PC software arena, continue to produce and market products on an "as is" basis, with a total disclaimer as to fitness or quality.

India could achieve the same competitive advantage with high-quality software and a legitimate software warranty as Japan did with its automobile industry in the 1970s. But this cannot be accomplished overnight: India must be willing to spend years creating and maintaining an image of high-quality software products.

A.3.3.4 Stage 5

The final stage, I believe, will involve the development of software-intensive products in an application area that incorporates some unique Indian expertise.

I don't have any idea what that area might be: I haven't spent enough time in India to get a good sense of the country's special skills, outside of the narrow area of computer technology. But an example borrowed from Singapore will help illustrate what I believe my Indian friends should be considering in their 10-year plan: Singapore, which has the fourth-largest deep-water port in the world, feels it has developed world-class expertise, over a period of centuries, in "port management." I have no idea what that involves, but that's just the point: whatever is involved in getting ships in and out of the harbor, scheduling the loading and offloading of oil tankers and container cargo ships, and managing the associated paperwork, regulations, tariffs, and so forth is something the Singaporeans know a lot about. Singapore is now actively involved in capturing that expertise in computerized expert systems, which it hopes to export to other major ports around the world.

And that's the concept India should be considering. Today, computer hardware is a universally available commodity. India can produce enough micros to meet its domestic needs, and it has had the good sense not to try building a hardware export industry to challenge the rest of the world. But in another 10 years, the vast majority of software products will be a commodity, too. There may be a short-term advantage if you can build a much cheaper and much higher-quality version of Lotus 1-2-3 or Microsoft Word, but within 10 years the advantage will have disappeared (and Lotus and Microsoft will have disappeared, too, if they continue producing expensive, low-quality products and delivering them to the marketplace two or three years behind their own announced schedules!).

What will become increasingly important is the human expertise incorporated within those software products. This is an area where the United States foolishly considers itself impregnable, as it introduces dazzling new products like HyperCard among the piglike behemoths like OS/2. Some of us, though, are already concerned that Japan's legendary creativity in the area of consumer electronics (best exemplified, perhaps, by the ubiquitous Sony Walkman) will soon carry over to software products.

How does India plan to compete on this level? That I don't have an answer to this question is irrelevant: I'm not an Indian. That India doesn't have an answer today is not crucial. That nobody appears to be even looking for an answer could, however, prove disastrous.

A.4 IMPRESSIONS

Toward the end of my trip, India was largely paralyzed by a *bandh*—a national strike organized by opposition political parties to gain support in an upcoming election. It was considered fairly peaceful, which means that only a dozen people were killed, only a few thousand arrested, and only one or two trains and buses burned during the one-day protest. The *bandh* organizers appealed to everyone to stay home from work, and it was widely rumored that anyone found driving in the streets might run into unruly agitators throwing rocks.

My hosts suggested I might prefer spending the day at a quiet seaside resort 35 kilometers south of Madras; it seemed the sensible thing to do. The evening before the *bandh*, NIIT's Arvind Thakur and his wife drove me out of the city, along a narrow two-lane road literally teeming with people, goats, bicycles, pigs, cars, cows, motorscooters, ox carts, and buses—all honking, yelling, weaving back and forth, and generally going about their normal business.

What I anticipated as a quick 15-minute trip turned into a 1-hour marathon; we all needed a strong drink when we arrived at the resort. Drinks blended into dinner, and for the next few hours we sat on a moonlit terrace overlooking the ocean, talking about the similarities and differences between life-styles and cultures in India and the United States. By the end of the evening, I was convinced you can't study technological developments in a country without taking into account some of the social, political, and cultural issues.

I knew, for example, that Indian companies have been slow to adopt CASE because imported software products are expensive compared to the salaries of programmers. I understood this intellectually. But I didn't really appreciate how pervasive this "people are cheap, machines are expensive" attitude is until Thakur explained to me that, for many, an automobile is a lifetime investment. So is a television.

"What about a dishwasher?" I asked.

"Oh, that's no problem," Thakur said. "We can get one for about a hundred rupees a month."

Mentally converting this to roughly US$6 per month, I expressed surprise. "That's a lot cheaper than our dishwashers! Where do you buy them? Japan? Korea? Taiwan?"

Thakur replied, "I was talking about a person."

Similarly, it takes a long time to get used to a political culture so different from that of the United States. The notion of public sector companies in all the key industries is strongly rooted in the Indian tradition of socialism. To me, it is unthinkable that a country as large as India has only three kinds of automobiles: something called an Ambassador, which looks as if it was designed in the 1940s; a vintage-1960s Fiat; and a newly designed Suzuki. Where are the Hondas, the Datsuns, the Toyotas—not to mention the BMWs, the Ford Escorts, and the Mercedes? The answer: if they aren't manufactured domestically, they don't exist. I was equally astounded to discover there is only one domestic (public sector) airline—passengers are completely at the mercy of the airline's capricious delays and flight cancellations. But that's the way things are done in India, and it's not likely to change in the near future.

On the other hand, the existence of a monolithic, centralized government bureaucracy does not mean that India is a land of homogeneous people, all carved from the same mold. Quite the opposite: there is probably more heterogeneity than you would find in the United States. India has 14 officially recognized languages, each with its own script and each with several dialects. English and Hindi are the two most commonly recognized languages, but the country is a hodge-podge of religions, castes, languages, and customs. It's a wonder anyone agrees on anything.

Indeed, Indians seem to thrive on disagreeing with one another—sometimes violently. During my visit, newspapers provided daily reports of terrorist killings in Punjab and Sri Lanka. Wary police and soldiers guarded the airports and searched baggage and passengers more vigilantly than in Rome or Tel Aviv or anywhere in the United States. My laptop MacLite computer was examined repeatedly, and in most airports the batteries were removed lest my computer should turn out to be a bomb. As a result, I wasn't able to begin writing my notes on the visit until my Air India flight left Bombay (I guess the theory is that it's okay to blow yourself up once you've left the country!). By then, the batteries were dead; I was forced to resort to paper and pencil for the next 16 hours.

When my colleagues learned I had just returned from India, they peppered me with questions: "What was it like? Was the poverty awful? Did the food make you sick?" Yes, the poverty is awful—indeed indescribable in parts of Calcutta. On the other hand, the slums I saw in Madras, Bombay, and Delhi were no worse than, say, those in São Paulo, and parts of Bombay and Delhi are quite cosmopolitan. No, the food did not make me sick; I love Indian food, and I actually gained weight on the trip!

The most unusual thing about India, for me, was the noise and the chaos in the streets—ironic for someone from New York City who is comfortable in the traffic jams of Paris and Rome. But Indian traffic is overwhelming. There are no regulations limiting automobile emissions, so billowing clouds of black smoke spew from every taxi, car, and bus. And since the streets are overflowing with pedestrians, cows, bicycles, goats, and carts, Indian drivers are forced to weave from one lane to the other, a hand firmly glued to the horn. The cacophony of blaring horns is deafening. I was astounded that I didn't see a single traffic accident during my trip.

To be fair, I should point out that Indians are just as overwhelmed by traffic in my hometown, New York: there are no people! One Indian told me that when he first visited New York, he thought everyone had died because he saw only cars on the highway. When, after riding several miles from the airport, he saw a pedestrian, he insisted the taxi driver stop so he could shake the pedestrian's hand.

On my last night in Bombay, someone asked me if I planned to come back to India. I glibly replied, "Not until your bloody telephones work a lot better!" But the serious answer is: yes. Not next month, and perhaps not next year. But India is a country that bears watching if you are interested in the global software arena. Like China, India has enormous resources and enormous problems; its progress, or lack of progress, during the next 10 years could well have an effect on all of us. India is indeed like a snake. And though its tail may wallow in medieval squalor for years, its head may move into the twenty-first century faster than any of us expect.

A.5 RESOURCES

National Institute of Information Technology
B 4/144 Safdarjung Enclave
New Delhi 110 029 INDIA
Attention: Mr. Rajendra Pawar, Managing Director
telephone: 60-0177
telex: 031-72343 IRIS IN
fax: 332-9598

Citicorp Overseas Software Limited
133/SDF V
SEEPZ
Bombay 400 096 INDIA
telephone: 630-1077
telex: 011-79113 COSL IN
fax: 634-9777

Citicorp Overseas Software Limited
(U.S. Representative Office)
4 Sylvan Way
Parsippany, NJ 07054
Attention: Mr. Rajesh Hukku, Manager
telephone: 201/397-7477
fax: 201/455-0929

National Association of Software and Service Companies (NASSCOM)
Sangha Rachana, 53 Lodi Estate
New Delhi 110 003, INDIA
Attention: Mr. Prem Shivdasani, President
telephone: 69-2655
telex: 031-65625 COMD IN
fax: 644-4169

Tata Engineering & Locomotive Co., Ltd. (TELCO)
Pimpri, Pune 411018 INDIA
Attention: Mr. S. D. Pradhan, Divisional Manager, Management
  Services Division
telephone: 84261
telex: 0146/223
fax: 212-82308

Interface Software
Resources Pvt. Ltd.
Unit 117-120, SDF IV
SEEPZ, Andheri (East)
Bombay 400 096 INDIA
Attention: Mr. Sunil Subhedar, Divisional Manager
telephone: 634-4017
telex: 011-79323 ISRL IN

Orissa Computer Application Centre
TDCC Building, Janpath
Bhubaneswar 751 007 INDIA
Attention: Mr. Subas Pani, Chief Executive
telephone: 50232
telex: 0675-399 OCAC-IN

Tata Consultancy Services (TCS)
12, Cathedral Road
Madras 600 086 INDIA
Attention: P. V. L. N. Rao, IBM Centre
telephone: 470459, 479315
telex: 041-6212

INTECOS Information Systems Division
7 Community Centre, East of Kailash
New Delhi 65 INDIA
Attention: Mr. Navyug Mohnot, Director of Systems

telephone: 643-2335
telex: 031-62554
fax: 644-0866

Computers and Communications Magazine (*C&C*)
Media Transasia
103, Anand Lok
New Delhi 110 049 INDIA
Attention: Mr. Sundeep Khanna, Business Editor
telephone: 644-0110
telex: 031-71313 MTIL IN
fax: 643-2950

Computers Today Magazine
Living Media India Ltd.
F-14/15, First Floor
Connaught Place
New Delhi 110 001 INDIA
Attention: Mr. J. Srihari Raju, Editor
telephone: 331-2199, 331-5801
telex: 031-61245 INTO IN
fax: 331-6180

Dataquest Magazine
D-74 Panchsheel Enclave
New Delhi 110 017 INDIA
Attention: Mr. Rajesh Kalra, Assistant Editor
telephone: 643-3999, 643-5999
telex: 031-71344 INDQ

PC World India
D-74 Panchsheel Enclave
New Delhi 110 017 INDIA
Attention: Mr. Debasish Ghosh, Editor
telephone: 643-3999, 643-5999
telex: 031-71344 INDQ

National Informatics Centre
'A' Block, CGO Complex
Lodi Road
New Delhi 110 003 INDIA

Attention: Dr. N. Seshagiri, Director General
telephone: 361504

SIPA News, The Newsletter of Silicon Valley Indian Professionals
Association
P.O. Box 3533
Santa Clara, CA 95055-3533
Attention: Sheela and Jayaram Kalpathy, Editors

END NOTES

1. Ernest-Jones, Terry. "Lines from the Coral Strand: UK Firms' Opportunities for Software Development in India," *Computer Weekly*, July 6, 1989, p. 24.
2. "ExIm Bank Finances Software Exports," *Dataquest*, July 1989, p. 30.
3. "Adam Osborne Looks for Big Bucks from Indian Schools System: New Micro Firm," *Computergram International*, June 23, 1989.
4. Desmond, John. "'CasePac' Triumvirate," *Software Magazine*, February 1989, pp. 8–9.
5. Chin-Leong, Kathy. "Offshore Programming: It's Not a Secret Anymore," *PC-Computing*, March 1989, pp. 177–178.
6. Raynor, Bruce C. P. "Gandhi: Foreign Investment in India Is Not an 'Open Door,' " *Electronic Business*, January 23, 1989, pp. 68–69.
7. Hallisey, Jane. "India Courts High-tech Business," *PC-Computing*, March 1989, p. 56.
8. Glatzer, Hal. "Software Intrigues India: Pools of Programmers Winning U.S. Business," *Software Magazine*, January 1989, p. 26.
9. Raynor, Bruce C. P. "Keeping the Pirates at Bay: The Job of Protecting Your Intellectual Property in India Is Perilous," *Electronic Business*, January 9, 1989, pp. 133–134.
10. Raynor, Bruce C. P. "Taking the Plunge: What You Need to Know About Doing Business in India," *Electronic Business*, January 9, 1989, pp. 132–133.
11. Bellinger, Robert. "Boston-to-India Software Link Planned," *Electronic Engineering Times*, May 1, 1989, p. 10.
12. Peterson, Stacey. "Antipirating Steps Urged," *Computer Systems News*, May 1, 1989, p. 3.
13. Furst, Al. "Third World Markets for 32-Bit Workstations," *Electronic Business*, December 10, 1988, p. 26.

14. Leibs, Scott. "Easing Programmer Deficit: Massachusetts and Indian Governments Plan to Code by Satellite," *Information Week*, March 20, 1989, p. 20.

15. Brown, Bob. "East Meets West for International Trade Network: Satellite Network Between Massachusetts and India," *Network World*, September 12, 1988, pp. 11–12.

16. Bennett, Chris. "Go East Young Man: India Develops its Computer Industry," *Electronics Weekly*, April 27, 1988, p. 18.

17. Rice, Valerie. "U.S. Electronics Firms Get Preferred Passage to India," *Electronic Business*, March 1, 1988, pp. 94–96.

18. Betts, Mitch. "High-Tech Pirates Said to Reap Billions," *Computerworld*, March 14, 1988, pp. 79–80.

19. Markoff, John, and Stephen Engelberg. "U.S. Debates Selling Supercomputers to 3 Nations," *The New York Times*, August 28, 1989.

20. Markoff, John, and Stephen Engelberg. "U.S. Fears Export of Supercomputers May Fuel Arms Race," *International Herald Tribune*, August 21, 1989.

21. "Computer Peripherals: Indo-USSR Venture in Tashkent," *Business Standard (of India)*, August 27, 1989.

22. "Great Future in Computers Forecast," *The Hindustan Times*, August 23, 1989.

23. "India to Lead in Computers," *The Patriot*, August 22, 1989.

24. "Big Scope for Export of Computers," *National Herald*, August 22, 1989.

25. "Software Base in Delhi: Siemens Establishing Software Operation in India," *Computergram International*, July 19, 1989.

26. "Bharat Bandh Partial; 11 Killed, Thousands Held," *The Times of India*, August 31, 1989, p. 1.

27. "IT Staff Stir Over Computers," *The Times of India*, September 2, 1989, p. 9.

28. "New Target for SW Exports," *Computers Today*, August 1989, p. 4.

29. Kamble, P. U. "Indian Computing Issues: At Stake," *Computers Today*, August 1989, pp. 65–67.

Appendix B

The Programmer's Bookshelf

I am often asked by programmers and systems analysts I meet, "What should I be reading in order to keep up with the field?" And there is the related question, "To what professional societies should I belong?"

You may be one of the very few people in the industry who finds these questions surprising. But the average American programmer has less than one computer book on his or her bookshelf (it was the late Karl Karlstrom, premier editor of computer books at Prentice Hall, who first pointed out to me that the total number of professional computer books sold was less than the number of programmers in the United States). The average American programmer reads no magazines, because they cost money. Even the free journals, like *Datamation*, are hard to find: the entire MIS organization gets only one copy to be shared among 200 Luddites.

There are three important things for you to realize if you're going to avoid getting left behind in the software industry: (1) it is vital to read important books and journals and attend key professional conferences, (2) it's an ongoing process since the information you read today will be obsolete within three to five years, and (3) the company you work for will probably provide limited support at best and no support at worst. The majority of programmers and systems analysts cannot depend on their companies to keep them professionally current; they have to be willing to invest some of their own time (even vacation time) and money to keep up with the field. (Conversely, an organization that implicitly dooms its technical staff to obsolescence has no call on its loyalty: that's one reason the turnover rate among programmers is so much higher in this country than in Europe and Asia!)

By the way, I strongly suggest that you keep your library at home. Chances are that it will be ripped off if you keep it in the office—and besides, the boss will never give you time to read any of the material!

So, without further ado, here is my list of the books that are absolutely "must" reading. (However, I feel that it would be in poor taste to include any of my books on this list.) The list includes a variety of golden oldies and new titles reviewed in various issues of my software journal, *American Programmer;* those that have been reviewed are marked with an asterisk, and the review is included in this appendix.

The books on this list are necessary for you to be a competent programmer, systems analyst, or DP manager, but they are probably not sufficient. If you work in a specialized area—operating systems, database packages, compiler construction, process control—you will need to add appropriate books that cover the specific subject matter. I have listed books that pertain to all systems development projects and all programming environments.

Check your bookshelf and fill in the missing titles. If you depend on your company library for this kind of thing, show these three pages to your boss and tell him that it's time to get out of the Dark Ages by buying these books. And then—most important—*read them.* If you read one per week it will take you about a year and a half to finish.

1. Andersen, Niels Erik, et al. *Professional Systems Development.* New York: Prentice Hall International, 1990.

2. Aron, Joel. *The Program Development Process, Part II: The Programming Team.* Reading, MA: Addison-Wesley, 1983.

3. Arthus, L. J. *Measuring Programmer Productivity and Software Quality.* New York: John Wiley & Sons, 1985.

4. Basalla, George. *The Evolution of Technology.* Cambridge: Cambridge University Press, 1988.

5. Beizer, Boris. *The Frozen Keyboard.* Blue Ridge Summit, PA: TAB Books, 1988.

6.* Bellin, David, and Gary Chapman, eds., *Computers in Battle.* New York: Harcourt, Brace, Jovanovich, 1987.

7.* Bentley, Jon. *More Programming Pearls: Confessions of a Coder.* Reading, MA: Addison-Wesley, 1988.

8. Biggerstaff, Ted. J., and Alan J. Perlis, eds. *Software Reusability.* Vol. 2, *Applications and Experience.* New York: ACM Press/Addison-Wesley, 1989.

9. Block, Robert. *The Politics of Projects.* Englewood Cliffs, NJ: Yourdon Press/Prentice Hall, 1983.

10. Boar, Bernard. *Application Prototyping.* New York: John Wiley & Sons, 1984.

11.* Boehm, Barry. *Software Engineering Economics*. Englewood Cliffs, NJ: Prentice Hall, 1981.

12. Bouldin, Barbara. *Agents of Change*. Englewood Cliffs, NJ: Prentice Hall, 1989.

13. Buxton, J. M., P. Naur, and B. Randell. *Software Engineering, Concepts and Techniques*. New York: Petrocelli/Charter, 1976.

14.* Brooks, Fred. *The Mythical Man-Month*. Reading, MA: Addison-Wesley, 1975.

15. Card, David N., with Robert L. Glass. *Measuring Software. Design Quality*. Englewood Cliffs, NJ: Prentice Hall, 1990.

16. Casti, John L. *Paradigms Lost*. New York: William Morrow, 1989.

17. Charette, Robert N. *Software Engineering Risk Analysis and Management*. New York: McGraw-Hill, 1989.

18. Connell, John L., and Linda Brice Shafer. *Structured Rapid Prototyping*. Englewood Cliffs, NJ: Prentice Hall, 1989.

19. Cutaia, Al. *Technology Projection Modeling of Future Computer Systems*. Englewood Cliffs, NJ: Prentice Hall, 1990.

20. Dahl, O. J., Edsger Dijkstra, and C. A. R. Hoare. *Structured Programming*. Englewood Cliffs, NJ: Prenticc Hall, 1972.

21. Date, Chris. *An Introduction to Database Systems*, Vol. 1, 4th ed. Reading, MA: Addison-Wesley, 1986.

22.* Davis, Stanley M. *Future Perfect*. Reading, MA: Addison-Wesley, 1987.

23. Dijkstra, Edsger. *Selected Writings on Computing: A Personal Perspective*. New York: Springer-Verlag, 1982.

24. Dijkstra, Edsger. *A Discipline of Programming*. Englewood Cliffs, NJ: Prentice Hall, 1976.

25. DeMarco, Tom. *Controlling Software Projects*. Englewood Cliffs, NJ: Yourdon Press/Prentice Hall, 1982.

26. DeMarco, Tom. *Structured Analysis and System Specification*. Englewood Cliffs, NJ: Yourdon Press/Prentice Hall, 1978.

27. DeMarco, Tom, and Tim Lister. *Software State-of-the-Art: Selected Papers*. New York: Dorset House, 1991.

28.* DeMarco, Tom, and Tim Lister. *Peopleware*. New York: Dorset House, 1987.

29. Dunn, Robert. *Software Defect Removal*. New York: McGraw-Hill, 1984.

30. Dunn, Robert, and Richard Ullman. *Quality Assurance for Computer Software*. New York: McGraw-Hill, 1982.

31. Feigenbaum, Edward, Pamela McCorduck, and H. Penny Nii. *The Rise of the Expert Company*. New York: Times Books, 1988.

32. Freedman, Daniel, and Gerald Weinberg. *Handbook of Walkthroughs, Inspections and Technical Reviews*. Boston, MA: Little, Brown, 1982.

33. Freeman, Peter. *Software Perspectives: The System Is the Message*. Reading, MA: Addison-Wesley, 1987.

34. Gane, Chris, and Trish Sarson. *Structured Systems Analysis: Tools and Techniques*. New York: Improved System Technologies, 1977.

35. Gilb, Tom. *Principles of Software Engineering Management*. Reading, MA: Addison-Wesley, 1988.

36. Grady, Robert, and Deborah Caswell. *Software Metrics: Establishing a Company-Wide Program*. Englewood Cliffs, NJ: Prentice Hall, 1987.

37. Halstead, Maurice. *Elements of Software Science*. New York: Elsevier, 1977.

38.* Hatley, Derek, and Imtiaz Pirbhai. *Strategies for Real-Time System Specification*. New York: Dorset House, 1987.

39.* Hetzel, William. *The Complete Guide to Software Testing*, 2nd ed. Wellesley, MA: QED Information Sciences, 1988.

40. Humphrey, Watts S. *Managing the Software Process*. Reading, MA: Addison-Wesley, 1989.

41. Jackson, Michael. *System Development*. Englewood Cliffs, NJ: Prentice Hall, 1983.

42. Jackson, Michael. *Principles of Program Design*. New York: Academic Press, 1975.

43.* Jones, T. Capers. *Programming Productivity*. New York: McGraw-Hill, 1986.

44. Kernighan, Brian, and P. J. Plauger. *The Elements of Programming Style*. New York: McGraw-Hill, 1974.

45. Kernighan, Brian, and P. J. Plauger. *Software Tools*. Reading, MA: Addison-Wesley, 1976.

46.* Kuhn, Thomas. *The Structure of Scientific Revolutions*, 2nd ed. Chicago: University of Chicago Press, 1970.

47. Laurel, Brenda, ed. *The Art of Human–Computer Interface Design.* Reading, MA: Addison-Wesley, 1990.

48. Lientz, B. P., and E. B. Swanson. *Software Maintenance Management.* Reading, MA: Addison-Wesley, 1980.

49. McClure, Carma. *CASE Is Software Automation.* Englewood Cliffs, NJ: Prentice Hall, 1989.

50. McClure, Carma. *Managing Software Development and Maintenance.* New York: Van Nostrand Reinhold, 1981.

51. McCorduck, Pamela. *Machines Who Think.* San Francisco: W. H. Freeman, 1979.

52. McMenamin, Steve, and John Palmer. *Essential Systems Analysis.* Englewood Cliffs, NJ: Yourdon Press/Prentice Hall, 1984.

53. Martin, James. *Strategic Data Planning Methodologies.* Englewood Cliffs, NJ: Prentice Hall, 1982.

54.* Martin, James, and Carma McClure. *Structured Techniques: The Basis for CASE.* Englewood Cliffs, NJ: Prentice Hall, 1987.

55. Martin, James, and Carma McClure. *Software Maintenance: The Problem and its Solutions.* Englewood Cliffs, NJ: Prentice Hall, 1983.

56.* Metzger, Philip. *Managing a Programming Project,* 2nd ed. Englewood Cliffs, NJ: Prentice Hall, 1983.

57. Mills, Harlan, Richard Linger, and Alan Hevner. *Principles of Information Systems Analysis and Design.* New York: Academic Press, 1986.

58. Minsky, Marvin. *The Society of Mind.* New York: Simon & Schuster, 1986.

59.* Musa, John, Anthony Iannino, and Kazuhira Okumoto. *Software Reliability: Measurement, Prediction, Application.* New York: McGraw-Hill, 1987.

60. Myers, Glenford. *The Art of Software Testing.* New York: Wiley-Interscience, 1979.

61. Myers, Glenford. *Software Reliability.* New York: John Wiley & Sons, 1976.

62. Myers, Glenford. *Reliable Software Through Composite Design.* New York: Petrocelli/Charter, 1975.

63. Naisbitt, John, and Patricia Aburdene. *Megatrends 2000.* New York: William Morrow, 1990.

64. Norman, Donald A. *The Design of Everyday Things.* New York: Doubleday/Currency, 1990.

65. Orr, Ken. *Structured Requirements Definition.* Topeka, KS: Ken Orr & Associates, 1981.

66. Orr, Ken. *Structured Systems Development.* Englewood Cliffs, NJ: Yourdon Press/Prentice Hall, 1977.

67. Page-Jones, Meilir. *The Practical Guide to Structured Systems Design,* 2nd ed. Englewood Cliffs, NJ: Yourdon Press/Prentice Hall, 1988.

68. Parker, Marilyn, and Robert J. Benson. *Information Economics.* Englewood Cliffs, NJ: Prentice Hall, 1988.

69.* Pirsig, Robert. *Zen and the Art of Motorcycle Maintenance.* New York: Bantam Books, 1975.

70. Pressman, Roger S. *Making Software Engineering Happen.* Englewood Cliffs, NJ: Prentice Hall, 1988.

71. Ravden, Susannah, and Graham Johnson. *Evaluating Usability of Human–Computer Interfaces.* New York: John Wiley & Sons, 1989.

72. Schindler, Max. *Computer-Aided Software Design.* New York: John Wiley & Sons, 1990.

73.* Sculley, John. *Odyssey.* New York: Harper & Row, 1987.

74.* Shlaer, Sally, and Steve Mellor. *Object-Oriented Systems Analysis: Modeling the World in Data.* Englewood Cliffs, NJ: Yourdon Press/Prentice Hall, 1988.

75. Shneiderman, Ben. *Designing the User Interface: Strategies for Effective Human–Computer Interaction.* Reading, MA: Addison-Wesley, 1987.

76. Shore, John. *The Sachertorte Algorithm.* New York: Penguin Books, 1986.

77. Swanson, E. Burton, and Cynthia Mathis Beath. *Maintaining Information Systems in Organizations.* New York: John Wiley & Sons, 1989.

78. Ward, Paul, and Steve Mellor. *Structured Development for Real-Time Systems,* Vols. 1–3. Englewood Cliffs, NJ: Yourdon Press/Prentice Hall, 1986.

79. Warnier, Jean-Dominique. *The Logical Construction of Programs.* New York: Van Nostrand Reinhold, 1976.

80. Weinberg, Gerald. *Rethinking Systems Analysis and Design.* Boston: Little, Brown, 1982.

81. Weinberg, Gerald. *An Introduction to General Systems Theory*. New York: John Wiley & Sons, 1975.

82.* Weinberg, Gerald. *The Psychology of Computer Programming*. New York: Van Nostrand Reinhold, 1971.

83. Weizenbaum, Joseph. *Computer Power and Human Reason: From Judgment to Calculation*. San Francisco: W. H. Freeman, 1976.

84. Wirth, Niklaus. *Systematic Programming*. Englewood Cliffs, NJ: Prentice Hall, 1983.

85. Wirth, Niklaus. *Algorithms + Data = Programs*. Englewood Cliffs, NJ: Prentice Hall, 1976.

86. Wood, Jane, and Denise Silver. *Joint Application Design*. New York: John Wiley & Sons, 1989.

87. Zuboff, Shoshana. *In the Age of the Smart Machine*. New York: Basic Books, 1988.

I was once told that a good way to understand someone's personality was to look at the books on his or her bookshelf. It's a personal thing—and my personal list of most important books may not match yours. I would be interested to hear from you if you feel that any of the books listed here should not be on the list. Or write me about any books on programming, systems design, systems analysis, database, project management, or software engineering that you feel should be on the list.

If you looked closely at the list, you might have wondered about number 46, Thomas Kuhn's *The Structure of Scientific Revolutions*. It has nothing to do with programming or software engineering, but it is one of the most important books on the list. We work in a field undergoing constant evolution and occasional revolutionary change; understanding the nature of such scientific revolutions and how people react to them is important to us as software professionals.

There is no question that the millionfold improvement in hardware technology over the past 40 years is a revolutionary development. But some colleagues of mine feel it is pretentious to suggest that developments in software technology are as revolutionary as the developments in quantum physics, biology, chemistry, or other scientific disciplines. There are, no doubt, a few software gurus who would like to compare themselves to Einstein or Newton, but the vast majority of the authors whose books are listed would agree that their accomplishments pale by comparison.

Even if the scale of scientific achievement is smaller in software than in quantum physics, the problems remain the same. Kuhn's book introduces the notion of "paradigm shifts," and it is a remarkably useful notion in our own field. For example, going from second generation programming languages (assembler) to third generation improved the productivity of programmers but did not cause a fundamental change in the way programmers worked. Fourth generation languages did cause a paradigm shift, however: development time could be cut by a factor of 10, and users could develop their own programs. Similarly, prototyping represents a significant paradigm shift away from the prespecified approach to systems analysis, in which data flow diagrams and other abstract modeling tools are used to document the user's requirements.

Kuhn gives us an excellent understanding of the politics of paradigm shifts. He shows how a new theory tends to be advocated by an angry, young radical who may spend years getting his ideas accepted. But then, gradually, the young radical mellows and ages until he becomes conservative; for reasons of pride, ego, and financial security, he continues defending his paradigm with fanatic zeal when his paradigm develops problems: exceptions and special cases arise and are handled with increasing difficulty. Finally, the once-new paradigm succumbs to the attack of an even newer paradigm, and the cycle begins anew.

One golden oldie, an absolute must for your personal library, is Gerald Weinberg's *The Psychology of Computer Programming*. Published in 1971, this book has gone out of print at various times and may be difficult to find. But it's a treasure and well worth stealing if you get the opportunity (someone stole mine, dammit!). Weinberg is an opinionated man, often difficult to get along with; worse, he lives in Lincoln, Nebraska, which is just about as far away from civilization as anyone would want to get. When visiting him several years ago, my wife (a native New Yorker) complained that the surrounding countryside was so flat she was able to stand on the coffee table in Weinberg's living room and see the West Coast. But none of that matters: *The Psychology of Computer Programming* is a gem, a classic. Here is the origin of "egoless programming" and "structured walkthroughs" that so many organizations try to practice. More important, this is probably the first book—certainly the best book—to emphasize that programmers are people, that they have egos, and that the "people issues" in a systems development project are often just as important as the technical issues.

Here's another classic: Robert Pirsig's *Zen and the Art of Motorcycle Maintenance*. Pirsig is (or was, when he wrote this book) a technical writer in the computer field. But it's not a book about computers per se; in fact, as Pirsig says in an introductory author's note, "it should in no way be associated with that great body of factual information relating to orthodox Zen Buddhist practice. It's not very factual about motorcycles, either." But if you substitute the words "program debugging" for "motorcycle maintenance" throughout the book, you will have one of the most useful and most inspirational books on debugging and software maintenance you will ever own. More than anything else, it taught me that if you have been looking for a bug for hours and you're getting frustrated, you will start making mistakes; you'll put more new bugs into the program than you take out. It's time to back off, put things away, and take a break. Pirsig talks about this in a long discussion about so-called "gumption traps":

> As far as I can see there are two main types of gumption traps. The first type are [sic] those in which you're thrown off the Quality track by conditions that arise from external circumstances, and I call these "setbacks." The second type are traps in which you're thrown off the Quality track by conditions that are primarily within yourself. These I don't have any generic name for—— "hangups," I suppose.

> The first time you do any major job it seems as though the out-of-sequence-reassembly setback is your biggest worry. This occurs usually at a time when you think you're almost done. After days of work you finally have it all together except for: What's this? A connecting-rod bearing liner?! How could you have left that out? Oh Jesus, everything's got to come apart again! You can almost hear the gumption escaping. Pssssssss.

All this is set within a story of intense drama, a man's quest for truth on a motorcycle ride across the country with his son. But I don't want to tell you anything more about it. Get the book. It may be a little hard to track down, but doing so is well worth the effort.

Back to the "real world" of software engineering: No programmer's bookshelf is complete without Barry Boehm's monumental tome, *Software Engineering Economics*. Published in 1981, it is crammed with 767 pages of encyclopedic information on measuring, modeling, and estimating just about every aspect of a systems development project. The book is somewhat dated—while it discusses analysis and design productivity tools, it obviously doesn't mention

PC-based CASE tools, which began to appear in the mid-1980s. And while it acknowledges the impact of structured programming and structured design, it doesn't cover structured analysis; the otherwise extensive bibliography doesn't mention DeMarco's *Structured Analysis and System Specification* or Gane and Sarson's *Structured Systems Analysis*. Still, it's a book I find myself referring to and rereading periodically; I hope Boehm will publish an updated edition to usher in the 1990s.

A more recent book on software productivity data is Capers Jones's *Programming Productivity*. Like Boehm, Jones has a reputation as one of the country's leading statisticians on software development: Don't pass up any opportunity to hear him speak. *Programming Productivity* is a study of the impact of every productivity technique you can think of on development costs, schedules, maintenance budgets, and the like. You may not agree with everything he has to say, but you can't afford to be ignorant of his data.

Another recent book I particularly recommend is *Odyssey* by Apple Computer CEO John Sculley. It documents Sculley's journey from Pepsi to Apple and tells his side of the battles with Steve Jobs. More important, it provides an eloquent description of the differences between small, innovative "third wave" companies and the older, stodgier "second wave" monolith for which you work. Reading Sculley's book won't necessarily make you an Apple fan or a Macintosh evangelist, but it will make you do a lot of thinking about the kind of environment in which you should be working.

On a very different subject, I recommend you read *Computers in Battle: Will They Work?* edited by David Bellin and Gary Chapman. It's a collection of roughly a dozen articles on such things as "Artificial Intelligence as Military Technology," "Computers and the Strategic Defense Initiative," "Computer System Reliability and Nuclear War," and other happy topics. One of the coeditors, Gary Chapman, is the executive director of the Computer Professionals for Social Responsibility (CPSR), and several of the papers, including one by David Parnas, seem to represent the philosophical viewpoint of CPSR. I happen to agree with their viewpoint but wish there had been a few papers representing the other side. Nevertheless, I think it is an important book; for those of us who have trouble satisfying ourselves that we have made a 100-statement program work correctly, it is almost inconceivable that the SDI folks may be trying to build a system with a hundred million lines of code. Now that Ronald Reagan has retired, maybe they'll just forget the whole thing . . .

Next on the "ya gotta read this" list of books is *Peopleware* by Tom DeMarco and Tim Lister. I put it in the category of airplane reading: it's short enough (188 pages) that you can read it on a typical airplane trip. The nice thing about plane rides is that they provide two to three hours of quiet, uninterrupted time—and that's what you should devote to this delightful collection of what the authors call "short essays, each one about a particular garden path that managers are led down, usually to their regret. What typically lures them into error is some aspect of management folklore, a folklore that is pervasive and loudly articulated, but often wrong."

Peopleware consists of 26 essay/chapters that can be read individually or in sequence. As you might guess from the title, it says little or nothing about hardware or software; nor does it discuss software engineering or the structured analysis methodology for which DeMarco is so well known. Instead, it discusses the cultural and sociological aspects of our strange profession—the people and what makes them tick. There are chapters on the office environment, including "The Furniture Police" and "You Never Get Anything Done Around Here Between 9 and 5." There are chapters on hiring the right people and motivating them for a systems development project, and there are several delightful chapters on growing productive teams.

When I say delightful, I don't mean that DeMarco and Lister spend all their time telling funny stories (though they're very good at doing that, too). Much of what they write is pretty blunt. Here are some excerpts from a chapter called "Vienna Waits for You":

> Historians long ago formed an abstraction about different theories of value: The Spanish Theory, for one, held that only a fixed amount of value existed on earth, and therefore the path to the accumulation of wealth was to learn to extract it more efficiently from the soil or from people's backs. . . .

> The Spanish Theory of Value is alive and well among managers everywhere. You see that whenever they talk about productivity. Productivity ought to mean achieving more in an hour of work, but all too often it has come to mean achieving more in an hour of pay. There is a large difference. The Spanish Theory managers dream of attaining new productivity levels through the simple mechanism of unpaid overtime. They divide whatever work is done in a week by forty hours, not by the eighty or ninety hours that the worker actually puts in.

> That's not exactly productivity—it's more like fraud—but it's the state of the art for many American managers. They bully and cajole

their people into long hours. They impress upon them how important the delivery date is (even though it may be totally arbitrary; the world isn't going to stop just because a project completes a month late). They trick them into accepting hopelessly tight schedules, shame them into sacrificing any and all to meet the deadline, and do anything to get them to work longer and harder.

Perhaps the most important chapter is the last, entitled "Holgar Dansk" (the title won't make any sense until you read the book). It addresses the ultimate question everyone has after reviewing all the things that are done badly in most EDP organizations: How can an ordinary programmer or project manager make things better? The standard answer to this sort of question (usually in the context of bringing in CASE tools or introducing walkthroughs) is something like this: "If you don't have the support and commitment of senior management, you'll never get anything changed." My own feeling is that life is too short to bother trying to change a large, screwed-up organization. It's much easier simply to walk out and find another organization whose priorities and values are more closely aligned with yours.

But DeMarco and Lister offer another solution—a quiet revolution. "If the silliness is gross enough," they point out, "people need no more than a gentle catalyst. It may be one small voice saying, 'This is unacceptable.' People know it's true. Once it's been said out loud, they can't ignore it any longer." They then cite several examples of quiet revolutions, including a department of a large government agency that has stuffed its telephone bells with tissues. There is no loud ringing of telephones now (you need to read Chapter 11 to see what the authors think of the modern telephone), only the gentle purr of the bell.

I called DeMarco in Camden, Maine, to ask him if he had had any more thoughts on the "people" issue since the publication of his book. "Well, I still feel that the sociological issues are far more important than the technological issues of systems development," he said. "But I'm a little worried that I'm spending too much time on 'soft' issues. Look what happened to Herb Grosch: he started off as a hard-core technician, and then he got softer and softer until he floated right up to Heaven." I think we can infer from this that DeMarco may return to "hard" technology issues. This means, we hope, that he is hard at work on a new edition of his classic, *Structured Analysis and System Specification*.

I strongly recommend that you buy one copy of *Peopleware* for yourself and another copy for your boss. If you are a boss, then buy one for everyone in your department, and buy one for your boss. You can order the book by calling Dorset's clever toll-free number, 1-800-DH BOOKS.

The next book that you really must buy is *Structured Techniques: The Basis for CASE* by James Martin and Carma McClure. I never thought I would find myself recommending a Martin book, because each new book seems just like his last book except for one or two new chapters. (To be fair, I should point out that the same thing has been said about my books!)

But I do look at each of Martin's new books, if only because senior managers in many organizations are so entranced by the miracles and magic that he promises. I disagree with much of what he says, and I don't think he really understands structured analysis or structured design. But it's just as important to read the work of people with whom you disagree as it is to read the work of people with whom you agree.

Structured Techniques: The Basis for CASE is actually a revised edition of *Structured Techniques for Computing*. The book looks comprehensive because of its size: in 776 pages it covers the gamut of structured programming, structured design, structured analysis, and data modeling methodologies, with extensive discussions of the CASE tools that support the methodologies. And it appears to be fairly well researched, with an extensive list of references to the classic books and papers on structured techniques. However, Martin and McClure either overlooked or ignored the important contributions of Paul Ward and Steve Mellor in their *Structured Development of Real-Time Systems*, which adds state–transition diagrams to the data flow models for real-time systems. And they seem to have missed *Essential Systems Analysis* by Steve McMenamin and John Palmer. Indeed, none of the six references at the end of the structured analysis chapter is more recent than 1978—and this is a book whose copyright date is 1988! Consequently, they promulgate the "old" structured analysis approach of building a "current physical" model and a "current logical" model before beginning to model the user's new system. But only bozos build current physical models today because it takes too long and involves too much wasted work.

Similarly, the chapter on structured design includes no references more recent than Meilir Page-Jones's 1980 *The Practical Guide to Structured Systems Design*. In case you thought nothing has happened since 1980, let me point out that Larry Constantine and I have found over 100 published papers on structured design since the publication of our original *Structured Design* in 1975. If there are flaws in the presentation of these two forms of structured techniques, I worry that there might be similar flaws in the discussion of the Warnier–Orr methodology, the Jackson methodology, the Gane–Sarson methodology, and so on.

Despite these criticisms (which may obviously be a little biased!), I still think this is a book that you should read. If you are opposed to structured analysis and design, Martin will provide you with some ammunition for the arguments in your office. And if you favor structured analysis/design, it's important that you read his discussion of the limitations and weaknesses of the techniques. This will help you avoid falling victim to the sales pitch of CASE vendors and consulting gurus who try to convince you that their approach truly is the "silver bullet" that will solve all software development problems.

Here is a book that is 16 years old and still gets quoted in almost every new book or paper on software engineering: Fred Brooks's *The Mythical Man-Month*. If you haven't read it, you should hang your head in shame and quickly shuffle down to the nearest technical bookstore and get a copy. If you have read the book, ask yourself how long ago it was; if it was more than five years (as it was for me), you should dust off the book and read it again (as I did in preparing this review).

Written as a series of essays, the book can be read in small chunks: read individual chapters during your next project status meeting while the project manager is droning on endlessly about the Urgent Need to get the project done in a hysterically optimistic period of time. A few of the chapter titles have become famous in themselves, including the one that forms the title of the book. The illusion, or myth, of the "man-month" occurs partly, as Brooks says, because of the "false assumption that underlies the scheduling of systems programming that all will go well, that is, that each task will take only as long as it 'ought' to take." Anyone who has worked on more than one or two systems development projects knows that people and calendar months are not interchangeable, and those who have read this chapter will forever remember Brooks's law: Adding manpower to a late software project makes it later. But it is amazing to see how many EDP managers and people outside the profession still don't understand that this is true.

The other chapter that still provides the basis for hot debate in today's world of structured analysis, prototyping, CASE, and so on is entitled "Plan to Throw One Away." Many people think Brooks is arguing that since we are incapable of building a system correctly the first time, we should just assume the first version of the system will have to be thrown away and replaced with a new, hopefully better, second version.

But Brooks never said the entire system had to be built and thrown away. Listen to page 117:

> Once one recognizes that a pilot system must be built and discarded, and that a redesign with changed ideas is inevitable, it becomes useful to face the whole phenomenon of change as a way of life, rather than as an untoward and annoying exception. . . .
>
> Far be it from me to suggest that all changes in customer objectives and requirements must, can, or should be incorporated in the design. Clearly a threshold has to be established, and it must get higher and higher as development proceeds, or no product ever appears.
>
> Nevertheless, some changes in objectives are inevitable, and it is better to be prepared for them than to assume that they won't come. Not only are changes in objective inevitable, changes in development strategy and technique are also inevitable. The throw-one-away concept is itself just an acceptance of the fact that as one learns, he changes the design.

But even if the first or second version of a system does meet its objectives when it is first delivered to the user, it will eventually decay, as Brooks eloquently points out at the end of this chapter. He quotes a study by Lehman and Belady indicating that the total number of modules in a system increases linearly with each new system release, but that the number of modules affected (i.e., modified or rewritten) increases exponentially with each new system release. Brooks concludes that

> All repairs tend to destroy the structure, to increase the entropy and disorder of the system. Less and less effort is spent on fixing original design flaws; more and more is spent on fixing flaws introduced by earlier fixes. As time passes, the system becomes less and less well-ordered. Sooner or later the fixing ceases to gain any ground. Each forward step is matched by a backward step. Although in principle usable forever, the system has worn out as a base for progress. Furthermore, machines change, configurations change, and user requirements change, so the system is not in fact usable forever. A brand-new, from-the-ground-up redesign is necessary.

Fred Brooks, once the architect and project manager for IBM's OS/360, is now professor and chairman of the Computer Science Department at the University of North Carolina.

I also recommend a "golden oldie" in the field of project management: Philip Metzger's *Managing a Programming Project*, 2nd ed. Even if you have no desire to ever be a project manager, you should have an understanding of the elements of project planning and organization. (For reasons why no intelligent programmer should consider a career path as a DP manager, take a look at Janet Ruhl's newly published book, *The Mainframe Programmer's Survival Manual*. There are lots and lots of books on project management; some of the newer ones deal with the impact of prototyping, end-user computing, structured analysis, and CASE tools on project management. That's fine, but you need to have a solid grasp of the basics before you explore today's new buzzwords and techniques. I think Metzger's book is the best of the lot.)

You have probably heard of object-oriented programming and design. Shlaer and Mellor's *Object-Oriented Systems Analysis* takes these concepts one step farther and suggests that an object-oriented view of the world can be useful during the systems analysis phase of a project. In an introductory section on "how projects go awry," the authors point out that one of the major problems in a systems development project is a form of floundering that I like to call "analysis paralysis":

> Many systems development projects begin with an analysis phase in which a great deal of information is transmitted from the various application experts to the systems developers. However, after a time, confusion sets in due to the quantity of information the analysts must take into account and the fact that they have few tools or techniques for managing that information. A protracted period of floundering then ensues, and the schedule suffers.

> Modern software engineering tools (dataflow diagrams) and automated computer aids (data dictionary packages, for example) have little impact on the flounder problem, since the origin of the problem is a lack of fundamental understanding of the conceptual entities that make up the application problem. Given such understanding, the tools and aids do help; lacking it, they serve only to provide an activity in which to flounder.

Thus, as the title of the book indicates, Shlaer and Mellor argue that the systems analyst should concentrate on modeling the user's world in terms of data. The modeling rules and structure described in the book are based on the well-known relational theories promulgated by Codd and Date. The diagrams, which the authors describe as information structure diagrams, are based on Bachman diagrams and on Chen's entity–relationship diagrams.

After two introductory chapters, the core of the book is devoted to chapters describing objects, attributes, relationships, and the representation of an overall information model of a system. If you are familiar with these basic concepts, you probably won't learn anything new in these chapters; on the other hand, if you have always had difficulty understanding what an information model is, you'll find the pedagogical approach used by the authors—a picturebook approach, with simple, straightforward explanations—makes this rather abstract concept very understandable.

For the practicing professional already familiar with the conceptual notion of data modeling, the real value of this book is its discussion of three major issues:

- How should one go about modeling a particular rule or observation?
- How can one depict a large model graphically?
- How should an information model be documented?

The last three chapters deal with these questions in detail; these three chapters alone are worth the price of the book.

For the systems developer who worries that he must make a binary choice between a data modeling approach and a process modeling approach (data flow diagrams), the last chapter of the book is invaluable. Shlaer and Mellor point out that, in fact, there are three models one can build for a system: an information model, a process model, and a state model (a model of the time-dependent behavior of the system). Classical books on systems analysis tend to discuss only one of these models (usually the data flow diagram, and rarely the state–transition diagram), without any indication of how they relate to one another. Mellor and coauthor Paul Ward discuss the three-model paradigm in their *Structured Development for Real-Time Systems*, but I like the presentation in *Object-Oriented Systems Analysis* even better. You can show this chapter to your programmers, systems analysts, managers, and users—and they should all understand it.

Two appendixes show the use of an information model for two different kinds of systems: one is a system that manages magnetic tapes in a computer center, and the other is a real-time process control system. The examples are taken from the authors' real-world consulting experiences.

Bottom line: this is a great book! Read it! Once you finish it, track down their newest contribution: *Object Lifecycles: Modeling the World in States* (Englewood Cliffs, NJ: Prentice Hall, 1992); in my opinion, this companion volume is even better than the first, though it's too new to include in my list of "classics."

Strategies for Real-Time System Specification, by Derek Hatley and Imtiaz Pirbhai, doesn't have the messianic zeal of Tom Peters's *Thriving on Chaos* or the literary grace of Patrick Conroy's *The Prince of Tides*, but it's one of a very small number of books on systems analysis that introduces some important, new ideas you need to know.

If you're familiar with software engineering and structured analysis, you've probably read Tom DeMarco's classic *Structured Analysis and System Specification*. And if you're concerned with the analysis and design of real-time systems, you may know Paul Ward and Steve Mellor's *Structured Analysis of Real-Time Systems*. Hatley and Pirbhai refer frequently to DeMarco's work as the foundation for their systems analysis approach, but they extend it into the realm of real-time systems. In this sense, they cover the same ground as Ward and Mellor, but they offer a substantially different approach. It's too early to tell which approach will become the standard, so it's important that you become familiar with both if you have any involvement with real-time systems.

The data flow notation popularized by DeMarco has been used for ten years for the analysis of business-oriented data processing systems. However, designers of process control, embedded avionics, and other types of real-time systems have found this notation inadequate because it lacks a mechanism for modeling interrupts and control flows. *Strategies for Real-Time System Specification* deals with this by adding a new kind of diagram to the systems analyst's repertoire: a control flow diagram. For example, Hatley and Pirbhai provide a model of a system to control a vending machine: it has both a data flow diagram (DFD) and a control flow diagram (CFD). Ward and Mellor, by contrast, would model the same system with a single diagram. Hatley and Pirbhai argue that for large, complex systems, there are advantages to keeping the control information and data flow information separate.

In addition to the DFD and CFD, Hatley and Pirbhai include a data dictionary, process specifications (which they refer to as PSPECs), and control specifications (CSPECs). The CSPEC consists of a state–transition diagram (STD) and a process activation table (PAT); the STD shows the states of the system and how they are influenced by control signals, while the PAT shows the circumstances under which the processes on a DFD are enabled and disabled. The relationship between these components of the requirements model is carefully explained in the book.

In addition to discussing systems analysis, or requirements modeling, *Strategies for Real-Time System Specification* also discusses systems design, or architecture modeling. Another set of modeling tools is introduced for this activity: the architecture flow diagram (AFD), the architecture interconnect diagram (AID), architecture module specifications (AMSs), and architecture interconnect specifications (AISs). I found it interesting that Hatley and Pirbhai provide a different graphical notation for the AFD than for the DFD. They also stress that the names in a DFD bubble should consist of a verb-object pair, while the names in an AFD box should consist of a noun phrase.

Though Hatley and Pirbhai make a good case for the need for all these diagrams, the novitiate is likely to be overwhelmed by the alphabet soup of DFDs, CFDs, AFDs, PSPECs, CPSECs, PATs, STDs, AIDs, AMSs, and AISs. More important, I think it would be virtually impossible to work with all these diagrams on anything larger than the trivial vending machine example unless one had the support of a CASE tool. However, the authors point out that Cadre, Iconix, Index Technologies, Tektronix, Promod, and Interactive Development Environments have CASE tools that support their method.

As with any book, there were things that I liked in *Strategies for Real-Time System Specification* and things that I didn't. What I liked best was the obvious wealth of practical, hands-on, real-world experience the authors provide the reader. From the examples they discuss (even the tiny vending machine system), it is evident they have used their method on a variety of large, complex real-time systems, and they have done this within the constraints of real-world standards and politics. In their Appendix B, for example, Hatley and Pirbhai give cogent advice for using their method on projects governed by MIL-STD-483A, MIL-STD-490A, and DOD-STD-2167.

I also liked the authors' emphasis on the separation of data and control. As they point out, designers of real-time systems are often tempted to overspecify the control aspects of a system when developing a requirements model, because they are far more familiar with (and interested in) the design and implementation of the system. Finally, I liked the emphasis on formal finite-state machines as a method of modeling the control requirements of a system; this has the benefit of drawing on many decades of formal work on finite state automata done by engineers.

What I didn't like about *Strategies for Real-Time System Specification* was what it didn't cover. Since it acknowledges DeMarco's work as its foundation for process models, it should have addressed the issue of building "current physical" models and "current logical" models before modeling the requirements of a new system. By not discussing this at all, it appears that Hatley and Pirbhai feel the analyst should not bother with models of a current system; perhaps this is because the systems development projects they have in mind involve development of a new system rather than the replacement, enhancement, or enlargement of an existing system (which is a more common phenomenon with business data processing systems).

I also felt that Hatley and Pirbhai ignored the difficult problem faced by the designer when he tries to go from a context diagram (in which one bubble represents the entire system) to the first-level data flow diagram. How does the analyst know whether that "level 0" DFD should have 3 bubbles, 7 bubbles, or 52 bubbles? McMenamin and Palmer first provided a practical solution to this problem with their "event partitioning" approach in *Essential Systems Analysis*, and it should be compatible with the overall approach proposed by Hatley and Pirbhai.

The third flaw in *Strategies for Real-Time System Specification* is the lack of a detailed discussion of information models (e.g., entity–relationship diagrams, or ERDs) and the relationship of information models to the process models and control models they introduce. A 4-page appendix at the end of this 412-page book gives a superficial presentation of ERDs and explains why the authors didn't discuss them at length. But I was left with the impression that they tacked the appendix on as an afterthought. I hope, in a subsequent edition, this material will be expanded so that readers can have a full treatment of all *three* dimensions of a system: process models, control models, and information models.

Having said this, I still insist this is a book you must read. Hatley and Pirbhai have used their method on major projects at Boeing and Lear-Siegler, and you are likely to see it used on a number of aerospace systems in the future. *Strategies for Real-Time System Specification* is an important contribution to the field of real-time systems analysis. It will serve, along with Ward and Mellor's *Structured Development of Real-*

Time Systems, as the foundation for future methodologies. After you have read both books, read "An Extended Systems Modeling Language (ESML)," by W. Bruyn, R. Jensen, D. Keskar, and P. Ward (*ACM Software Engineering Notes,* January 1988) to see the efforts currently being made to combine the best features of the Hatley–Pirbhai and the Ward–Mellor approaches.

Since first publishing my selection of the greatest computer books in the June 1988 issue of *American Programmer,* I have received a steady trickle of suggestions from readers. In fact, one reader, Bill Hetzel, even gave me a copy of one of his books and suggested it should augment, if not replace, Glen Myers's classic, *The Art of Software Testing.*

And indeed this is a book that should sit beside the Myers classic on your bookshelf. It's called *The Complete Guide to Software Testing,* 2nd ed. Hetzel is a veteran of the testing field, having published an earlier book, *Program Test Methods.* He and his partner, Dave Gelperin, run a consulting firm called Software Quality Engineering, which has taken a leadership role in organizing the International Conference on Software Testing during the past several years.

The Complete Guide to Software Testing makes the important point that testing is not just something done once, after code has been written, until the project team runs out of time and money; it is something that accompanies each phase of the systems development life cycle. Thus it is meaningful to talk about "analysis testing" and "design testing" as well as the more traditional testing of code; the wise project manager will build these into his schedule. Indeed, throughout the book, Hetzel emphasizes the importance of tracking and measuring the testing work done on a project—not only to keep the project under control but to provide data that can be used on future projects.

Hetzel also furnishes a wealth of practical advice and guidance on the use of automated tools for testing; while this material may become dated fairly quickly, *The Complete Guide to Software Testing* provides a sufficient framework so that a project manager can easily evaluate new vendor tools as they appear. In general, checklists are provided for almost all aspects of testing; the book can and should be a bible for project managers. For the MIS organization that plans to purchase packaged software rather than developing its own, Hetzel advises budgeting 25 percent of the purchase price for testing one or more candidate products; this is advice you won't find in many places!

The best part and the worst part of the book occur at the very end: the best part of the book is the collection of appendixes and references. The appendixes include a nationwide survey of software testing practices, a sample testing policy, and a quality measurement diagnostic checklist. The references are extensive and fairly complete; as you would expect, they provide a wealth of new references that supplement the 1979 Myers textbook.

Alas, the book lacks an index, which makes it difficult to track down information by keyword, subject heading, or author name. For those who don't have time to read the book from cover to cover, the absence of an index is a royal pain. However, it's the only negative thing I can think to say about this otherwise excellent book. I suggest that you call QED and order your copy today.

The next book on my list covers a related topic, software reliability. The book is entitled *Software Reliability: Measurement, Prediction, Application*, by John Musa, Anthony Iannino, and Kazuhira Okumoto. At 621 pages, this is definitely *not* an "airplane book" you can read on your next New York-to-Chicago flight. In fact, even if your plane is delayed on the runway for an hour, delayed over O'Hare for another hour, and ultimately rerouted to Atlanta, you still won't finish by the time you land. This is a heavy-duty book, with more mathematics than I've seen since my student days at MIT; it took me several weeks of slow, careful reading to get through it all.

Given the difficult nature of the book, Musa, Iannino, and Okumoto have done an admirable job of partitioning the material into three sections to meet the needs of three different audiences. Part I, as the authors point out, was written for "those who need to develop a general understanding of software reliability measurement and what it can be used for, even though they may not directly apply it. This category includes high-level managers, engineers who use or whose designs interface with software, and people who purchase, lease, or use software." This group may not wish to read further in the book—meanwhile, everyone else can begin with Part I and not be overwhelmed.

The second part of *Software Reliability: Measurement, Prediction, Application* is written for people who will actually be using and applying software reliability measurement. The five chapters in this section cover failure definition, test run selection, determination of the parameters for both execution time and calendar time components of the reliability model, and performance of studies and computation of useful quantities. These chapters assume that the reader already understands the basics of software reliability models and now wants to learn "how to do it."

The average reader will skip Part III; it is intended instead for researchers and students of reliability, as well as people carrying out research in software engineering, applied statistics, operations research, and anyone else who wants a deeper understanding of the theoretical background of software reliability. However, even if you're not a researcher, you should take a look at Chapter 9 (which provides a logical and historical perspective on most of the published reliability models) and Chapter 13 (which presents criteria for comparing different reliability models).

As the authors state at the end of their final chapter,

> In summary, the field of software reliability measurement and prediction has made substantial progress in the last decade. It cannot yet provide a standard cookbook approach for widespread application. There are several problem areas that need work. However, it is clearly beyond the pure theory stage and it can provide practical dividends for those who make the modest investment in time required to learn and apply it.

Anyone involved in the design and development of large, complex information systems today must certainly be concerned with the reliability of his or her system. Even if management and customers don't know how to ask for meaningful reliability models, we should be providing them. It's something that only a tiny subset of the systems development profession knows how to do, but it's something we must *all* learn how to do in the 1990s. *Software Reliability: Measurement, Prediction, Application*, by Musa, Iannino, and Okumoto, may well become our bible for software reliability in the next decade.

Next, I direct your attention to a slim volume, *More Programming Pearls: Confessions of a Coder*, by Jon Bentley. This is a follow-up to an earlier book called (surprise!) *Programming Pearls*. It consists of a collection of 15 essays that are meant to be read one at a time. The first 4 describe techniques for manipulating programs, essays 5 through 8 sketch some tricks of the programmer's trade, essays 9 through 12 deal with the design of input and output, and essays 13 through 15 describe three useful subroutines. There is a definite UNIX and C flavor to the book, but it's not intrusive; you'll find it interesting reading even if you program in COBOL.

Why would anyone want to read a programming book? They tend to be deadly dry and boring, and the idea of actually reading one is enough to instantly put programmers and nonprogrammers alike to sleep. But this one is different. The closest comparison I can make is to Fred Brooks's *The Mythical Man-Month*, which *everyone* loves. You'll feel the same way about Bentley's book. It's filled with wit, charm, little anecdotes, pointers to further reading on various topics, and examples that are definitely more interesting than the turgid stuff of most programming books. The essay on designing graphic output concludes, for example, with the famous map of Napoleon's disastrous Russian campaign of 1812, first drawn by the French engineer Charles Joseph Minard in 1861.

Question: What do you do on a 13-hour plane ride to Argentina? Answer: A lot of reading. I sometimes pick up a spy novel at the airport, but long plane rides are my favorite time to catch up on the interesting books, manuscripts, and journals that lie in disorganized heaps around my office. Sometimes I choose books outside my normal categories of software engineering and data processing. Because they focus on different engineering disciplines or management problems, they often turn out to be eminently important reading material for those of us with careers as programmers, systems analysts, and DP managers.

Future Perfect, by Stanley M. Davis, is just such a book; it is also important reading for CEOs and end users of information systems. *Future Perfect* talks about computer hardware and software, about artificial intelligence and distributed systems—but it's not a computer book per se. It may be the most important book you read this year because it draws a clear picture of the *context* in which information systems will operate in the 1990s. The business organizations we create in the 1990s will be quite different from current dinosaur organizations, and those new organizations will require new types of information systems—which in turn will require new approaches to systems analysis and design.

As Davis points out at the beginning of the book, organizations are the last thing to change in a chain that consists of universe → science → technology → business → organization. "It is no accident," says Davis, "that Sir Isaac Newton came before Adam Smith, whose theories in turn had to be spelled out before Henry Ford could create the assembly line and Alfred Sloan could then devise the divisional corporate structure." But just as it is often said that military generals build weapons to refight the last war, so it seems that organizational structures reflect the previous wave of business and technology. Specifically, says Davis, current organizational models are based on the assembly-line business paradigm of the 1920s.

Other recent authors have pursued this argument, but I find Davis's perspective particularly persuasive. The basic characteristic of the new business of the next decade, says the author, is that it will provide increasingly intangible, "no-matter" products and services. The notion that we are moving to a service economy is not new, of course. However, Davis provides some interesting statistics that suggest that services already account for far more than 70 percent of the U.S. GNP, as is commonly reported. If you are a lawyer working for General Motors, for example, you are counted as part of the industrial sector because GM is considered an industrial company. Obviously, there are lawyers and accountants and other service-related people in all manufacturing companies; indeed, it is estimated that at least 5 percent of the GNP in the United States is created in the central administrative offices of companies. As Davis points out, only 6 percent of IBM's employees are directly involved in the manufacturing of products; services play a critical role in *every* sector of the economy, even in such mundane "smokestack" industries as automobiles.

In the 1990s, customers will demand access to products and services *any* time and *any* place. Current organizational structures are ill-suited to operate in this fashion; they will have to change to match the new business paradigm. The notion of an "any time" business is provocative to anyone who grew up 20 or 30 years ago. Then "banker's hours" was an apt description of a business culture that transacted business only when it was convenient for the business, with little or no concern for the convenience of the consumer. "Speaking practically," says Davis, "whatever your business, think about how you can create products and services in real time that you can deliver instantly. Even in the slowest-moving company, this contextual shift will speed things up." The operating rules here are

- Consumers need products and services *any time* (that is, in their timeframe not the providers).
- Producers who deliver their products and services in *real time*, relative to their competitors, will have a decided advantage.
- Operating in real time means no *lag time* between identification and fulfillment of the need.

It would be comforting to think existing organizations could adapt to these new possibilities . . . and perhaps some of them will. However, *Future Perfect* argues against this. It suggests most "problem solvers" and planners will continue applying patchwork, Band-Aid solutions to *symptoms*, rather than addressing underlying *causes*—just as doctors are often criticized for focusing on remediation of illness, rather than prevention of illness (wellness). As Davis says,

> People who identify problems generally identify themselves as problem solvers, yet the irony is that they then have a stake in the problem staying identified but unsolved. They adopt the posture that the problem is so large the best they can do is whittle away at it.

> Socially meaningful lives can be devoted to curbing addiction, bureaucracy, crime, disease, and so on through the alphabet. What all these people share in common is a baseline presumption—the problems are so great that totally eliminating them is an absurd and ridiculous thought.

Future Perfect asserts another important aspect of the business of the next decade will be the "any place" business—that is, putting the business in the consumer's hands rather than making the consumer come to an arbitrary manufacturing or distributing location. Much of this is made possible by the continuing trend toward miniaturization—a trend we in the computer field are well aware of, but whose significance we don't always appreciate. As Davis points out,

> The technological ability to transform micromatter, by compacting it in space, is very much at the heart of the new economy: transforming time, space, and mass to be more useful to people. The cornerstone of the transformation lies in seeing them as resources rather than roadblocks. Thus, *when a spatial limitation is reached, rather than viewing it as a constraint, space needs to be redefined so that it can accommodate the new need.*

The next step will be allowing consumers directly to create and control the manufacturing of goods and services. One rather mundane example of this was Coca-Cola's proposal to place the manufacturing of its product—that is, the mixing of soda water and syrup—in the consumer's refrigerator, thus eliminating any need to visit the grocery store. A more familiar example is software: many of the products and services of the next decade will be software based and should/will have the facility for allowing consumers to create their own products.

All this involves managing space—the space in which products are manufactured, distributed, and consumed. The organizational analog to this is that of managing the space that the company itself occupies. But as Davis points out, "a tremendous amount of space in the marketplace is taken up by intermediation. Finding ways to disintermediate is a way to create space for new opportunities." Disintermediation is the process of removing the intermediaries that stand between the consumer and the ultimate producer. Disintermediation can even be a business in itself, as exemplified by the direct-mail form of retailing. The move toward disintermediation is illustrated by the downsizing and elimination of middle management in large organizations. It leads away from hierarchical organizational models (exemplified by military organizations) to flat network models, where everything and everyone is connected. And it is part of the reason for the boom in small businesses, as Davis points out:

> What kind of agent is most likely to create disintermediation? The answer is small business, where most people do for themselves what in large businesses they would have specialists do for them. Two out of every three new jobs created in the past ten years have been in businesses with less than twenty employees, whereas the *Fortune* 500 created no additional jobs during that same decade.

While this may seem a familiar philosophical view, Davis also provides some rather blunt, pragmatic advice when he discusses burcaucracies. The author defines a bureaucracy as "a business, or any other institution, that exists to carry out an organization," and goes on to state "Davis's law of bureaucracy: any company giving less than two-thirds of its energies to its business, and more than one-third of its energies to its organization." Where this exists, he says,

> . . . it is not merely that the company's organization is lagging behind, nor that the organization-tail is wagging the business-dog. Something even more serious is operating: The mindset that began in the universe, and wound its way through science and technology to business and organization, has reached a dead end and collapsed. It is time for a new world view.

The discouraging note in *Future Perfect* is the prediction that it will take 10 years for even the most forward-thinking organization to advance from the assembly-line paradigm to the "any time, any place" paradigm. Many organizations, says Davis, will take even longer, because the tcchnology required to implement the new organizational structures is just now becoming practical and readily available. He goes on to say

> New concepts for management are more likely to be accepted in new businesses, run by new leaders, who are building new organizations than they are to take hold in established businesses, with established organizations, and established people running them.

However, he offers one detailed case study—Federal Express—as an example of an organization that can rise to meet the challenges of the 1990s.

A comment in the concluding chapter would make the entire book worth reading, even if you had skipped over the first several chapters. Davis interviewed a manager of future development in a large organization, a manager who lamented that his greatest concern was about the things his people didn't know that they didn't know. For those of us in the fast-moving computer field, this is a sobering thought.

Future Perfect won't show you how to improve the productivity and quality of the next software system you build. But it will make you step back and look at *everything* you're doing from a much broader perspective. This book is definitely required reading.

Now all I have to do is decide what to read on my *next* 13-hour plane ride to Argentina, which takes place just as I am printing out the last page of this manuscript and sending it on its merry way to the publisher. Hmmm . . . what about the follow-on to *Zen and the Art of Motorcycle Maintenance*, by Robert Pirsig? It's called *Lila: An Inquiry into Morals* (New York: Bantam Books, November 1991) and I should be able to pick it up at the airport bookstore. . . .

Index

Get the guaidance you need —
all delivered in Ed Yourdon's
candid, witty, one-on-one style
— and for just $49 per year!
That's less than a dollar a week
to receive the inside scoop from
one of the best thinkers in
managing computer tech-
nologies. You'll find it all in *Ed
Yourdon's Guerilla Programmer*.

***Ed Yourdon's Guerilla
Programmer*** is published by
Cutter Information Corp.
37 Broadway
Arlington, MA 02174-5539 USA
Phone: (617) 648-8702
　　　　or (800) 964-8702
Fax: (617) 648-1950
　　　　or (800) 888-1816